W0230116

DESIGNING CREATIVE
DATA VISUALIZATIONS

CHART

FROM
CHARTS
TO ART

NEIL RICHARDS

TABLEAU VISIONARY
HALL OF FAME, AUTHOR
QUESTIONS IN DATAVIZ

CHART is a fantastic resource showcasing Bremer's stunning portfolio of artistic data visualizations and data art while offering an engaging glimpse into her thought processes and creative journey. A valuable source of ideas and inspiration for both newcomers and experienced practitioners.

COLE NUSSBAUMER KNAFLIC

AUTHOR OF *STORYTELLING WITH DATA* AND
FOUNDER OF STORYTELLING WITH DATA

From sketching ideas to combining chart types and finding inspiration in the unexpected, Bremer brings the process to life with vivid examples, inviting readers to reimagine what's possible when we embrace creativity in data storytelling. *CHART* is a gift to anyone who works with data—Nadieh's insights will inspire you to experiment, think differently, and create visuals that connect with your audience in new ways.

FIL RIVIÈRE

CARTOGRAPHER
AND DATA
VISUALIZATION
ENGINEER AT
OBSERVABLE

A grand chef of data visualization, continuously crafting new dishes that are always—whether sweet or tasty—a feast for the eyes, Nadieh excels at sharing meticulously documented recipes that blend technique and art. This beautiful cookbook will undoubtedly inspire you to bake your most yummy charts.

GIORGIA LUPI

PARTNER AT PENTAGRAM, FOUNDER
OF ACCURAT AND AUTHOR OF *THIS IS
ME AND ONLY ME* AND *DEAR DATA*

In the evolving world of data visualization, *CHART* offers a fresh and thoughtful perspective. Having explored similar ideas myself, which I've called Data Humanism, I really appreciate how Nadieh brings her own unique voice to the conversation, embracing complexity and creativity in ways that inspire new thinking about data.

Bremer's data visualizations are beloved for good reason. She embraces the complexity of data to create beautiful experiences that delight, spark curiosity, and reveal meaning. Her work feels magical, seemingly beyond reach. Yet, in *CHART*, Nadieh generously shares her process, speaking to the reader as a friend and peer. Nadieh describes concrete, specific actions we can each take to bring similar richness into our own creative processes and data-driven work.

ZAN ARMSTRONG

DATA VISUALIZATION EXPERT WHOSE WORK HAS BEEN USED BY SFMOMA, STANFORD, GOOGLE RESEARCH, THE WHITE HOUSE, AND THE DALAI LAMA

STEPHANIE EVERGREEN

AUTHOR OF 3 BOOKS ON DATA VISUALIZATION AND FOUNDER OF THE EVERGREEN DATA VISUALIZATION ACADEMY

Everyone has seen Bremer's beautiful work and wondered how she came up with yet another creative idea. *CHART* walks you through her process, revealing her thoughtfulness, attention to detail, and willingness to iterate. Yes, you'll be inspired by her final products. But your own process of creating data visualization will change by her model. Bremer gifts readers a structure for exploring data to find a story and pulling together a visual influenced by the data.

Bremer excels at creating captivating and memorable information-rich data displays. In *CHART* she provides a series of prompts and recommendations—informed by her own experiences—for other data designers who are hungry for inspiration. If you're stuck in a world of bar charts and line charts and looking to stretch your own capabilities beyond standard visualization forms, this book is for you.

JEN CHRISTIANSEN

SENIOR GRAPHICS EDITOR AT *SCIENTIFIC AMERICAN* AND AUTHOR OF *BUILDING SCIENCE GRAPHICS*

ANDY KIRK

INDEPENDENT DATA VISUALISATION EXPERT AND AUTHOR OF *DATA VISUALISATION: A HANDBOOK FOR DATA DRIVEN DESIGN*

Through showcasing her exquisite back catalogue of work, Nadieh takes us to the boundaries of the possible. She generously coaches us through what it takes to strive for and achieve the most enigmatic qualities of charm, elegance, and impact. Nobody is more uniquely talented, more evidently qualified, and more capable of inspiring others to unlock their x-factor.

CHART is a glorious celebration of the art and craft of creative data visualization—data with soul! I deeply appreciate Nadieh's relentless creative explorations, pushing past the obvious and embracing a playful sense of wonder. Whether you're a seasoned designer or just beginning your journey, this book will challenge you, encourage you, and remind you why we fell in love with data visualization in the first place.

MORITZ STEFANER

INDEPENDENT DATA VISUALIZATION EXPERT AT TRUTH & BEAUTY

JAN WILLEM TULP

DATAVIZIONEER, TULP INTERACTIVE

This beautifully crafted book is an invaluable source of inspiration for creating innovative and visually striking data visualizations. The meticulous documentation, including detailed sketches and early prototypes, offers readers a rare glimpse into the evolution of each project. This comprehensive guide is essential for anyone seeking to expand their horizons and explore the boundless potential of data visualization, from novices to seasoned practitioners.

SHIRLEY WU

CO-AUTHOR OF *DATA SKETCHES* AND INDEPENDENT DATA VISUALIZATION EXPERT

Our much-needed antidote to predictable and ordinary charts. Bremer is a luminary of our generation, and this book is a generous invitation into her creative process. Each page is a visual feast, packed with real case studies and stunning visuals from her many client and personal projects. *CHART* is the essential companion for data designers striving to create beautiful, informative visuals in an increasingly complex and nuanced world.

Bremer has distilled a splendid series of lessons from her deep reservoir of spectacular custom freelance visualization work to show us all how to go above and beyond: beyond the defaults, beyond the basics, beyond the boring, beyond the standard chart types, beyond the same old stuff, beyond the simplistic, beyond our previous limits! This book will inform and intrigue every designer, from fledgling to veteran, through Nadieh's thoughtful yet approachable voice.

TAMARA MUNZNER

PROFESSOR, DEPARTMENT OF COMPUTER SCIENCE, UNIVERSITY OF BRITISH COLUMBIA. AUTHOR OF *VISUALIZATION ANALYSIS AND DESIGN*

ROBERT KOSARA

DATA VISUALIZATION DEVELOPER AT OBSERVABLE AND PROPRIETOR OF THE VISUALIZATION BLOG EAGEREYES.ORG

Data visualization can be a bit same-y, especially if you're used to the usual charting and BI tools. Not so Bremer's work! She makes data exciting and beautiful while staying thoughtful and truthful. Taking us through her process with sketches and prototypes. Imploring us to think outside the usual confines of techniques. *CHART* is a book that not only contains spectacular charts but is itself spectacularly designed. It is a joy to read and will be an incredible resource to come back to for inspiration again and again.

AK Peters Visualization Series

Visualization plays an ever-more prominent role in the world, as we communicate about and analyze data. This series aims to capture what visualization is today in all its variety and diversity, giving voice to researchers, practitioners, designers, and enthusiasts. It encompasses books from all subfields of visualization, including visual analytics, information visualization, scientific visualization, data journalism, infographics, and their connection to adjacent areas such as text analysis, digital humanities, data art, or augmented and virtual reality.

RECENT TITLES

The Golden Age of Data Visualization: How Did We Get Here?
Kimbal Marriott

Data Visualization for People of All Ages
Nancy Organ

Data Visualization in Excel
Jonathan Schwabish

Building Science Graphics
Jen Christiansen

Joyful Infographics
Nigel Holmes

Making with Data
Edited by Samuel Huron, Till Nagel, Lora Oehlberg, Wesley Willett

Questions in Dataviz
By Neil Richards

Mobile Data Visualization
Edited by Bongshin Lee, Raimund Dachselt, Petra Isenberg, Eun Kyoung Choe

Data Sketches
Nadieh Bremer, Shirley Wu

CHART: Designing Creative Data Visualizations from Charts to Art
Nadieh Bremer

For more information about this series, please visit: *routledge.com/AK-Peters-Visualization-Series/book-series/CRCVIS*

Back in the 1970's Václav Havel wrote that "life, in its essence, moves towards plurality, diversity, independent self-constitution and self-organization" and "towards the fulfillment of its own freedom." On the other hand, authoritarian systems of power demand "conformity, uniformity, and discipline," and, contrary to life, which "strives to create new and improbable structures," they "force life into its most probable states."

Havel was referring to how autocracy in his own country, Czechoslovakia, diluted dissidence through enforced civil mediocrity, silence, and comfortable acquiescence, but it's possible to infer much broader themes from his words: the constant tension in human existence between the drive to think and act independently, as autonomous individuals, and the pressure and constraints imposed by the structures, legitimate or not, we all operate into.

To Havel, life itself, if lived well and in truth, is an act of dissidence. So is work done ethically, with care and attention to detail.

What does this have to do with the book that you have in your hands? Nadieh Bremer's work is an act of creative dissidence within a world—the world of data visualization—where inherited heuristics and conventions were enforced by community pressure, and went barely challenged, for too many years.

All visualizations, typical thinking went, have to be efficient, effective, simple, and ought to stick to a bare and sanitized modernist aesthetic.

Times have changed for the better. Nadieh belongs to a new generation of visualization designers who explore boundaries and cross them. This book doesn't dismiss conventional graphic forms—the bar graph, the line graph, the pie chart, and the choropleth map will fortunately always be with us—but it reminds us that the language of visualization doesn't need to remain static, and that expanding it can be thrilling.

Like Havel's "life," this language, if unshackled, can evolve instead towards plurality and diversity and, as Nadieh's book exemplifies, it can create new and improbable structures, most mysterious and wondrous ones.

ALBERTO CAIRO
& TAMARA MUNZNER

SERIES EDITORS, AK PETERS VISUALIZATION SERIES

First edition published 2025
by CRC Press
2385 NW Executive Center Drive, Suite 320, Boca Raton FL 33431

and by CRC Press
4 Park Square, Milton Park, Abingdon, Oxon, OX14 4RN

CRC Press is an imprint of Taylor & Francis Group, LLC

Title: CHART
ISBN: 9781032797755
was successfully transmitted to the Library of Congress.

ISBN 978-1-032-79775-5 (hbk)
ISBN 978-1-032-80632-7 (pbk)
ISBN 978-1-003-49780-6 (ebk)

DOI: 10.1201/9781003497806

Designed by Julie Brunet datacitron

For Product Safety Concerns and Information please contact our EU representative:
GPSR@taylorandfrancis.com
Taylor & Francis Verlag GmbH, Kaufingerstrae 24, 80331 München, Germany

NADIEH BREMER

DESIGNING CREATIVE DATA VISUALIZATIONS

CHART

FROM CHARTS TO ART

EDITED BY EMILY BARONE

CRC Press
Taylor & Francis Group
Boca Raton London New York

CRC Press is an imprint of the
Taylor & Francis Group, an **informa** business
AN A K PETERS BOOK

To my parents,

whose unwavering support and boundless belief gave wings to my dreams and whose love put me on the path to all I have achieved.

PART III

AIMING FOR VISUAL DIVERSITY

PART IV

DIVING INTO DATA ART

INTRODUCTION

UNLOCKING CREATIVE DATA VISUALIZATION

0.1

We live in a world surrounded by data. The sheer variety and abundance of data—whether public or private—is ripe for exploration and discovery. The insights we find might be revelatory or shocking. Yet, all too often, we present them in the same old ways, relying on charts that are mundane, repetitive, and uninspiring. Such charts blend into the background, failing to capture people's full attention or spark any sense of wonder. But it doesn't have to be this way.

Think about the difference between elevator music and a live concert. Both are musical experiences, but one exists only in the background, nonintrusive and emotionless, whereas the other will leave a lasting impression. What if we could make every data visualization more exciting and engaging? What if we could transform the way people perceive and interact with data, making it not just informative but also captivating and memorable? There's a whole range of musical experiences between elevators and stadiums. The same type of continuum exists for data visuals.

I did not write a typical educational textbook, with formulas and hard rules about how to make visuals better. This book is extremely personal to me, almost like a professional diary. From my decade of working in the field of data visualization, I've distilled my experience, personal stories, and tips I've picked up along the way into practical lessons and strategies. I've drawn from countless hours working with international organizations, major businesses, startups, non-governmental organizations (NGOs), and public institutions. Each lesson shows how I create custom pieces for each client. I've organized these lessons so they showcase the full spectrum of visualizations, starting with ordinary charts that focus solely on conveying numbers, and ending with data artworks that evoke emotions.

To begin, I will show how to enhance ordinary charts with unique design elements, and experiment with uncommon chart forms to create something entirely new. I'll share strategies to make data more human, more relatable, and more memorable. From there, I'll explain the benefits of sketching and introduce techniques such as what I call "amplified encoding," and visualizing data both at the most granular level and as aggregated clusters. I will add visual diversity (my personal mantra) using design strategies that provide context and nuance. Finally, I'll open the door to the world of data art, which goes beyond data visualization but offers inspiration and techniques that can enhance traditional data visualization work.

Figure 0.1

Photo by Piek.cc

As you absorb the examples in the coming pages, my greatest hope is that you will adopt a mindset that embraces creativity and innovation, allowing you to craft truly striking and unique visuals. Whether you are a proficient journalist, a seasoned data analyst, a (data viz) business professional, or someone with a budding interest in the field, these lessons will equip you with the skills to elevate your work.

This book invites you to go beyond the conventional boundaries of data visualization. By the end, you will have the knowledge and inspiration to transform the ordinary charts and graphs that populate your reports, presentations, posters, dashboards, websites, and apps into visuals that not only inform but also delight and engage your audience.

Join me in this creative adventure! It's time to move beyond pre-programmed defaults, to think outside the chart. It's time to unlock the full potential of data through innovative design and produce visuals that resonate long after the numbers have been crunched.

Welcome to the world of creative data visualization.

NADIEH BREMER

DATA VISUALIZATION DESIGNER
AND DATA ARTIST

A BLUEPRINT

A quick note to orient you with the various parts of this book

This book begins with a few brief chapters that cover my background, my general project process, and my preferred tools. These chapters provide useful context for the projects that I'll present.

From there, the book is organized into four parts, each adding progressively more creativity to data visualization. As you read, you'll move along a spectrum of innovation that starts with ordinary charts and ends with data art.

Within these parts, you'll find three or four lessons. Each lesson begins with a general introduction to the subject, followed by case studies showing how I applied the lesson to real-world projects.

Each project includes a brief description at the start, such as "Business | 2018 | UNESCO," indicating whether it was a client (business) or personal project, its publication year, and the client's name or the project's title (if personal). While this book contains images of all the case studies, some are best viewed on screen because they are animated or interactive in some way. I've provided a URL so you can explore them directly.

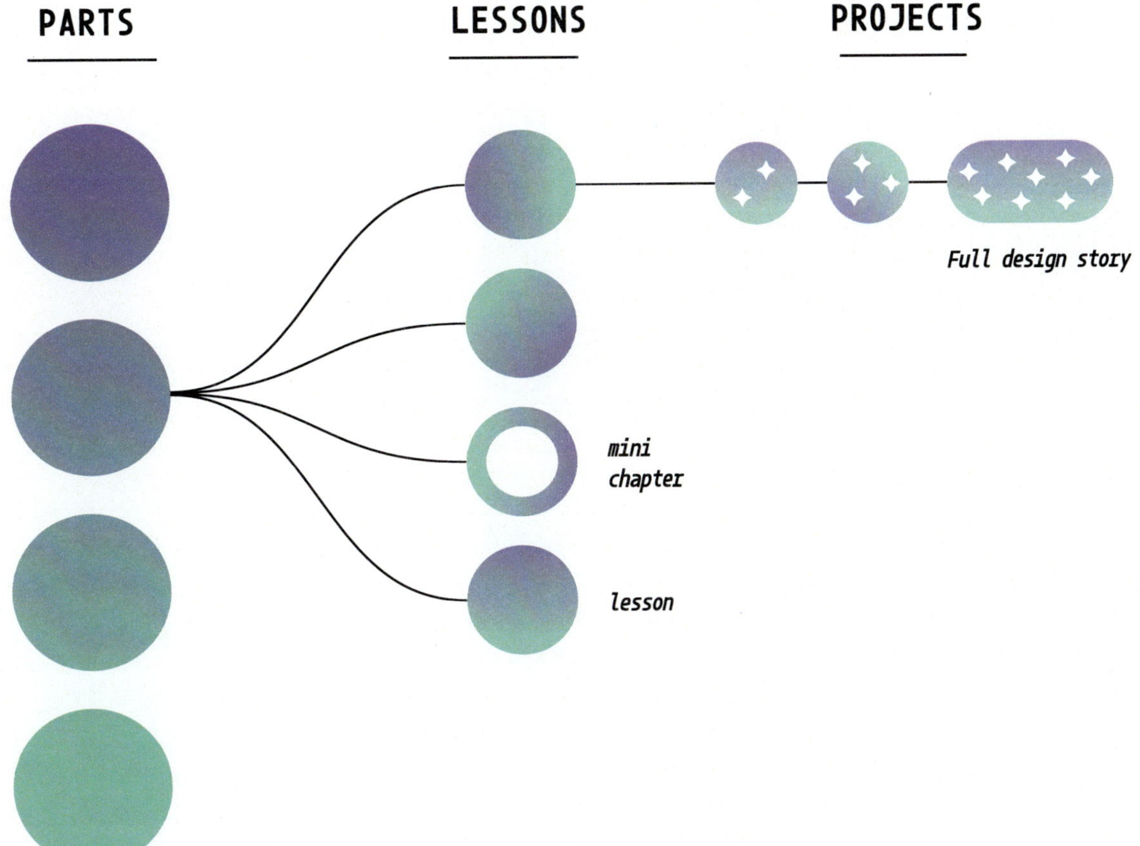

One lesson in each of the four parts features an in-depth project breakdown—a complete design story. Here, I take you through the entire creative process, from the client's initial goals and my early design sketches to the final visual, with numerous work-in-progress images along the way. While these detailed narratives align strongly with the lesson's theme, you'll find they also reinforce ideas from other lessons elsewhere in the book.

At the end of the book, you can find a list of all the case studies, along with information about the main tools, and their QR codes for easy reference of the online versions.

Sprinkled along the creative spectrum are six mini chapters that offer quick tips and general insights that don't require a full lesson. The information in these chapters applies broadly, whether you are creating ordinary charts or data art.

Together, these lessons, case studies, and tips will inspire you and guide you as you push your creative limits.

MY JOURNEY INTO DATA VISUALIZATION

How my path through astronomy and data science led me to my true passion

When I first realized my passion for the visualization of data around 2014—a decade ago at the time of writing—there weren't any data visualization courses offered at schools or universities that I was aware of. Every data visualizer I knew had wandered into the field in their own way, coming from their own unique backgrounds and professional experiences.

I've often been asked how an astronomer like myself ventured into this field. My journey is a series of seemingly unrelated experiences that, in hindsight, connected in just the right way to land me where I am now.

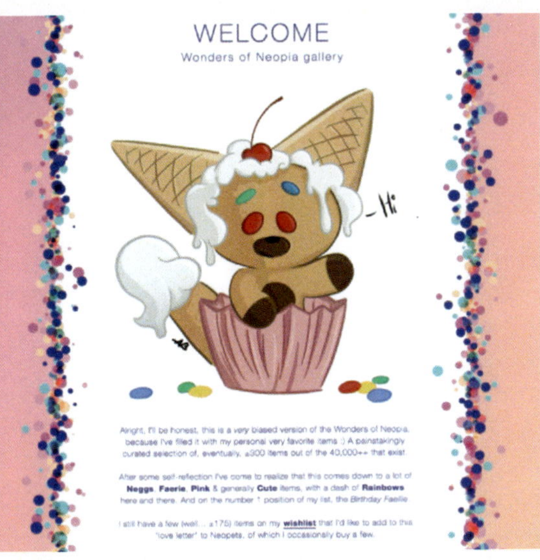

0.2

Figure 0.2

Screenshot of my customized gallery of favorite "Neopets" items, taken a few years after I started building "Neopets" pages.

EARLY YEARS

1987–2005

As a child, I always needed a creative outlet. Through drawing, cross-stitching, or molding clay, I found joy in creating things that were aesthetically pleasing. I had little interest in making anything functional; my goal was always to create something beautiful, something that you wanted to look at, something that could be worn or displayed.

For a while during my teenage years, I was obsessed with "Neopets," a virtual pet website where users can create and care for digital pets, play games, and explore a quest-driven fantasy world filled with shops and communities. I made custom designs for my own pets using Photoshop, and I dabbled in basic HTML and CSS to create a custom pet page (figure 0.2). Looking back, this was my first real exposure to coding.

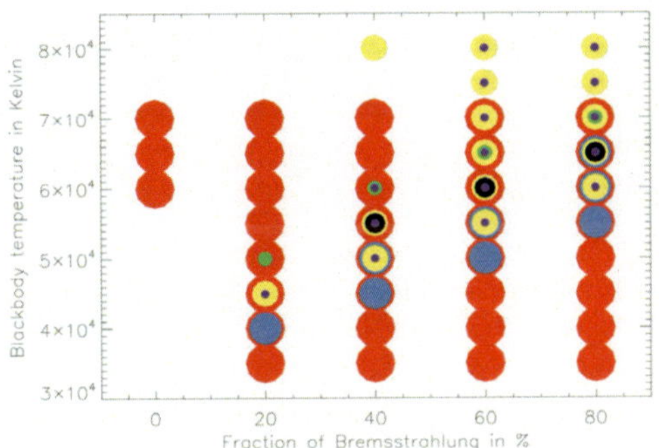

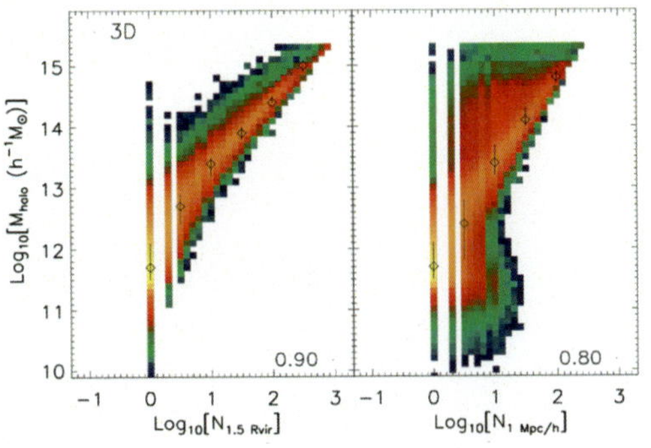

0.3

Figure 0.3

Two of the more visually creative images from my astronomy thesis papers; I've sadly forgotten much of what they convey.

STUDYING ASTRONOMY

2005-2011

I first fell in love with the cosmos at ten years old, after randomly picking a book about our solar system from the school library. After high school, I felt destined to study astronomy at Leiden University. In my first year, I was introduced to programming through a C++ course, and though it was challenging, I quickly became captivated by how code could "make things happen." However, after that initial course, I didn't code anything for almost three years, as there was no need to apply such skills in my calculus, linear algebra, and astronomy courses.

In the final year before receiving my Bachelor of Science degree, I was reintroduced to coding through IDL, a language used primarily in the field of astronomy. By the time I was tackling my master's thesis, coding had become second nature, and I regularly wrote scripts to analyze data, create images, and extract insights from simulations (figure 0.3).

0.4

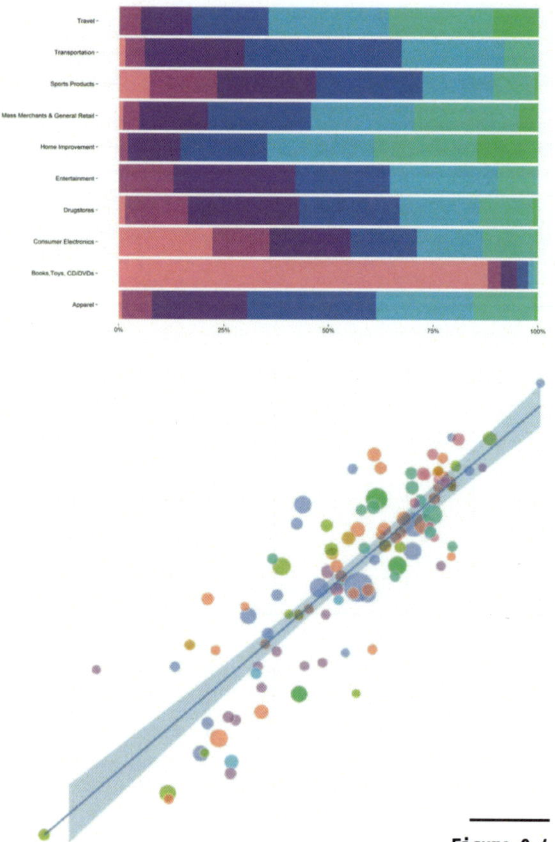

WORKING AS A DATA SCIENTIST

2011–2014

After completing my Master of Science degree in cosmology, I decided not to pursue a PhD. I still loved the field, but I wanted to work on projects with more practical applications. This led me to Deloitte in Amsterdam, where I joined the consulting division's newly formed analytics team as a data scientist. My studies had taught me how to gather, prepare, and analyze data; how to come up with hypotheses and test them; and how to solve a big problem through small, programmable steps. Instead of using these skills to uncover the mysteries of the cosmos, I was now using them to understand the patterns of consumer behavior—what meals they ordered at fast food restaurants, how much mortgage debt they held, what they purchased at the supermarket, and so on. I learned various new programming languages, including R, which became my go-to tool for data preparation and analysis (figure 0.4).

Figure 0.4

Charts I created with R that I deemed worthy enough to save on my laptop for over a decade (purposely stripped of titles and explanation)

As consultants, my team and I had to give many data-centric presentations to clients, typically at least one per week. As you might guess, we included a lot of data visualizations in our slides. Despite the countless number of charts I made during my first years at the company, I used only a very narrow selection of chart designs (notably, bar charts, line charts, box plots, and scatter plots).

At the start of 2013, I attended a data science conference where I was introduced to D3.js, a JavaScript library for creating interactive, web-based data visualizations. I immediately fell in love with its capabilities. After returning home, I spent the next week of my free time trying to build an interactive bubble chart that could switch between different variables and animate on mouse hovers (figure 0.5). The learning curve was steep, largely because writing commands in D3 was so different from the data analysis languages I was used to. I had to adjust to a new way of communicating how I wanted my charts to look and perform. I also had to learn JavaScript, with a sprinkle of HTML and CSS. It was a lot, all at once. Nevertheless, the creative potential of D3 excited me.

Figure 0.5

The first chart I ever created using D3.js, my primary tool for creating visualization to this day. I believe it was about mortgages. The chart could switch between different variables on the x- and y-axis on a click.

Variables are typically the columns in a data set that say something about the data points, such as country name, or building height, or person's age.

0.5

A TURNING POINT

2014

In late 2014, I created a few D3 visualizations at work, experimenting with less conventional chart types like hexagonal heatmaps. I still saw myself as a data scientist, but I wasn't sure I was enjoying the nature of the data analysis and machine learning work as much as I used to. Wrangling a predictive model to make it ever so slightly more accurate left me with more frustration than joy.

At my yearly review I had no good answer when my boss asked me about my goals for the coming years. On the heels of that sobering meeting, I attended another data science conference. I still remember feeling a bit empty as I went through the motions of attending presentations. Little did I know how quickly things would turn around.

I was early to a session and sat down, waiting for the presenter Mike Freeman, to set up. He plugged in his laptop, and his title slide appeared on the big screen: "Data Visualization Specialist."

It's like I was hit by lightning.

"That's a thing on its own?" I asked myself. "You can specialize in data visualization?"

In that instant, I knew where I wanted my career to go. This epiphany reignited my passion, and from that point on, I spent every free moment improving my skills and diving deeper into the world of data visualization. I started reading any book about data visualization best practices that I could get my hands on. I still remember the profound impact that Alberto Cairo's *The Functional Art* had on me.

I was actively searching for more data visualization content online, and that's how I found the works of data designers who were creating visuals as their main job! In particular, the works of Giorgia Lupi, Moritz Stefaner, and Jan Willem Tulp were, and still are, great inspiration for me. All of them embrace complexities within data sets and make very creative and custom visuals. I've gravitated to complex and richly layered designs with my own work, as you'll see more and more toward the end of this book.

Even more importantly, I created personal projects to put my knowledge to use (figure 0.6) and began to share my work publicly. Data visualization became my hobby. Sometimes I used data I found online, while other times I played with data sets from work to see what else I could do with them. I was genuinely enjoying myself.

0.6

Figure 0.6

Screenshots of a special kind of interactive chart, a chord diagram, that shows how people switch between phone brands. I had originally only created a static version for a report for Deloitte. See the full version at *nbremer.github.io/Chord-Diagram-Storytelling*

PIVOTING TO DATA VISUALIZATION DESIGN

2015–2016

With newfound clarity, I discussed my desire to focus on data visualization with my mentor and my boss. They were supportive of my efforts, and I began taking on a few projects with a larger data visualization focus than before. This new role wasn't just about analyzing data to develop market strategies. It also involved creating reports and posters, for example, to reveal the insights to an audience.

To try and connect with others in the field, I started a blog called "Visual Cinnamon" to share my personal projects and what I was learning with the wider (online) data visualization community.

In 2015, I joined Adyen, a fintech company that handles payments on behalf of businesses, as a full-time data visualization designer. I was working on prototypes of dashboards and custom visualizations for the company's client portal. Effectively, I would dream up and build standalone examples that my front-end colleagues could adapt for the website and client portal.

A major career milestone came in 2016, when I began a collaboration with the inspirational artist and solopreneur Shirley Wu (who is now also an amazing friend). We had met in the spring of that year at the OpenVis data visualization conference, where we'd both presented. That fall, we launched "Data Sketches" (datasketch.es), a project where we individually created an extensive data visualization on the same topic—ranging from lighthearted themes like movies to more abstract ones like nostalgia—each month for a year. These 24 visualizations (half hers, half mine) were not just creative outlets, but also learning experiences as we gave each other feedback, refined our work, and documented the entire process, from data gathering and preparation to sketching and finalizing our ideas. It took a few more years, but this collaboration eventually culminated in our book of the same name, celebrating the fusion of creativity and data (figure 0.7).

Figure 0.7

My first book, *Data Sketches*, published in 2021, which I co-wrote with Shirley Wu, about our extensive collaboration to explore creative data visualizations.

0.7

BECOMING A FREELANCER

2017-PRESENT

0.8a

0.8b

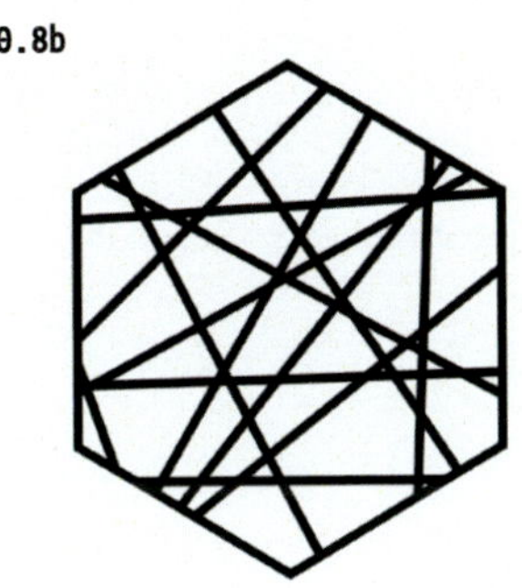

Figure 0.8a & b

The logos from Visual Cinnamon between 2017-2022 (a) and 2022-2025 (b).

After a year of primarily creating dashboards at Adyen, I realized I missed the diversity of consulting—working with different clients, exploring a range of industries, and solving various problems. Then, at the end of 2016, Google News Lab asked Shirley and me if we were interested in creating a project using some of Google's data for one month of "Data Sketches." I saw this as my opportunity to set out independently, with Google being my first paying client!

If you had asked me a few years earlier if I would ever consider freelancing, I would have said, "Absolutely not." Not having a steady paycheck felt too financially stressful. However, through "Data Sketches," I realized that I loved working on bespoke, custom, and creative data visualizations. If I wanted to work with a mix of clients, industries, and data, I knew I had to do it as a freelancer.

Initially, freelancing as a data visualization designer was daunting. But I had the fortune to continue working part-time with Adyen for a few months, which gave me peace of mind as I established myself.

Now, as I write this book in 2024, I've been freelancing for about eight years. My work is varied and rewarding. I've had the privilege to collaborate with clients and explore data sets I could have only dreamed of, and I continue to set my own schedule and explore new creative boundaries, even carving out time to write books!

Looking back, I can clearly see how all the pieces of my journey led to data visualization and data art. To me, data visualization is the perfect blend of math, science, and finding insights within data—fields I've always loved—combined with a deep-seated need to create something visually engaging. That creative itch I had as a child never left me. Even during my time in the corporate world, I spent weekends experimenting with origami lamps, melting crayons on canvas, and trying out any craft that caught my interest.

These days, I get to channel my creative energy directly into my work, crafting visualizations that are both functional and artistic. I am able to leverage my blend of skills, including analytics, science, art, and problem-solving to create insightful pieces. Data visualization, which sits at the intersection of logic and imagination, continues to excite me. I look forward to seeing where this adventure takes me next.

MY DATA VISUALIZATION PROCESS

The five stages that are common to all my projects

Every piece I create is different. But the work process I use is generally the same. In this chapter, I'll walk you through my sequence, from gathering insights to sketching ideas, to creating the final product. This will give you some background to better understand the full scope of the work behind the projects in this book. To me, this process is critical if you intend to nurture an environment for creative data visualization. Let's dive in!

1%-5% of a project's time

1 | FOUNDATIONAL WORK

To start any new visualization project, I need two things: the goal and the data. I obtain these in different ways, depending on whether I'm working on a client project or a personal project.

When I'm working on a client project, I have to:

In this book, client projects encompass work I've done for both my freelance clients and stakeholders I worked for as a corporate employee earlier in my career.

- **Understand the goal.** What does the client want to achieve with the visualization? Why do they want their data visualized? What should the audience learn, feel, or be convinced of? What story should it tell? Where—and in what form—will the final visual be published?

- **Get familiar with the data.** What variables are available? How much data is there? Are there multiple data sets (with different variables), or just one?

For personal projects, there are some subtle differences. First, I need to define the goal myself. This could either be a story or insight that I want to share visually (e.g., "show all gold medal winners in the Summer Olympic Games such that people can discover trends and patterns across the years"). However, sometimes, my goal is to learn a new technique or tool, in which case data insights are secondary. Once I know my goal, I'll generally look for a relevant and topical data set. Occasionally I stumble upon a fascinating data set before I've set a goal, in which case, I explore the data a bit to see if it's worth establishing a goal and turning the data set into a project. If you'd like to learn more about my process for personal projects, I highly suggest reading *Data Sketches,* a book I co-authored that walks through the entire process of 24 elaborate data visualization projects.

For now, let's assume that I'm working on a client project.

My process always starts with a conversation so I can understand the client's needs and hear more details about the data. Sometimes, the client will walk me through a spreadsheet via screen sharing; other times, they'll send over the full dataset or a sample for me to dive into.

It's also important for me to understand the intended target audience. Is the audience familiar with this particular data already, or are they new to it? Are they an informed audience (like company employees) that already has background knowledge or context, or a general audience? In what setting will the visual be displayed? There is a large difference between a fleeting social media post and a museum installation, to give you two extremes. In what form will the visual be presented: a website, a magazine, an Instagram post, a report? All of these answers have a large impact on the general direction of the design and how elaborate and creative I can be.

Furthermore, I need to know any technical constraints. Is the client looking for a static or interactive visualization? If it's static, what size are they envisioning? If it's interactive, should it resize for different screen sizes, like mobile or desktop? I sometimes have clients who don't specify their desired interactivity, in which case I give my advice on what would best suit their intended goal and also discuss the impact their decision has on the cost, as creating an interactive visualization takes far more time than a static one.

These are some of my typical questions, but there could be others depending on the nature of the project.

With this foundational information, I can evaluate the project's scope. I compare the scope to my past projects to see which are similar in complexity, cost, and time. This lets me estimate the budget I would need. After we've gone through the administrative steps and signed the contract, I can really dive in!

5%-30% of a project's time

2 | DATA CLEANING AND ANALYSIS

Worry not! I'll run through the software and tools that I use for all my data analysis, sketching, and programming in the next chapter.

The first step is cleaning the data: checking it for errors and missing values. I check each variable to ensure that the data has been loaded into my program correctly and note whether anything seems odd: Are the numeric variables all numbers? How many unique values does each variable have?

Next, I roughly explore the data. I look for trends, patterns, and outliers by analyzing the data and calculating basic statistics like minimums,

0.9a

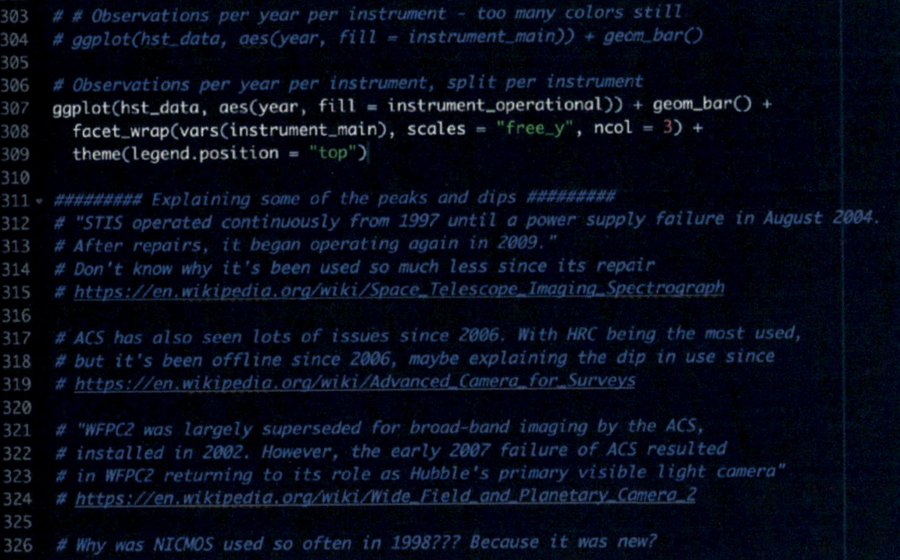

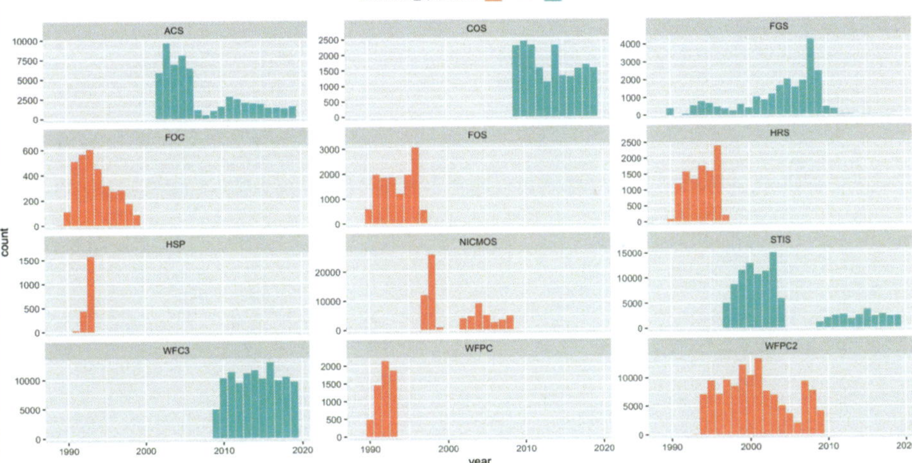

0.9b

Figure 0.9a & b

Snippet from my R code analyzing Hubble's instruments and the notes I added for context (a), and the accompanying plot showing the number of observations by operational (turquoise) and non-operational (red) instruments (b).

maximums, and averages. I also create simple charts—line charts, bar charts, scatter plots, box plots—anything that helps me build a mental model of the data. Data cleaning and data analysis usually go hand in hand—I jump between checking the data and understanding it continuously.

I take a lot of notes during this phase, writing down anything that stands out or seems unusual. For instance, while analyzing data for the Hubble Space Telescope project (which you'll see in Lesson 10), I noticed certain telescope instruments weren't used for stretches of time. Curious, I did some research and discovered that those instruments occasionally failed and were repaired by astronauts (very cool!). I wrote my research findings alongside the code that analyzed the instruments data (figure 0.9). Keep in mind, this preliminary research may end up on the cutting room floor once I start assembling the visual. Ultimately, there was so much other interesting information in the Hubble data that I didn't even get to use the instrument findings in the final visual!

This process may take less than an hour for very small data sets. But it could also take a week or two (in case of the Hubble data set, for instance), and lead to follow-up emails full of questions for the client. I think of this phase as a jigsaw puzzle, where I need all the pieces in place to truly understand the data.

5%-10% of a project's time

3 | SKETCHING DESIGNS

Once I've cleaned and analyzed the data, it's time to come up with a way to visualize that data. I start by creating a mood board for the project: a collection of inspiring visuals that I think align with the project in some way. I don't share this mood board with the client, as they may not understand why I might have selected certain images. (In the end, I'll pick a few of the images that best reflect my ideas and sketches of the final product, which I then share with the client via email or in a more formal presentation.)

With my mood board open on my computer for reference, I begin sketching. Yes, I hand draw sketches on my iPad or in my notebook (as you'll learn more about in Lesson 5). Sketching helps me explore different design approaches (Figure 0.10). If I can, I'll try to create multiple concepts and sketches. These sketches are often very abstract, focusing on the main shape(s) that I want to use for visualizing the data.

Sometimes, I present all the options to the client; other times, one concept stands out, and that's the only one I show. After presenting the sketches and gathering client feedback, I'm ready to build the final visualization. This sketching phase generally takes about a day, perhaps two days for projects with multiple visualizations.

Figure 0.10a & b

Initial, hand-drawn sketch in my notebook for a project for Mozilla about noteworthy contributors to a GitHub repository (a), and a second digital sketch to refine some of the colors and details (b). The final result is shown in Mini Chapter IV.

0.10a

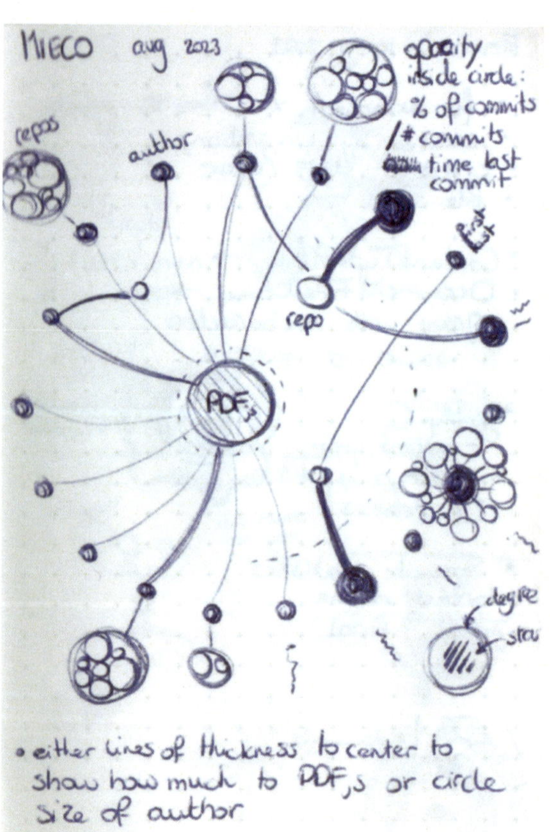

0.10b

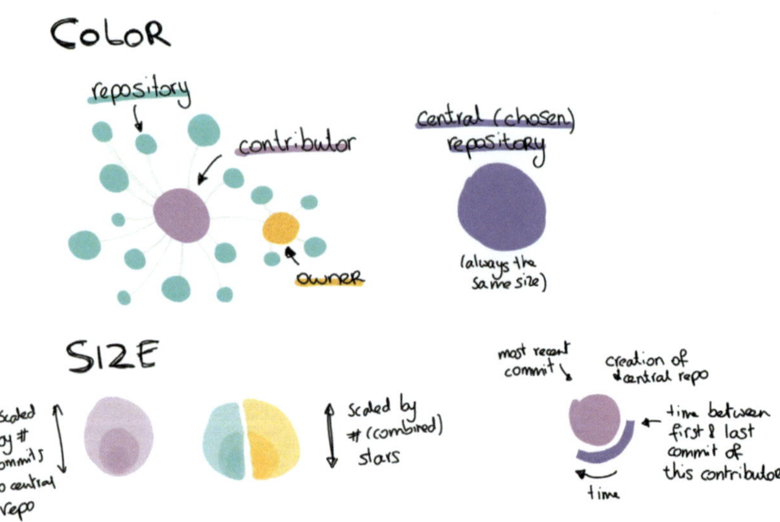

70%-90% of a project's time

4 | CREATING THE DATA VISUALIZATION

Next, I translate the rough sketch into an actual, but basic, visual on my screen. At this stage, I'm not concerned with axes, colors, labels, or details—just the shapes and overall structure. Despite my earlier analysis, the data can often surprise me as it comes to life on my monitor. For example, while sketching, I may have thought that 3,000 data points would fit in the given space, but in practice, it didn't work. Catching these quirks early allows for adjustments or even a redesign if needed (usually, a compromise or deviation from the original approach will solve the problem).

I always program my visualizations. Even for small datasets, I prefer programming, because I can plot all of my data exactly according to the values. It can take a long time to set up, but once it works, it doesn't matter if I have 1 or 1 million data points (apart from the computer taking more time to draw them all). Plus, it's fairly straightforward to make small adjustments, like scaling the circles to a different size, because the program will apply those adjustments to all the points at once. This makes it fast and pain-free to iterate the design.

Figure 0.11

Interactive visualization showing results from "ranked-choice votes" for the Democratic candidates during the 2020 US election. See more about this project at *visualcinnamon.com/portfolio/swayable-preferential-polling*. Conceptualized with James Slezak at *Swayable.com*

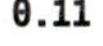

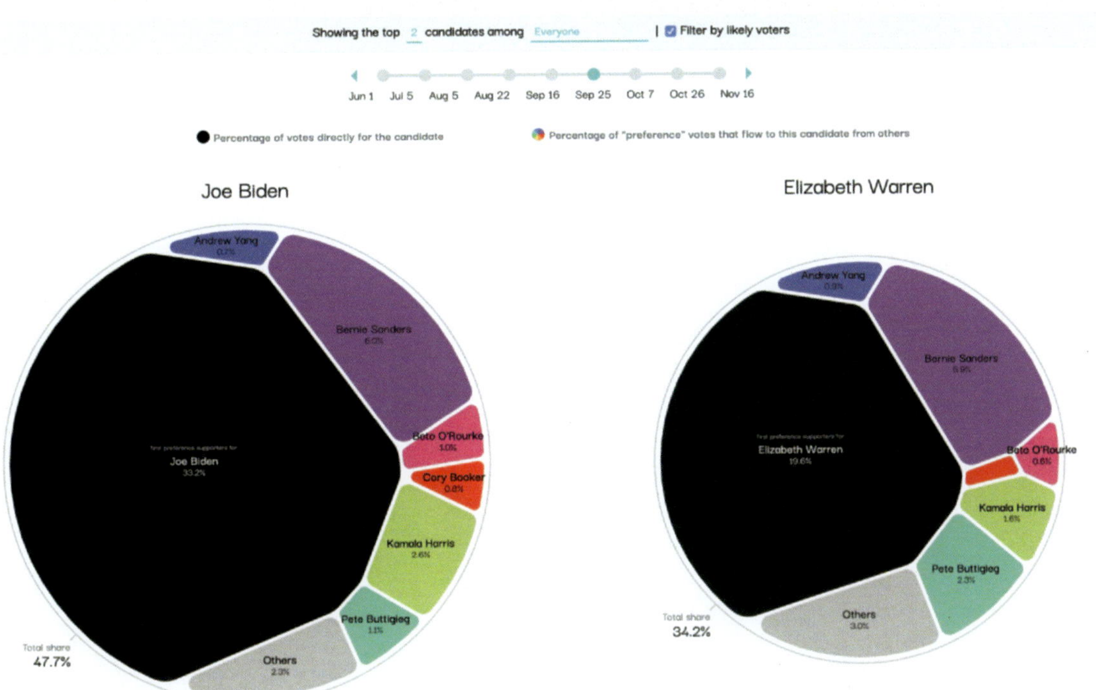

Once the structure is in place, I focus on the finer details. In the course of the project, this is where I spend most of my time, thinking about how to make the visualization not only functional but also engaging. It's also the part of the process that can look different from project to project, as I always customize my visualizations to each client and data set.

Throughout the design process—but especially early on, when many things are still changing—I send the client updates on my progress, generally in (long) emails with many screenshots, and disclaimers about how the look is still rough. These touch points allow the client to provide feedback, keeping them involved and excited about the visualization.

I will say that for 90% of my projects, the client provides useful feedback that improves the result. Nevertheless, there are times when I'll disagree with clients' ideas or feedback. I will try and convince them that another approach would be better. However, in the end, if they wish to not heed

Figure 0.12

The first work of the "Imagine" collection, which creates fictional skies and constellations inviting the viewer to engage their imagination and find objects, animals, and mythical heroes within the shapes and patterns. See more versions at *visualcinnamon.com/art/axiom-space*

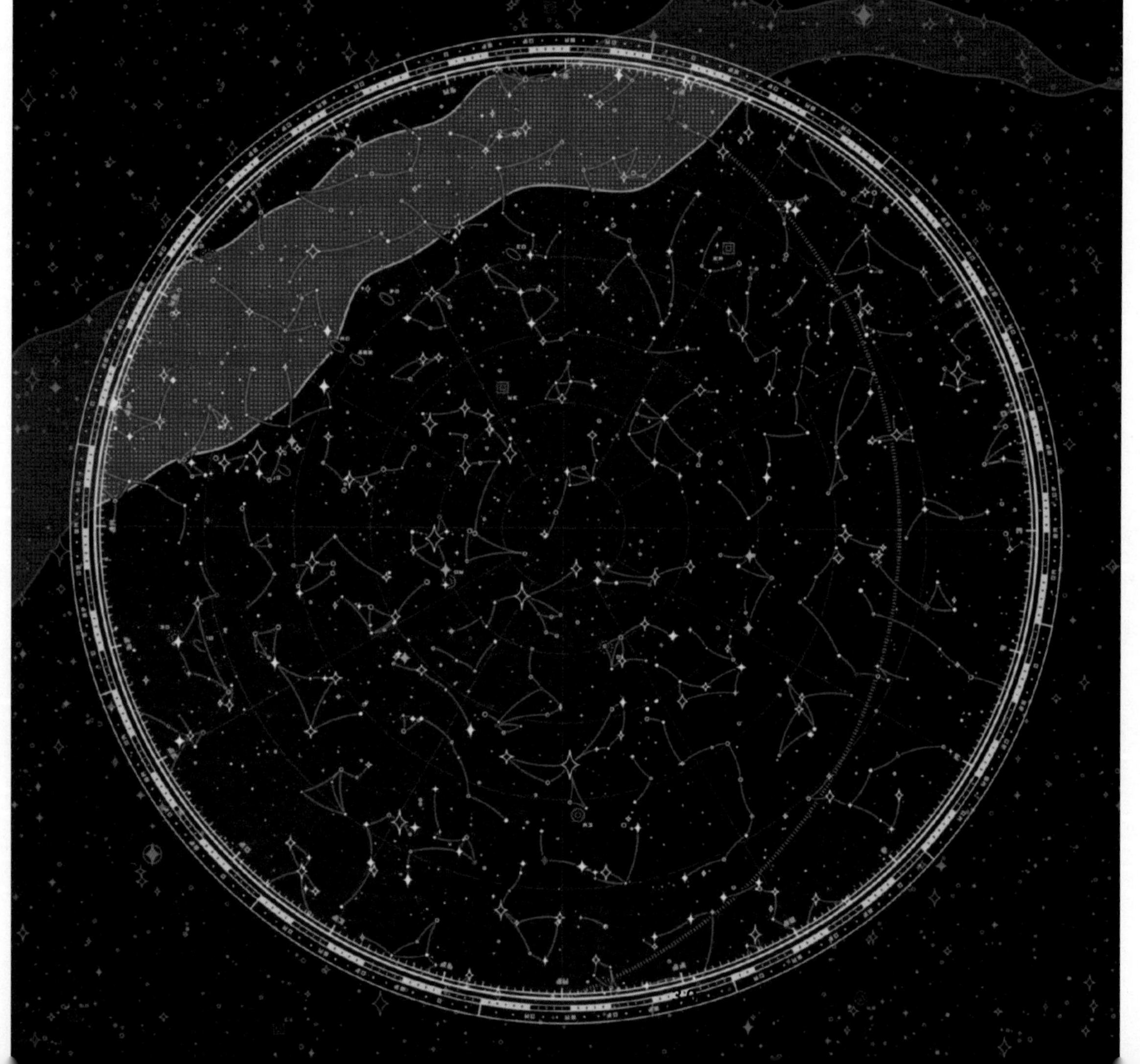

0.12

my advice, I will follow their wishes, as they have the final say. (That said, I never agree to manipulating the design in a way that would inaccurately present the data.)

For smaller projects, I typically offer two rounds of feedback. For larger projects, I incorporate feedback throughout the process whenever it's given. In those cases, I fully embrace my perfectionist side and continue until the client and I—though usually I'm the stricter judge—think it's done.

1%–5% of a project's time

5 | DELIVERING THE FINAL RESULT

When the result is a static visual, I often program it until it's between 90% and 95% complete. Next, I copy the result into a vector program to add the final touches by hand. I find that this manual process is actually faster for some details, especially elements that appear only once, such as a title, introduction text, legends, and annotations (though when there are many annotations, I program them). Finally, I will send the image files to the client.

If the final visual is interactive or is meant for the web, I generally send the code to the client. I add clear documentation, so their developers can integrate my work into their systems or website.

And that's my "typical" process. I try to be very flexible with my clients' wishes, so the finer steps of each project might look a little different, but the broad strokes stay consistent. I've produced interactive prototypes, websites, posters, images, videos, and (giant) framed prints—and just about everything in between (except for a painted mural, which is still on my wishlist). While these formats may not seem to have much in common, they all are custom-designed. Every project is a little different—the subject of the data set, the client and its industry, the place where the piece will be displayed—which is part of the reason why I find my job to always feel interesting.

MY TOOLS AND SOFTWARE

A quick look at my trusty companions

I'd like to introduce you to the typical tools that I use in my data visualization process. They are mentioned in roughly the order that I work with them during a project. This is by no means an exhaustive list, and what works well for you can be something entirely different. It gets a bit technical and niche here and there, but I want to give you the complete picture. Don't worry if some of the software and programs mentioned in this chapter are foreign to you; none are a requirement to understand the concepts in this book.

HARDWARE

I'm currently working on a MacBook Pro. Due to the big data sets that I often work with, I opted for a powerful laptop. For 90% of the time, I have it plugged into my extremely wide 38″ Dell monitor, as I can work much faster if I have the space to see a browser, the code, and debugger open side-by-side. A webcam (Logitech C920), a wireless keyboard (Apple), and a good ergonomic mouse (Logitech MX Master 2S) round it out.

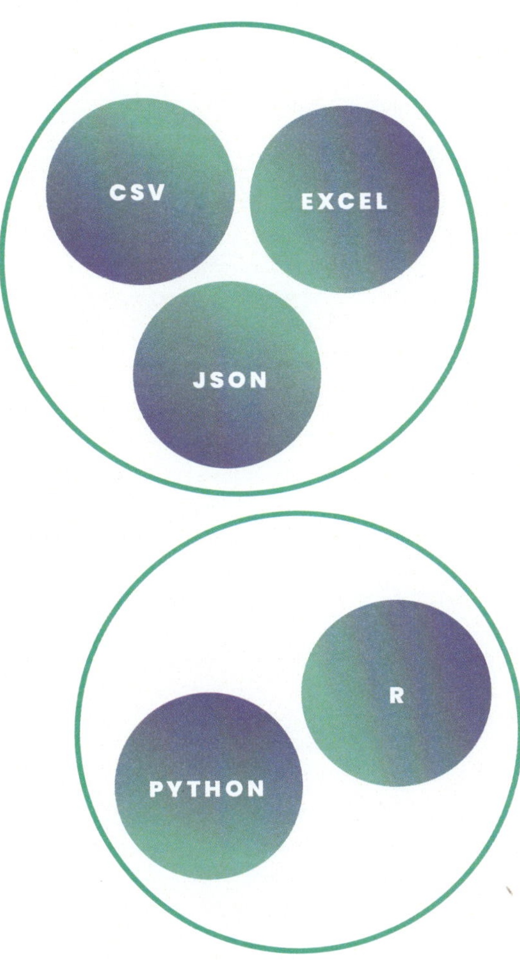

DATA PROCESSING

In terms of data, I work with CSV (comma separated values), JSON (JavaScript Object Notation), and Excel files for almost all of my projects. There are the very occasional exceptions, when I use more exotic file types, or image (JPEG/PNG) files.

For data cleaning and analysis, I use R, a programming language specifically designed for statistical computing and data analysis. Its programming style suits me perfectly—I use it for both the quick data explorations and the deep dives. I also rely on it to help shape my initial visualizations.

I occasionally work with Python, another programming language used for data analysis (and many other applications). However, this is only when I need to use a function that R doesn't support.

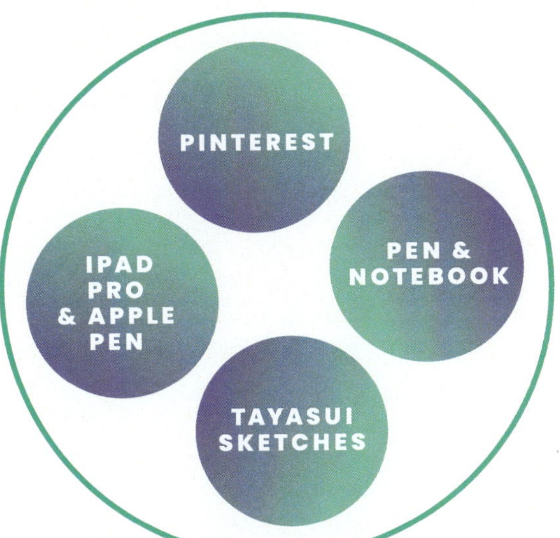

SKETCHING

During the design phase, I turn to my Pinterest boards (found on pinterest.com/visualcinnamon). Some boards are about data visualization, and some hold interesting images on other topics. I look through the boards and I copy anything that sparks inspiration to a private "client mood board" for later reference.

For the ideation process, I rely on sketching. I'll dive deep into this in Lesson 5, but I firmly believe in sketching initial ideas by hand. For this, I use the most analog tools of them all: a pen and a little pocketbook notebook that I can easily carry with me at all times. That way, I can sketch both at home and during downtime (e.g., waiting for public transport).

However, I also have an 11″ iPad Pro and an Apple Pen if I want to more easily work with colors and layers. Effectively, I can make the sketches more elaborate without losing the freedom of drawing anything I want. Tayasui Sketches is an app that I find has just the right number of options that I need for my minimal sketches, which is important because I don't want to be distracted by extra or overwhelming bells and whistles.

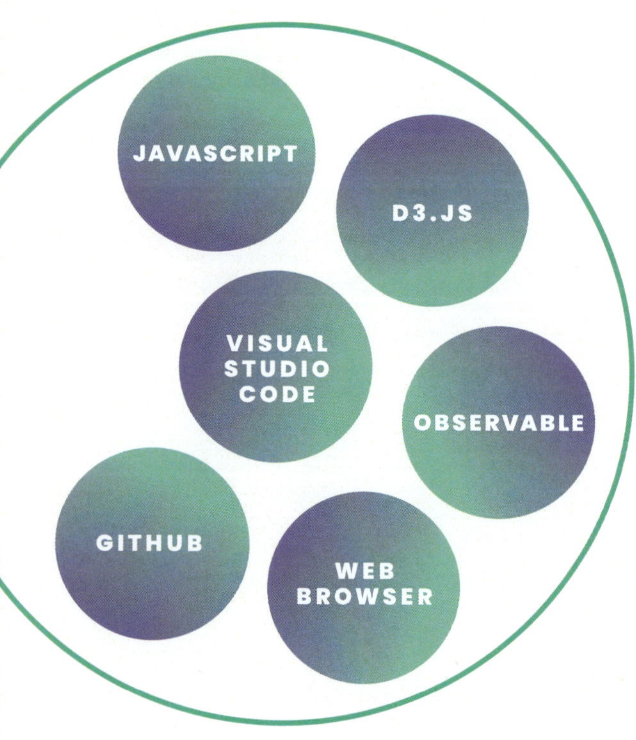

PROGRAMMING

Once I have the rough design in hand, I start programming with JavaScript, the programming language used for creating interactive and dynamic content on websites. I almost always bring in (or "import," in computer speak) D3.js, a JavaScript library that creates custom, dynamic, and interactive data visualizations for the web. I recommend it for its versatility, as it can handle everything from simple charts to complex, interactive stories. I appreciate the extreme amount of freedom I have to fine-tune even the smallest details of the visual. There is a steep learning curve with D3, which I've experienced myself. Nevertheless, it was worth the pain because I've not found better tools to execute static and interactive creative ideas (other than doing it manually, which isn't possible when the data sets are too big).

Although frameworks such as React, Vue, and Svelte are widely used in web development, I don't incorporate any of these into my process. I try to have as few dependencies as possible to avoid a clash with the software already embedded in the client environment/ website. But also, I get joy from creating the visualization, not from the technology and coding itself. Therefore, I have not (yet) found the drive, or need, thankfully, to learn any framework.

I might look up some sample visuals on Observable, which is an interactive data visualization platform created by Mike Bostock, the original author of D3. It features a giant repository of "notebooks" containing the underlying code for any featured visual. Most of these are based on D3, making it a great place to get the base code for a certain chart form.

I write my code in Visual Studio Code, which has many convenient extensions to streamline the process. It features a code spell-checker, a "live server" that automatically reloads the webpage every time I save my script, and dozens of other helpful capabilities. It also implements GitHub Copilot (an AI-powered code completion tool) to make writing code faster and less tedious.

I look at the resulting visual using a web browser. I check that my visual works in all mainstream browsers so I can correct functionality glitches and account for any browser bugs.

GitHub is for my version control, a means to manage and track changes in my code. It also serves as an online backup of my work in case something happens to my laptop. Furthermore, GitHub offers a straightforward way to turn code into a private website (called GitHub Pages) that I can regularly share with my clients.

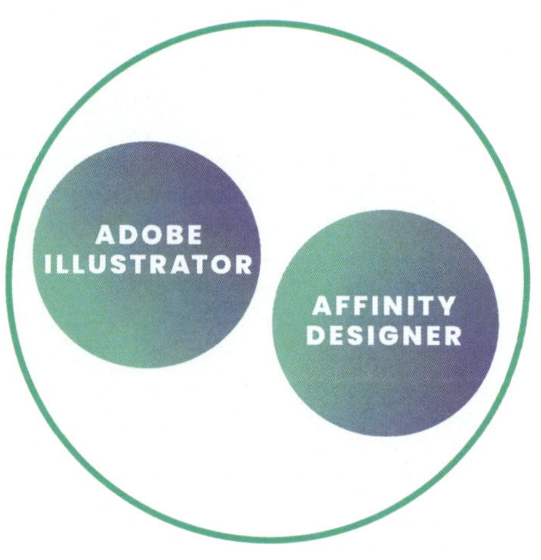

For projects that are static images, I often copy the visual to a vector program such as Adobe Illustrator or Affinity Designer to add some final elements (such as legends) and make minor adjustments.

And with that, you're familiar with the core tools of my day-to-day work. Most of them are also free and open-source. I encourage you to give them a try!

To be sure, I also like to experiment with other tools. Sometimes, a certain design style or a certain data set might demand a different kind of tool, such as WebGL, which I needed for the "Breathing Earth" project in Lesson 4, and Blender, which I learned while making the "Nintendo Switch Games" visual in Lesson 11.

Figure 0.13

My desk setup at home between 2017 and 2023, with prints from Dan Catt, Gemma O'Brien, Matt DesLauriers, and Shirley Wu displayed on the walls, alongside some of my own work.

Figure 0.14

My paper notebook and iPad Pro with sketches.

0.13

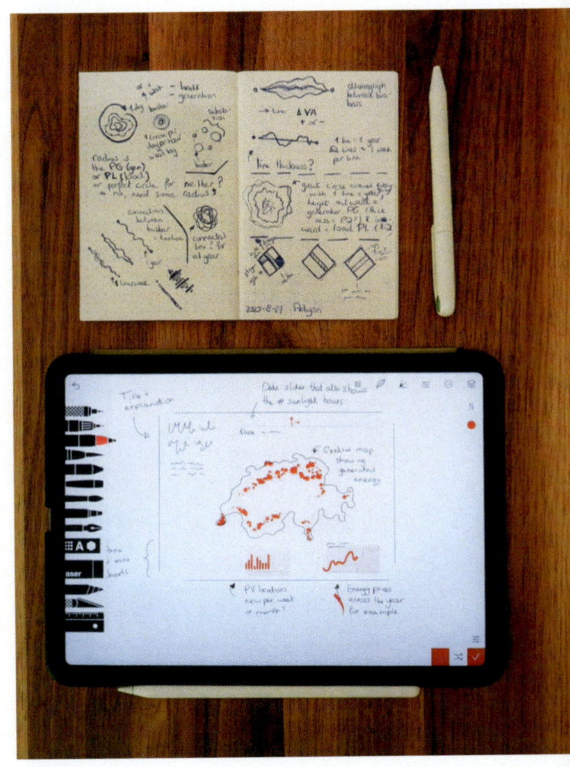

0.14

PART I

STAYING CLOSE

Charts have become ubiquitous in the corporate world. You can't go through a report or view a slide deck without seeing a chart. And business dashboards are full of them, of course! Most of these fall into what I call the "ordinary charts" category. You could also call them standard, traditional, or straightforward charts. They include line charts and bar charts, and their sole purpose is to show the data. Many chart purists glorify extreme versions of these charts and believe that every pixel should be dedicated to showing data in its most minimal form.
No embellishments allowed!

It's hardly a wonder that these straightforward charts are everywhere: These days, many people know how to interpret them without needing an explanation. They are hugely important because they allow people to grasp data-based insights quickly and easily.

ORDINARY CHARTS

But therein lies the crux. How do you make an impact if your audience has seen hundreds of line charts? How do you make yours stand out? How do you inject some creativity into even the most common chart without diminishing its effectiveness?

In this section, I'll demonstrate design techniques that can enhance a traditional chart. I'll explain how to add small but significant touches to the design, use uncommon chart forms, and even merge two standard charts to create something completely new and exciting.

By the end, you'll be able to take the ordinary chart forms that we all know and love and make them more suitable for your data, more memorable, and more effective!

LESSON ONE

GIVE A CHART

The topic or subject of the data can be great inspiration to elevate a straightforward chart

I love to customize each project according to the data set, even if there isn't much data to work with. I try to add something to catch the viewer's eye, to make them curious about a visual that they haven't seen before.

Consider bar charts. Bar charts are everywhere! It's impossible to recall all the bar charts you've seen. I've personally created more bar charts than any other chart type, particularly in my preliminary analysis stage, when I'm exploring and trying to wrap my head around a new data set. I also often use them as smaller, supplemental charts around a central, more prominent visual. However, when a bar chart (or any other straightforward chart type) needs to be the primary visual, I try to go beyond the default. I look to elevate it in a unique way and make it stand out from all the other bar charts in the world.

Depending on the data you're working with, this process can be easy or challenging. I find that when working with data that has lots of elements (rows) or variables (columns), customization happens more naturally. I see myself as "painting with the data." The more data I have available, the bigger my toolset. I have more opportunity to create something visually diverse using a variety of shapes, in various sizes and colors. Smaller data sets don't often allow me to paint so freely. I need to sit down and think about how to make the visual more memorable and engaging.

Whether I'm working with an expansive data set or a succinct one, I first consider the data's topic and what each data point represents. If the data set is about people, cities, technology, or nature, for instance, I'll tap into those categories for creative inspiration.

SOMETHING

UNIQUE

MAKE IT MORE HUMAN

When I'm representing individuals within my data visualization, I try to make each person visible—showing each as a separate entity.

An almost stacked bar chart

BUSINESS | 2019 | ADYEN
investors.adyen.com/financials/h2-2018

Figure 1.1

Adyen's employee growth from 2017 to 2018, by office.

For example, the grid of (somewhat) stacked bar charts in figure 1.1 puts a twist on traditional stacked bar charts. Of all my creative work, this is the closest I've gotten to featuring a standalone bar chart as the primary visual. I created it for a bi-yearly shareholder letter for Adyen, a payment technology company in the Netherlands. It shows the one-year growth of full-time employees (or FTEs) in each office. The number of employees at year-end 2017 is in bright green and the number of added employees at year-end 2018 is in dark green.

Since I was creating a chart about a relatively small number of people, I wanted to draw each person separately. I especially wanted to emphasize the individuals running an entire office by themselves. After some rough sketches, I eventually made a visual that looks like a stacked bar chart (if you squint your eyes a little), but where each employee is a single diamond.

For as far back as I can remember, I've been a big believer in turning data into relatable, captivating visual experiences. After reading Giorgia Lupi's 2017 "Data Humanism" manifesto, I realized that my style aligned with a movement to make data, as she says, "unique, contextual, intimate." Giorgia's work continues to be a touchstone for me as I've developed my personal ideas about data design, many of which are now expressed in this book.

Initially, I used a square to represent each person. However, I found that rotating the squares 45 degrees to form diamond shapes was a little more visually attractive (and as a metaphor, I felt that a diamond shape looked more like a "human" shape than a square).

I could have styled each diamond a little differently. Humans are all unique, and adding a little randomness to the icons makes them appear more organic, more natural, more human. (I'll dive deeper into randomness as a creative tool in Lesson 12.) However, in this case, it was better to show restraint and make each icon look the same. Embellishing the diamonds further simply wouldn't have been a good visual match for Adyen's brand style and the report's overall design. In addition, making each diamond a little different (in size, for example) would obfuscate the stacked bar chart shape I was going for.

There are no strict rules that determine how far you can go in turning a more standard chart into something unique. You have to rely somewhat on your gut, and ask yourself, "Does it feel right?"

1.1

You develop this intuition with experience, but, along the way, you should:

- Consider the importance of the visual. This was one of many charts in the whole report and not the most important one. I made the most important charts in the report as visually attractive and memorable as possible and while keeping the others more straightforward.
- Make it fit with the overall brand style (if applicable).

- Ensure the chart still reveals the same insights as the more standard version would have.

Just two intentional design decisions—to plot individuals instead of grouping them and showing them as diamonds instead of squares—was all it took to spruce up a standard chart. By preserving simplicity, this visual has all the benefits of traditional stacked bar charts while sparking intrigue and offering a little more detail.

DRAW INSPIRATION FROM PHYSICAL SHAPES

Let's look beyond human-centric data. If your data points represent any kind of tangible entity (cats, clothes, computers) or have a relationship to something physical (such as data about daylight hours corresponding to the sun), you can use that physical subject for inspiration. You can also find inspiration for concepts with a clear visual mark or metaphor (such as showing love through the heart shape). Basically, you have the liberty to use any form, silhouette, or shape—whether simple or complex—that represents the data.

I'm not against icons completely; there's always an "it depends." However, I would caution you to apply icons only when you've considered them thoroughly, and even then, use them sparingly and make sure they complement the rest of the visual.

Personally, I try not to be too on the nose. Icons might come to mind quickly. However, an overload of icons makes a visual appear less refined. It puts the viewer's focus more on the icons themselves, not the data. Furthermore, using many icons often creates visual clutter. The more complex the icon's shape, the less elegant I generally find the result.

Nevertheless, that doesn't mean an icon can't be a good jumping-off point.

1.2

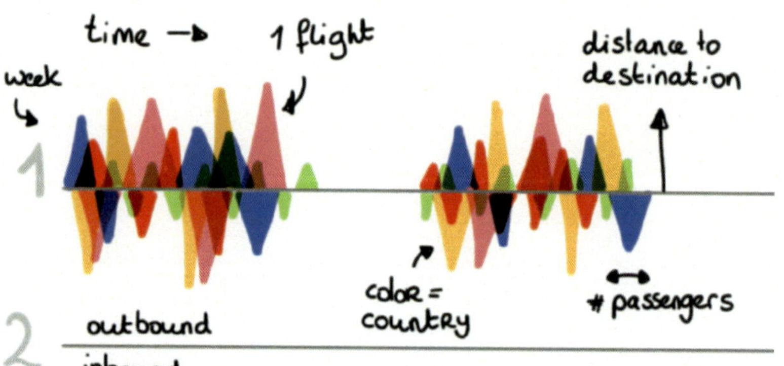

Triangle flights

BUSINESS | 2017 | TRANSAVIA

visualcinnamon.com/portfolio/a-year-in-flights

Often, when I want to represent a single data point, I opt for the tried-and-true circle. Circles are universally recognized as individual data points. A circle is the most minimal shape, perfectly symmetrical; dot your pen on a piece of paper and you have a circle. It's a fundamental shape, and available in any graphical software. But there are

1.3a

Figure 1.2

A sketch of the various ways each flight is encoded through its triangle shape, orientation, position, and color.

Figure 1.3a & b

The final poster of "A Year in Flights," showing a year of Transavia's flights, using triangles to represent each plane.

other options that fall somewhere between circles and very complex shapes that are ripe for exploration.

Consider, for instance, the piece I created for Transavia, a Dutch airline. I placed all their tens of thousands of flights from the previous year in one visual. I didn't use tiny airplane icons to represent airline flight data. Instead, I used a more schematic idea of airplanes: elongated triangles. As shown in my sketch in figure 1.2, there were various ways that I encoded the flight data into triangles. For instance, the taller the triangles, the farther the distance to the destination. The wider, the more passengers. Up or downward pointing triangles represent outgoing or incoming flights, respectively. Color shows the country the flights were going to (for outbound) or coming from (inbound).

In figure 1.3, you can see the final result that was printed on a canvas spanning almost 3 meters wide by 1 meter high (9′10″ by 3′3″).

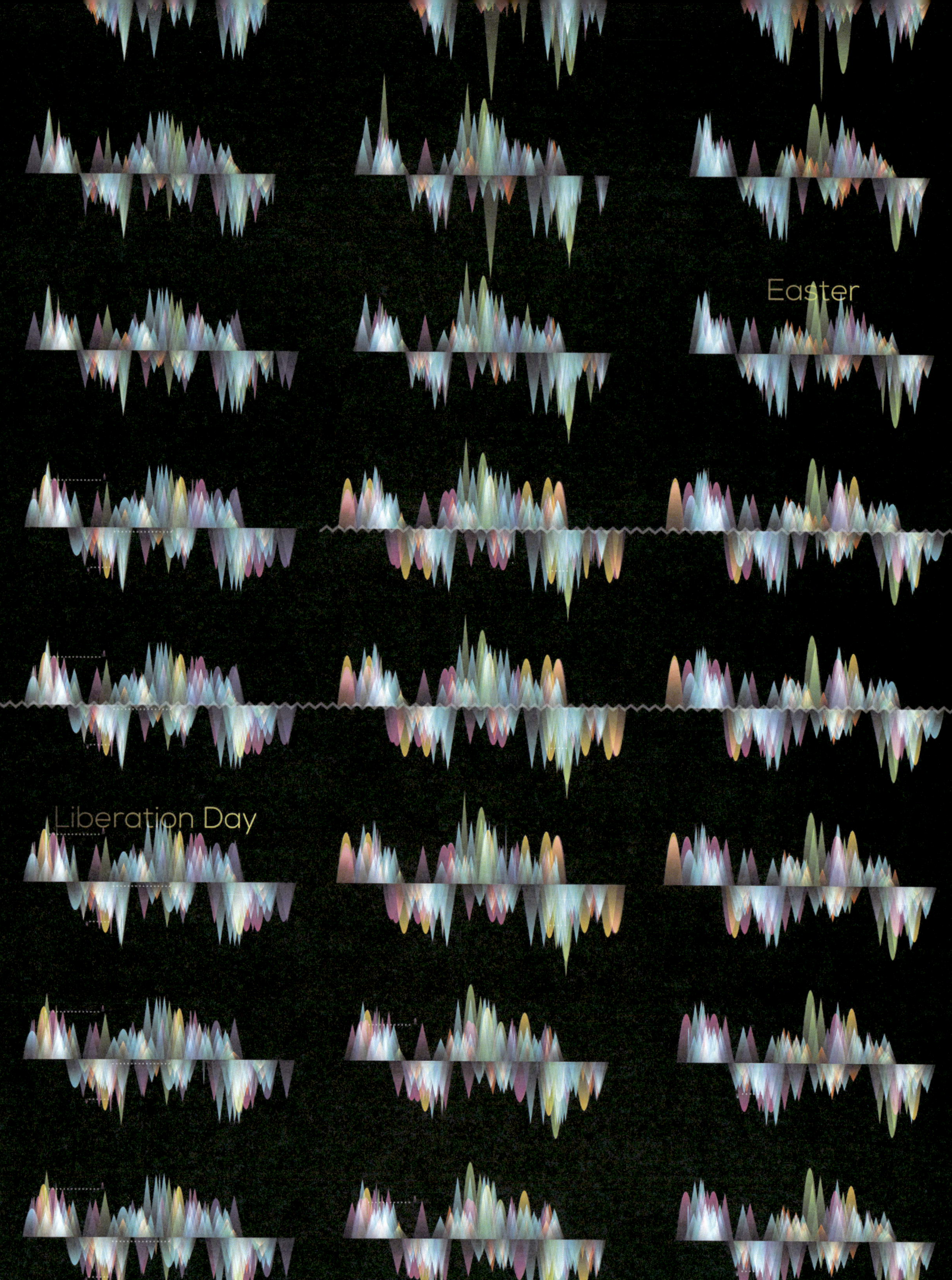
Easter
Liberation Day

I also thought the elongated triangles evoked the airplane exhaust trails that fan out as the particles dissipate. This symbolism, in addition to the schematic airplane shape, made triangles a more natural shape than dots to represent each flight.

Figure 1.4a & b

A zoom in of "The Top 2000 ❤ the 70s & 80s" visual (a) and the full poster on the next page (b).

Vinyl record circles

PERSONAL | 2016 | THE TOP 2000 ❤ THE 70S & 80S
top2000.visualcinnamon.com

Figure 1.4 shows a poster I created for "Data Sketches." It explores the top 2,000 best songs—as chosen by a Dutch audience—where each song is a circle. The songs are clustered by year of release and plotted along a diagonal axis with 1960 at the bottom-left and 2010 at the top-right. The bigger the circle, the higher the position in the top 2,000.

1.4a

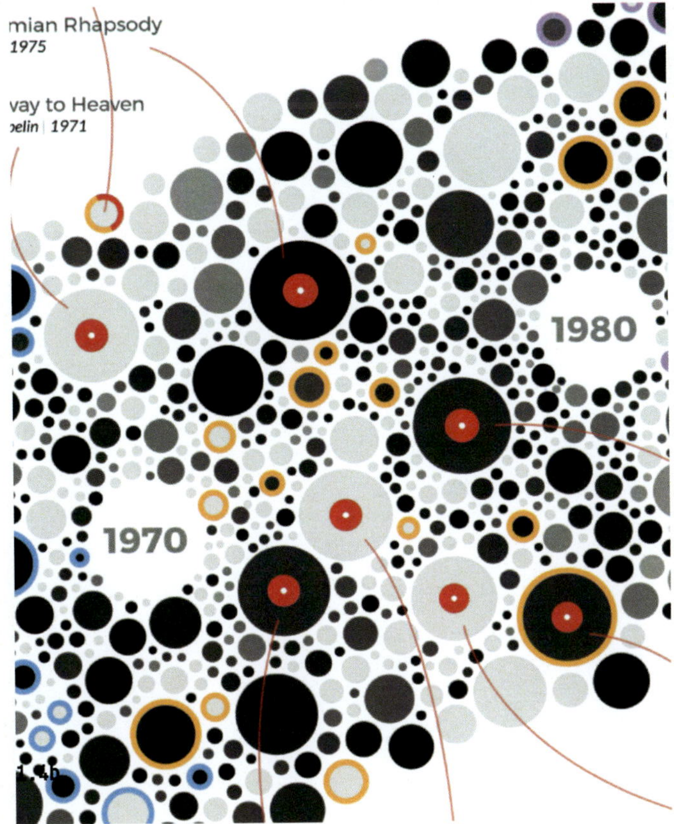

As this data set represented music across the decades, I made the top 10 songs stand out by designing them to look like vinyl records. I was lucky that a vinyl record is circular and quite schematic in its basic design; I only had to add two smaller circles to the main black/gray circle to create the record's label (in red) and the tiny hole in the middle (in white).

Making each of the 2,000 circles look like vinyl records would have overloaded the visual, resulting in a cluttered mess. Instead, by only applying this embellishment to the top 10 songs, I made those data points stand out. The vinyl records add that small "something" to make the visual more unique.

TOP 2000 ❤ 70's & 80's

Since 1999 the 2000 most popular songs of all time, as voted by the show's audience, are played on Dutch national Radio 2 in a yearly marathon. The 2000 songs are on the air between noon on December 25th until New Year's Eve and over half of the Dutch population listens to the Top 2000 each year.

Each ● to the right represents a song in the Top 2000. It is placed according to its year of release. In the legend below you can see what the size and color of a song means.

The bulk of the songs and most of the top 10 are from the 70's & 80's...

Newly discovered
Although already released in 1972, *Starman* from David Bowie is the highest new song in the list. It never appeared in the previous 17 editions of the Top 2000 and entered in 2016 on position 270.

Prince
Another legend who passed away in 2016 (on April 21st). It seems that new people discovered his works, with all 9 songs that were in 2015's list rising significantly and 8 more songs joining in 2016.

Position in Top 2000

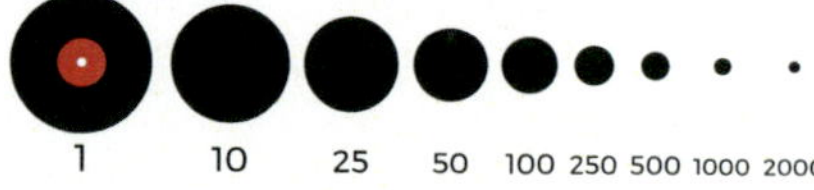

Highest position reached in weekly Top 40

never reached the top 40*

1 Bohemian Rhapsody
Queen | 1975

3 Stairway to Heaven
Led Zeppelin | 1971

1980

1970

Golden oldie
The oldest song in the list, Billie Holiday's *Strange Fruit*, is from 1939. It's 17 years older than the second-oldest song. If it will make the 2017 edition remains to be seen, it's barely in now, on position 1989.

Year of release

The Beatles
No other artist or band has more songs in the Top 2000 as the Beatles. With 38 songs they are responsible for 14% of all titles before 1970. Nonetheless, only 5 years ago they still had 50 songs in the list.

4 Piano Man
Billy Joel | 1974

5 Child in Time
Deep Purple | 1972

Spread across release years of the 2000 songs
For 4 editions of the Top 2000

The charts on the right represent all 2000 songs from 3 past editions of the Top 2000 (held in 2000, 2005, 2010) and the most recent 2016 edition.

The songs are stacked according to their year of release. The higher a rectangle, the more songs that are in the Top 2000 list from that release year.

The black dotted line represents a smoothed curve over all 2000 songs. This makes the comparison between the 4 charts easier.

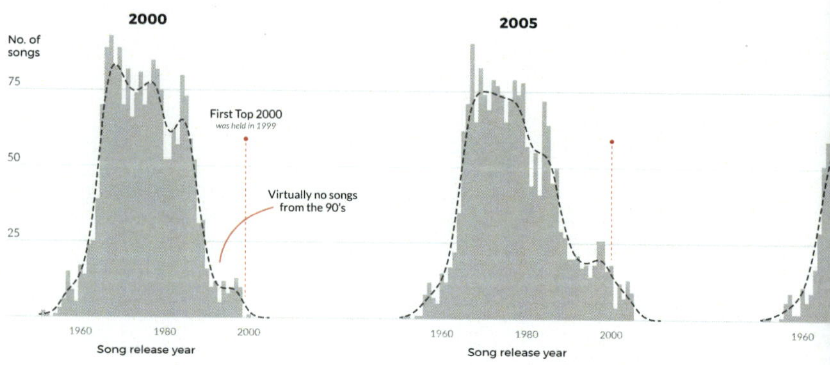

Created by Nadieh Bremer | VisualCinnamon.com for the December edition of data sketch|es

Visit tinyurl.com/2016top2000 for the

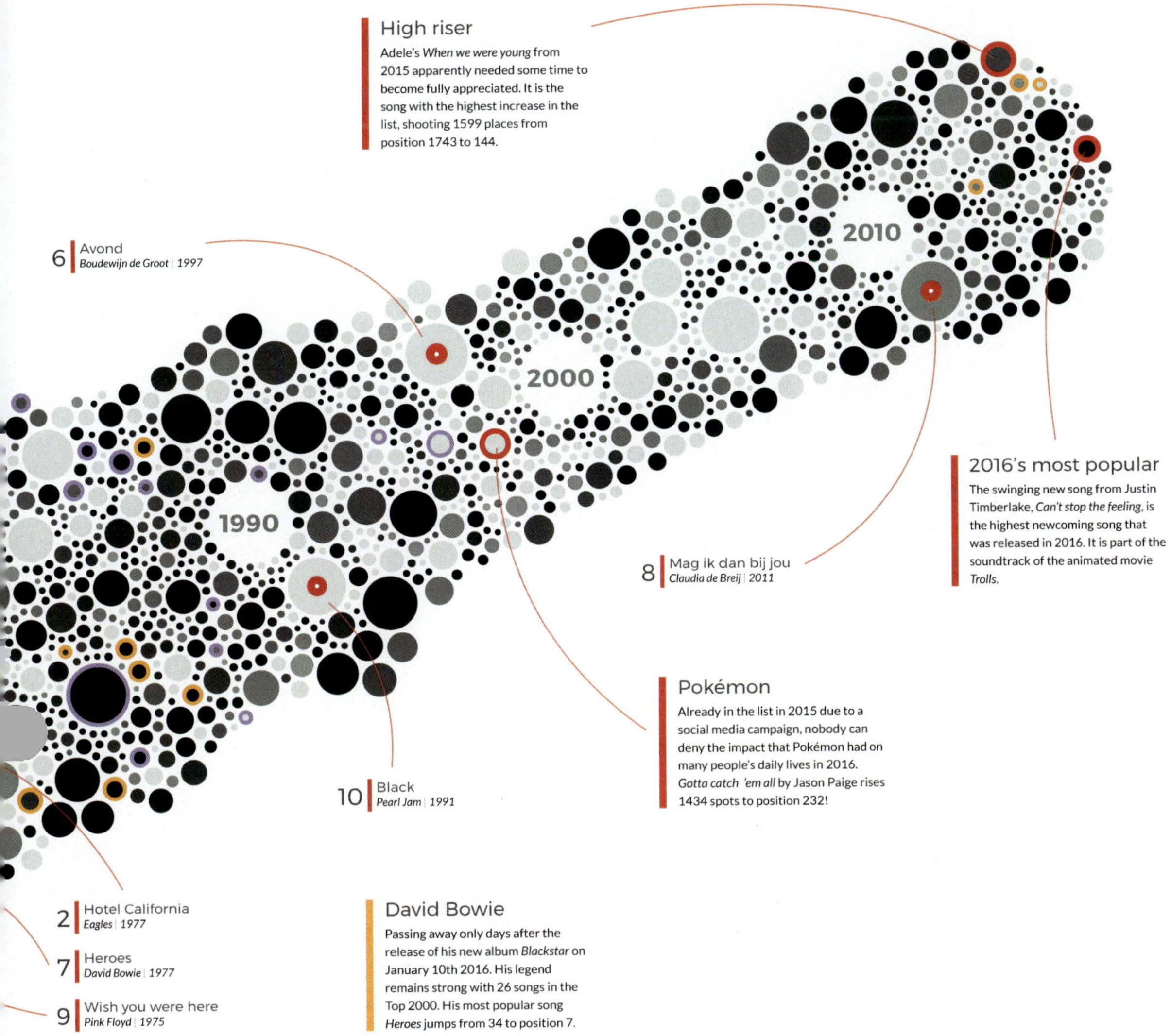

High riser

Adele's *When we were young* from 2015 apparently needed some time to become fully appreciated. It is the song with the highest increase in the list, shooting 1599 places from position 1743 to 144.

6 Avond
Boudewijn de Groot | *1997*

2010

2000

1990

2016's most popular

The swinging new song from Justin Timberlake, *Can't stop the feeling*, is the highest newcoming song that was released in 2016. It is part of the soundtrack of the animated movie *Trolls*.

8 Mag ik dan bij jou
Claudia de Breij | *2011*

Pokémon

Already in the list in 2015 due to a social media campaign, nobody can deny the impact that Pokémon had on many people's daily lives in 2016. *Gotta catch 'em all* by Jason Paige rises 1434 spots to position 232!

10 Black
Pearl Jam | *1991*

2 Hotel California
Eagles | *1977*

7 Heroes
David Bowie | *1977*

9 Wish you were here
Pink Floyd | *1975*

David Bowie

Passing away only days after the release of his new album *Blackstar* on January 10th 2016. His legend remains strong with 26 songs in the Top 2000. His most popular song *Heroes* jumps from 34 to position 7.

But they're losing tracks to the new Millenium

It makes sense that the Top 2000 will be more spread out for each new edition, since there are more songs to choose from. However, if we compare the distributions of the Top 2000 songs over 4 editions, we see that, especially, the 90's has been gaining a lot of popularity.

Even though all songs from the 90's were out in the 2000 edition, only a few songs from that decade were chosen. Whereas in the 2016 edition the number of songs from the 90's has risen significantly. This could be due to a new generation who has grown up during the 90's taking over from those who voted in the early 2000's (who apperantly didn't appreciate the new music).

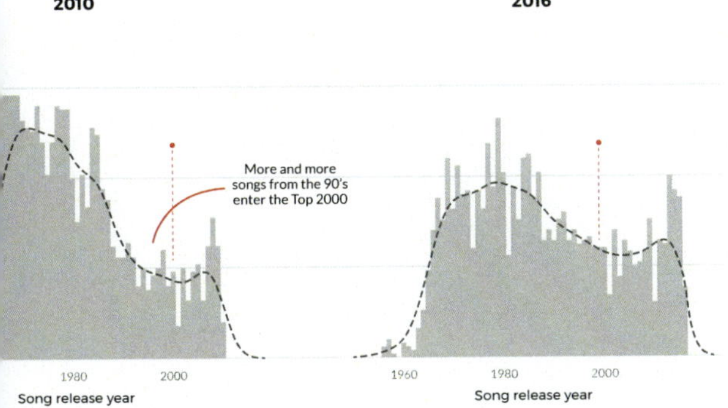

e interactive visual and see the name & title of each song

Data | Top 2000 list from Radio 2 | Top 40 info from Mediamarkt's Top 40

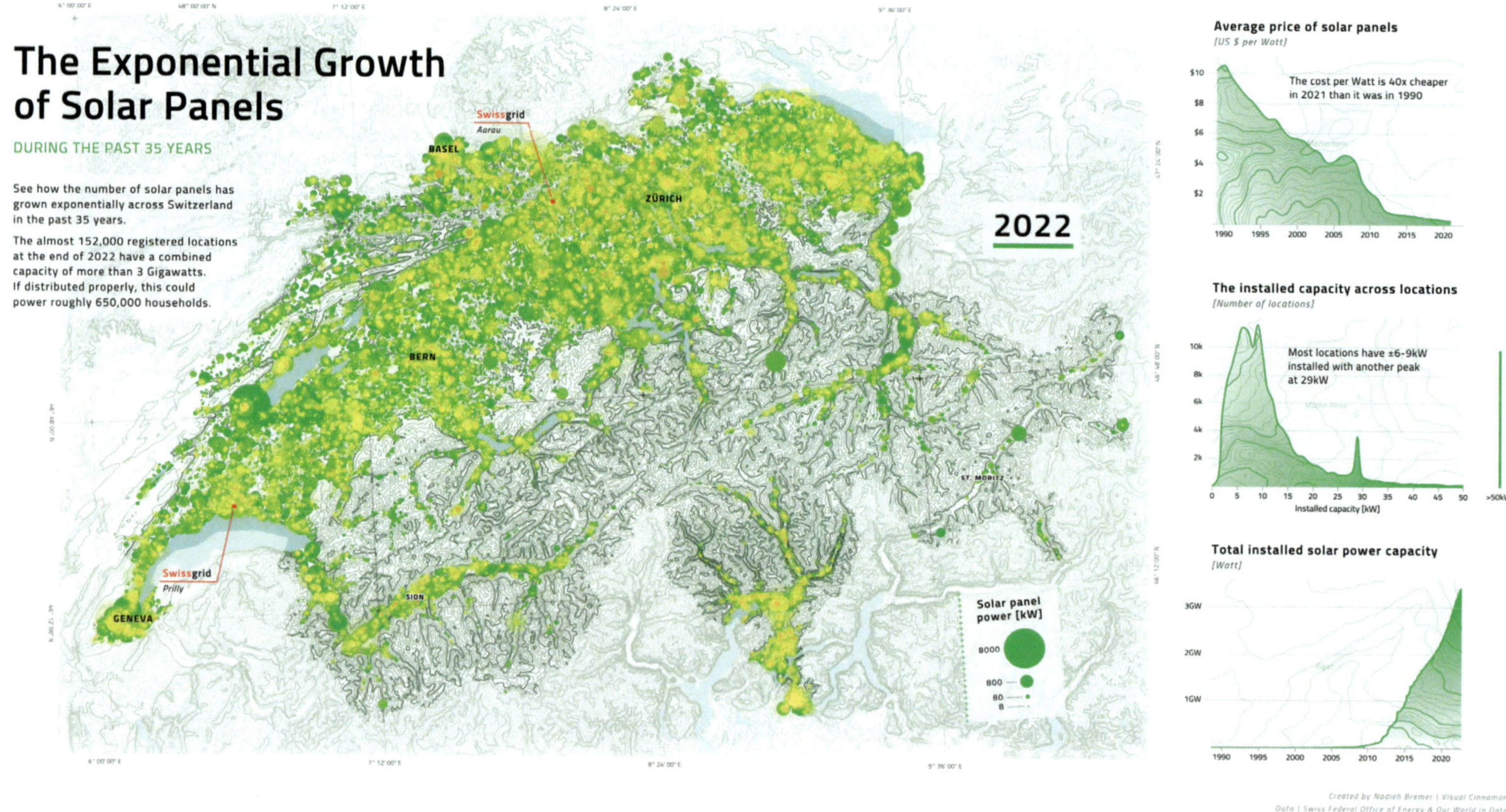

1.5a

USE THE DATA'S TOPIC

Instead of focusing on the data points (like individual people or individual songs), you can also take a step back and look at the data set as a whole. The overall subject can often act as a form of creative inspiration. Is the data set about something as broad as movies? About something more narrow, such as science fiction movies? Or something super specific—data that perhaps dives deep into one particular movie?

Line charts with map backgrounds

BUSINESS | 2023 | SWISSGRID

visualcinnamon.com/portfolio/swissgrid-gencoop

Figure 1.5a & b

One of the final frames in an animation about the rise of solar panels in Switzerland over the past 35 years (a) and a zoomed-in view of the top line chart (b).

Figure 1.5 shows one of the final frames in an animation about the growth of solar panels across Switzerland. The main visual is a map of Switzerland with circles that "pop up" at each new location that added solar panels over the past 35 years. The circles first appear in yellow and slowly turn green as the animation progresses. My client, Swissgrid, the Swiss national electrical grid company, wanted to add a few extra

Average price of solar panels

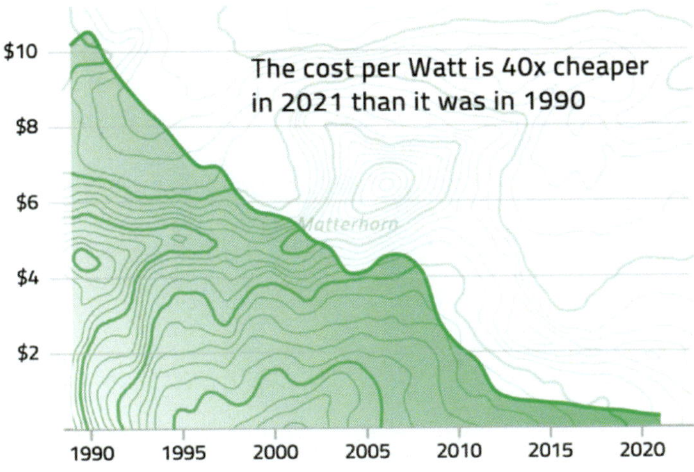

1.5b

insights to contextualize the main map, such as the decrease in the average price of solar panels. Line charts made the most sense for these smaller data sets. However, the simple line charts I initially created looked too plain compared with the detailed map. Design-wise, the elements didn't go well together.

Since the three line charts looked a little like mountains, and the primary visual was a map of Switzerland, a country known for its peaks, I applied the topographic contour lines from the main map to the background of each line chart. I selected contours from the regions around three famous Swiss mountains. The background contours don't add data insights, but they bring the design style of the central map into the line charts, visually connecting them. In addition, the contour lines made the line charts a bit more interesting to look at and more memorable.

It's subtle, but if you look closely, the contour lines below the chart's plot line are green and thicker than the lines above the plot line. Furthermore, a subtle green gradient from the top-right to the bottom-left adds a little extra touch to the design to make the area below the line chart stand out more against the background.

Five circles instead of one

PERSONAL | 2016 | OLYMPIC FEATHERS
olympicfeathers.visualcinnamon.com

The visual in figure 1.6 shows every gold medal winner in the Summer Olympics from the first games in 1896 up to 2016, split by sport, edition (year), event, gender, and continent of the winning country. It was another personal project I created for "Data Sketches."

I'm not saying that inspiration can never come from anything else than the data or its topic. Sometimes, inspiration strikes out of the blue. This doesn't happen often, and I generally think the ideas that relate to the data or topic are stronger.

Figure 1.6

"Olympic Feathers" showing some 5,000 gold medal winners from every Summer Olympics.

Around the time that I was looking at the data, I randomly happened to see an image of a fanned peacock tail. I began sketching circles, as I was inspired by both the circular shape of the tail and the symmetry of the individual feathers. However, after analyzing the data set and drawing some sketches (figure 1.7), I realized that one large circle wouldn't fit all of the data points unless I made each gold medal really, really small. Then it occurred to me to use the five rings of the Olympic symbol since it's so iconic and recognizable! Although the final design did not have the feather shape, I still named the project "Olympic Feathers" as feathers had been in my mind during the whole process.

1.6

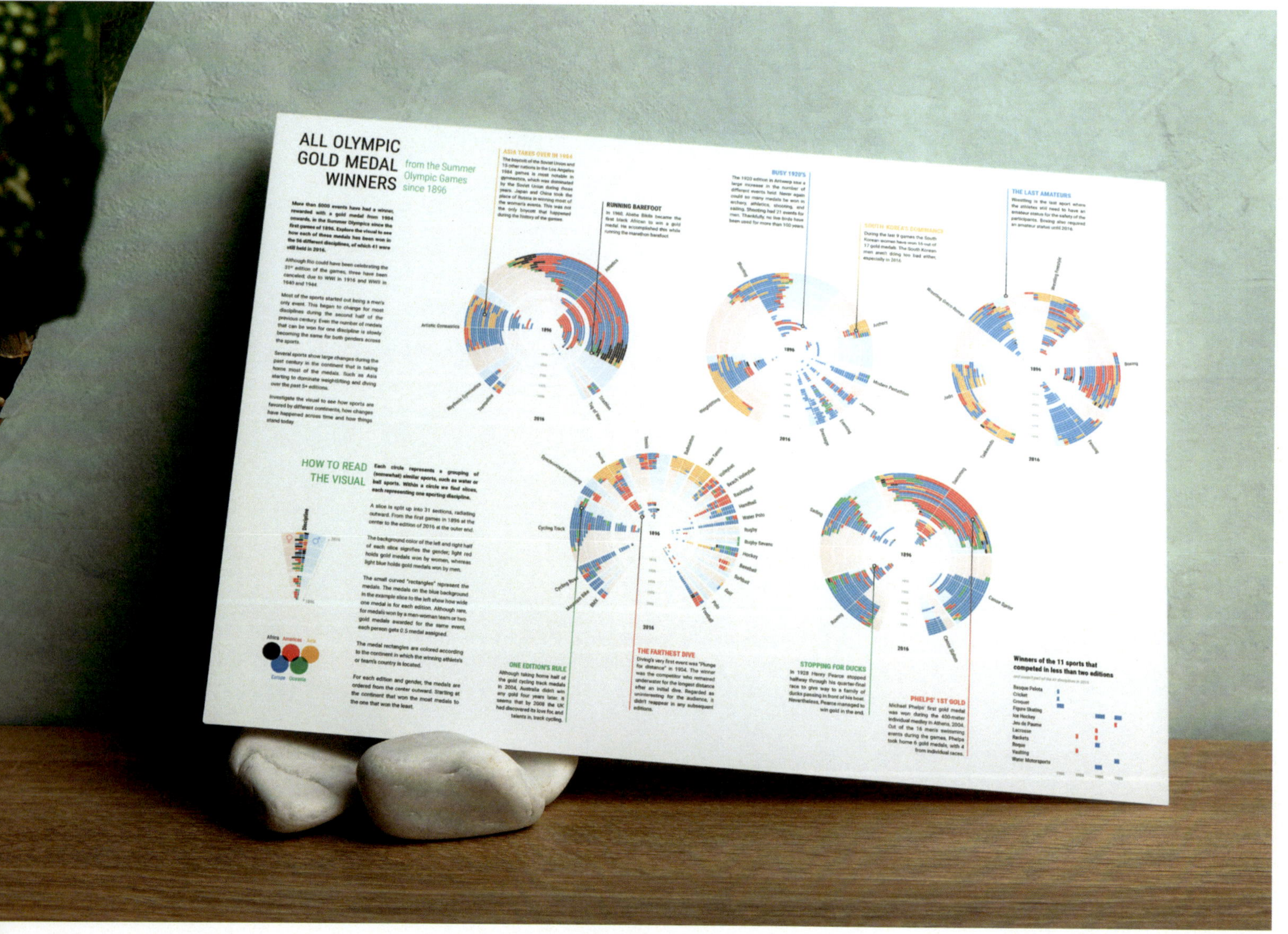

1.7

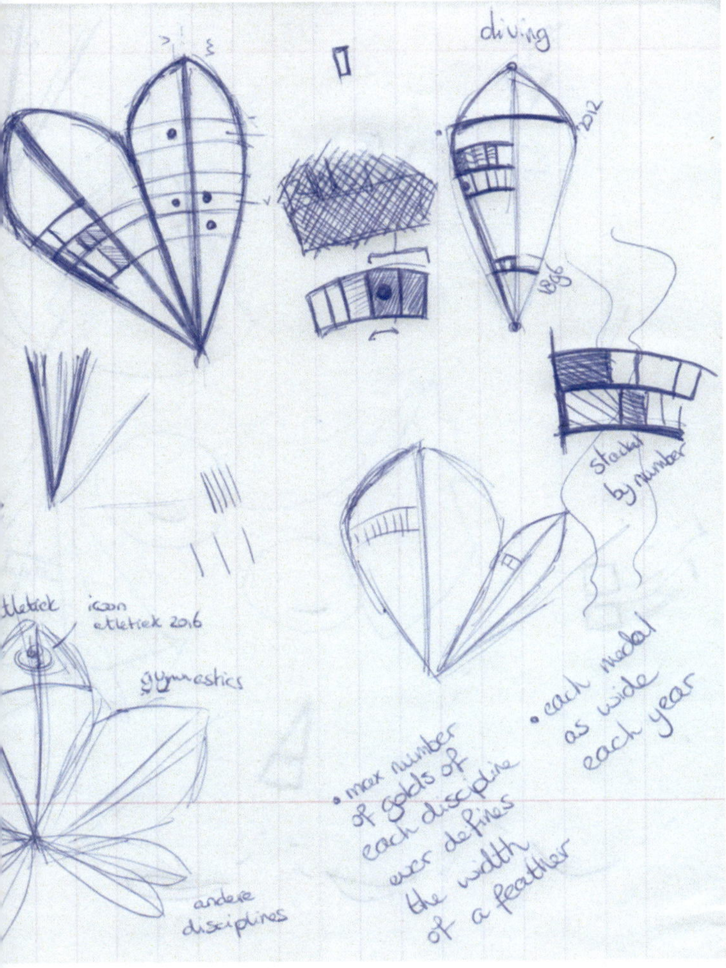

Figure 1.7

A sketch where I was trying to figure out how to lay out all of the medals.

Thinking back on it now, I'm surprised that I hadn't thought of using a layout with the five circles from the very start. However, I often dive in straight away when I find a new, exciting project to work on; I get pulled by the "current" of whatever idea or thought I have in that moment. Only once I stumble across my first big problem do I "come back up for air" and think about it more holistically. To this day, it's a habit that I'm struggling to break!

I'll admit some topics aren't terribly inspiring, especially the more stuffy ones, such as financial data sets from banks. No more dollar signs or stacked coin icons, please. As an alternative, I suggest focusing your creative energy on the chart's *design*, such as the use of subtle color gradients (which I'll go into in Mini Chapter IV), the font choices, or the color palette.

There isn't one specific way to take an ordinary chart beyond the default, to make it stand out and be memorable. Nevertheless, I hope the specific examples I've shown here give you new ways to think about using the data points—as well as the data themes and associations—as a source of inspiration.

LESSON TWO

CONSIDER

Nontraditional charts can be more expressive and communicate certain data insights more effectively

There are many more ways to visualize numbers than the default options available in software tools. Like window shopping, you can peruse a wide variety of chart types on display on websites such as the Data Viz Project (datavizproject.com), which showcases over a hundred different options. A significant benefit of standard charts—like bars, lines, pies, and scatter plots—is that many people are familiar with them and can quickly and intuitively get their message. However, a downside of standard charts is that they can oversimplify the data and the story. If you find this to be the case for a particular data set you're working

UNCOMMON CHART TYPES

with, I urge you to see if a nontraditional chart can convey that underlying story more effectively and with more nuance and care. Furthermore, because these often overlooked charts are less common, they can add a unique and creative flair that piques a reader's interest based simply on their novelty factor.

Visualizing money flows

BUSINESS | 2019 | ADYEN

investors.adyen.com/financials/h2-2018

Figure 2.1

The sketch of the Sankey diagram showing the money flows.

I'll start with my favorite example of how one particular uncommon chart type—which, thankfully, is appearing more often these days—was a perfect match for the data and wowed the client's stakeholders.

Let's return to the Adyen report from the previous lesson. In addition to that diamond-based stacked bar chart about employee growth, I got to create several more charts for that report. The most important one summarized Adyen's earnings and costs over a given period.

2.1

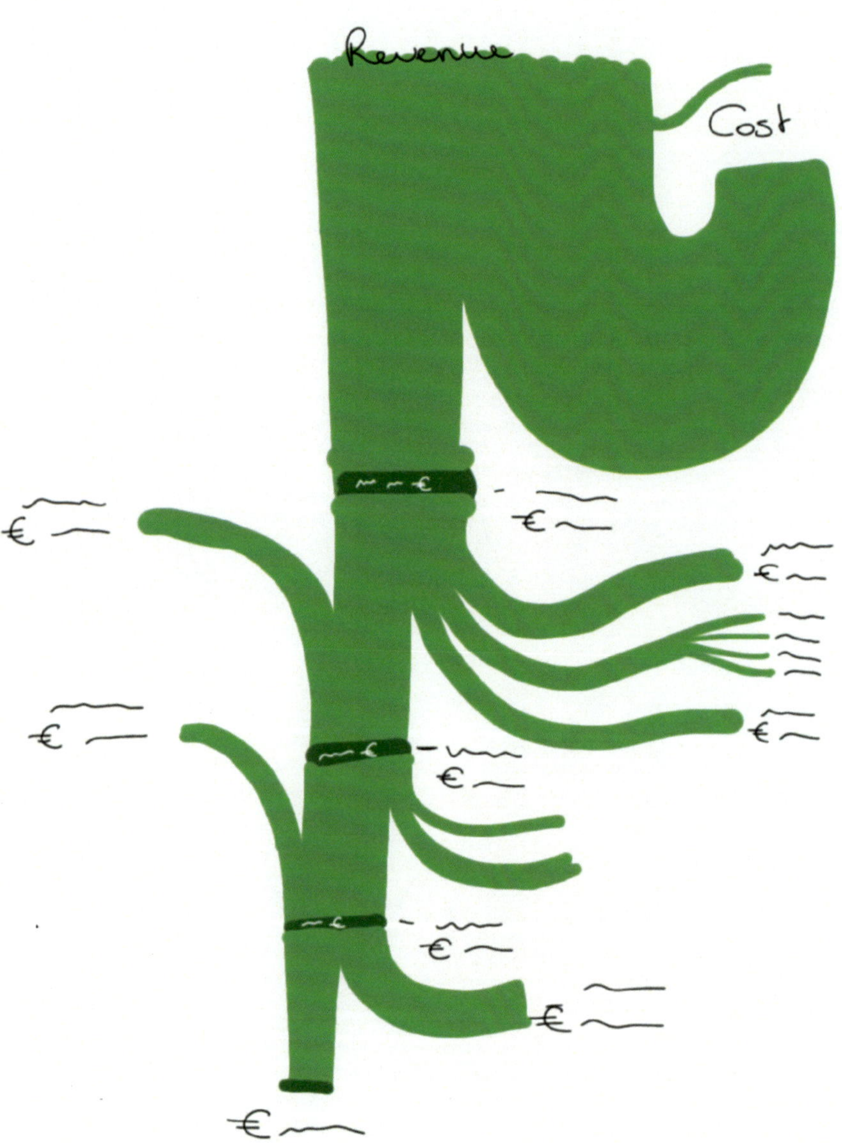

The raw data table contained numbers about the money coming into and going out of the company. These numbers represented a money flow, which is often illustrated well through Sankey diagrams, where the value of a specific entity (money, in this case) scales to the width of the lines in the diagram.

To find inspiration for this project, I looked for examples of Sankey diagrams and saved the ones I liked to a mood board I had set up on Pinterest. Then, using the financial numbers in the data table as a reference, I drew the rough sketch in figure 2.1.

Sankeys are usually drawn horizontally, with the flows progressing from left to right. However, I knew the report would be printed in a portrait layout. Therefore, in my sketch, I made the money flow vertically, starting at the top and ending at the bottom.

It took me considerable time to make this sketch a reality. I used D3's handy Sankey plugin to create a basic

2.2

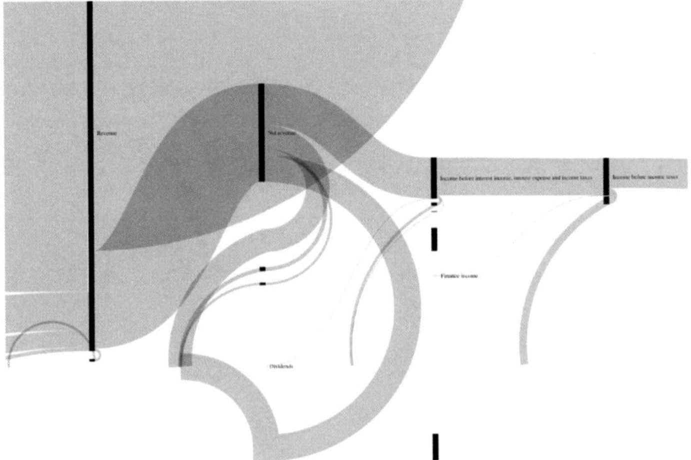

Sankey diagram. However, I wanted things to look different than the default. For one, I wanted the money flowing out of the company to curve in a perfect quarter circle, away from the vertical line, and fade away. (You can see this concept in the small flows bending to the right in figure 2.1).

I also wanted the share of the money that flowed all the way to the end to be a straight line down. This meant I had to calculate how to precisely position all the flows on the page. Thankfully, my rough sketch made it easy to know what I was trying to achieve, even if the attempts along the way sometimes looked hopeless (case in point, figure 2.2). This is one of the reasons I always like to sketch my designs first, especially the smaller data sets where I can get a good handle on all the numbers.

Figure 2.2

An early work-in-progress screenshot where I was trying to wrangle D3's Sankey plugin into my design, with minimal success.

Figure 2.3 shows the final published result. I learned that the visual was received very well by Adyen's shareholders, even though many of them had never seen a Sankey diagram before.

My general strategy for piquing clients' interest in a less common chart type is by showing them how the chart will look. For this project, I only had to show the rough sketch of the Sankey to convince my client that it was a great way to present the data. Often, a sketch is enough to do the trick, but I also like to add several screenshots of other good examples of the chart type. Sometimes, I first have to make a simple prototype using their data. In an extreme case, for a different client and a different Sankey, I had to create the visual entirely before I could convince them of my idea, which was certainly a risk, but one I was willing to take as I believed it was the optimal approach for that particular data set.

Figure 2.3

The final result of the Sankey visualization in Adyen's shareholder report.

There may be times when you simply can't convince your client or manager to go for a less conventional chart. They can be too set in their ways, or there may not be a budget for the extra time a new chart might require, or they don't see the benefits of your idea as clearly as you see them; there can be many reasons. In those cases, let it go, as I've learned to do. Use the standard chart, and keep your eyes open for another opportunity in the future.

Visualization H2 2018 Income statement

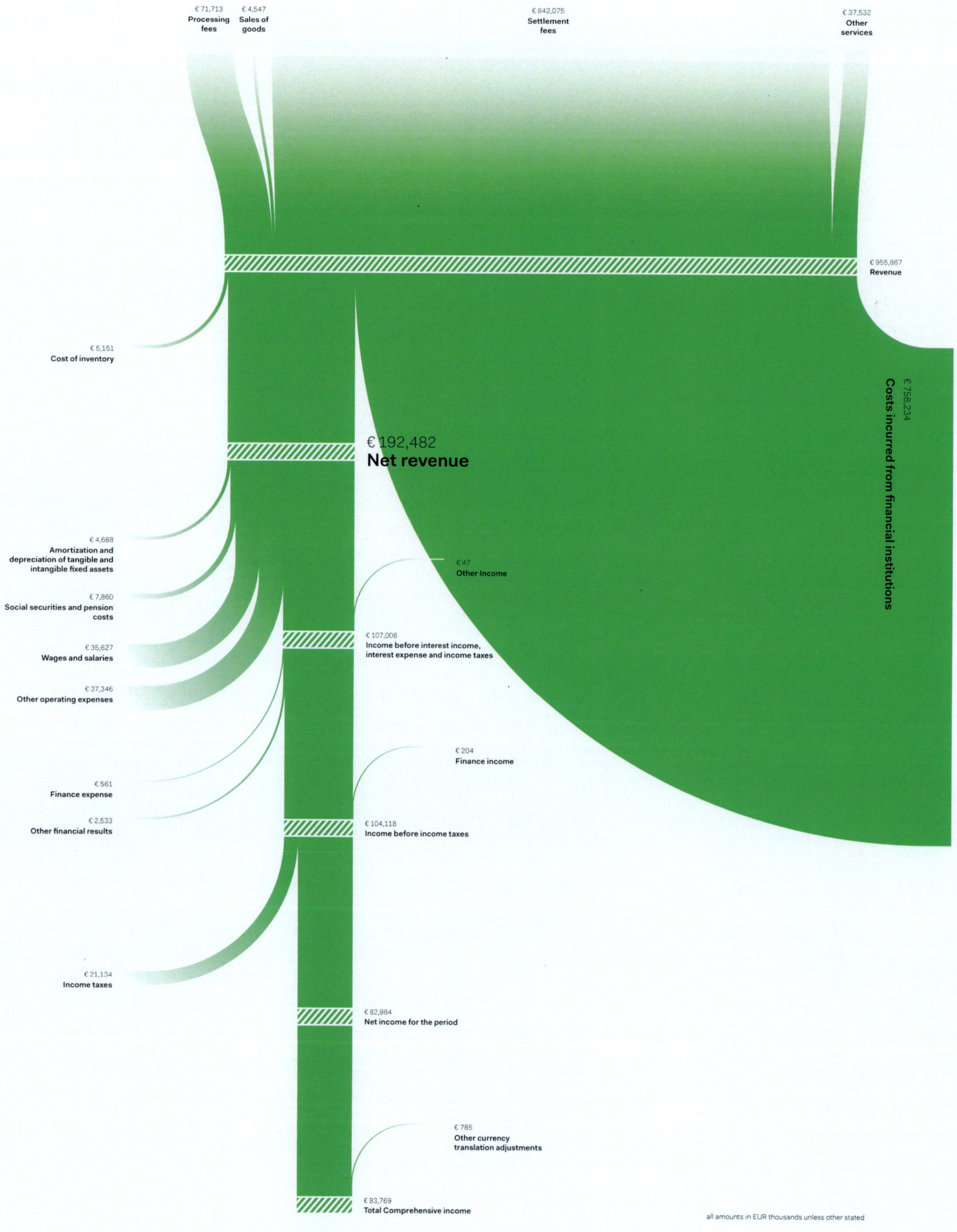

all amounts in EUR thousands unless other stated

Visualizing the most popular names

PERSONAL | 2015 | THE TOP 10 BABY NAMES

nbremer.github.io/babynames

Each year, the United States Social Security Administration releases a list of the most popular baby names by sex. I was surprised to find that the data goes back more than a century! Wanting to increase my skills with D3 at that time, I thought it would be interesting to visualize the shifts among the most popular baby names over time. Figure 2.4 shows my initial sketch. It looks like a line chart, but it's a line-chart variation known as a "bump chart." With bump charts, the y-axis shows the rank order, with the highest rank at the top. They are specifically suited to explore changes in ranks over time—exactly what I wanted to do with the baby names.

I had hoped that the data would also contain the number of babies given each name so I could add circles around each point, sized to that number. However, the data only contained the rankings, which was still quite a trove.

Figure 2.4

My sketch (with notes in Dutch) to reveal how the list of top 10 baby names changed over time.

I learned a lot about interactivity while creating this visualization. I added hover interactions for each line, a search box, a button to switch between girls and boys, and more. With over 135 years of data, the full timeline, crunched to fit the width of a screen, made it simply too small. So instead, it served as a tool below a bigger version of the chart, where you could select a span of time that the larger chart would focus on. (Highlighting a subset of data in this way is called "brushing.") The final result is in figure 2.5.

2.4

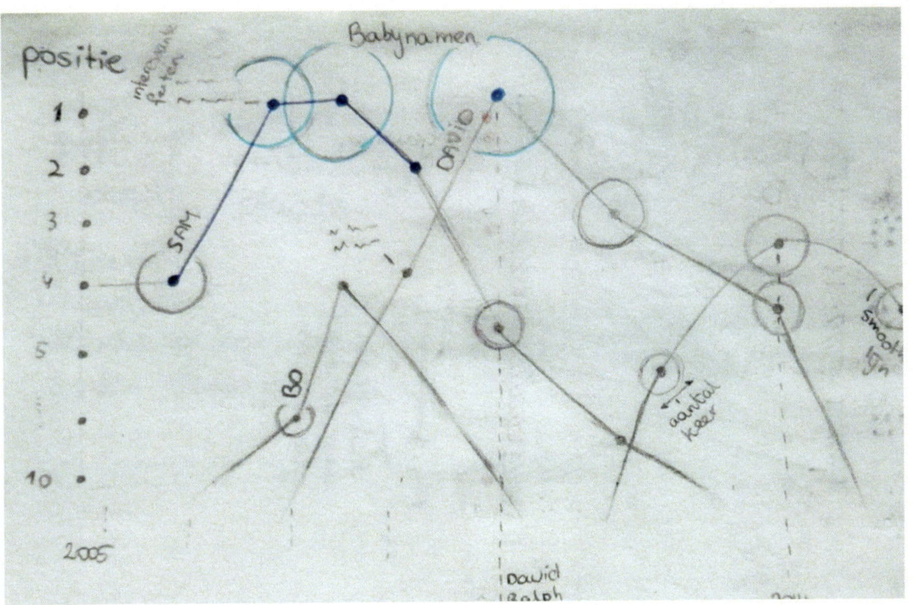

If I hadn't previously seen an example of a brushable chart, I probably would have never thought to use it here. And that's a bit of a catch: In order to pick an uncommon chart form, you have to know it exists in the first place. I'll dive more into this concept in the next chapter.

2.5

Figure 2.5

The final result of the "Top 10 Baby Names" visual for girls.

2.6

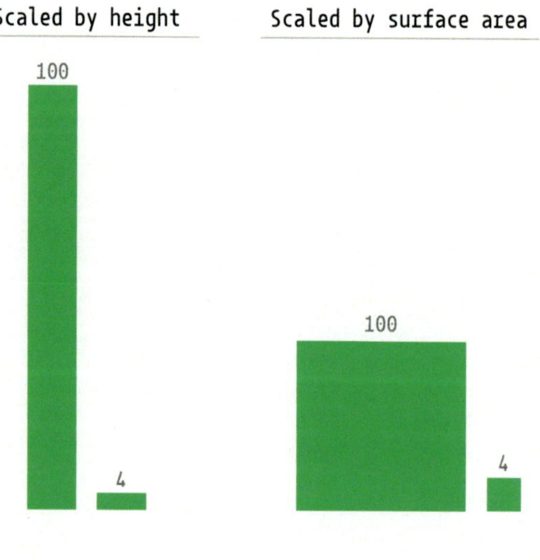

Figure 2.6

Showing the same two values as bars (using height) and as squares (using surface area), where the latter brings the values visually closer together.

Squares instead of bars

BUSINESS | 2019 | ADYEN

investors.adyen.com/financials/2018

Sometimes the case for using an uncommon chart is less obvious. It may be more appropriate than a standard one, but for small or subtle reasons. I want to return to that Adyen report one last time. The data, which broke down operating expenses, was presented as numbers across several tables.

I could have taken the easy path and simply put all the numbers in a bar chart of expenses (wages, taxes, inventory, etc.). Alternatively, I could have opted for a stacked bar chart, which shows the part-to-whole relationship (the total costs broken down into the sub-parts). But I didn't go with either of these standard charts. Instead, I used a treemap, as shown in figure 2.7. A treemap is also appropriate for showing part-to-whole relationships, and I had several clear reasons for taking this path over a stacked bar chart.

For one, this visual was about conveying a general sense of the costs and relative size of each expense. Because there were tables in the report presenting the actual numbers, I didn't mind using surface area (rectangles, in this case) to represent the expenses, even though length (like bars in bar charts) makes it easier to compare them.

A second reason was the considerable difference between the largest and smallest expenses. In fact, there was a massive gap between the largest expense and every other expense. In a bar chart, this would

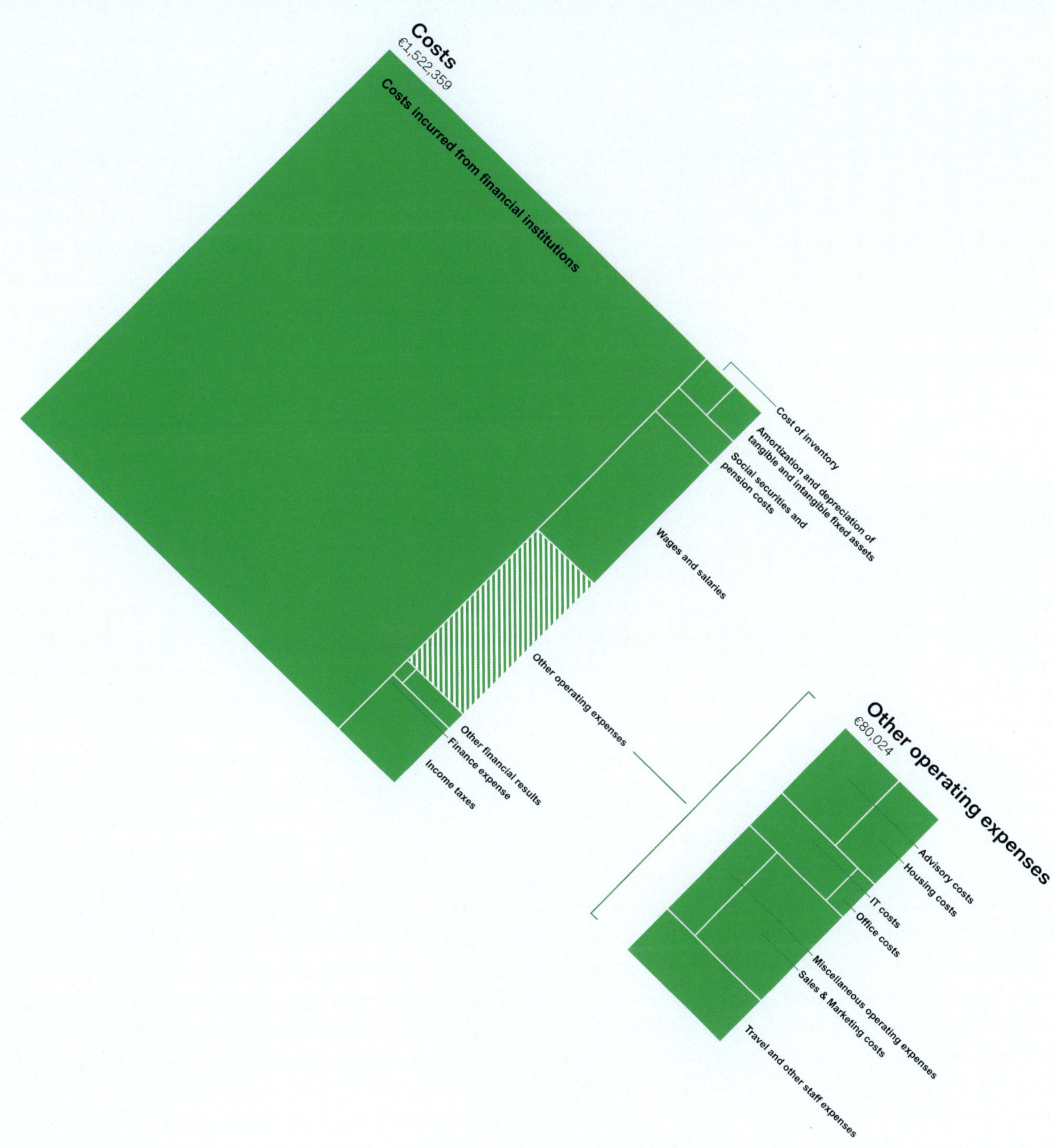

2.7

Figure 2.7

A treemap conveying the breakdown of Adyen's 2018 operating expenses, published in its annual report.

have resulted in a chart with one giant bar and an array of tiny bars. The visual would have been faithful to the data but not great at presenting all the operating expenses. Using area to encode the data, such as with rectangles or circles, brings large differences in values "visually" closer together. See figure 2.6 to compare the same values as bars (using height) and squares (using surface area).

And third, a treemap is a less common chart form that is relatively easy to interpret. It has a higher novelty factor than the standard charts, making it generally more intriguing and memorable.

Several of my favorite nontraditional chart types besides Sankey diagrams, treemaps, and bump charts are:

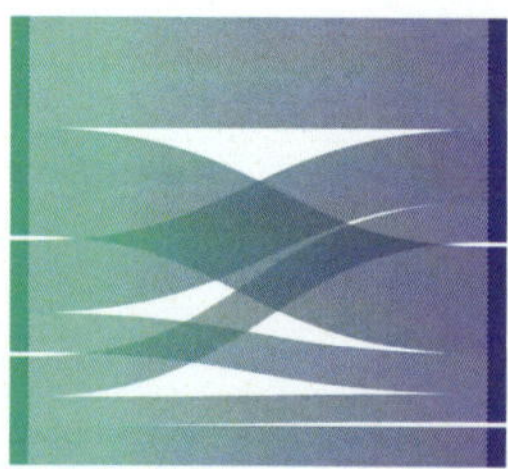

Alluvial diagrams

Another type of flow chart subtly different from Sankeys. I created a curved version about how people transition from studies to occupations in figure 5.1b.

Beeswarms

This is what the "Top 2000 ❤ the 70s & 80s" from Lesson 1 uses, in figure 1.4.

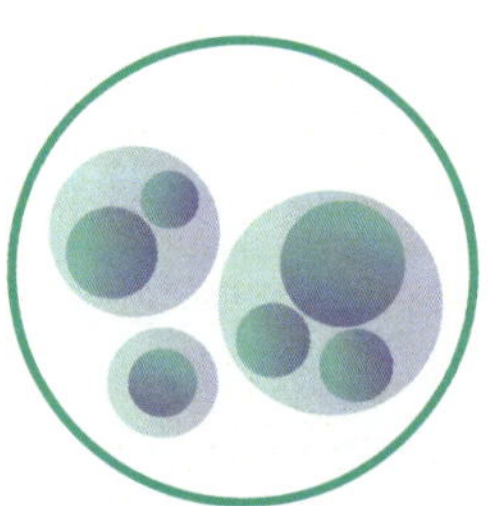

Circle packing

The "A Closer Look at Labor" project from Lesson 3 uses this, in figure 3.1.

For these reasons, the final result was both more effective in portraying the data insights and also more visually interesting than a standard stacked bar chart.

Why rotate it 45 degrees, though? Well, I liked how it made the whole presentation that bit more visually appealing. Moreover, the orientation made the two treemaps fit better on the (portrait) page and complemented the design style of the diamonds from the employee chart in Lesson 1 (figure 1.1).

I've often asked my clients, "Is it important that the viewers can read the exact number, or is it good enough for them to get a sense of the numbers?" I then explain that doing the latter generally gives me more opportunity to make an attention-grabbing, beautiful, and memorable visual. This project nicely exemplifies this distinction.

I want to stress this again: The chart form you choose has to convey the information effectively. It's not about picking something unusual for unusual's sake. It's about realizing that although you can visualize many data sets with standard charts, a less common chart might be just as good—or even better—at conveying the central insight.

Like all chart types, the nontraditional ones have their strengths and weaknesses. However, because it's highly likely that your target audience hasn't encountered them (very often), the uncommon charts have to be quite a bit more effective or visually intriguing than the standard option would be.

But how do you know if a different chart form is effective and if people will be drawn to it? For me, the answer comes down to whether people understand the insight or goal I'm trying to convey. And to determine that, I deploy a multi-step process.

My first step is always to use myself as a test case—not my current self, but my past self. I look back at my initial notes and recall what it was like when I was new to the data. What was unclear to me at the time? Does this visual provide clarity? My projects generally span two weeks to two months, so it is relatively easy to think back to that initial moment of encountering the data.

Chord diagrams

You've already seen one in the Introduction about how people switch between phone brands, in figure 0.6.

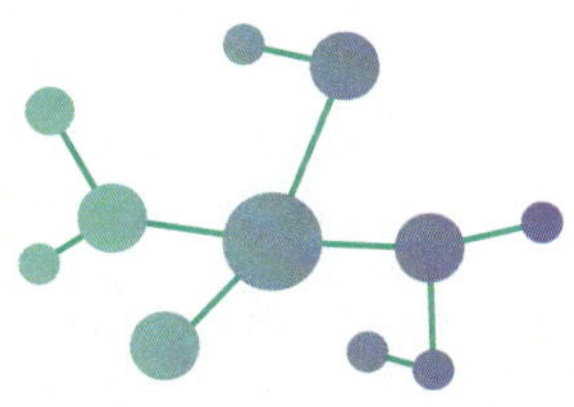

Networks

Which you'll see in my "Why Do Cats & Dogs?" project in Lesson 7, in figure 7.7.

Voronoi treemap

A treemap but with a more organic-looking layout. You've seen one in the "Design Process" chapter in the Introduction (figure 0.11), and you'll see a more elaborate example in Lesson 8, with figures 8.1 and 8.2.

My second step is to ask my client for feedback. Sometimes, I'll ask them to show the visual to their colleagues who aren't involved with the project (but who could be an intended audience). You should ask for feedback every time you share an update. What's more, make sure you share rough initial versions (with an explanation on how to interpret them) instead of disappearing for a while and coming back with something that looks very polished. If the feedback indicates that the chart isn't effective, you want to address that critique as early as possible.

For bigger projects, I might ask my data visualization friends or colleagues for feedback. If possible, I might share a sneak peek on social media and see what reaction it gets. And if the intended audience is really general, which is often the case for newspaper visuals, I will perform the "Dad Test," and yes, ask my dad if he gets it.

For the type of projects I work on, those steps have always been more than enough to realize whether my visual is effective, or whether it feels like "homework." However, the more serious the impact your visual can make, the more serious you need to be in researching the pros and cons of your chart choice.

In all cases, if someone has difficulty understanding the visual, I try to find the root cause of their confusion by asking questions like, "Why was this unclear?" or "How did you come to that conclusion?" Sometimes, their problem isn't with the chart type. But other times, my choice simply isn't working, and I need to revert to a traditional chart type after all.

So, the next time you make an important data visualization, experiment with a number of chart types to see if a nontraditional one stands out as the best way to convey your data. If it does, it will probably have an added bonus of being more unique and eye-grabbing.

Thankfully, more and more visualization tools support uncommon charts, making them faster to test and easier for data professionals to create. Any benefit this might have in improving the data literacy of the general public would be wonderful!

BROADEN YOUR HORIZON OF VISUAL FORMS

Being aware of a wide range of chart types is essential to harnessing the most efficient and engaging visual forms for your data.

As the Venn diagram in figure I.1 shows, there is a large universe of visual possibilities. A subset of this universe will fit your specific data set, resulting in something that properly conveys the insights of your data.

Within this subset, there may be a few good and maybe one or two amazing chart forms for your data. However, you may not know that those great options exist! By making your "knowledge circle" bigger, you will have a larger pool of chart forms to consider. Hopefully, this will make it more likely that you'll find a highly optimal solution during your creative process.

Although increasing your data visualization knowledge happens naturally as you get more experience visualizing data (it did for me), I urge you to give yourself a boost and actively broaden your horizons.

I suggest starting by browsing through some data visualization catalog websites that feature hundreds of different chart types. After that, I highly suggest following fellow data visualization creators whose work you like. Their social media posts or newsletters can be great resources. Get inspired by others. Remix instead of reinvent.

Another resource I recommend is the "Information is Beautiful Awards." During the selection process, the competition organizers publish a list of entries that make it to the longlist. (This list gets further downsized to a shortlist and, eventually, a handful of winners.) If I can spare the time, I like to check out each longlisted entry.

In general, keep your eyes open for data visualizations when you browse the web. If something draws your eye, take a minute to look at it inquisitively. Why do you think it stood out to you? How is it visualizing the data? If you think it looks beautiful, try to understand exactly what parts you find beautiful. The colors, the typography, the shapes? These little thought experiments should be fun. If it feels more like homework than leisure, you're pushing yourself too hard. Do it in a casual way that works for you in the long run.

Figure I.1

A Venn diagram illustrating the benefits of having a large "knowledge circle" of visual forms.

LESSON THREE

COMBINE CHARTS

Fusing chart types together can create distinctive and compelling visuals

Once you have a good handle on the universe of chart types, I find that combining them is the next natural creative step to explore. This lesson will walk through two ways to do this: placing one chart into another and merging the best of two chart forms.

PLACING ONE CHART INTO ANOTHER

Let's start with the simplest way to combine two charts: inserting one chart into another. I especially like it when the outer chart has large circles that can act as containers for the inner ones.

Bars inside circles

PERSONAL | 2015 | A CLOSER LOOK AT LABOR
nbremer.github.io/occupationscanvas

Figure 3.1

The highest level of "A Closer Look at Labor" showing all of the occupations in a circle packing chart.

This one is from a while ago! I hadn't been using D3 for that long and wanted to improve my skills. So I created many personal projects around this time, including one that looked at the US labor force.

3.1

I took a nice, clean data set from the US Bureau of Labor Statistics that broke out employed people by occupation and age. This data set contained the number of people working in a hierarchy of occupational groups. Additionally, the data split the number of people in those groups into eight age categories.

I used a circle packing approach to visualize the hierarchy of occupations. Each occupation (e.g., dentist, psychologist) is a white circle sized according to the number of people in that occupation. Those circles are grouped together in larger circles and then those circles are grouped in even larger circles, all based on the hierarchy. For instance, firefighters, police, and detectives are all part of the "protective service" occupations, which are, in turn, grouped with the other "service" occupations such as personal care, healthcare, and food preparation.

You can see the complete overview of occupations and their groupings in figure 3.1. Hovering on a circle triggers a tooltip showing the name of the occupation or occupational group. Clicking on a circle zooms into that group.

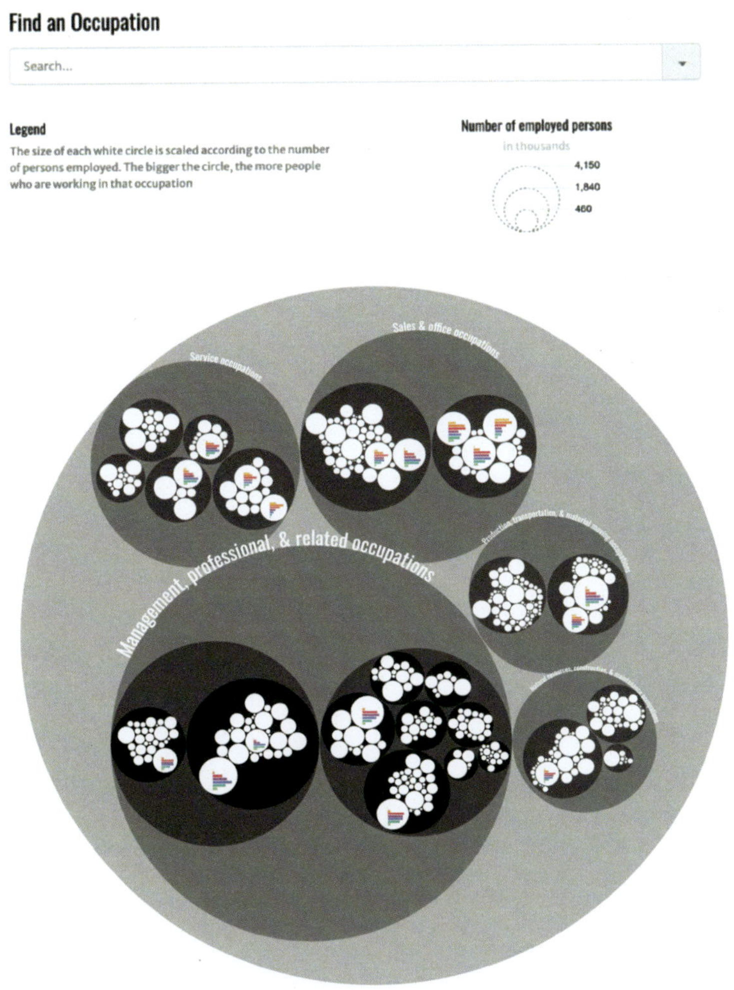

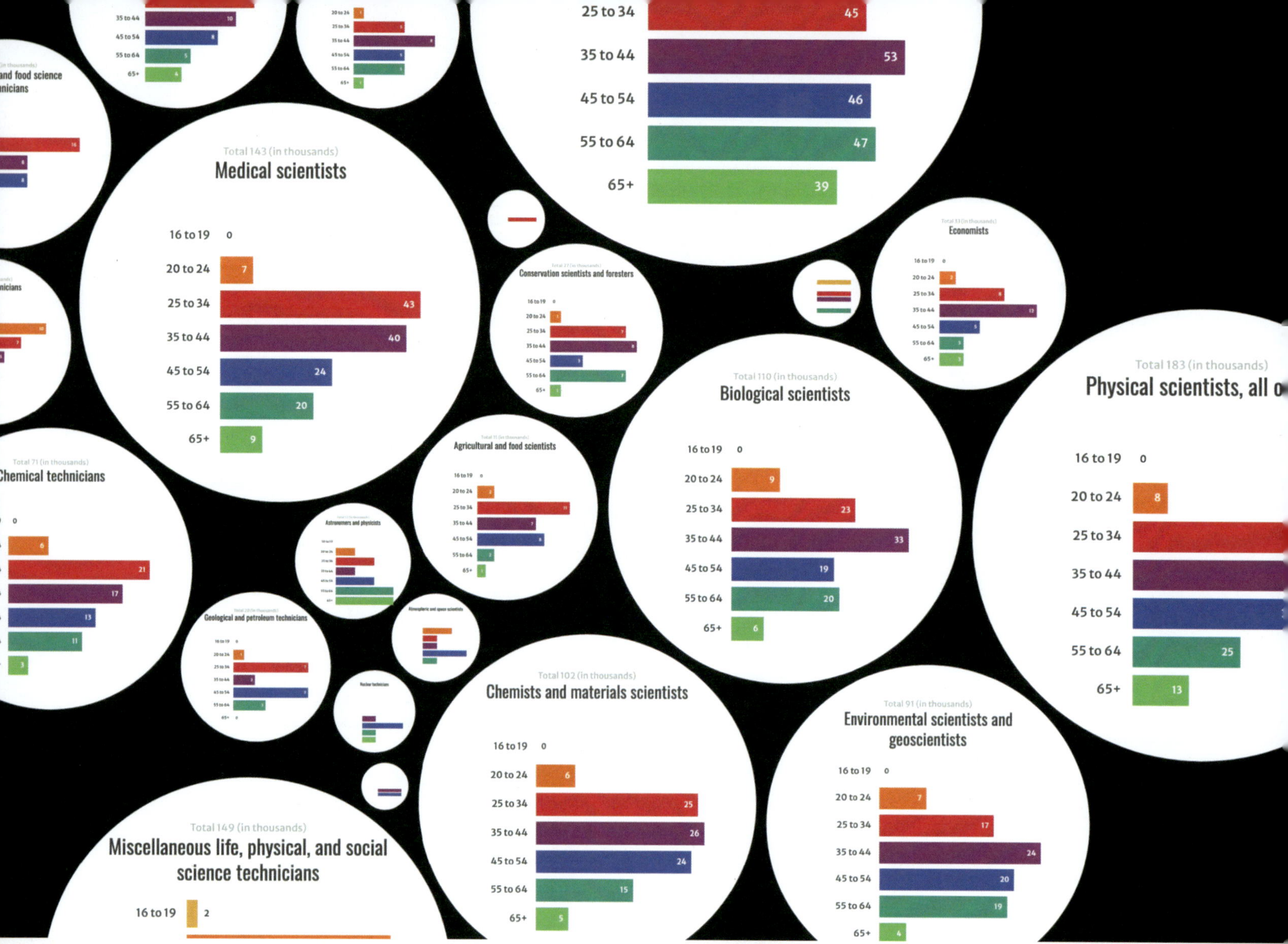

3.2

Figure 3.2

A zoomed-in view of the "life, physical & social science" group, where the inner occupation circles are large enough to hold bar charts.

I also wanted to convey age data. Age categories would present nicely as a bar chart. And so, I thought, why not place bar charts inside each white occupation circle? Zoomed out, the white circles were too small to fit an entire bar chart. But thanks to the wonder of interactivity, which I was still very new to at the time, I devised a solution: reveal the bar charts only when zoomed in close enough for the enlarged circles to contain them.

Figure 3.2 shows a zoomed-in view of the "life, physical & social science" group, which is inside the right circle of the "management, professional, and related" group in figure 3.1.

By embedding bar charts into the circles, I provided an extra layer of context and insight into each occupation (lifeguards have a very different age distribution than judges, for instance) while making the visual a little more unique and memorable.

MERGING TWO CHART TYPES

One of my favorite approaches is to cherry-pick elements from two (or even more) chart types and see if I can blend them. Some of the charts that are listed in chart catalogs are hybrids, such as violin plots that are a mix of box plots and histograms. I'll admit that this method doesn't always work, but when it does, the results can be outstanding.

Stacked bar charts in a radial heatmap

PERSONAL | 2016 | OLYMPIC FEATHERS
olympicfeathers.visualcinnamon.com

I already introduced the "Olympic Feathers" project in Lesson 1. In figure 3.3, I've zoomed in on one of the five circles, showing athletics and gymnastics gold medals. Each ring represents a different Olympic edition, from 1896 (inner ring) to 2016 (outer ring). Each section of the circle is a sporting discipline, with female events in one half (pale red background) and male events in the other (pale blue background). Finally, each gold medal is a rectangle, colored according to the continent of the winning country. Finally, Olympic or world records are white dots within the rectangles.

Figure 3.3

Zooming in on the top-left circle from the "Olympic Feathers" project in Lesson 1.

3.3

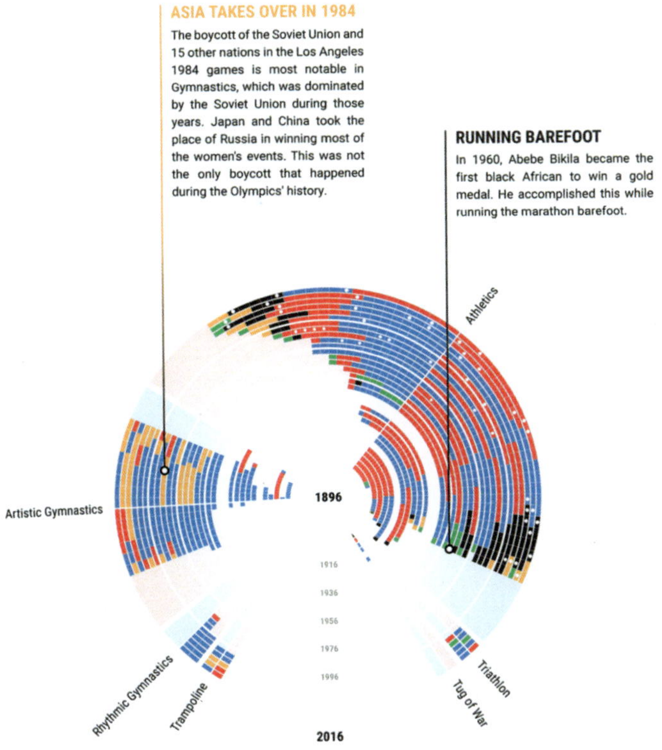

In essence, this visual form is hundreds of stacked bar charts merged with a circular heatmap. This hybrid design wraps all the stacked bars into a radial form. If you were to "unfold," say, the female events from Athletics, you would end up with a more typical stacked bar chart—one stack of gold medals for each Olympic game.

As you may recall from the last chapter, it was a decidedly strange inspiration that led me to this design: an artistic image of a peacock's tail. The symmetry of a single feather somehow clicked for me as a way to show female and male events of one sporting discipline on each half of a feather.

As I sketched, I began to recognize the elements of a circular heatmap. However, a traditional circular heatmap has a fixed grid, which wasn't

ALL OLYMPIC GOLD MEDAL WINNERS

from the Summer Olympic Games since 1896

More than 5000 events have had a winner, rewarded with a gold medal from 1904 onwards, in the Summer Olympics since the first games of 1896. Explore the visual to see how each of these medals has been won in the 56 different disciplines, of which 41 were still held in 2016.

Although Rio could have been celebrating the 31st edition of the games, three have been canceled; due to WWI in 1916 and WWII in 1940 and 1944.

Most of the sports started out being a men's only event. This began to change for most disciplines during the second half of the previous century. Even the number of medals that can be won for one discipline is slowly becoming the same for both genders across the sports.

Several sports show large changes during the past century in the continent that is taking home most of the medals. Such as Asia starting to dominate weightlifting and diving over the past 5+ editions.

Investigate the visual to see how sports are favored by different continents, how changes have happened across time and how things stand today.

ASIA TAKES OVER IN 1984

The boycott of the Soviet Union and 15 other nations in the Los Angeles 1984 games is most notable in gymnastics, which was dominated by the Soviet Union during those years. Japan and China took the place of Russia in winning most of the women's events. This was not the only boycott that happened during the history of the games.

RUNNING BAREFOOT

In 1960, Abebe Bikila became the first black African to win a gold medal. He accomplished this while running the marathon barefoot.

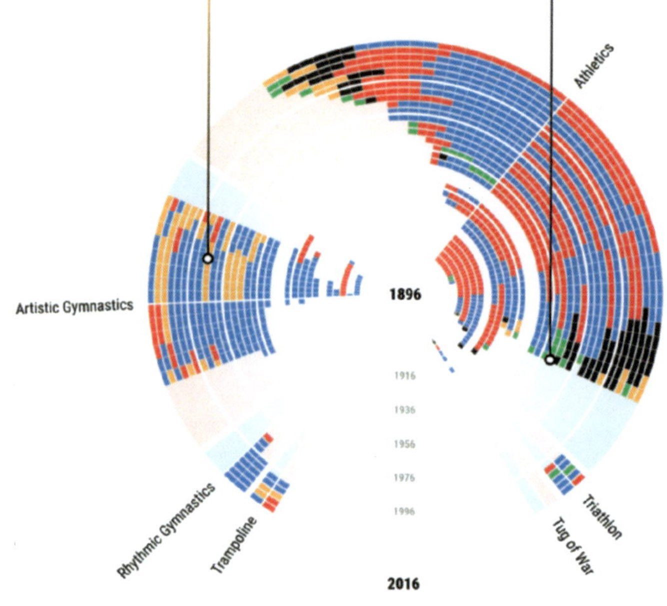

Tennis
Badminton
Diving
Synchronized Swimming
Cycling Track
1896
1916
1936
1956
1976
1996
2016
Cycling Road
Mountain Bike
BMX

HOW TO READ THE VISUAL

Each circle represents a grouping of (somewhat) similar sports, such as water or ball sports. Within a circle we find slices, each representing one sporting discipline.

A slice is split up into 31 sections, radiating outward. From the first games in 1896 at the center to the edition of 2016 at the outer end.

The background color of the left and right half of each slice signifies the gender; light red holds gold medals won by women, whereas light blue holds gold medals won by men.

The small curved "rectangles" represent the medals. The medals on the blue background in the example slice to the left show how wide one medal is for each edition. Although rare, for medals won by a men-woman team or two gold medals awarded for the same event, each person gets 0.5 medal assigned.

The medal rectangles are colored according to the continent in which the winning athlete's or team's country is located.

For each edition and gender, the medals are ordered from the center outward. Starting at the continent that won the most medals to the one that won the least.

Discipline
♀ ♂
2016
1896

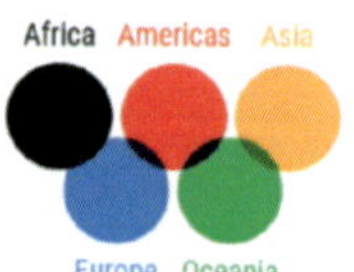

ONE EDITION'S RULE

Although taking home half of the gold cycling track medals in 2004, Australia didn't win any gold four years later. It seems that by 2008 the UK had discovered its love for, and talents in, track cycling.

THE FARTHEST DIV

Diving's very first event w for distance" in 1904. T was the competitor whc underwater for the longe after an initial dive. Re uninteresting for the a didn't reappear in any s editions.

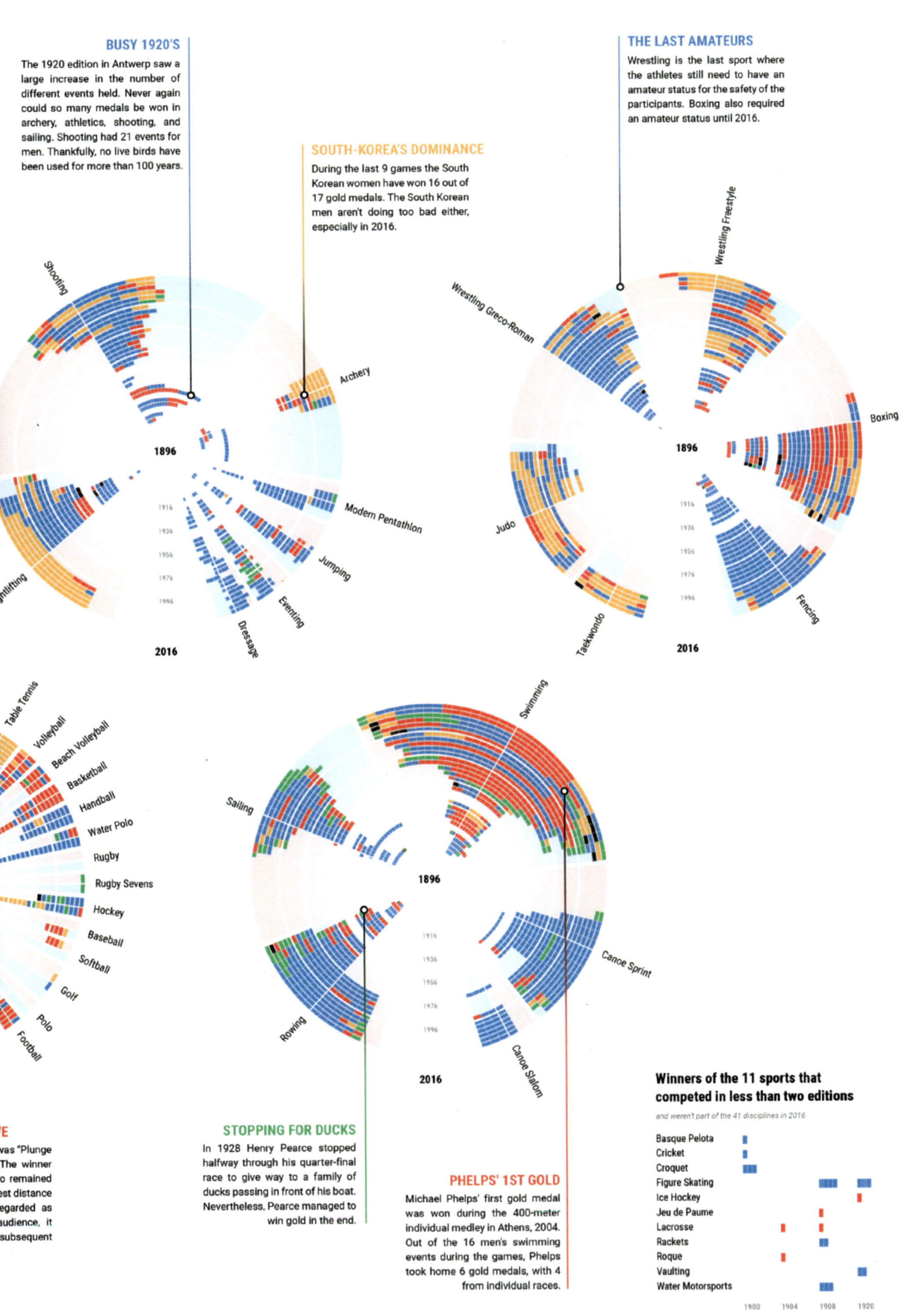

BUSY 1920'S
The 1920 edition in Antwerp saw a large increase in the number of different events held. Never again could so many medals be won in archery, athletics, shooting, and sailing. Shooting had 21 events for men. Thankfully, no live birds have been used for more than 100 years.
SOUTH-KOREA'S DOMINANCE
During the last 9 games the South Korean women have won 16 out of 17 gold medals. The South Korean men aren't doing too bad either, especially in 2016.
THE LAST AMATEURS
Wrestling is the last sport where the athletes still need to have an amateur status for the safety of the participants. Boxing also required an amateur status until 2016.
Shooting
Archery
Modern Pentathlon
Jumping
Eventing
Dressage
1896
1916
1936
1956
1976
1996
2016
Wrestling Freestyle
Wrestling Greco-Roman
Boxing
Judo
Taekwondo
Fencing
Table Tennis
Volleyball
Beach Volleyball
Basketball
Handball
Water Polo
Rugby
Rugby Sevens
Hockey
Baseball
Softball
Golf
Polo
Football
Swimming
Sailing
Canoe Sprint
Canoe Slalom
Rowing
STOPPING FOR DUCKS
In 1928 Henry Pearce stopped halfway through his quarter-final race to give way to a family of ducks passing in front of his boat. Nevertheless, Pearce managed to win gold in the end.
PHELPS' 1ST GOLD
Michael Phelps' first gold medal was won during the 400-meter individual medley in Athens, 2004. Out of the 16 men's swimming events during the games, Phelps took home 6 gold medals, with 4 from individual races.
Winners of the 11 sports that competed in less than two editions
and weren't part of the 41 disciplines in 2016
Basque Pelota
Cricket
Croquet
Figure Skating
Ice Hockey
Jeu de Paume
Lacrosse
Rackets
Roque
Vaulting
Water Motorsports
1900
1904
1908
1920

Figure 3.4

The landscape poster version that I created some time after the release of the online (more portrait-style) version.

possible here due to the number of events changing each edition. After some more sketching, I realized that I could instead display the data as a stacked bar chart, but shaped into the layout of a circular heatmap. It resulted in a chart form I hadn't seen before that accommodated 5,000(!) gold medals without being too overwhelming.

FULL DESIGN STORY

For this next example, I want to walk you through my whole design process. It took quite a lot of trial and error before I found a good way to visualize the data.

Inventing a depth circle

BUSINESS | 2019 | ALIS_
visualcinnamon.com/portfolio/alis-os

Before we dive in, let me give you some background. The client, alis_, was a South African startup (now operating under a different name) that was developing a machine learning system that, at the time, was aiming to help people spot investment opportunities. At the heart of their business was alis OS, an operating system that drives everything they do.

Alis OS executed "services," or tasks, ranging from copying files to running predictive models. Each service belonged to a specific domain, or group of services with similar tasks. Often, these services triggered others, creating chains of tasks and connections that resemble a network.

The client wanted a way to visualize this network, to see their system in action—what tasks were running, which had failed, and what services had created new ones. They also hoped the final visualization would double as a marketing piece, taking center stage on their landing page. It needed to be informative yet visually striking, fully aligned with the brand's bold black, white, and bright red palette. Balancing these requirements presented quite a challenge for a single data visualization!

THE INITIAL IDEA

Figure 3.5

"Royal Constellations" shows the intertwined family tree of European royal houses going back hundreds of years. See the interactive visual on *royalconstellations.visualcinnamon.com*

Alis_ came to me because they felt the style of my "Royal Constellations" visual (figure 3.5) would suit their data perfectly. That project shows the family tree of 3,000 people connected to European royal houses, with each circle representing a person and each line representing ties to their parents, partners, and children. Dates of birth run along the vertical axis. The current royal leaders are displayed as

Royal Constellations

A 1000 years of ancestral connections in the European royal families

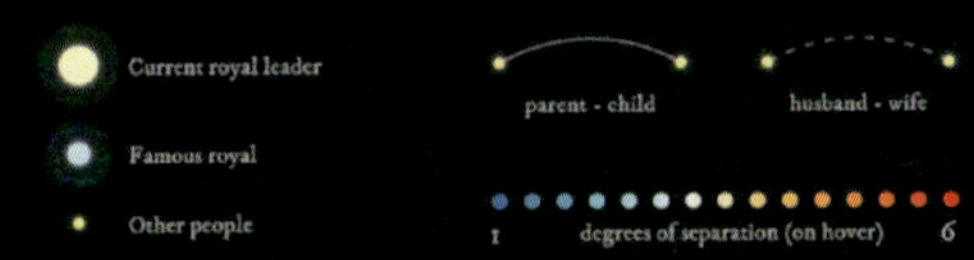

Discover the shortest path between two royals

If you click on a star you will select & fix that person. By clicking on another star the visual will show you the shortest path between the two (although sometimes multiple shortest paths exist. The algorithm will then show one of these). To clear the fix on the first person, click anywhere outside of the star filled area.

Royal & aristocratic families are known for their fondness of marrying within their own clique. Restraining aggression between two families, creating a stronger front towards a third family, increasing territorial acquisitions, legal claim to a foreign throne through inheritance are some of the most common reasons.

This leads to very interesting & entangled family trees which the visual below tries to convey. It shows how all 10 of the current hereditary royal leaders of Europe can be connected to each other through their ancestors. We don't have to look very far back. Even the most distant royal relatives have their shared forebears born after the year 1700.

Each "star" below is a person, placed approximately on their year of birth in the vertical direction and to their closest relative who is a royal leader today in the horizontal direction. Hover over a star to see how many relatives can be connected to that person in "6-degrees of separation". For highly connected royals, such as Pauline of Württemberg, born in 1810, who is a relative of 6 current royal families, it may take a second to calculate all connections.

This genealogy is far from complete, or perfect, probably many more interconnections exist, but this peek into the history of Europe's royals shows that it's all one big (happy?) family.

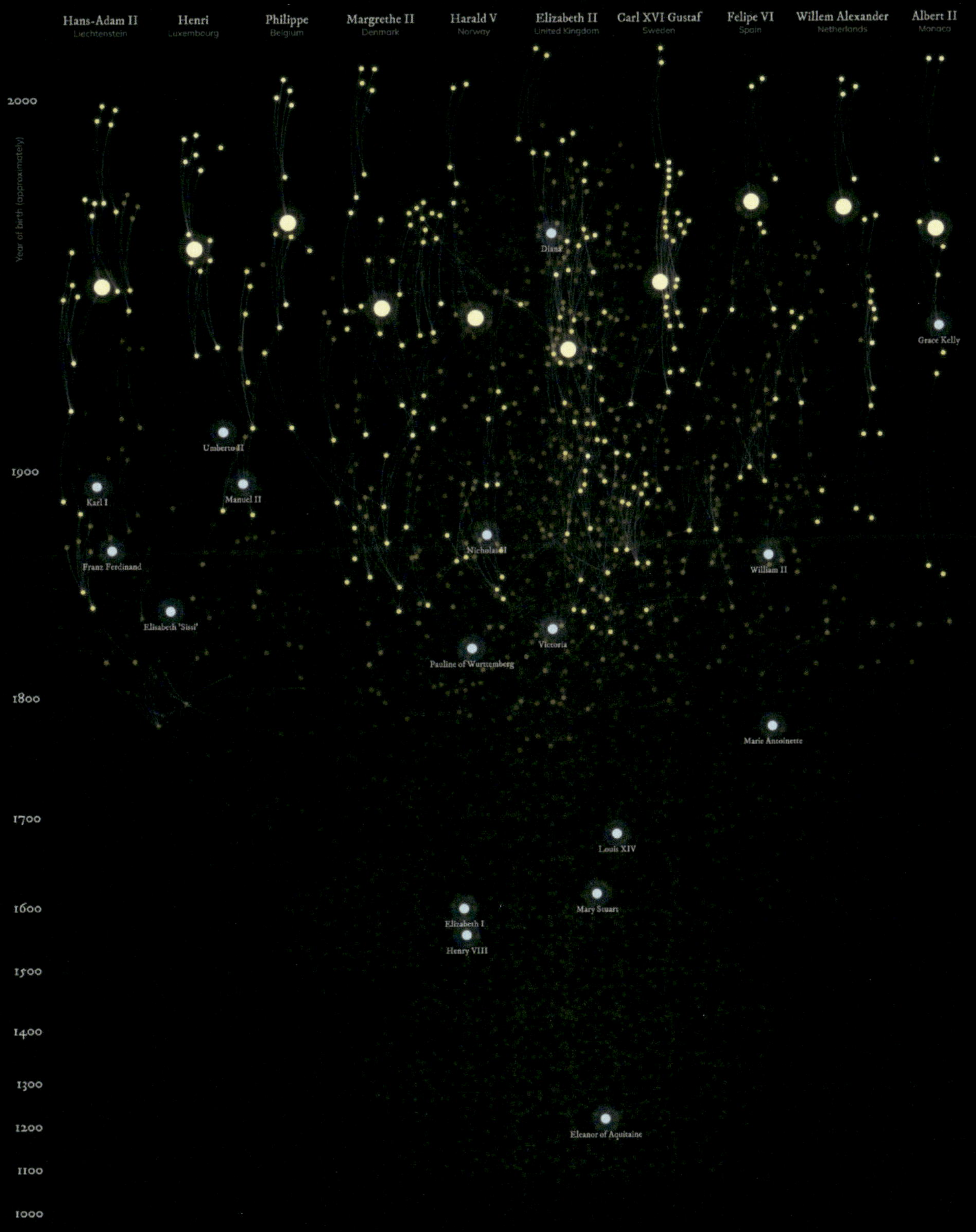

Hans-Adam II
Liechtenstein
Henri
Luxembourg
Philippe
Belgium
Margrethe II
Denmark
Harald V
Norway
Elizabeth II
United Kingdom
Carl XVI Gustaf
Sweden
Felipe VI
Spain
Willem Alexander
Netherlands
Albert II
Monaco

Year of birth (approximately)

2000
Diana
Grace Kelly
Umberto II
1900
Karl I
Manuel II
Nicholas II
William II
Franz Ferdinand
Elisabeth 'Sissi'
Victoria
Pauline of Württemberg
1800
Marie Antoinette
1700
Louis XIV
Mary Stuart
1600
Elizabeth I
Henry VIII
1500
1400
1300
1200
Eleanor of Aquitaine
1100
1000

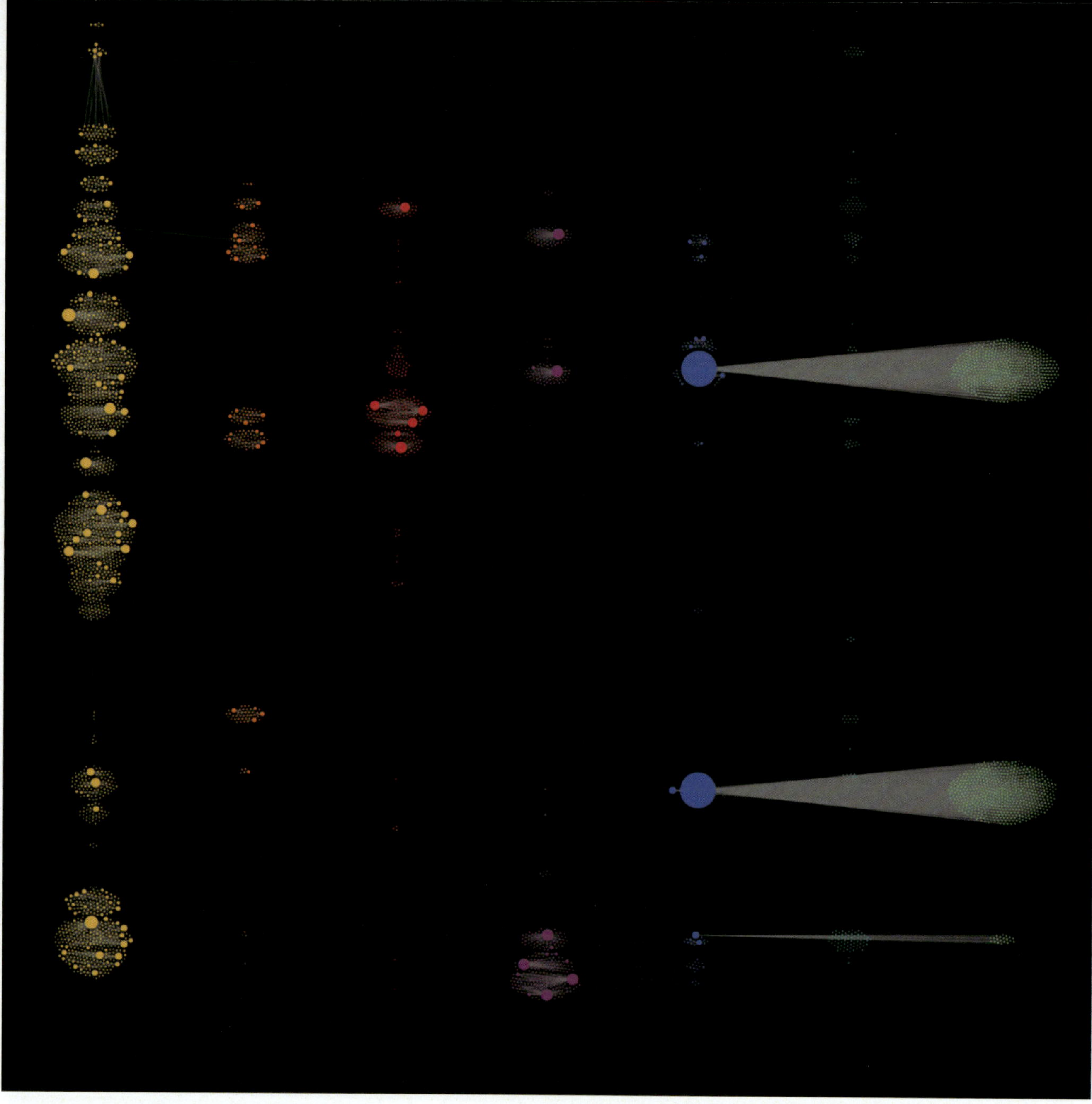

3.6

Figure 3.6

A very rough first result after placing the alis_ data into the "Royal Constellations" template.

bigger circles toward the top. Everybody else is placed horizontally, based on the position of their closest relative among the current royal leaders.

Applying this visual structure to the alis OS data, each dot (person) would be a service. The vertical axis (birth date) would show the creation time of the service, while the horizontal arrangement (current royal leaders) would hold the service domains.

After a call with the client and seeing the data, this seemed like a very plausible option, and I started with the same template. It didn't take long to get a very rough first result of the network on my screen (figure 3.6).

I realized immediately that the "Royal Constellations" approach did *not* work with their data.

There were two significant issues. For one, a service hardly ever created another service in a different domain. Therefore, having the seven domains spread horizontally did not allow the network to spread out horizontally. It's not even apparent from figure 3.6 that this data is, in fact, an interconnected network at all!

The second, bigger issue was that the process of services creating new services generally happened within a few (milli)seconds. After which, nothing might happen for a while, relatively speaking. This meant all those services, the circles, wanted to sit at the exact same points along the timeline, resulting in vertically stacked blobs of packed circles.

Figure 3.7

Dropping the domains and stretching out the services along a spiraled time axis.

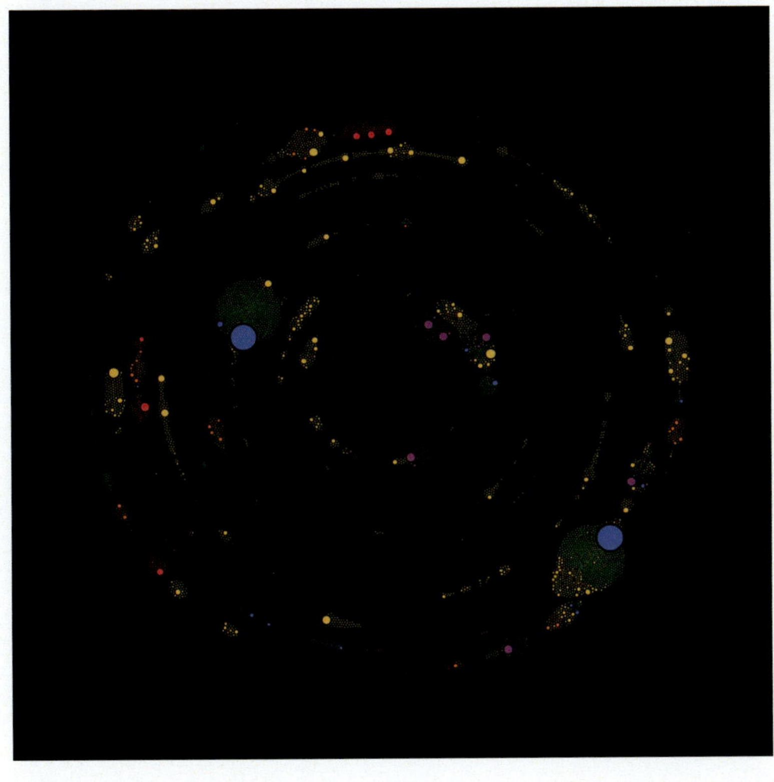

3.7

I tried removing the domains to stretch out the time axis along a spiral line (figure 3.7). However, even that wasn't enough to erase the blobs. Furthermore, there was no sense for which services were creating others.

I reached out to my contact at alis_ to explain why the "Royal Constellations" approach wasn't effective for their data. I emphasized that to move forward, we needed to restart with my usual process: creating a design tailored to the data and the project objectives. Fortunately, we were able to reallocate some budget to accommodate a proper design phase.

TRYING TO FIND A GOOD DESIGN APPROACH

This is where the chart-merging finally happened, though it took many iterations. I'd like to take you through some of the design attempts. The following images are very minimal. I'll explain the concept behind each one, but don't worry if everything doesn't make perfect sense! These early designs were all about exploring the potential of different layouts.

In the previous images, I had arranged the services along a timeline, with each dot precisely marking its creation time. For my first attempt at a new design, I wanted to see how it would look if I focused on the *order* in which services were created, rather than precise creation time. This would ensure equal spacing between each one, whether they were created seconds or minutes apart. Since many services were created almost simultaneously, the exact time wasn't as important as the order in which they appeared.

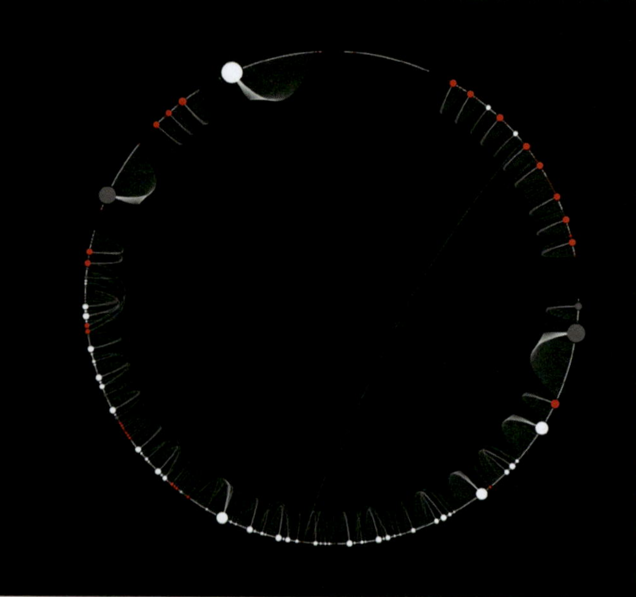

3.8

I chose to place the services along a circle, if only because I like spherical shapes and when I'm in doubt, I seem to default to them. In figure 3.8, I clustered services of the same domain together and added gaps between them to visually separate one domain from the other. Within the domains, I ordered the services chronologically. The lines reveal connections between each service and the subsequent (or downstream) services it triggered.

I also did away with the rainbow scheme (which I usually test early in a project for some visual fun) and settled on a simple white-on-black motif. The only exception was if the service had failed, in which case I used red—the only branded color available but also appropriate for what it represented.

However, the circular layout made it difficult to see the hierarchy of services. That is, which services were the "initiating" services, and which were created from another service.

So I tried a very different approach, although I sadly don't remember how the idea came to me. I placed the domains as "spokes" radiating from a central point (figure 3.9), with each spoke containing the associated services. Here, again, there was no timeline; I placed the dots in order of their creation along the spokes.

Figure 3.8

Services (dots) by domain, ordered chronologically, with gaps between the domains.

Figure 3.9

Placing the services in "spokes," one spoke per domain.

3.9

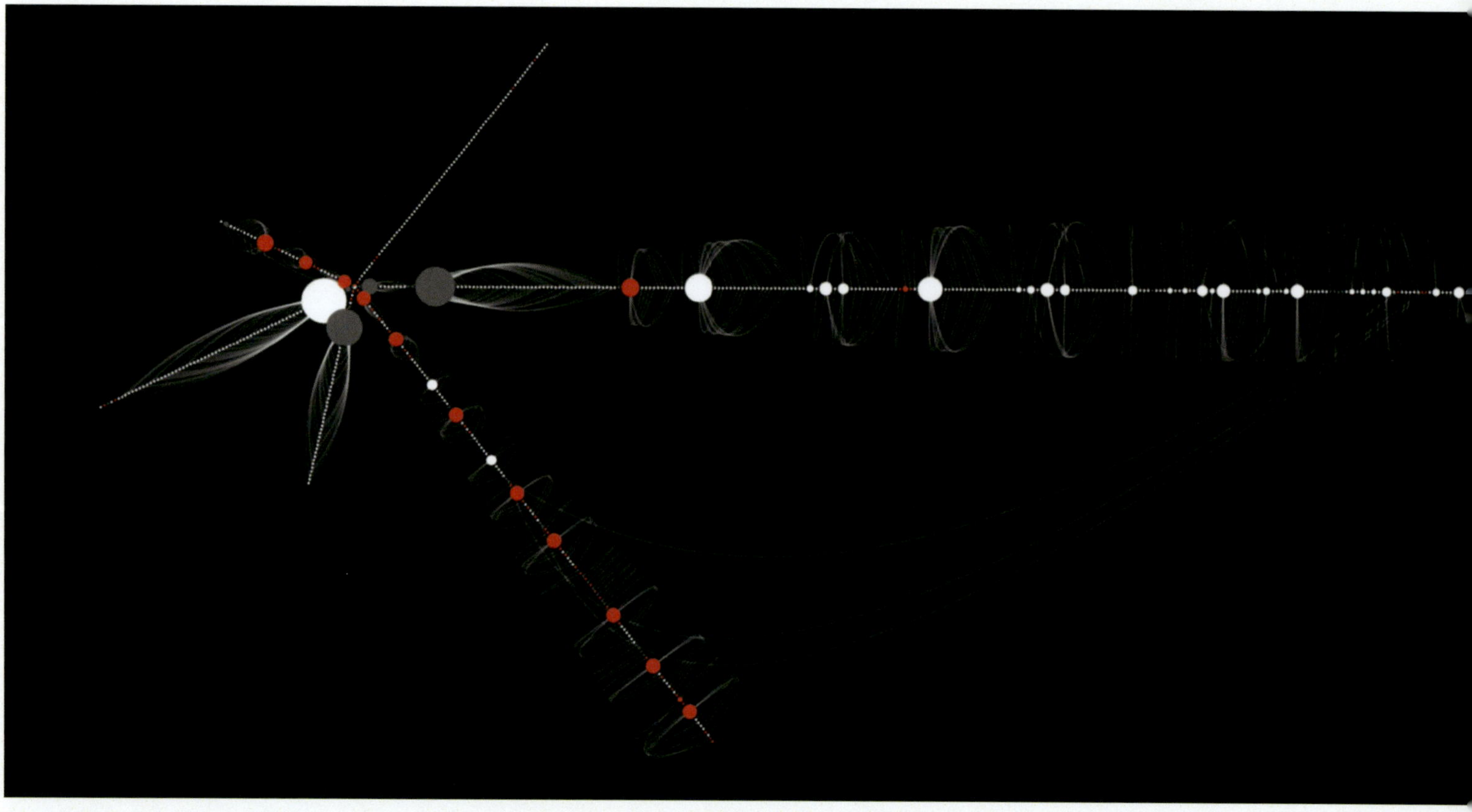

Figure 3.10

Visualizing the services as seven little (force-directed) networks.

Clearly, one domain was much larger than the others, creating an undesirable, off-balanced visual. I might have tried to address this issue visually, but, remember, this data was not static; the visual needed to be flexible, so it would work even as the underlying data changed. I worried that a domain could, at some point, grow so large that it wouldn't fit on the screen. Alas, I moved on to other ideas.

3.10

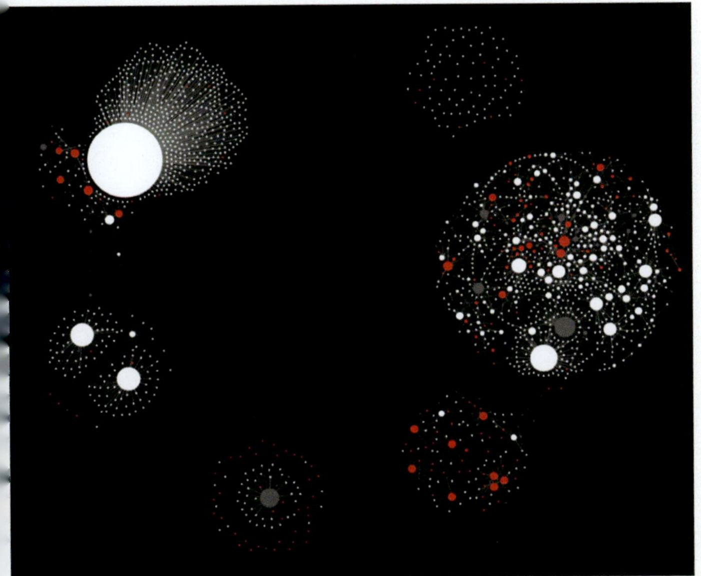

I then wondered how this data set might look as a force-directed graph—the chart type most often used to visualize networks, where entities appear as dots and their connections are lines linking them. I applied a separate force algorithm to each domain, and the result was seven little clumped-up "hairballs." Obviously, not great!

After tweaking the network algorithm's settings, I got some less hairball-y configurations (figure 3.10). However, it didn't feel like a stable solution that could adapt easily to the evolving data set. Furthermore, the visual conveyed a sense of chaos first and foremost. It wasn't providing any insight.

But then again, this data set was more like a tree than a network: A service would only ever appear if a user initiated it, or if it was triggered by an upstream service. Therefore, I tried a tree layout, which is often horizontal or vertical but can also bend into a radial format.

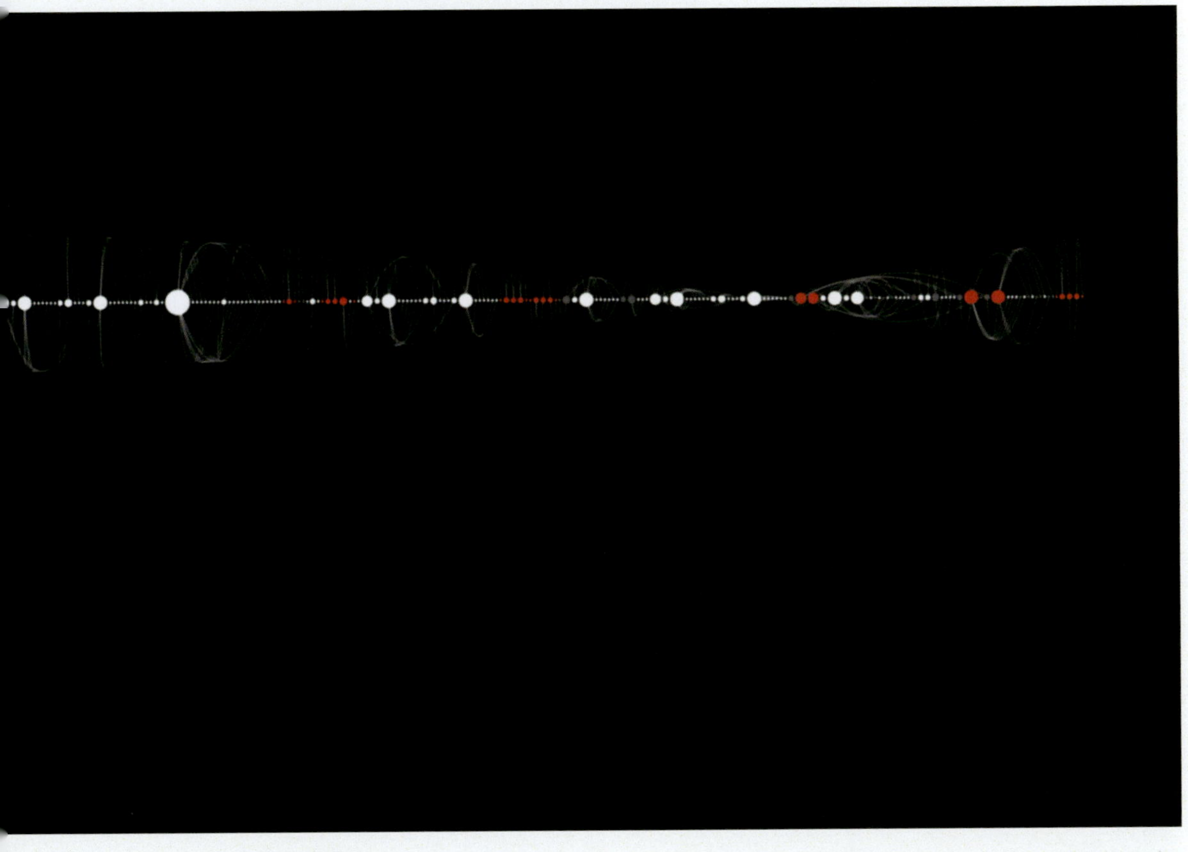

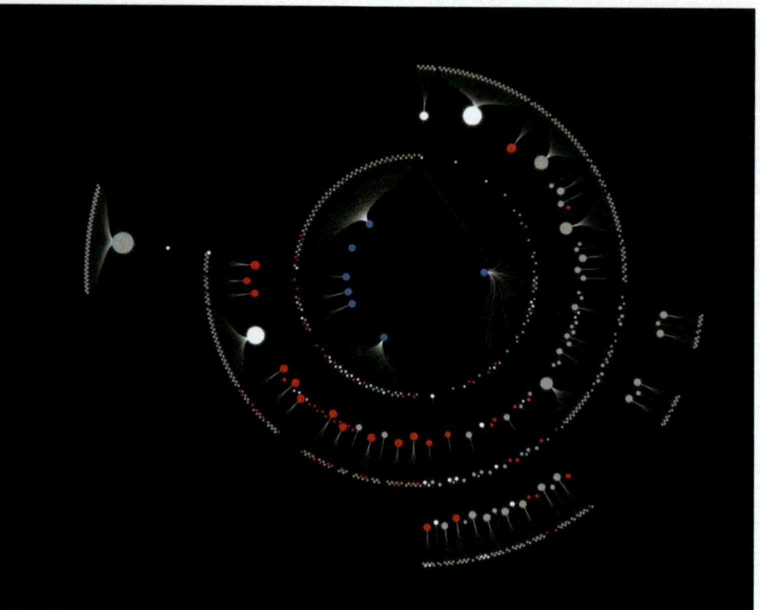

3.11

Figure 3.11

A radial tree clearly shows the hierarchy of created services, up to four levels deep.

Figure 3.11 shows the result for a radial tree where each inner blue dot represents a domain, and all the dots directly connected to them are their associated services. I liked being able to see the hierarchy of services clearly. It's apparent that one service can trigger a secondary service or even a series of secondary services. In turn, those secondary services spawn their own tertiary services, and so on.

There was a good chance I would have stuck with the radial tree layout if not for one major issue: domain crossing instances, where one domain's service created a secondary service in a different domain. Sadly, that information was lost entirely in the radial tree.

At this point, I was running out of ideas. I tried a few more outlandish concepts that didn't pan out. Eventually, I returned to my original circle idea and tried to refine it (figure 3.12). I emphasized different domains along the circle by adding dotted lines in the gaps between them and thin solid arcs outside the main circle. I drew the inter-domain connections on the inside of the circle (long red lines) and intra-domain connections on the outside of the circle.

3.12

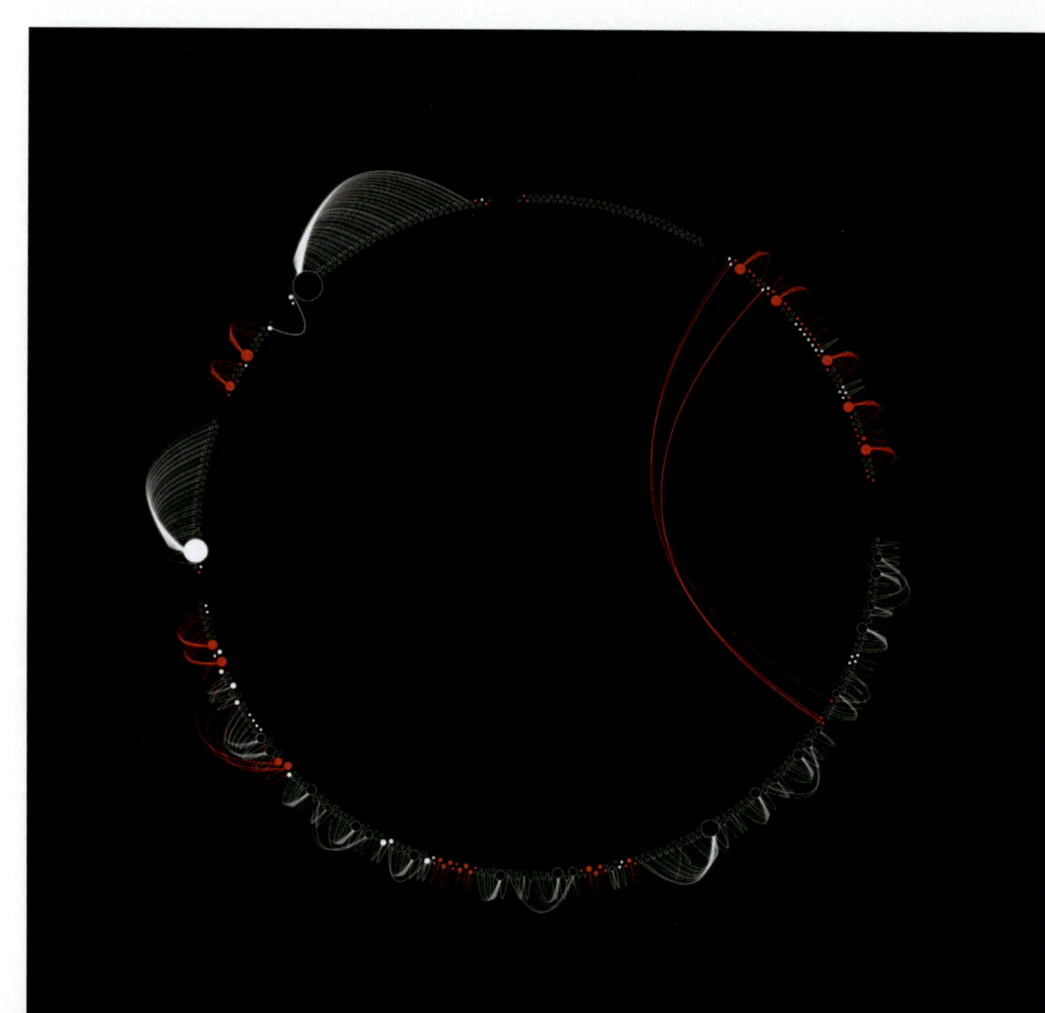

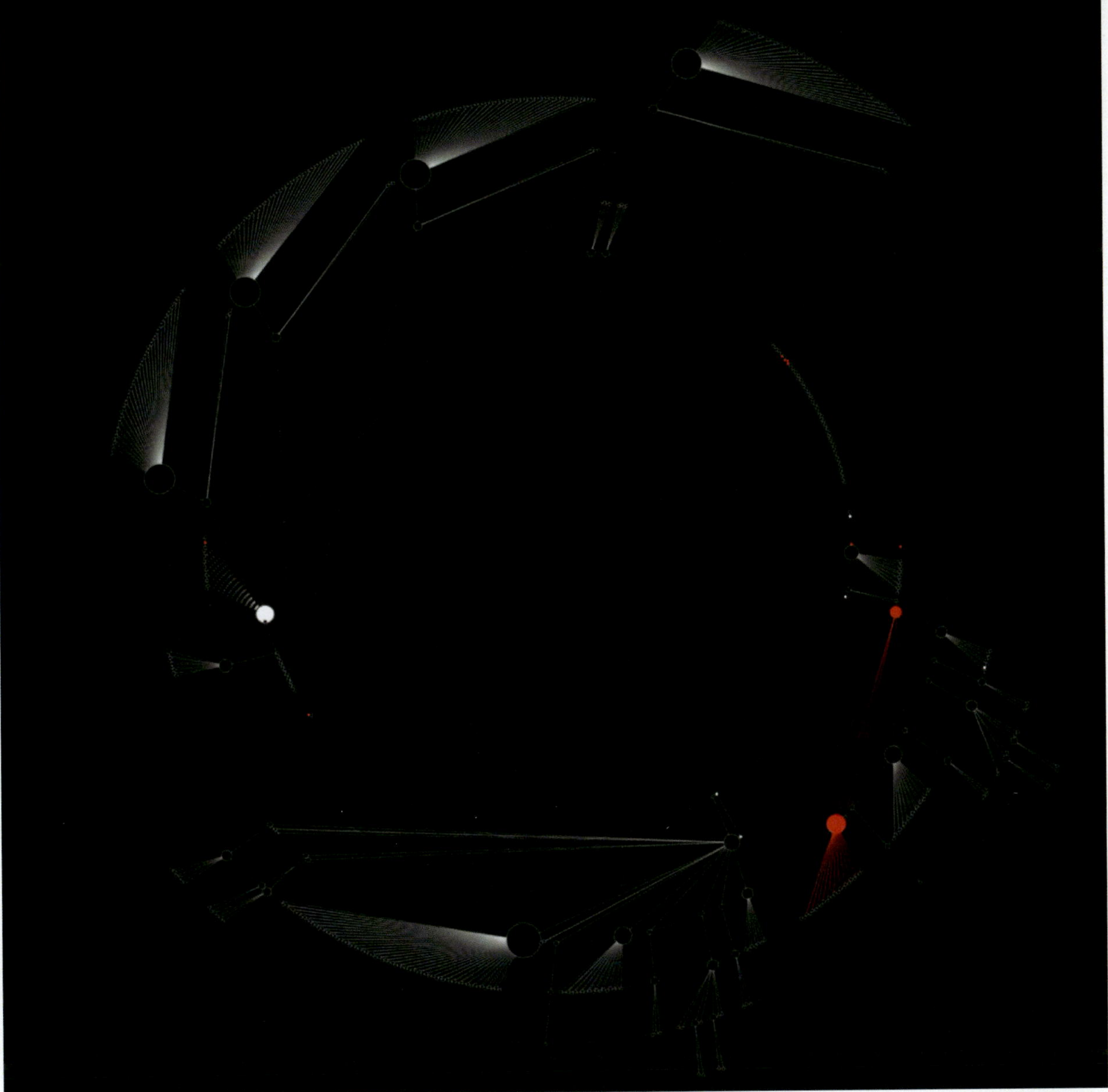

3.13

Figure 3.12

Fine-tuning the original circle idea by making the domain sections more apparent and connecting the services with lines running inside and outside of the circle.

Figure 3.13

Moving services one level outward from their parent to show the hierarchy of service creation.

It had some potential, but it wasn't quite there. It didn't clearly show the hierarchy of services.

I had completely run out of ideas. Nothing I tried worked well enough, so I took a step back to reflect on all my designs. My two favorites were the straightforward circle layout in figure 3.12, which arranged services by domain and time, and the radial tree in figure 3.11, which clearly highlighted the hierarchy of services. Perhaps I could combine the strengths of both into something new—starting with the circle layout and applying the hierarchy concept from the radial tree. In this way, I'd position each service on a series of concentric circles, with each downstream service one step farther outward from its parent service.

MERGING TWO CHARTS INTO A DEPTH CIRCLE

In figure 3.13, you can see the first rough attempt at creating this new chart form, which I called a "depth circle." When I first saw the result, I instantly felt I was onto something.

I could finally see which services had created others, and I could even spot when a service farther outward had failed (shown as red dots), triggering a cascading failure inward, as it caused the original service to fail, too (see the bottom right in figure 3.13). This likely happened because the original service depended on information from the service it had created in order to be successful.

The hybrid approach let me precisely control the position of each service, so I knew that I could ultimately group them together by domain—something the radial tree alone couldn't achieve.

I reintroduced some design elements from the radial circle design (figure 3.12), transforming the straight lines into curvy ones and adding

Figure 3.14

The depth circle after curving the lines, separating the domains again, and giving the operational processes a warm white glow and the failed services a red glow, inspired by car lights in the dark.

3.14

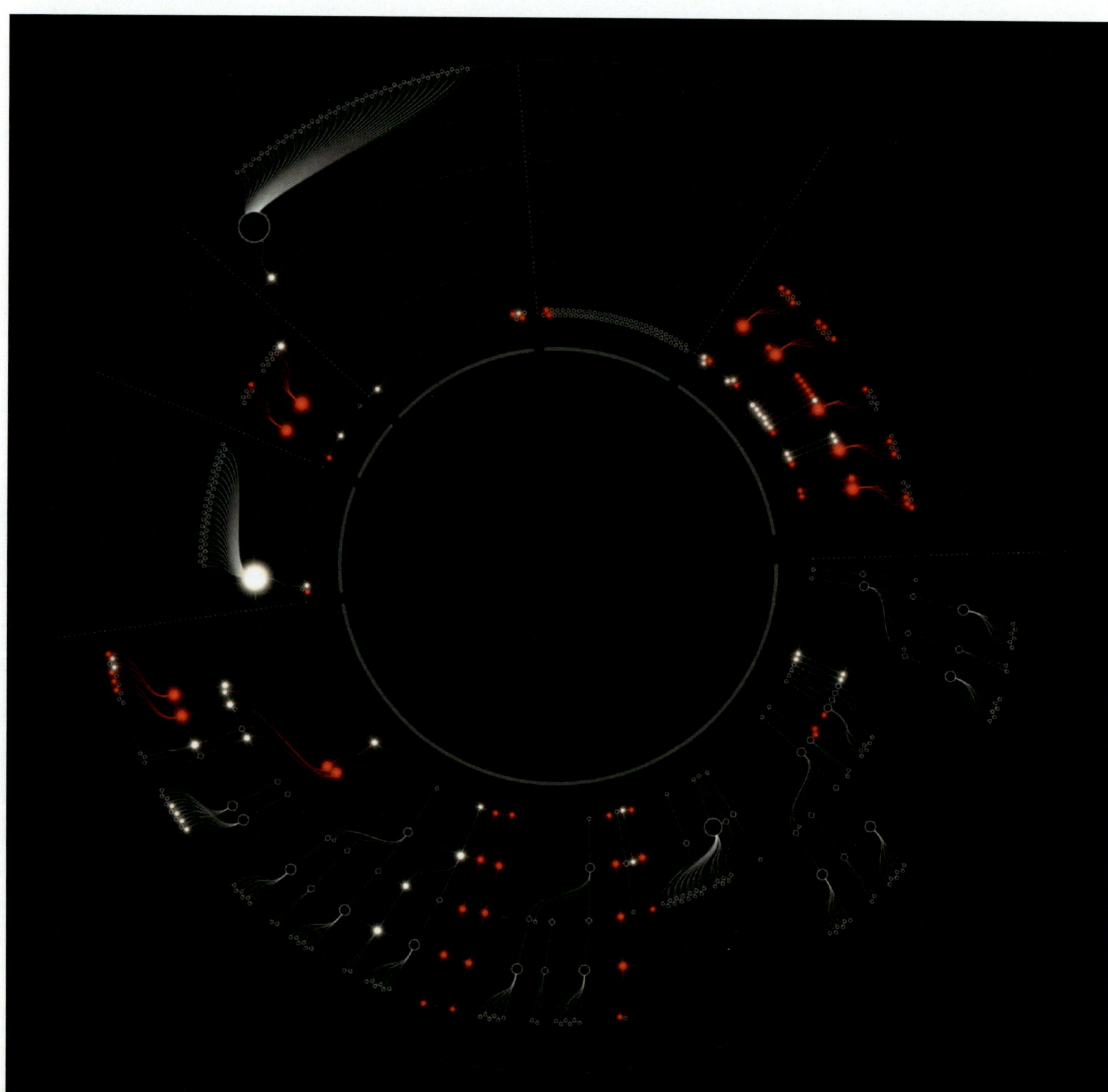

3.15

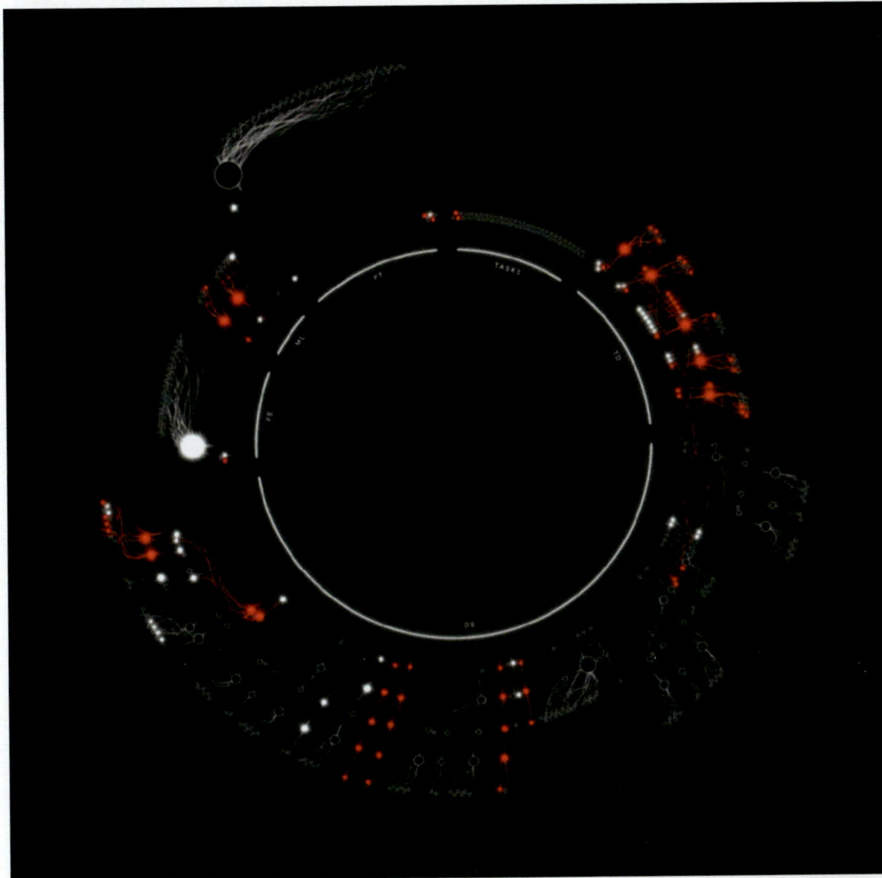

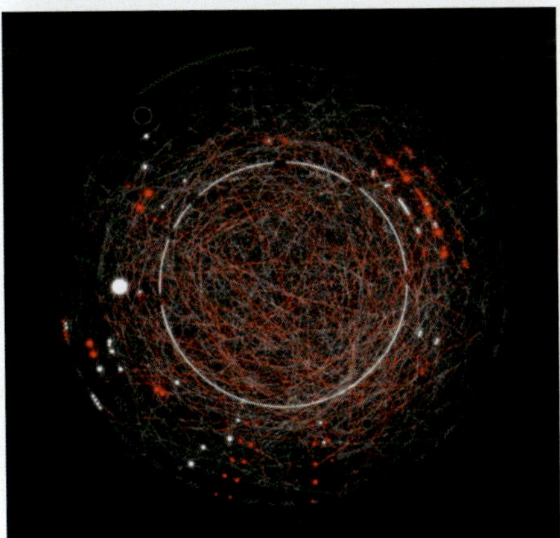

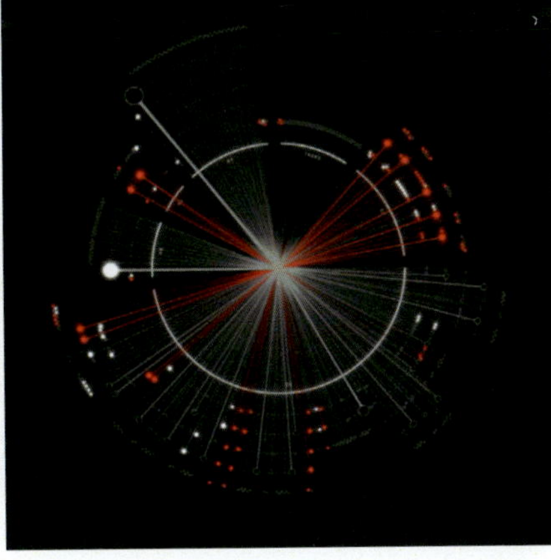

Although unrelated to this lesson, I'd like to offer this advice: any network or tree visualization benefits from a custom approach because the most effective design depends so heavily on the specific connections within the data set.

details that aligned with the client's brand. A key aspect of alis_' branding was long exposure photos of car lights passing at night. Drawing on Lesson 1 about incorporating the topic, or in this case, the brand style into the design, I gave any operational services a bright, warm white glow, while the failed ones emitted a red glow. A small thing to add that had quite the visual effect.

By the time I'd gotten to the visual in figure 3.14, I had all the things I'd aimed for. I could understand how the system was working: I could see the hierarchy, I could see how some services had failed (due to others failing), and I could see the split between the domains through the larger gap and dotted lines separating the domain sections. And! It looked intriguing. To someone who has never seen it before, it's not immediately clear what it's representing, but I believe that the visual form entices a new viewer to want to know. I was ready to share this version with my client. Thankfully, they were delighted with the result!

Figure 3.15

Several "blooper" screenshots from trying to get wobbly lines.

Further inspired by the long exposure photos of car lights in the dark—and to apparently give myself an extra challenge—I wanted to enhance the lines between the services. So I drew a dozen near-transparent lines between a pair of dots, each with a slight wobble, to represent cars taking a slightly different path to the same destination.

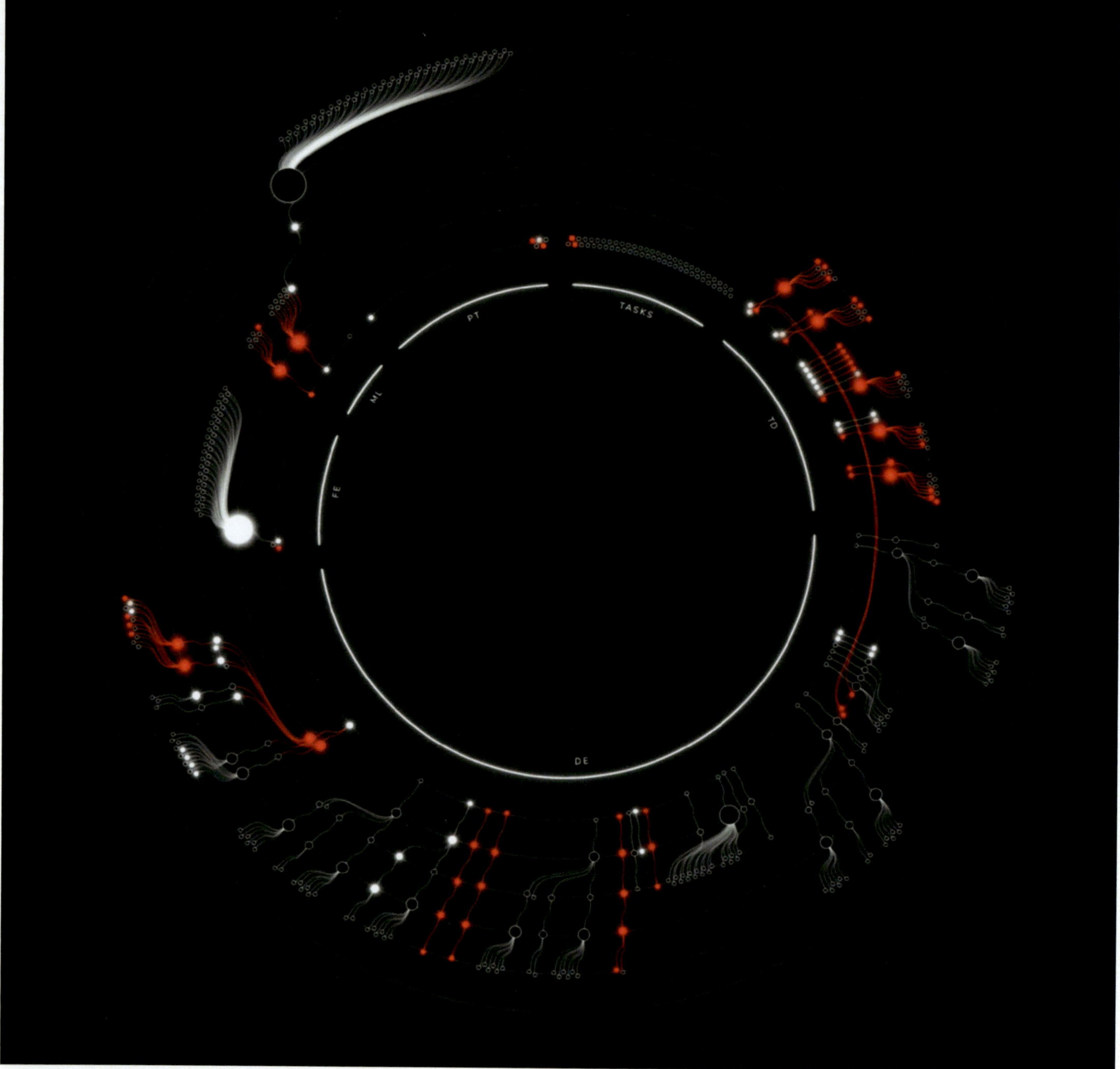

3.16

Figure 3.16

Slightly wobbly lines inspired by car lights in the dark.

Figure 3.17a & b

The final result, with some extra information in the center (a), which gets updated when the user hovers over a specific service (b).

It took a lot of experimenting with the mathematical formulas to draw a subtle wobbly line (built up from the near-transparent lines), as the work-in-progress shots in figure 3.15 show.

Figure 3.16 shows the final result of this process, where all the lines have subtly gained more character. You can now more clearly see a domain crossing on the right side, where the red lines span almost a quarter of a circle.

3.17a

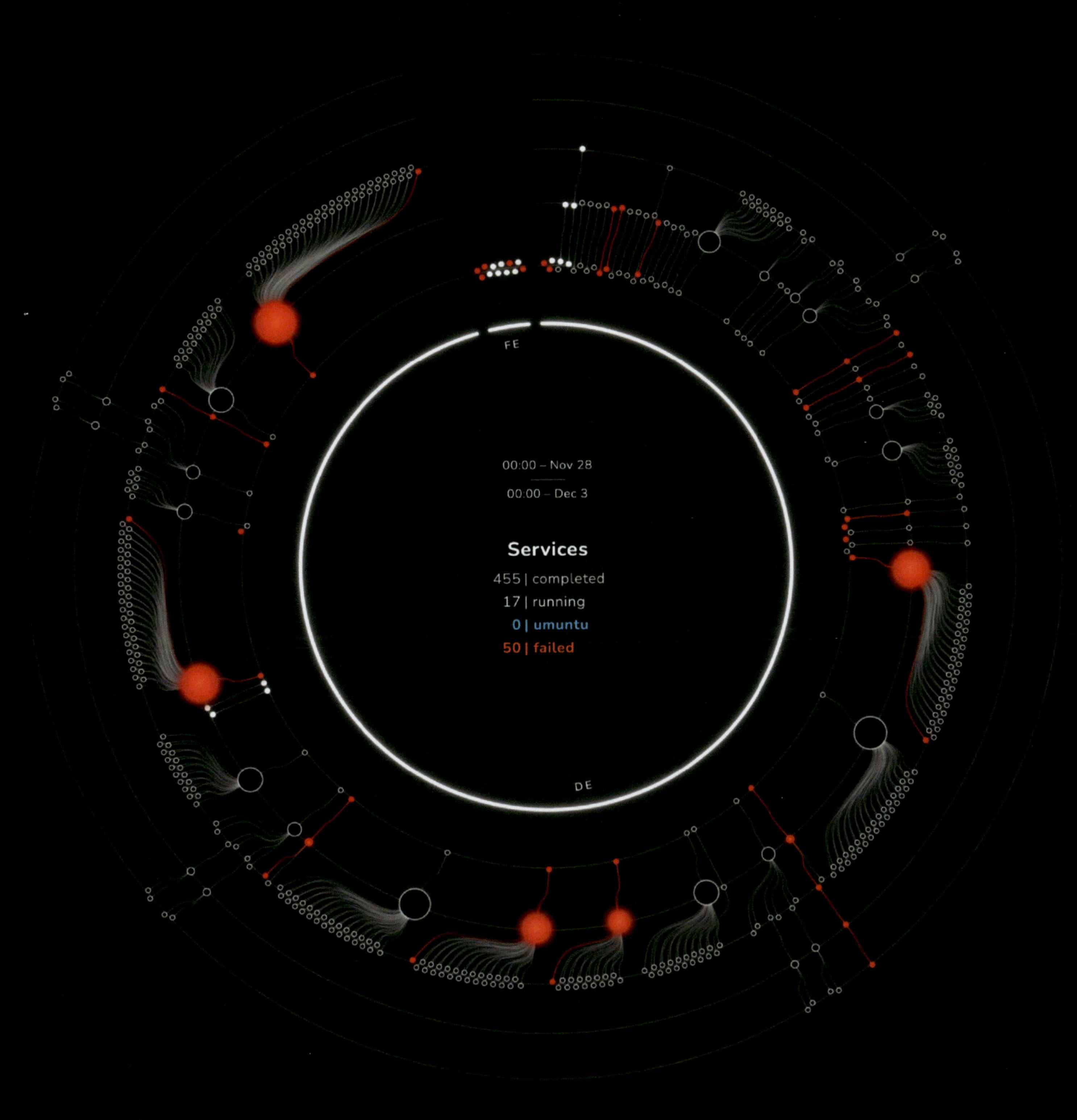
FE
DE
00:00 – Nov 28
00:00 – Dec 3
Services
455 | completed
17 | running
0 | umuntu
50 | failed

3.17b

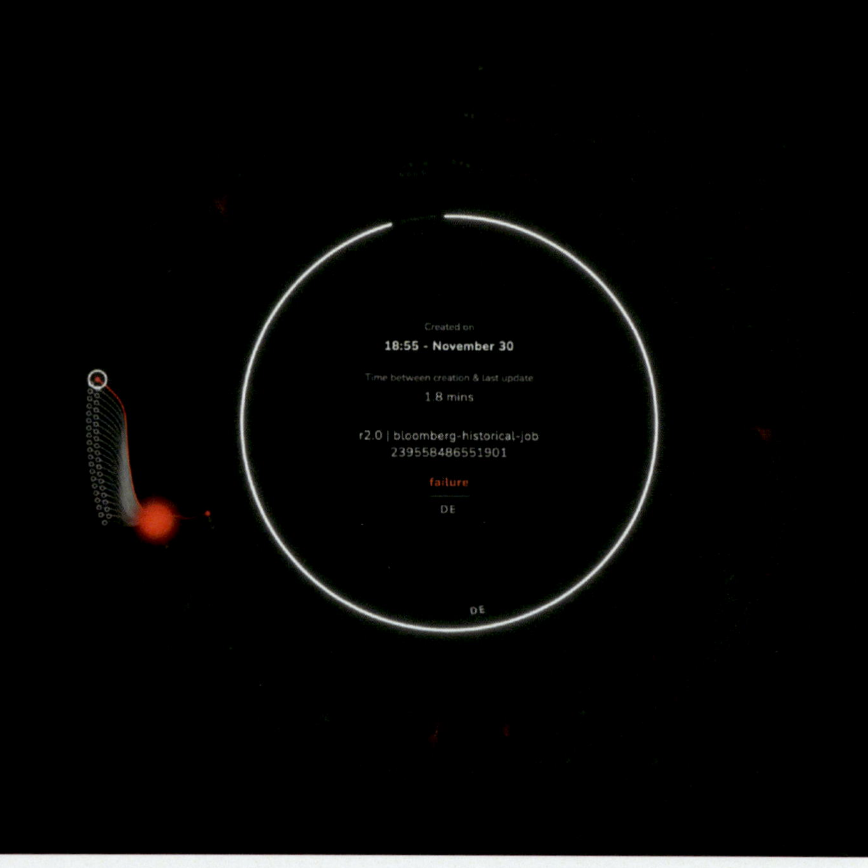

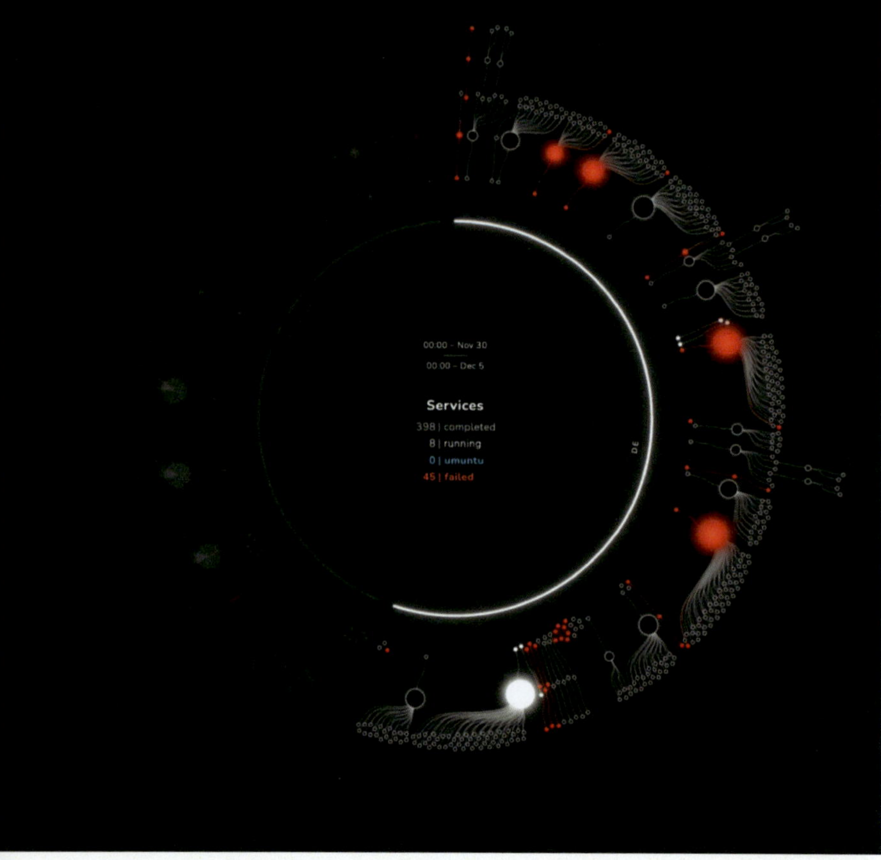

3.18

ADDING INTERACTIVITY

The last significant step was making the visual interactive, through hovers and clicks, and able to handle continuous data updates.

Instead of building a tooltip for each dot, I used the central part of the circle to display information about all of the services (figure 3.17a) or just the selected one (figure 3.17b).

Figure 3.17b shows a hover on a failed service (the little red dot on the left with a white circle around it) and the cascading effect up the hierarchy, impacting its parent, and their parent service.

You can also hover over a specific domain arc (along the inside of the circle) to highlight only those services (figure 3.18) or click on it to make the visual animate and visually remove all the other domains.

I'm very happy to have found a way to reveal the connections in this complex system of services, especially considering how unsuitable the initial "Royal Constellations" concept was for the data.

In the end, merging my favorite elements from a circle layout and a radial tree created something truly effective—and totally unique—for alis_' data.

Figure 3.18

Hovering over a specific domain arc highlights only the services that belong to that domain.

Starting with a straightforward approach—placing one chart within another—is a great way to ease into the technique of combining charts. But merging two chart types is where the real magic happens. This approach takes more effort, though; it requires thoughtful planning to come up with the concept, requiring sketches and likely some rough prototypes to gauge the potential. Yet the results can absolutely be worth it. When a well-executed hybrid chart comes together, it creates a new visual that stands out and is far more impactful than either of the individual charts could have been alone.

USE CIRCULAR SHAPES

People are drawn to circular shapes. The introduction to Manuel Lima's *The Book of Circles* is a wonderfully thorough analysis of why this might be and how circles are a fundamental part of, well, nearly everything. It's not hard to come up with examples: The sun and moon, two essential elements of our world dictating human lives (especially before civilization) are round. The "window into our soul," our eyes, are round. Circles are simple, smooth, endless, and calming.

With this in mind, I constantly iterate on my visuals by adding more circular shapes and rounded curves to my designs to see if it will increase their visual appeal. For example, I often prefer to use circles instead of squares to represent individual data points (see all of the images from Lesson 7). I opt for smooth, curved lines when possible (as with the solar panel line charts in figure 1.5). I like to (subtly) round the corners of spiky or rectangular shapes (as I did in a visual about pesticides, shown in figures 8.1 and 8.2). I also use arcs between two points in a network diagram instead of straight ones (see the royal families visual in figure 3.5).

There are most certainly cases when squares, rectangles, or straight lines better fit the chart form, the visual design, the client's brand, or the data (the employee stacked bar charts in figure 1.1). However, after analyzing all of the projects in this book, I would say four out of five rely heavily on circles, circular layouts, or curvy elements (where straight lines or sharp corners were deliberately replaced by rounded alternatives).

Figure II.1

A very round piece from my "Coiling Curves" collection where I played around with spirographs. I've been fascinated with spirographs since I was a child. I keep returning to them and iterating on them every now and then.

II.1

PART II

GETTING

Now that you are comfortable making those ordinary charts more effective and memorable, you can send your creativity to the next level. The lessons in this section will introduce techniques to help you start deviating from the straightforward charts. You will learn how to push the boundaries of your creativity and come up with original concepts.

First, I'll demonstrate a quick and simple technique that adds more visual appeal by encoding the same data value with several visual aspects. Next, we'll really flex our creative muscles and step away from the computer. I'll showcase the benefits of sketching designs first—and getting the most out of that legwork. This will prepare you for the following lesson, where you'll move away from thinking in chart types altogether and let the data and your goals take the lead as you come up with effective ways to showcase insights.

CREATIVE

By the end of this section, you will understand how to take ordinary charts one step further and even go beyond the scope of the existing charts to create custom designs for your data. This will be especially important for cases where traditional charts cannot capture the data's complexities and context.

LESSON FOUR

AMPLIFIED

Present the same variable in diverse ways to achieve something more visually captivating

I hardly ever see charts that represent the same data point in multiple ways. Generally, a data variable is set to one visual channel, such as size, color, *or* opacity. But it's perfectly acceptable to set the size, color, *and* opacity to the same variable. This technique feels most taboo in business settings, where the dogma of having very clean and minimal charts reigns supreme. It's as if you're breaking some unwritten rule about what's "proper" in the world of data visualization.

But let me tell you, applying "single variable amplified encoding," or, more simply, "amplified encoding," as I like to call this technique, is one of my favorite and quickest ways to infuse creativity into a chart. Some might have heard of it as "double encoding," but that sounds like there's a limit to encoding a variable only twice. In contrast, with amplified encoding, I want to convey that although encoding twice is fine, there is no limit to the number of ways you can encode the same variable to different visual channels.

ENCODING

4.1a

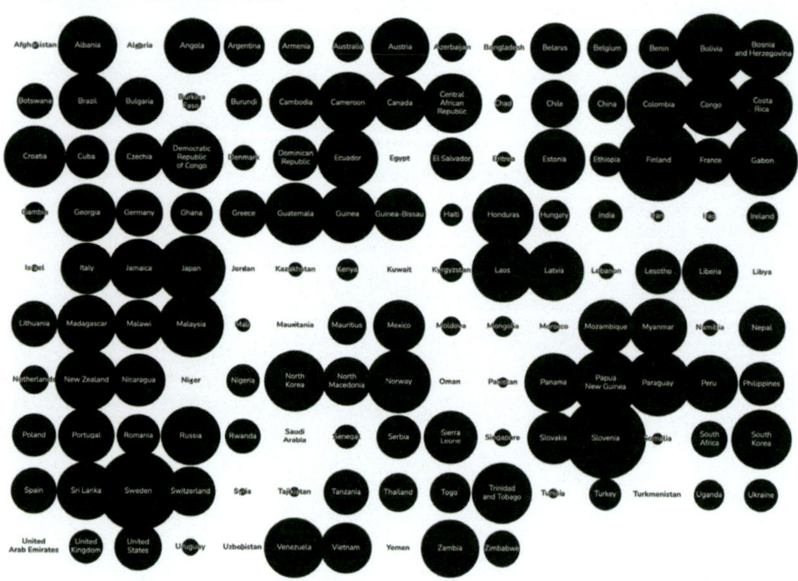

4.1b

Figure 4.1a & b

Each circle is a country, scaled in size to the number of trees per square kilometer (a). With amplified encoding, size, color, and opacity represent the number of trees (b).

Imagine a grid of about 150 circles, each representing a country. Now, scale the size of each circle to, say, the number of trees per square kilometer—the denser the trees, the larger the circle. Sure, that's a fine chart; you can read and interpret it (figure 4.1a). Yet, it feels like you could give it a little more flare to break up the monotony and make it easier to interpret.

You might try coloring the circles, going from a light yellow (sparse tree cover) to a lush green (dense tree cover). And while you're at it, play with opacity, going from almost transparent for low values to fully opaque for the highest values. That will result in a more engaging grid than 150 monochromatic circles (figure 4.1b), because you've applied three different visual channels (size, color, and opacity) to the same value (trees per square kilometer).

I applied this exact styling and amplified encoding to a "Data Sketches" project called "Breathing Earth," except that each circle (50,000 in total!) represented a small area on Earth, and the value was the amount of "greenness" as measured from space (figure 4.2).

Besides making the visual more captivating, amplified encoding generally makes it easier for someone to interpret the value of the data because several visual clues convey and reinforce the message. This also helps with accessibility, as there are more ways to interpret the value if one specific visual channel isn't ideal for the audience (such as people with color blindness). See, for example, that it's easier for your eyes to notice the largest circles in figure 4.1b versus 4.1a.

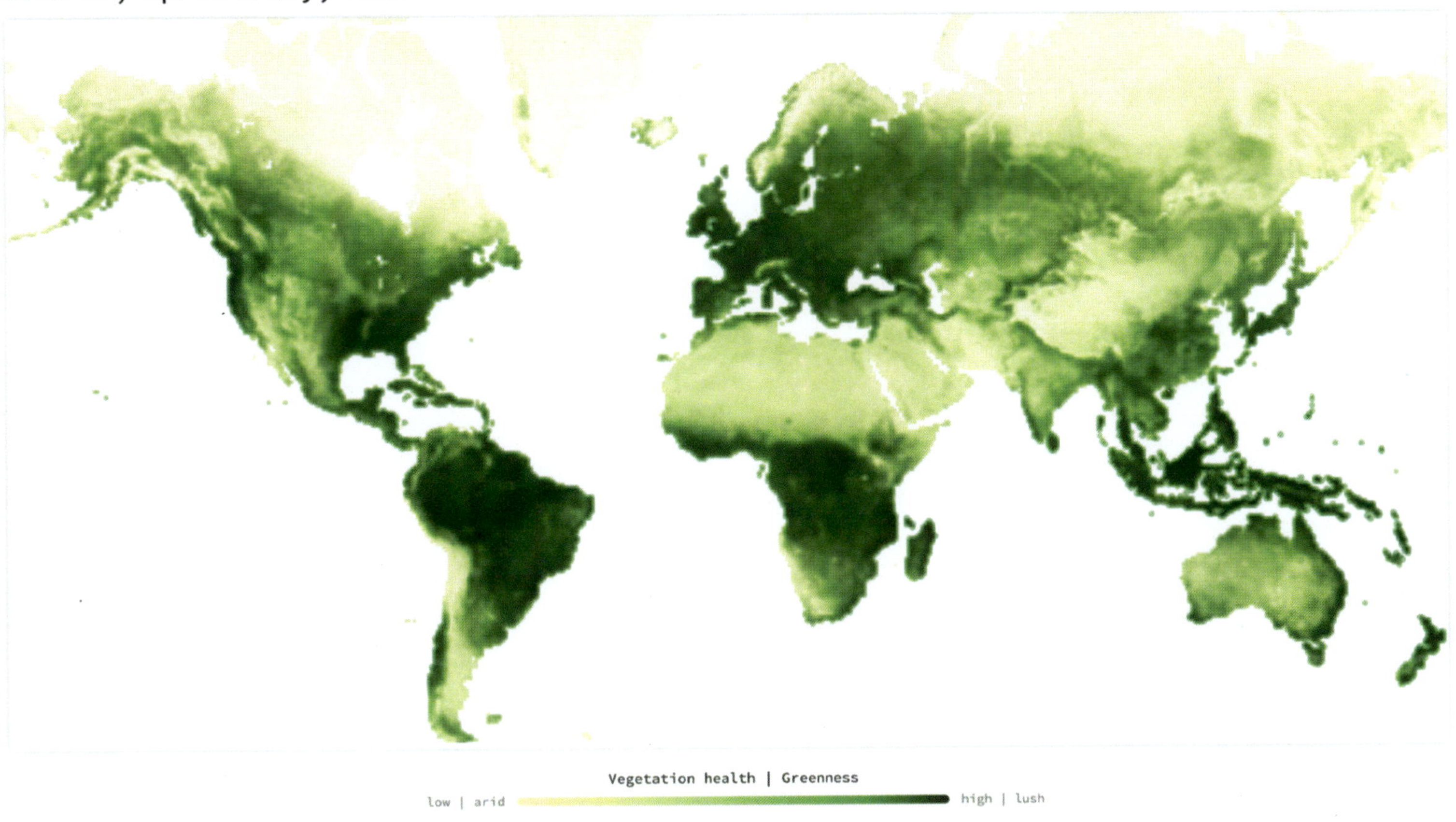

4.2

Figure 4.2

"Breathing Earth" is a land map made of small circles that uses amplified encoding to show "greenness" through circle size, color, and opacity. See the visual on *breathingearth.visualcinnamon.com*

Once you've set one visual channel to a variable, adding others is usually straightforward. In many data visualization tools, it often takes just an extra drag-and-drop action or a few additional lines of code to assign, for instance, opacity to the variable after you've already assigned size. This approach makes it easy to experiment with amplified encoding without requiring a significant investment of effort or time.

4.3a

4.3b

Figure 4.3a, b, c & d

Some of the projects I created while studying with the Fab Academy.

Figure 4.4

The electronic board with the phototransistor (a little white rectangle at the bottom).

Visualizing just one number

PERSONAL | 2021 | FAB ACADEMY

fabacademy.org/2021/labs/waag/students/nadieh-bremer/blog/week-15

I use amplified encoding in various examples throughout this book, often in subtle ways. But I've also taken amplified encoding to the extreme. I want to show you a project where I visualized just one number in various (silly) ways, overflowing it with encodings. I wanted to experiment with some unconventional techniques that I'm unlikely to use for visualizing data in more serious contexts.

At the start of 2021, I stopped working for six months to enroll in the Fab Academy program through a so-called "Fab Lab" in Amsterdam (a workshop with fabrication machines). This was a 20-week course, partially online, partially in the lab, headed by Neil Gershenfeld from MIT. He and his team of global instructors teach students "how to make almost anything" in Fab Labs across the world. I learned how to design for, and work with, laser cutters, 3D printers, CNC machines (precision cutters), and more, as well as how to design and construct electronics. It was intense, and I loved every second of it.

4.3c

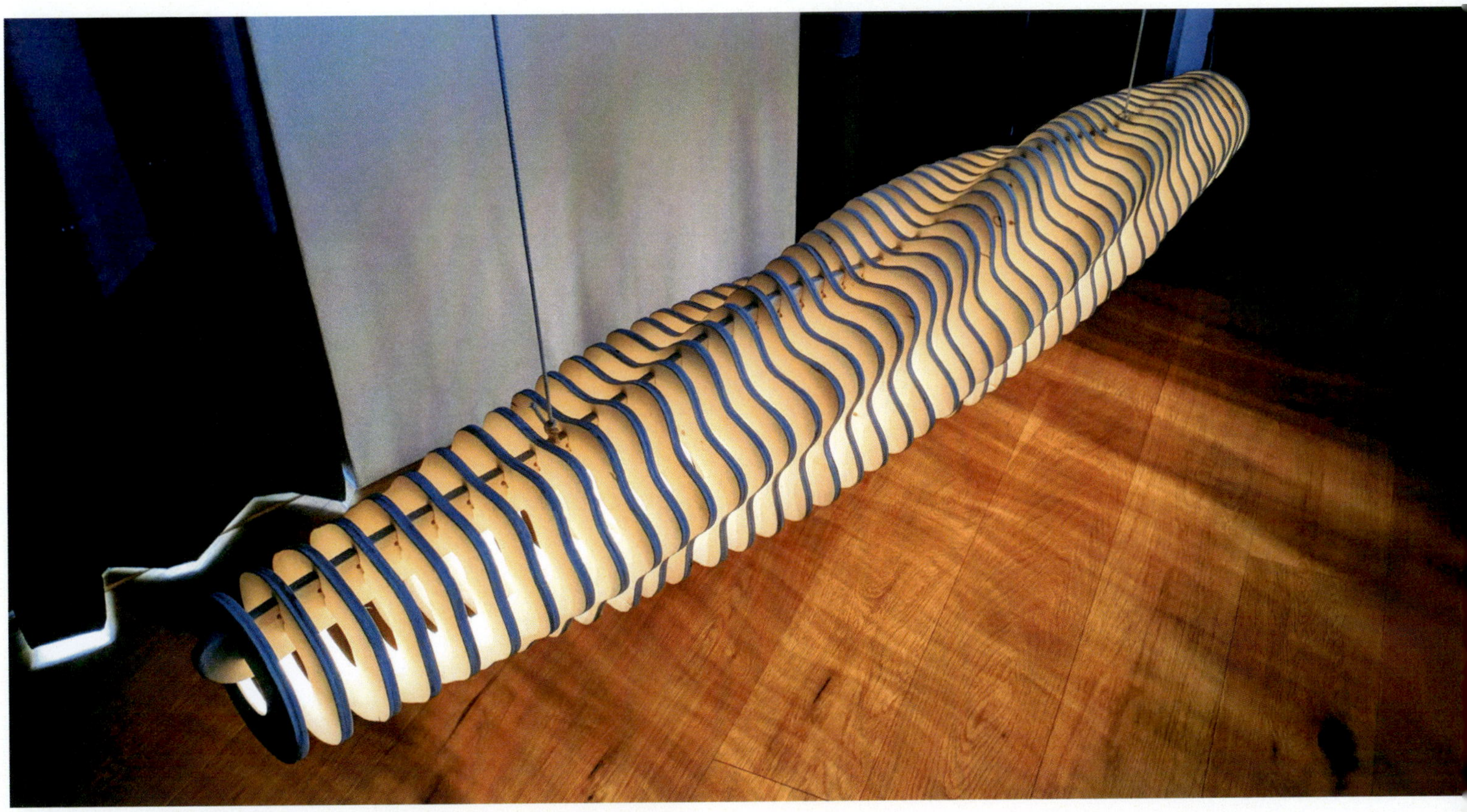

4.3d

4.4

As a technical note, I used four different tools to create these visuals, where I tried to use the particular strengths of each tool to guide the design direction. The jumping bars from figure 4.5 are made with D3.js + SVG, which is great for visuals with fewer elements, especially if they involve animations or interactions. The confetti circle from figure 4.6 uses the HTML5 Canvas API, which can handle tens of thousands of elements all moving about. However, it's more complex to program than using SVGs, especially if you want animation and interaction, and I therefore only use it when visualizing a large number of elements. The 3D blocks in figure 4.7 are made with Three.js and WebGL, as this is one of the main ways to create 3D visuals on the web. Finally, the flow fields from figure 4.8 use p5.js, which is a great library for a more general form of creative coding and has a great noise function to quickly create flow fields.

During one of the weeks, the assignment was to visualize a value from one of the sensors on an electronic board we'd made in the previous weeks. On my first board (about 5 centimeters in diameter) was a tiny phototransistor measuring the light intensity of its environment (figure 4.4). I realized that I had never actually tried to visualize just one number. I wondered how I would approach such an assignment, not once but multiple times—trying to come up with various ways of visualizing this single (yet continuously changing) value. And things got a little wilder with each attempt.

VARIATION 1 / EQUALIZER BARS

For the first attempt, I wanted to recreate an audio equalizer bar but applied to light instead of sound. The bar increases or decreases in height depending on the amount of light measured.

Figure 4.5 shows three states of the resulting visual: when the phototransistor measures a lot of light (a), an average amount of light (b), and hardly any light (c). The digits represent the phototransistor

4.5a

4.5b

4.5c

4.6a

4.6b

Figure 4.5a, b & c

Visualizing the light intensity for when it's bright (a), average (b), and dark (c).

4.6a & b

Visualizing the light intensity as ejected confetti when it's bright (a) and dark (b).

numbers, ranging from 0 for extremely bright light to 1,024 (which is 2^{10}—a computer thing) for total darkness. If you feel that the other way around makes more sense (more light = more photons = higher number), then I fully agree with you, by the way. Nevertheless, the height of the bar, divided into equal horizontal slices like an audio equalizer, reflects the number value; a high bar for a high number, which means there wasn't much light measured.

But I didn't stop there. I also used the value to encode the background color on a spectrum from yellow (bright) to pink (average) to purple (dark), making it immediately more apparent that a high value is actually associated with darkness. In contrast, a low value (bright light) has a vibrant yellow background. In addition, each slice of the bar has a different color depending on the value of the light it represents. Finally, the giant text in the middle is technically a fourth way to encode that value, just in case the other ways didn't make it clear enough. In short, every pixel in the visual connects to that one number in some way.

VARIATION 2 / CONFETTI ALONG A CIRCLE

For my second attempt, I created an invisible "particle ejector" that moves in a circle and spews lots of "circular confetti" as it travels (figure 4.6). The confetti are circles of various colors and sizes that slowly get smaller and eventually disappear. I based it on an example I found online years earlier that I had saved in an "inspiration board." (The upcoming Mini Chapter III after this lesson will go deeper into gathering inspiration.)

The background color continues to change with the light intensity. The big number in the center is still there, too. However, the radius of the circle that the confetti ejector travels on, along with the speed and number of confetti circles, are all tied to the light intensity: The higher the number, the larger the radius of the circle, the faster everything moves, and the more particles get ejected (figure 4.6b). The darker it becomes, the bigger the "party," was my thinking there.

4.7a

4.7b

4.7c

Figure 4.7a, b & c

Visualizing the light intensity when it's bright (a), average (b), and dark (c), as 3D boxes descending into, or rising from the ground.

Figure 4.8a, b & c

Flow fields that change depending on the light intensity. These images show bright (a), medium (b), and dark (c).

VARIATION 3 / BOXES VANISHING INTO THE GROUND

Next, I decided to go back to the equalizer bar but see if I could make the result feel different. Instead of 2D rectangles stacked on each other, I placed 3D boxes inside a square plane—1,024 of them. Then I programmed the boxes to slowly descend into, or rise from, the ground depending on the light intensity (figure 4.7). Why do it like that? I actually couldn't tell you; there's no deeper reason than that it seemed like it would create something fun to look at as the boxes moved up and down.

As I mentioned, the visual encoding is a play on the first variation: The background color, the number of boxes, the color of the boxes, and the giant number in the center are all driven by the light intensity in the same way. Nonetheless, I think most people wouldn't notice how similar the two are.

It was a way for me to explore the idea that assigning the same visual channels (rectangles/boxes, background color, the text in the middle) could still yield a very different looking result.

VARIATION 4 / COLORFUL RIVERS

As my final variation, I dove into the data art realm. (This example will give you a little taste of what to expect later in this book.) I used "flow fields" to create gorgeous, amorphous shapes and patterns. They look incredibly complex but are much easier to create than you might expect. If there were a "hello world" example for the field of generative art (which I'll explain more in Lesson 11), flow fields would be it.

4.8a

4.8b

4.8c

Figure 4.8 shows the results. Thousands of circles constantly appear, drawing over each other. Their positions are determined by the underlying "current" of the flow field. The circles' color, thickness, and speed are all based on the measured light intensity: bright light is yellow, big, and fast (figure 4.8a), while dark is purple, small, and slow (figure 4.8c).

In all these examples, the multitude of visual channels made each example look much more visually attractive than if I'd only used the background color, or only the height of the bars, or only the number of particles.

As I mentioned at the start, these were playful examples. Nevertheless, as you can see, there are various ways to amplify the visual encoding for just one metric. Color, size, opacity, thickness, and shape are some of the most straightforward and often used. However, I also used the speed of the particles to spice things up. Usually, you have to take some time to think about more unconventional encodings and play around with them to create something surprising and perhaps even fun.

I think more about amplified encoding when working with smaller data sets, because it elevates my visuals and charts beyond the expected default. Nevertheless, this technique can be applied to data sets of all sizes, and from the ordinary charts all the way to data art.

Amplified encoding is incredibly versatile and can be subtle if you want it to be. Very subtle encodings often don't need to be explained through a legend because they're barely noticeable—the slight roundness of rectangle angles, a minor shift in color or gradient, or the order in which things are plotted, for example. Don't be afraid to experiment. You'll be amazed at how even such small adjustments can, almost unconsciously, make a chart look more intriguing or beautiful because you've stepped away from having things look "too uniform." So embrace amplified encoding in your designs!

PROJECTING YOUR DATA ONTO OTHER VISUALS

When designing a new visualization, I often like to mentally project my data onto existing visualizations. This helps me generate more ideas and go beyond the bubble of what I could've conceived on my own.

When "projecting," I imagine how a data visualization would look if it had used my data instead. I see if there's a way to replace each of its variables with a variable from my data and consider if the result would make sense. I can only do this exercise once I've done exploratory data analyses, as I need to have a good grasp of the data and the distribution of each variable in my head before I can project it.

I want to emphasize that the goal isn't to create an exact replica, with your data imposed directly on the original chart. Rather, projecting should allow you to assess whether the visual channels used in the original effectively convey the data for your context. If it does, you can follow the

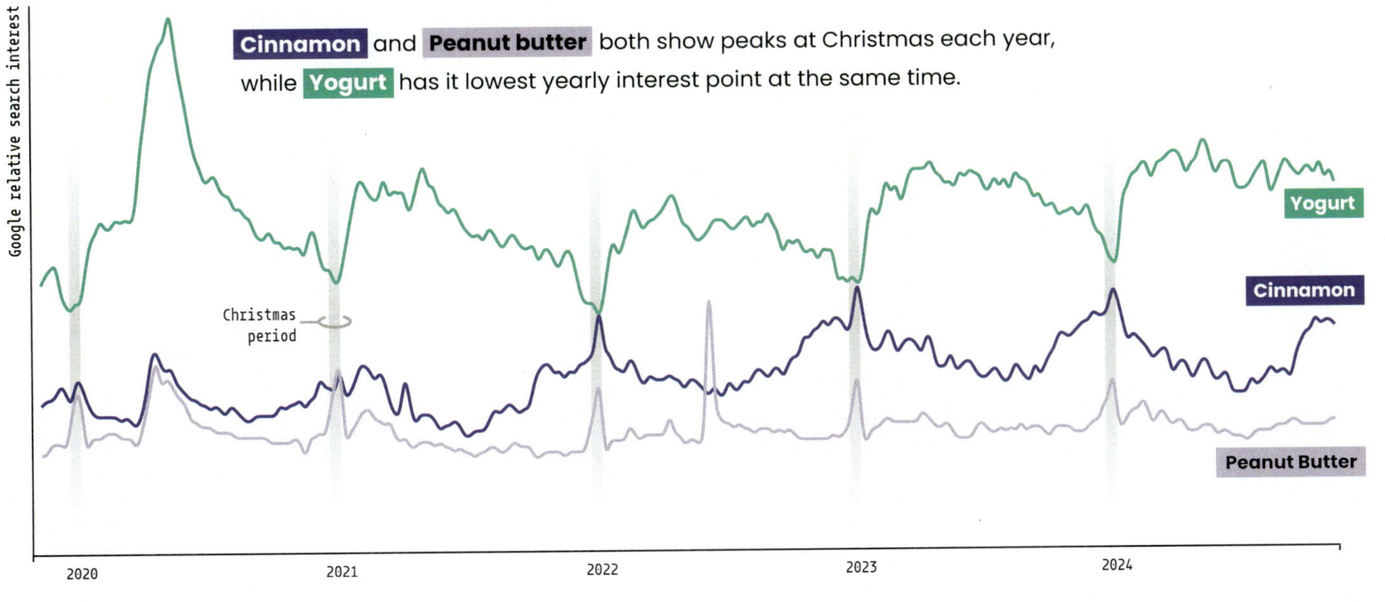

Figure III.1

A line chart of the relative Google search interest in yogurt, cinnamon, and peanut butter, showing their spikes or dips around Christmas.

same approach to set up the visual but then transform it into something customized to your goal, data, and topic.

As I move through my projections, I'll write notes and draw little sketches for designs that show promise. I refer back to these references when I explore the ideas further with more detailed sketches. What's great about this process is that I gain something even if I find that my data doesn't project well onto the existing visual. Finding out why data doesn't work in a particular visual template is often very insightful. I still walk away with a better understanding of when and how I might use that design in the future, if I happen to have a more suitable data set.

To give you an idea of the process, let's say I have a data set on Christmas Day snowfall over the past 50 years in various capital cities. The data includes the country name, capital city, year, and amount of snow that fell.

The existing chart I'm projecting onto is a line chart that shows the relative Google search trends of cinnamon, peanut butter, and yogurt. Searches for cinnamon and peanut butter tend to rise and fall in tandem, while searches for yogurt are inverse. This is especially true around Christmas (keeping with the theme!), where cinnamon and peanut butter spike, and yogurt dips. (See figure III.1.)

This is an oversimplified example of a chart to project onto. It would be more practical to directly plot a line chart from the snowfall data and check the result. In general, I project onto visuals that are more complex or have something unique, as they would take a long time to recreate. However, I've chosen an extremely common chart type here to illustrate the projection concept.

Figure III.2

The Christmas card I sent out to my past clients in 2023 showing snowfall on Christmas days over the past 50 years in various cities. Find the interactive version at *nbremer.github.io/christmas-card-2023*

III.2

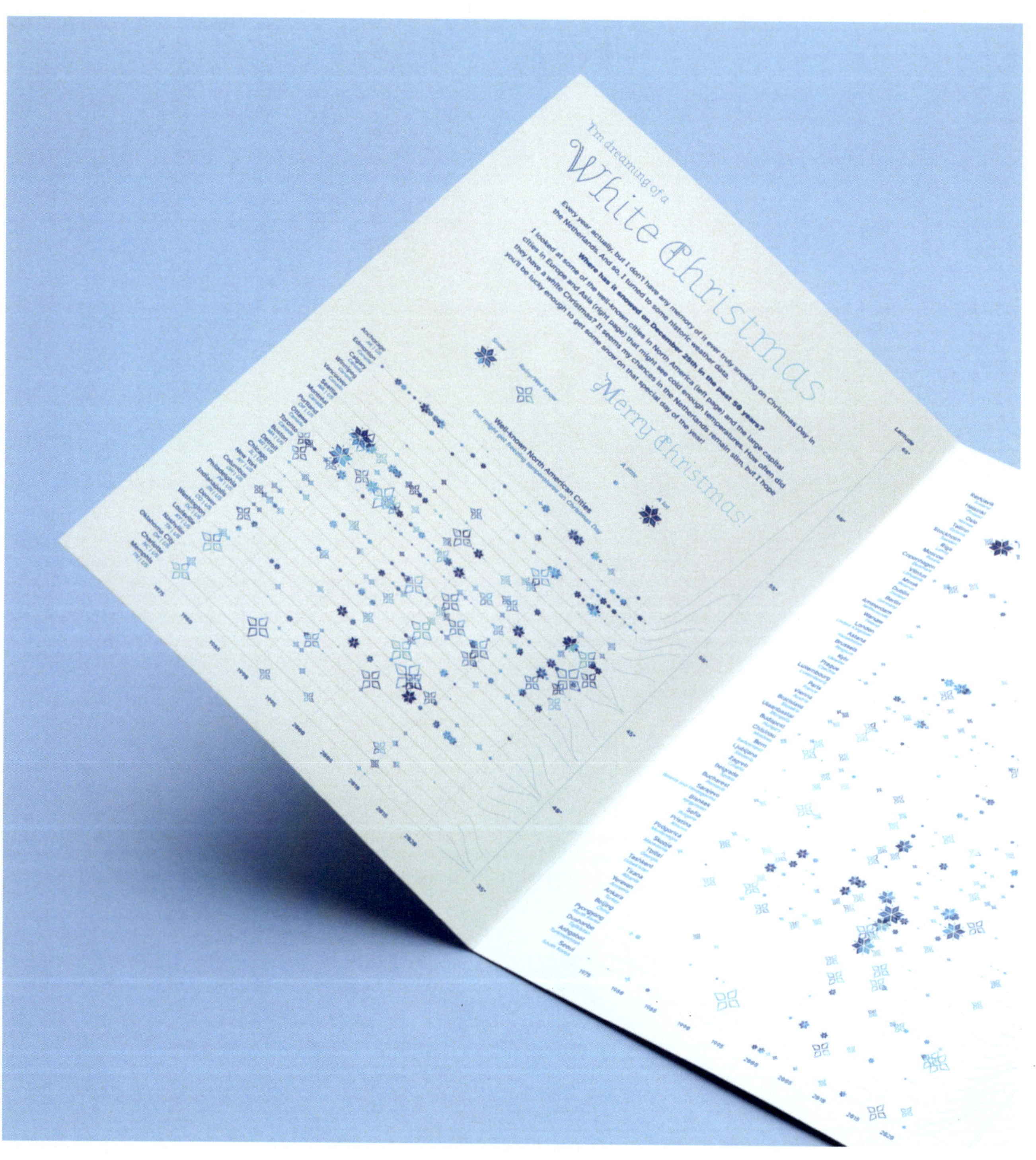

Let's imagine each step. The food lines would become city lines, one per capital city, each running back 50 years. I could replace the y-axis search trend values with the amount of snow each Christmas. But here's the issue: For most years, snow on Christmas Day is rare (an insight I'd have noticed during the data analysis), so this value would often be zero for most capitals. This would lead to mostly flat lines along the bottom with the occasional upward spike for snowy years. Therefore, although I could theoretically fit my data into the line chart, it wouldn't be a very effective approach to portray the snow data. But I still gained valuable information from the projection process—I realized that my design would need to accommodate a lot of zeros.

The challenge was making sure the visual emphasized the Christmases with snow and not all the snowless ones. So I placed each city on its own row, adding a little snowflake mark for each Christmas it snowed, sized according to the amount of snowfall (figure III.2). That way, the snowing years visually filled the space, and the snowless years were simply empty, not drawing any attention.

COLLECTIONS TO INSPIRE

I have several image collections of data visualizations (and more) that I find beautiful, interesting, or inspiring in some way. When I'm looking to project my data, it's great to have these collections handy. I curate boards on Pinterest (pinterest.com/visualcinnamon) for different types of data visualizations, such as radials, networks, geospatial, infographics/full posters, data art, and others. However, you can use whatever organizational method is best for you, such as saving it to a specific folder on your computer.

To start and grow such a collection, look for images and data visualizations whenever you browse the web, and save the ones you think are interesting. If you don't want to build and maintain your own more customized collection, you can also save links to websites, collections, lists, boards, and other places where aggregations already exist.

HOW TO ASSESS POTENTIAL CANDIDATES

Not every chart I keep in my inspiration trove is worth a test projection. For instance, a donut chart wouldn't make sense for the snow data because I wanted to showcase each value instead of showing parts to a whole. I also wouldn't use a treemap because treemaps aren't meant to show a timeline. To efficiently decide which charts are worthy of this projection exercise, I look at my collection of example charts and pick those that convey the data in a way that aligns with my goals for my data set. For example, am I trying to show connections, compare values, or show a timeline (like in the snow example)? I've found that the more often I do this exercise, the faster I can assess an existing chart's potential.

LESSON FIVE

SKETCH DESIGNS FIRST

Use plain pen and paper to sketch rough concepts and develop more expressive ideas

Sketching is a fantastic way to design more creative and effective data visualizations. Whether you use a plain pencil and paper or a digital pen and a tablet, you'll get good results from this practice—as long as it's your hand that's drawing.

5.1a

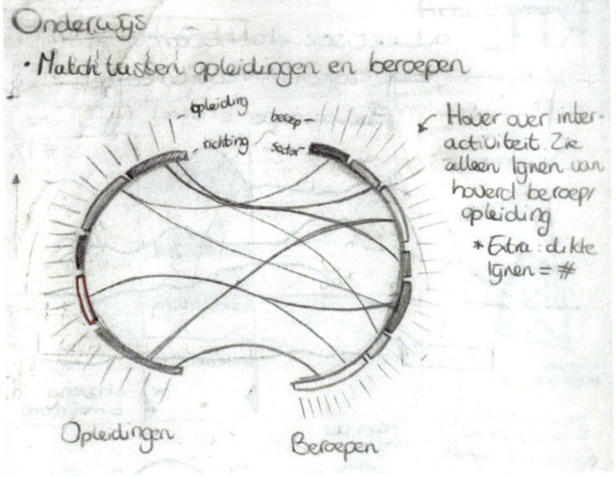

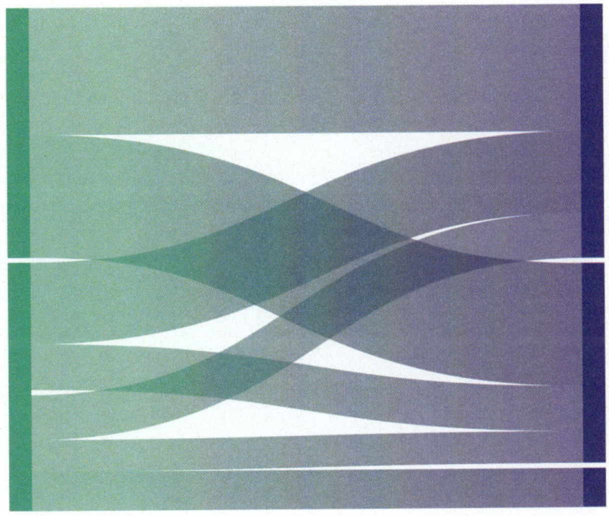

5.1b

Figure 5.1a & b

My sketch (including notes in Dutch) that bends the left side (Studies / "Opleidingen") and right side (Occupations / "Beroepen") (a) versus a standard rectangular alluvial diagram (b).

WHY SKETCHING UNLEASHES CREATIVITY

When sketching, you're not constrained by your knowledge of a certain software program. You don't have to interrupt your thought flow to search online for "how to draw a hexagon," for example. Furthermore, if you rely on a charting program, it can be really hard to think outside of its defaults. When you sketch, you're taking time to think about the design instead of going straight for the pre-set chart options in your tool. Sketching will help you focus on the task, removing digital distractions.

With a pen in hand, you're free to play with shapes to see which might make a chart effective and visually interesting. You can be experimental and more easily mold the data visualization to fit your particular data set and the insights you want to reveal. If anything were possible, what visual forms would you like to use?

Perhaps you'd draw something curved instead of straight...

Turning a normally rectangular chart into a circle

BUSINESS | 2015 | DELOITTE
visualcinnamon.com/2015/08/stretched-chord

While working as a consultant at Deloitte (my very first job after graduating), I created several interactive data visualizations for a report on the state of education in the Netherlands. The goal was to show whether students entered occupations tied to their studies, and, if not, where they ended up instead. I had a data set of thousands of people in the Netherlands with their degree and their occupational industry 1.5 years after graduating.

I started to draw, and in figure 5.1a, you can see the idea I wanted to create: a distribution of studies on the left (as a curved stacked bar chart) and a distribution of occupations on the right. It seemed like an interesting approach because I could connect the studies and

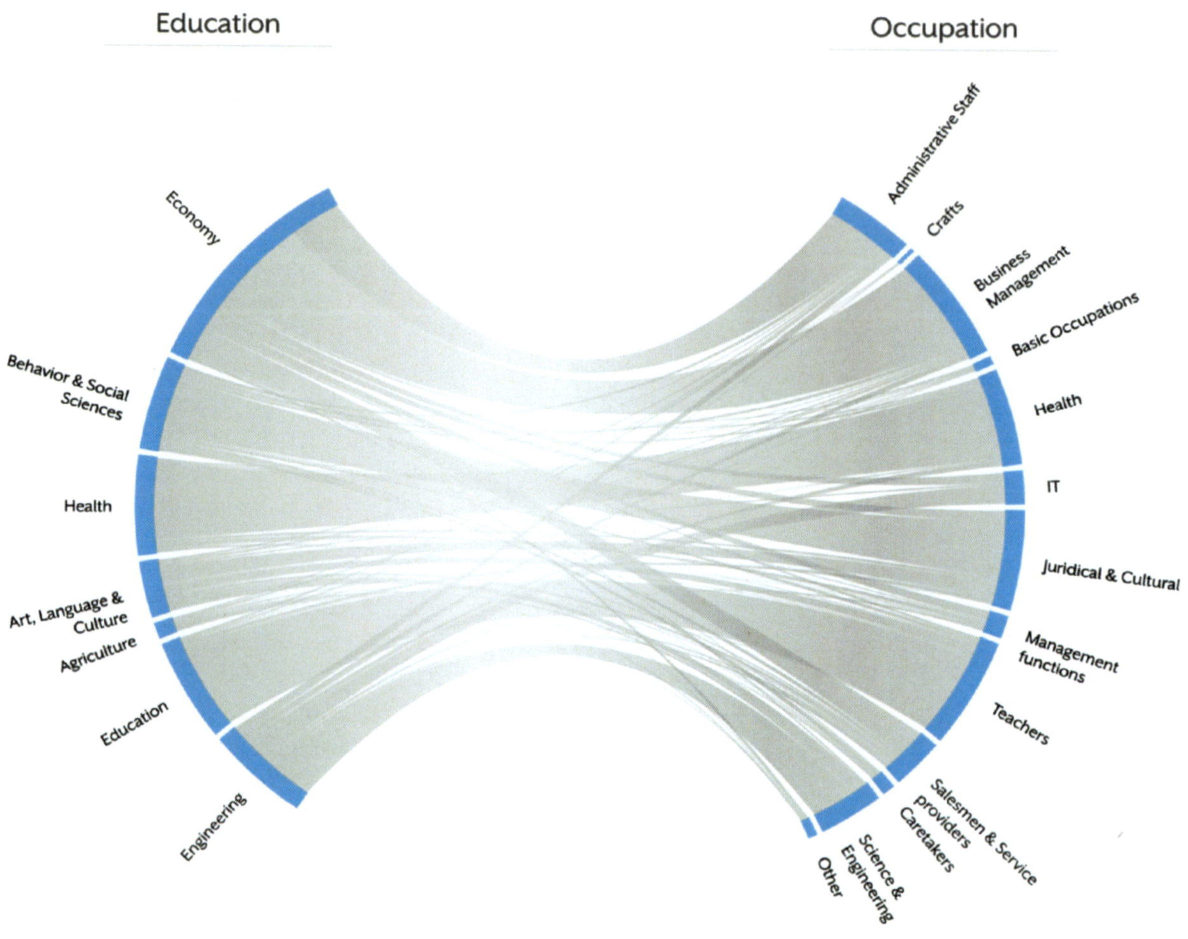

5.2

Figure 5.2

The final result of the custom "curved" alluvial diagram that I created based on my simple initial sketch.

occupations with lines, where the thickness of the lines scaled to the number of people who moved from a particular study to a specific occupation.

I had, in essence, created something known as an alluvial diagram (figure 5.1b), which is similar to a Sankey diagram but generally shows how the entities within the data are grouped according to different variables (studies vs. occupations). However, I did not constrain myself to the typical alluvial diagram shape, which has straight stacked bar charts on either side, as I thought semi-circles would look much more visually attractive.

Mind you, I had no idea how to turn this sketch into a reality. However, it gave me a clear "dot on the horizon" to follow. It took a lot of learning, a lot of testing, and even asking a question on a forum, but I managed to turn the sketch into a reality (figure 5.2). Once the piece was published, I was proud of myself for making the final result look visually intriguing. I had never seen a design like that before.

During the sketching phase, my imagination isn't considering—or hindered by—the possible technical limitations I might encounter later on. I know that translating my sketch into a digital format may require learning new skills, using a new tool, coming up with some hack, or finding a compromise to get as close as possible to the sketch. But I don't fret over those things as I move my pen across the paper.

5.3

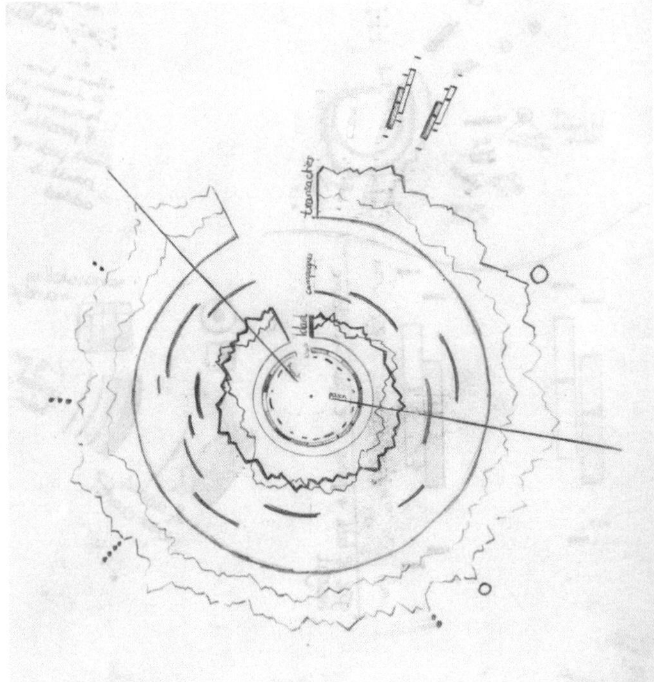

Figure 5.3

After a few rough sketches to test the design idea, I sometimes use my ruler and drawing compass to make a more refined sketch. The result is still crude, but I find that straight lines and decent circles can help to fine-tune the more elaborate ideas.

MORE REASONS WHY YOU SHOULD SKETCH

The main benefits of drawing are breaking from software constraints and coming up with more unique and compelling ideas. But there are many other advantages to sketching data visualization designs:

Sketching designs is fast | I don't think there's a quicker way to iterate on data visualization ideas than drawing them by hand.

You're less likely to fall in love | Sketches are always crude drawings. Software programs make it too tempting to perfect the design. This takes time—which becomes wasted time if you realize later that the idea doesn't work. The fear of wasting time may lead you to keep trying to salvage it. The sunk cost of a sketch is much lower.

Sketching helps you catch logical errors | You're much more likely to catch conceptual and logical errors in the concept or design early on by sketching it out. I often have an idea that seems to make sense. However, once I try to draw it, I realize I've overlooked some minor but crucial aspect of the data or how I want to visualize it. If you can't make your idea work on paper, there's no way it will work once you move to a computer and try to work with the actual data.

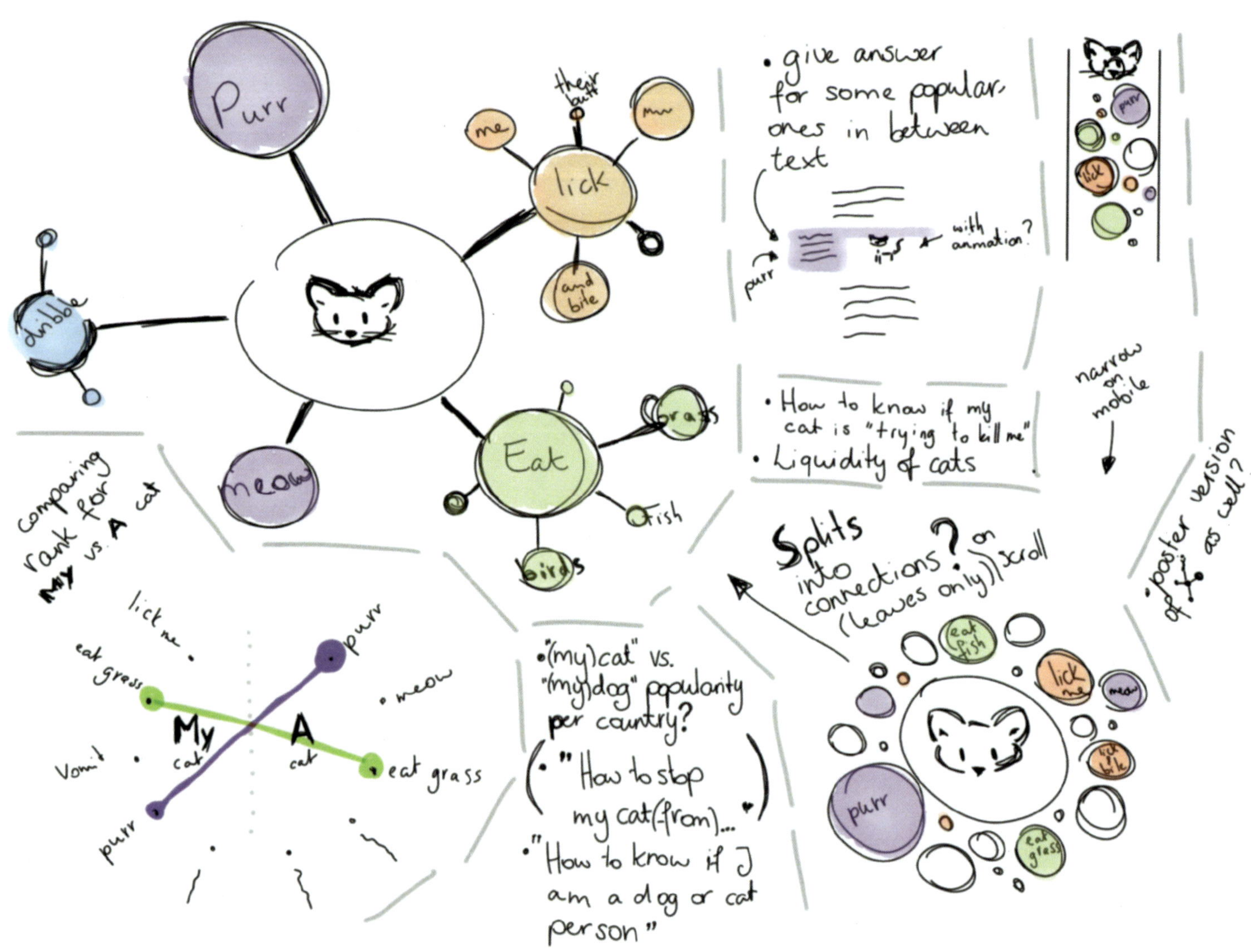

5.4

Figure 5.4

The sketches and ideas that I created for the "Why Do Cats and Dogs...?" project for Google News Lab.

Sketches are easier to discuss with clients | This might seem strange, but I find it much easier to present and talk about my data visualization designs with my clients when the sketches are hand drawn. They inherently convey that "this is not how it's actually going to look." With hand-drawn sketches, I can talk with my client about the *concept* of the design, whereas with digital tools, the client may feel they need to discuss the exact colors, sizes, or fonts I used.

Sketches give you a target | When I sketch a bespoke design, I have a clear "guide" for what I want to aim for visually. The project described earlier in this lesson about the studies and occupations is one example; I needed to expand my digital abilities to execute the sketch. But throughout my career, I recall hand-sketching basic shapes—circular arcs, dashed lines, gradients, etc.—that I didn't know how to make on my screen. And guess what? I figured them all out! Furthermore, once I have a really solid design on paper, I'm much more driven to learn how to turn my sketch into a reality, even if the learning process takes some extra time.

These benefits don't just apply to trained artists! Sketching is a very accessible practice; you don't need to have "drawing skills." My sketches usually consist of simple lines, curves, and rectangles. They don't need to be perfect; lines don't need to be straight; circles can be weird blobs. The only objective is to show, on paper, how you're going from data to visual elements.

I don't mean to imply that you should sketch designs for every chart you create. Sketching is most critical for visuals that are important in some way, that need to present an argument, make an impact or an impression on an audience.

Figure 5.5

The final result of the "word tree" visual that turned out somewhat differently than the original sketch. The sheer size of the data set literally did not fit with the original idea and I therefore had to adjust it somewhat. Central cat illustration by Juliana Chen.

5.5

Sketches with lots of cats

BUSINESS | 2019 | GOOGLE NEWS LAB

WhyDoCatsAndDogs.visualcinnamon.com

One of the biggest (and most fun) projects I've ever worked on was the "Why Do Cats and Dogs...?" visual exploration website I created for Google News Lab. It shows how people use Google to understand their cats and dogs better. I requested the most popular questions that people ask on Google that start with "Why do cats..." or "Why does my cat..." (or some similar variation), and the equivalent for dogs. After some sketching, I knew that my main visual would organize those thousands of questions into a tree-like structure that would reveal which questions were most popular.

Figure 5.4 is what I presented to Google—an extremely rough sketch with various thoughts and ideas on how I wanted to visualize the fascinating data set. I got the green light, and that visual eventually transformed into what you see in figure 5.5.

GETTING THE MOST OUT OF SKETCHING

I follow five guiding principles during my sketching phase that have a significant impact on the efficiency and success of the process:

Analyze the data first | I suggest analyzing the data before you start thinking about designs and sketching, such as making histograms for all the numerical variables to see the range and distribution of values. Check for outliers and general trends that might be interesting as callouts or highlights. You'll create much more relevant sketches once you've grasped the rough structure of the data.

Be inspired by others | After I've analyzed the data, but before I start sketching, I often look for some inspiration to hit the ground running. I quickly scroll through some of my data visualization Pinterest boards. I look at what others have made and get inspired by their work (as I covered in Mini Chapter III).

Only sketch the abstract layout | Sketches are only meant to convey the rough shape of the visualization. It should show how you will translate the data into visual elements. Will each data point become a circle? Will those circles scale to a variable? Will they be connected by lines? Will they be placed on an x-axis and y-axis or something circular? Colors, fonts, and other visual design choices only start to matter in the next phase when creating the chart with actual data.

Figure 5.6

I created a page full of sketches for the "Space Wars" visual for *Scientific American*, where I showed all active satellites in space. I started with a simple treemap (middle-left page) and also tried a circular Voronoi diagram and a beeswarm chart (top-right page). Then, I combined the treemap with the circles (bottom-right page), which became the chosen design approach. You can find the final result in figure 8.4. There are no colors or fonts; these sketches only focus on establishing the fundamental layout.

As a mini-tip, write down your available variables so you can quickly reference them, as I did in the top-left of the notebook in figure 5.6.

Sketch more than one idea | Try to sketch at least three ways to visualize the data to help you develop better options. I used to give a workshop where one of my favorite exercises was to ask the participants to sketch six visuals for a specific data set. The catch? They had exactly one minute to draw each sketch. Afterward, I asked how many would choose the first thing they drew as their final design. Rarely did anyone raise their hand.

Test early with larger datasets | The more data points you need to visualize, the sooner you need to test the rough sketch with the actual (and complete) data set. I've drawn many sketches that seemed like great ideas on paper, but when I applied the data values, the design simply didn't work. Sometimes, the data had several outliers that forced

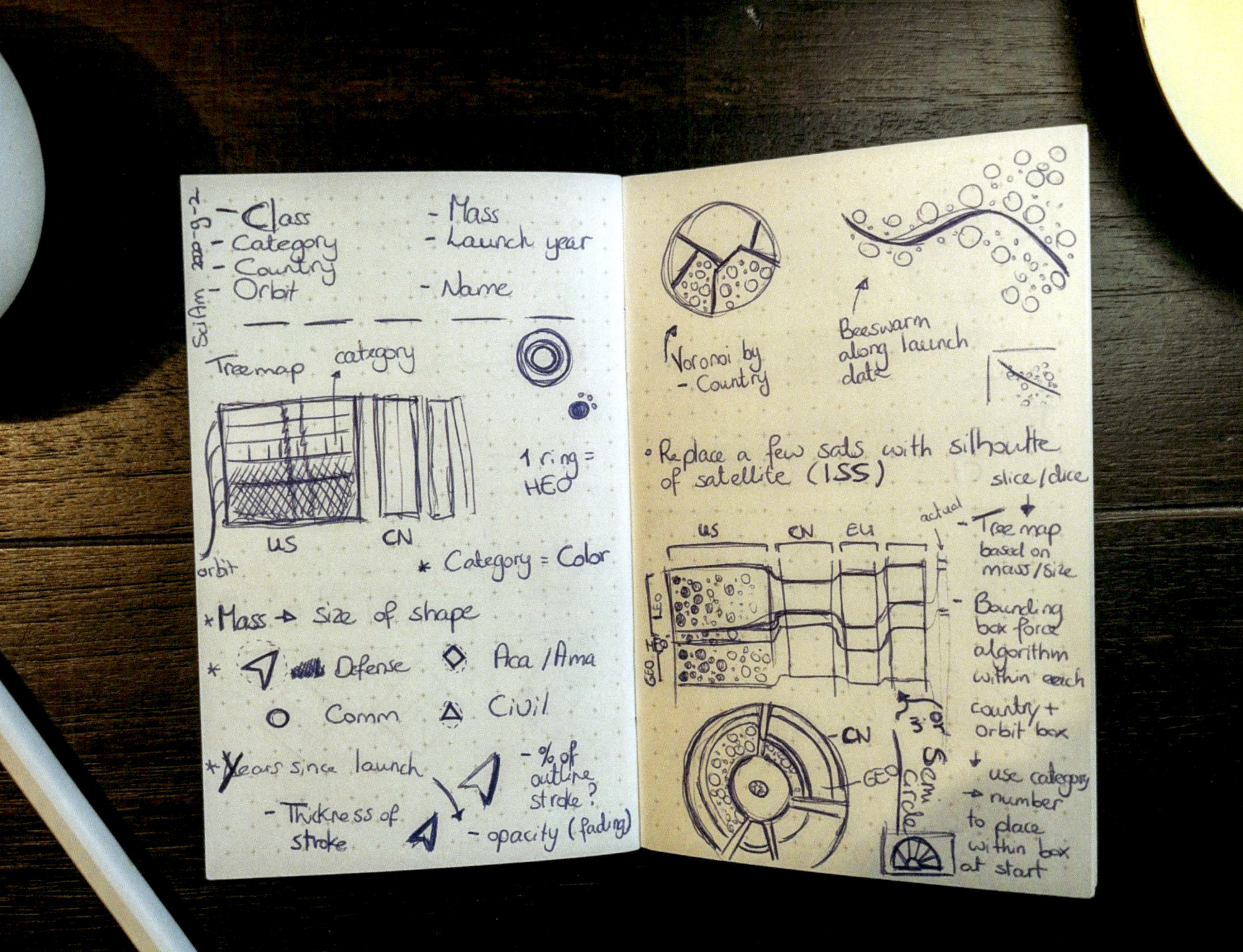

SciAm 2020-9-2
- Class
- Category
- Country
- Orbit
- Mass
- Launch year
- Name
Treemap
category
1 ring = HEO
US
CN
orbit
* Category = Color
* Mass → size of shape
* Defense
Aca/Ama
Comm
Civil
* Years since launch
- Thickness of stroke
- % of outline stroke?
- opacity (fading)
Voronoi by - Country
Beeswarm along launch date
• Replace a few sats with silhouette of satellite (ISS)
slice/dice
actual
- Treemap based on mass/size
US
CN
EU
LEO
GEO
- Bounding box force algorithm within each country + orbit box
CN
GEO
Semi circle
use category number to place within box at start

all the other data points into the same spot. Other times, my intention to apply intricate designs to each data point didn't work, as the large quantity of data made each point too small to see.

For small data sets, it's easier to get a good sense of the data values, and your sketch can be quite close to the final result. But when you have thousands of data points—and hand drawing a thousand dots isn't realistically doable—the sketch becomes an *approximation* of the idea. The more approximate the sketch, the higher the chance you've missed a vital aspect of the data that will prevent the design from working.

I failed to follow my own advice for the "Why Do Cats and Dogs...?" project, which is why the final result didn't (quite) look like the initial sketch: There was too much data to fit around the original word tree idea, so I had to break it up into dozens of smaller trees, each enclosed in its own circle (figure 5.5).

Figure 5.7

A slide from the design deck I created for Swissgrid showing several plots I made during my data analysis phase.

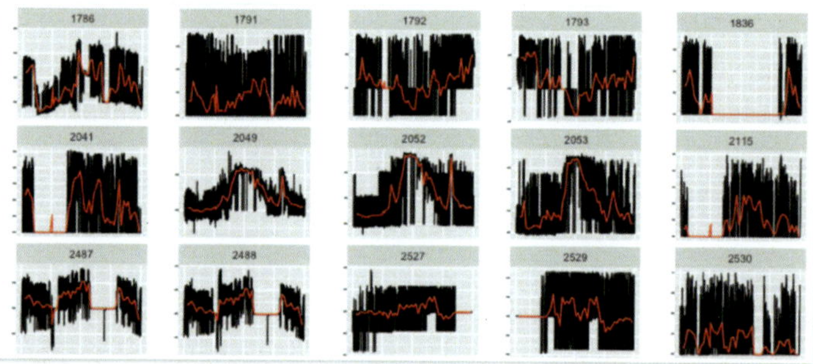

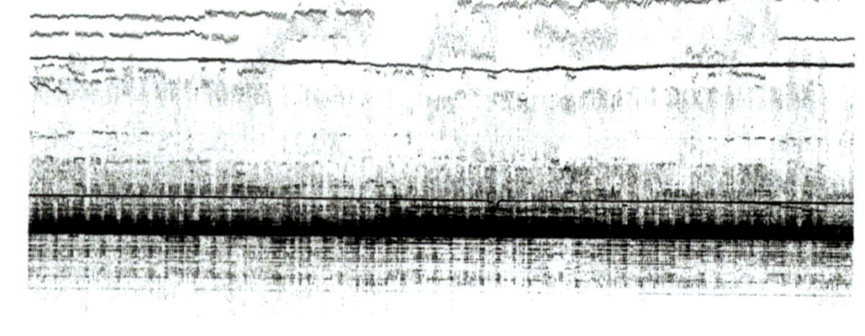

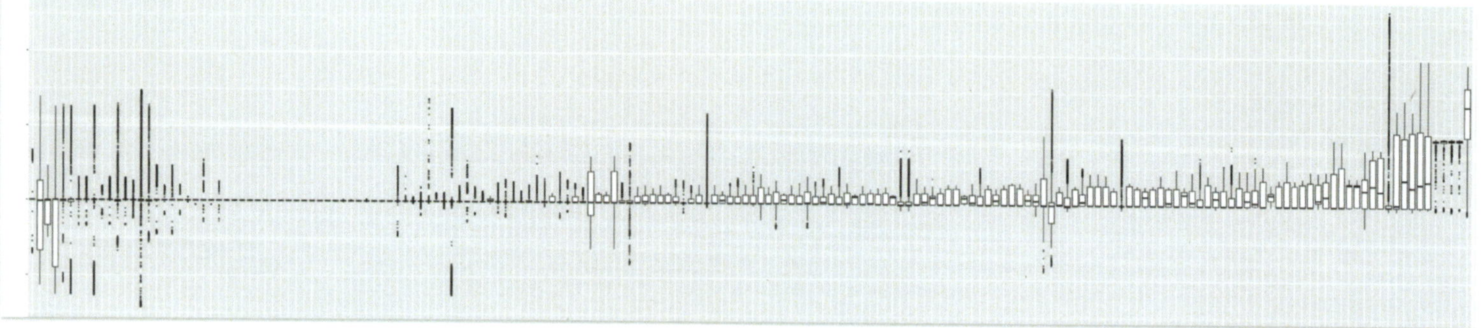

5.7

Figure 5.8a, b & c

Each slide shows a different design concept for visualizing the piece as a whole: a map (a), a circle (b), and in a grid (c). The gray rectangles originally showed some inspirational images to convey the idea better.

5.8a

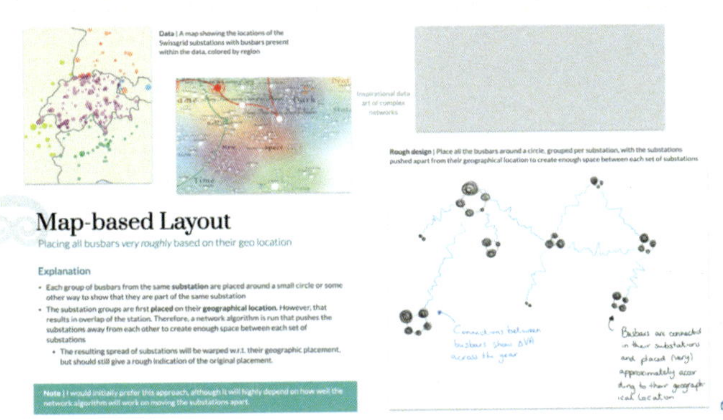

5.8b

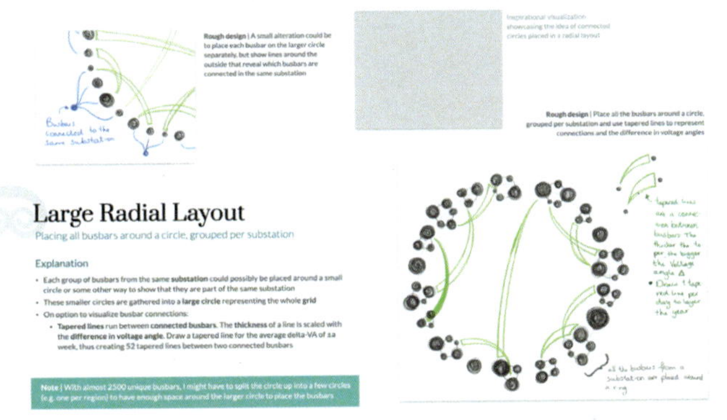

5.8c

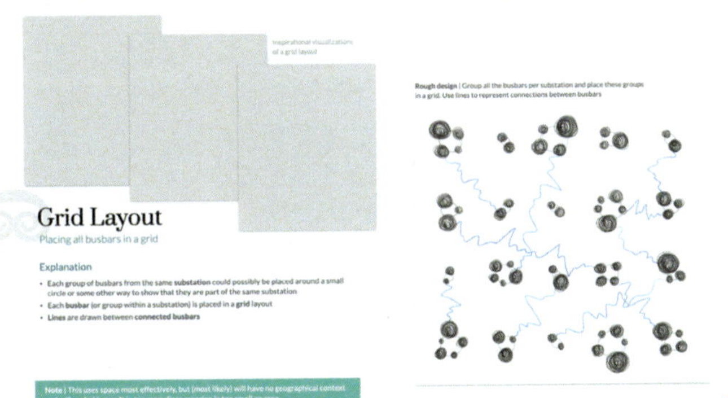

How to convey over 60 million data points in a static piece

BUSINESS | 2020 | SWISSGRID

swissgrid.ch/en/home/newsroom/blog/2021/20210701-01.html

Swissgrid, the company in charge of the electrical high-voltage network in Switzerland, wanted to visualize the data generated in its network with an artistic touch.

I got a data dump of the workings of their entire high-voltage grid in 2019, including how much power was generated, transported, and used per minute. It was over 60 million rows in multitudes of data sets. It is still the biggest overall data set I've ever worked with and visualized.

With such a large data set, I spent a long time **analyzing the data** to understand what made this electrical grid run. I created dozens of charts to help me understand the numbers. See figure 5.7 for one of the slides that I presented to the client with my findings from the analysis phase. Don't worry about trying to understand the details of the data or the exact sketches. I just want you to see the concept of what I'm showing to a client when presenting designs.

I **sketched rough designs** that transformed all those numbers into visual elements. I came up with **multiple ideas** on how to structure the overall design. I could show the data according to a map of Switzerland, or along a circle, or in a rectangular grid (figure 5.8).

I also came up with multiple designs for more fine-grained aspects of the data, such as visualizing stations that generated or dispersed energy (called "busbars").

5.9

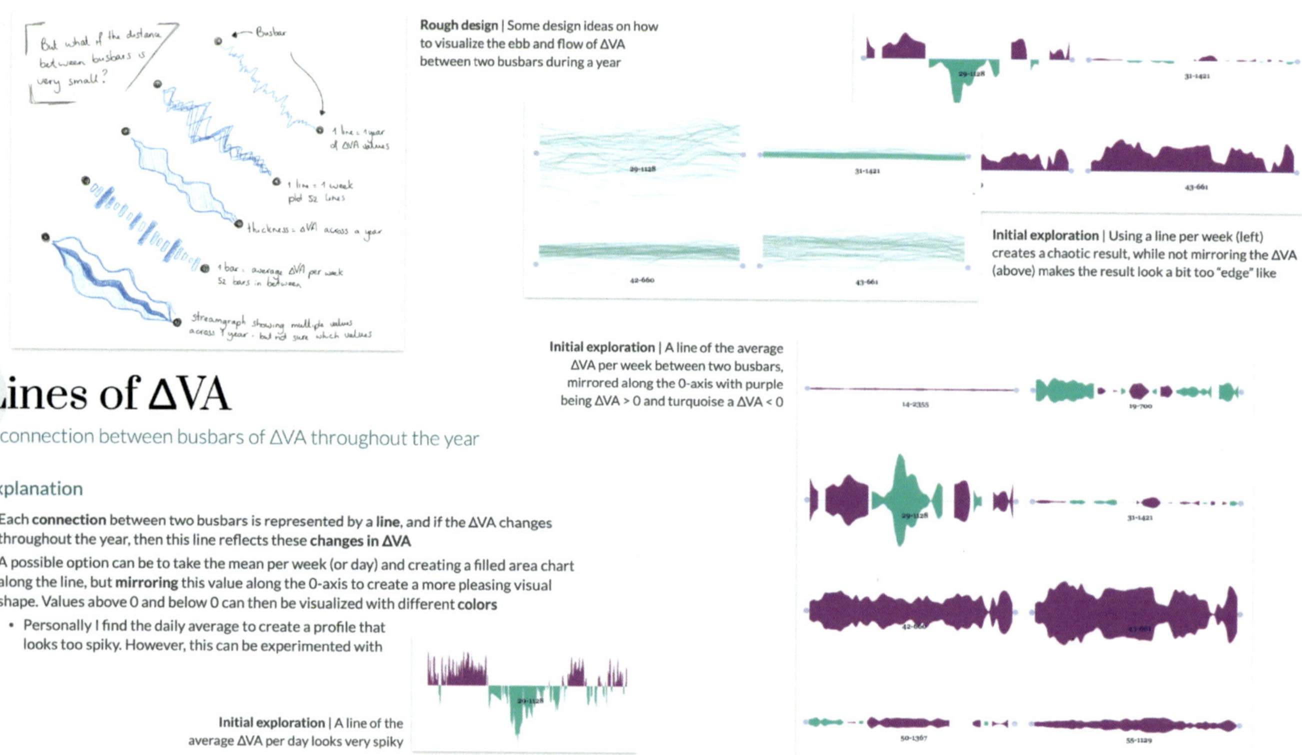

Figure 5.9

A slide with the sketched idea in the top-left and screenshots from initial tests using the actual data.

Because the data was massive, I also **tested** the design ideas I thought were most promising (figure 5.9). I wanted to check that it would look as I had envisioned it.

In short, I used all of my sketching guiding principles.

Finally, I packaged it all into a slide deck I presented to my client so we could discuss the ideas and decide which design concepts to pursue. Once we had a plan, it would still take hours and hundreds of iterations to get the details right. However, the extensive data analysis and sketching phase laid the groundwork to build the idea into a unique and visually striking piece of informative data art. (I say "informative" because you could still make out trends and patterns.)

5.10a

Figure 5.10a & b

The final result, "Landscape of Power Flows," printed on a 3m x 2m (9′ 11″ x 7′ 7″) canvas and hung in the Swissgrid lobby (a), and a zoom in on the next page (b).

Sketching is an integral part of my process. It is a major creative catalyst in my data visualization work and is the main reason why I'm able to create bespoke and original charts.

Sketching will provide you the freedom to draw any shape you want with relative ease, to quickly grab hold of an inkling of an idea, to get something on the page, to strengthen it, and just see where it goes. (Even if it leads nowhere, there's no harm, as it didn't take up too much time anyway.) All that freedom to explore boosts your chances of striking gold and ending up with a data visualization design that will be effective, loved, shared, and remembered.

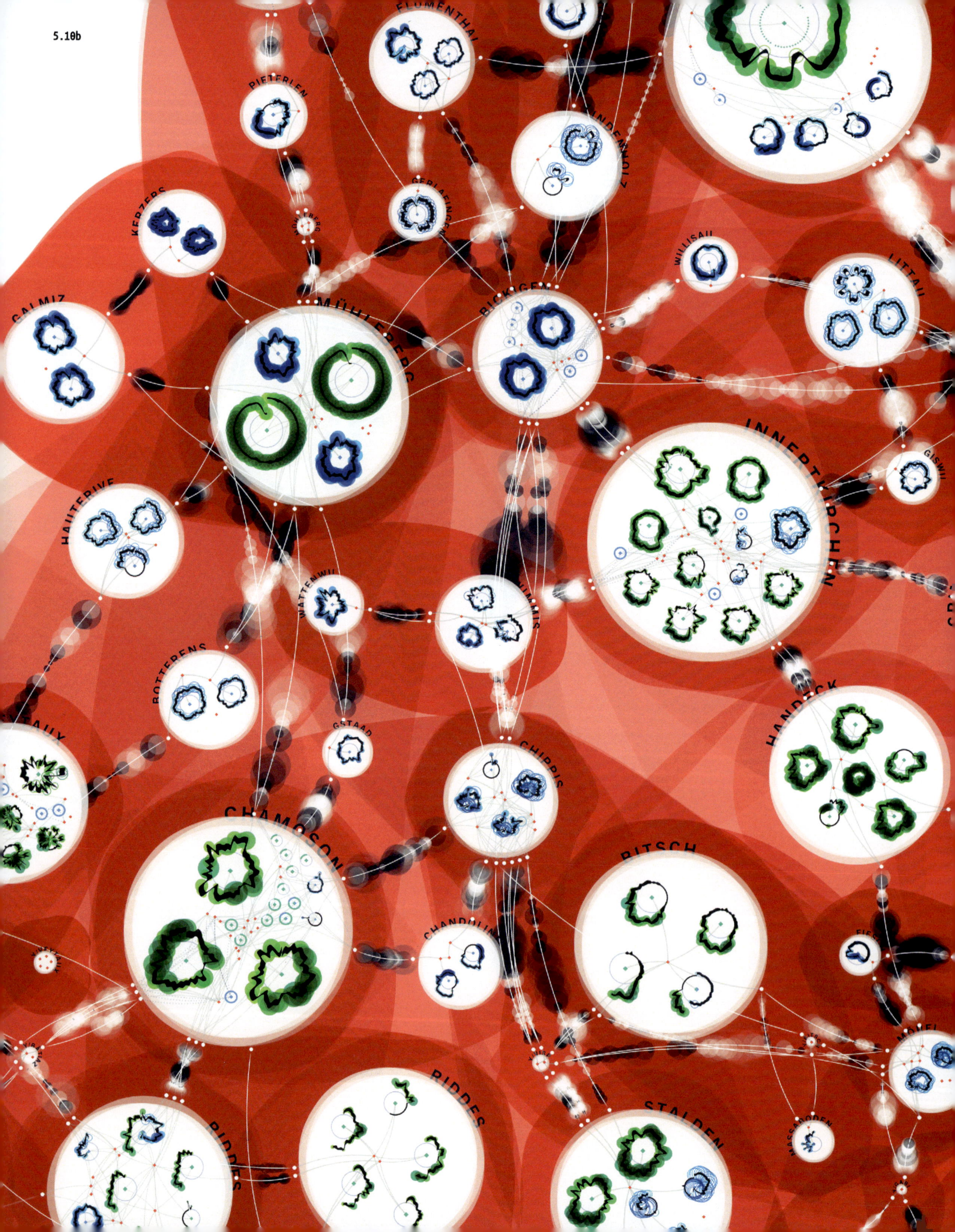
5.10b
FLUMENTHAL
PIETERLEN
LINDENHOLZ
GERLAFINGEN
KERZERS
WILLISAU
LITTAU
GALMIZ
MÜHLEBERG
BICKIGEN
INNERTKIRCHEN
GISWIL
HAUTERIVE
WATTENWIL
BOTTERENS
GSTAAD
HANDECK
CHIPPIS
CHAMOSON
BITSCH
CHANDOLIN
RIDDES
STALDEN
MASSABODEN

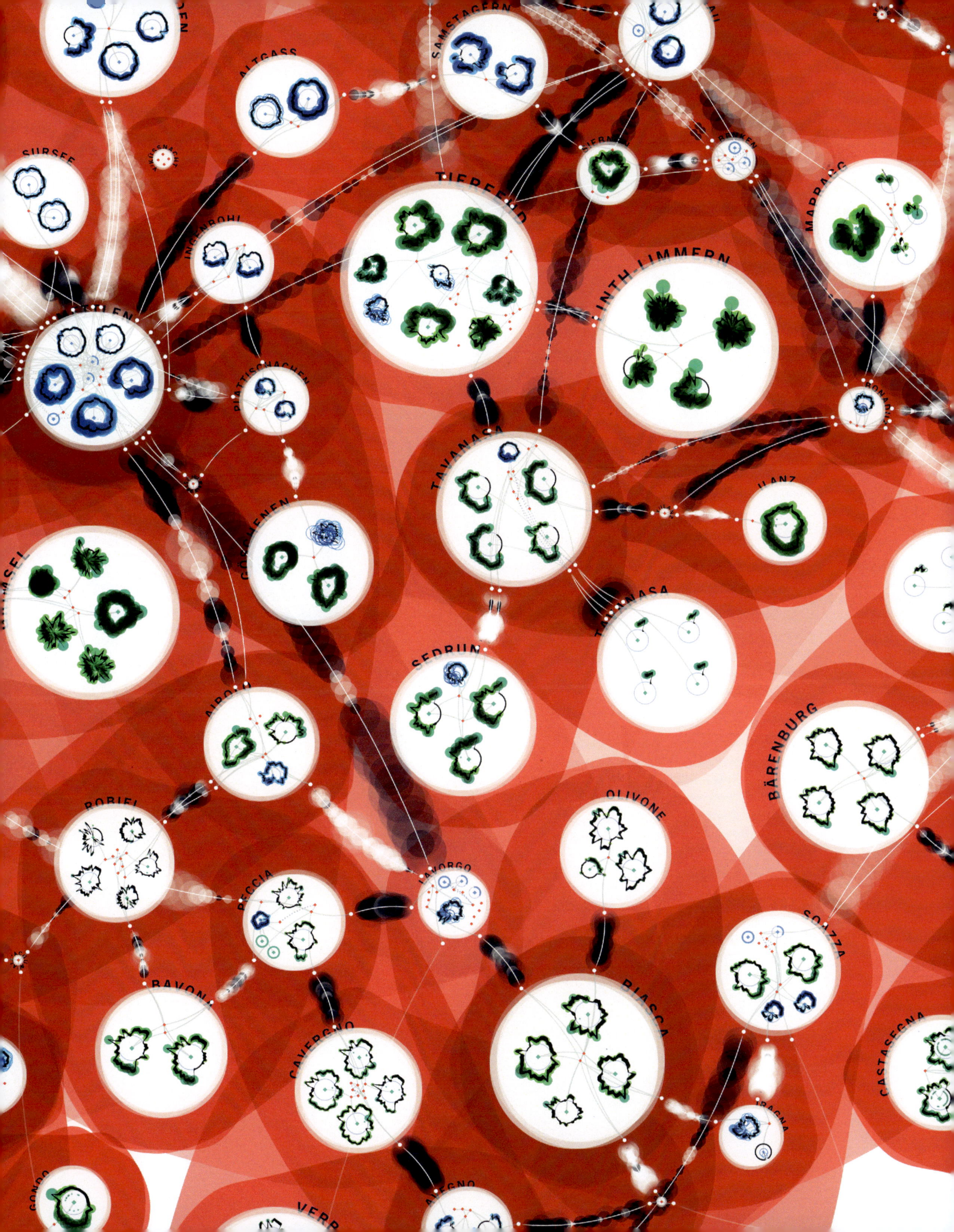

ALTGASS
SAMSTAGERN
SURSEE
INGENBOHL
LINTH LIMMERN
TAVANASA
ILANZ
SEDRUN
BÄRENBURG
OLIVONE
PECCIA
LAVORGO
BAVONA
CAVERGNO
BIASCA
SOAZZA
CASTASEGNA

LESSON SIX

DON'T THINK

Think less about "chart types" and more about what information, patterns, and stories to reveal

When creating a data visualization, it's helpful to start by thinking about the end. In other words, focus on the ultimate goals for your data. Consider the information, patterns, and stories you want to reveal. Consider the message you aim to convey. Consider your audience and how they'll engage with the visualization.

If it feels overwhelming to consider all these things, you may be stuck thinking in "chart types." When you're in this mindset, you may feel tempted to push data into several different charts to see what fits best. You might ask, "Am I going to visualize this data as a bar chart or violin plot?"

IN CHART TYPES

This is not an ideal place to start your project. Such limited thinking will snuff your innovation before it has the chance to spark. When I don't think in chart types, my creativity opens up, and I can find even more effective visual forms to reach my end goals.

Now, you may conjure a design that's similar to a common chart type. That's fine! Line charts and bar charts are popular for a reason: They often work well. However, the key is to arrive at a design by putting the data, story and goals first—not the chart type. That mental shift makes all the difference.

When the data has many (complex) facets, the whole story can't easily fit within the constraints of the traditional charts. They would oversimplify the multi-layered insights. The more intricate the data, the greater the need to make something more custom, driven by the data, its story, and your goals.

ADOPTING A DATA, STORY, AND GOALS MINDSET

When you get a new project, you may want to jump to the creative part immediately. But before you design, analyze the data set to get a good understanding of what variables are in there and how they look (distributions, ranges, etc.). Once you have grasped the data, you may feel ready to design, but hold off just a bit longer! This is the point at which you need to actively adopt an end-game mindset. Think about what you want to show with the data. What is the fundamental goal? Do you want to show connections, comparisons, evolutions, or something else? Chart classification resources, such as the "Visual Vocabulary" from the *Financial Times* or "The Graphic Continuum" by Severino Ribecca and Jon Schwabish, often start with these questions.

Personally, I prefer to describe what I want my visual to show in a few detailed sentences. For example, my goal for the "Education to Occupation" visual from the previous lesson was: "Show whether students ended up in occupations tied to their studies, and, if not, to which sector they moved instead."

Finally, with a mental model of the data variables in your head and the goal written down, it's time to start designing. This is the tricky part and is hard to put into a formula. But here are some key pointers:

Think about metaphors: Are there any visual encodings in shape, color (or more) that connect to the data or topic? Metaphors make it easier for the audience to understand and remember your data encoding. A few examples are the often-used "red equals hot, blue equals cold" color associations. Or the triangle shapes representing airplanes and the circles that look like little vinyl records in Lesson 1.

Continuously evaluate: This may seem obvious, but at various points during the design phase, take a step back and see if what you're working on still makes sense. Is it (still) conveying the insights or story? Do this outside of any user testing, as you, yourself, will always be the first person to evaluate your visualization.

Test and iterate—a lot: It's perfectly normal for your first idea to be less than perfect. Hop back and forth between sketching and visualizing the data to make adjustments and think of new ideas if the current one isn't working. At the end of the process, iterating becomes more about fine-tuning the design: trying color palettes, finding the best stroke width for your lines, the exact placement of the annotations, etc.

The design phase starts with sketching ideas. I experiment with basic shapes like dots, circles, squares, rectangles, blobs of any shape, and lines. The goals-oriented mindset is critical here. "I want to show a flow, so something with lines could work," or "I want to show different groups, using circles or squares for each group member," or "I want to show each data point separately, so I'll start with a few simple dots." I keep my hand moving as I logically consider the possibilities—don't feel the need to have the complete idea in your head before you start sketching it!

I also want to make the following very clear: It's okay if the sketch ends up making no sense, or if the idea doesn't encompass all the details you were aiming to show. This is where iteration comes in. Start again. Try re-using pieces of a previous idea or sketch that worked well, but adapt it for a new variation. After a while, also try to let go of the concept you've been working on and come up with something different to shake things up. As I mentioned in the previous lesson, try drawing at least three distinct ways of visualizing the data.

When I'm in the goals mindset, I tend to work in layers. I will first focus on the most essential aspects. Once I have achieved my topline goals in a visual form, I will add other variables to the design.

I realize this is a lot of process to follow. Therefore, let's review everything with the help of some specific visual examples.

FULL DESIGN STORY

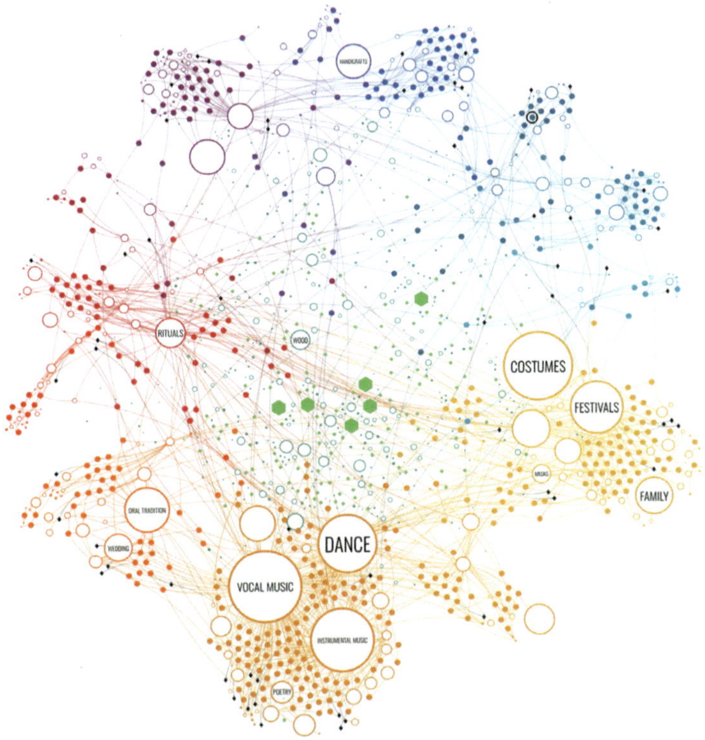

Customized rings of information

BUSINESS | 2018 | UNESCO

ich.unesco.org/en/dive

Since 2003, UNESCO has maintained a list of Intangible Cultural Heritage. This repository goes beyond monuments and objects; it includes traditions and living expressions passed down through generations, including oral traditions, performing arts, social practices, rituals, festivals, and traditional crafts. The wide-ranging list includes cultural elements such as lacemaking in Croatia or the tango in Argentina and Uruguay. Each year, UNESCO adds roughly 40 new elements. In 2023, the list had 730 entries.

6.1a

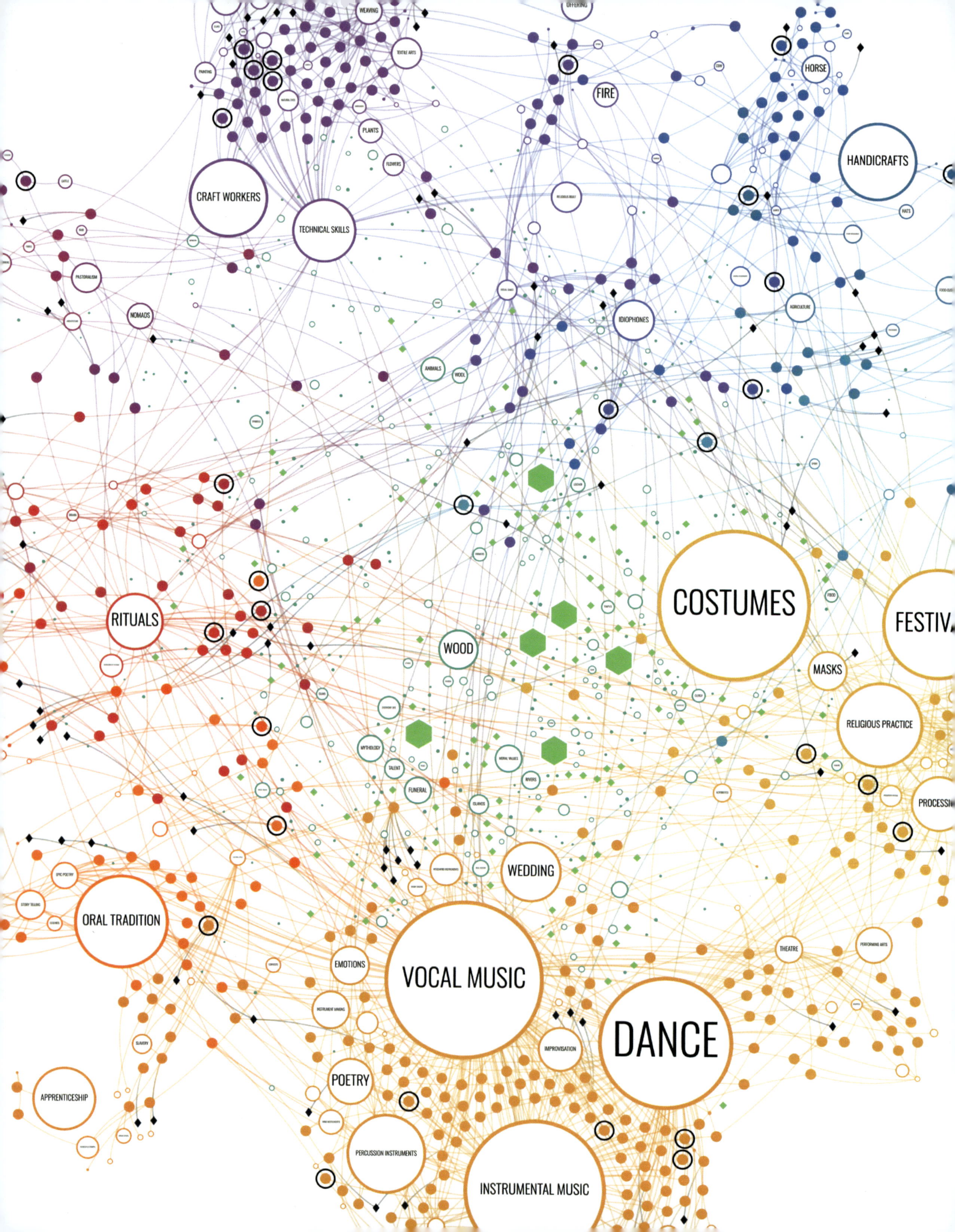

WEAVING
TEXTILE ARTS
PAINTING
PLANTS
FLOWERS
CRAFT WORKERS
TECHNICAL SKILLS
FIRE
HORSE
HANDICRAFTS
HATS
PASTORALISM
NOMADS
IDIOPHONES
AGRICULTURE
ANIMALS
WOOL
COSTUMES
FESTIV
RITUALS
WOOD
MASKS
RELIGIOUS PRACTICE
FOOD
MYTHOLOGY
TALENT
FUNERAL
MORAL VALUES
RIVERS
ISLANDS
PROCESSI
WEDDING
EPIC POETRY
STORY TELLING
ORAL TRADITION
EMOTIONS
VOCAL MUSIC
THEATRE
PERFORMING ARTS
INSTRUMENT MAKING
IMPROVISATION
DANCE
SLAVERY
POETRY
APPRENTICESHIP
PERCUSSION INSTRUMENTS
INSTRUMENTAL MUSIC

6.1b

Figure 6.1a & b

The network visual of Intangible Cultural Heritage that shows the roughly 450 cultural elements (at that time) and their connections to hundreds of different concepts, countries, regions, and even UNESCO World Heritage Sites.

At the start of 2018, I created a highly interactive network visual for the UNESCO website that showed how the cultural elements (as of 2017) connect to each other through their shared expressions or essential components, called "concepts," such as dance, family, and handicrafts, among hundreds of others (figure 6.1).

TRYING TO CREATE A COMPLEX VENN DIAGRAM

A few months later, UNESCO asked me to create several more interactive visuals for the website, each focusing on a different aspect of cultural heritage. One of these was cultural "domains." There are five overarching domains, such as "performing arts" and "social practices."

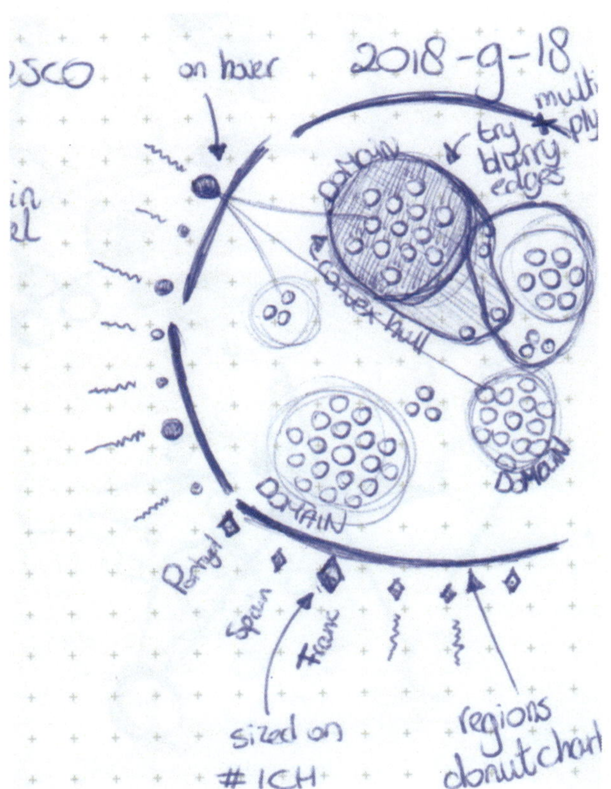

6.2

Figure 6.2

The first sketch for the domain visualization.

The tricky part, which I learned from analyzing the data, is that one cultural element could belong to any number of domains, and most were tied to multiple domains. UNESCO wanted a visualization that lets people explore all the cultural elements and their varied combination of domains.

With that goal in mind, I grabbed my notebook to sketch ideas. (I was already quite familiar with the data from the previous project in figure 6.1.) You can see the first idea sketched out in figure 6.2.

I started by drawing a bunch of dots, each a cultural element, in five different clusters, with a rough ring enclosing them (and the word "domain" alongside it). Those would be the elements that belonged to only one domain. I then drew smaller clumps of dots between these clusters, representing cultural elements belonging to multiple domains.

My first goal was to show which cultural elements belong to which domains. So I used a blobby shape to enclose all the dots assigned to a specific domain. (Note the two amorphous shapes in the top-right of figure 6.2.) That would be my first "layer," which achieved my primary goal. The approach ended up being similar to a Venn diagram, but with five categories.

The countries were a second important aspect. Therefore, this became the next layer to tackle. Because the central layer had an overall circular shape, I felt that adding an outer circle could work well. I drew an outside ring of dots and diamonds that represented the countries, grouping them by their region. I also drew some fainter lines from the countries to the cultural elements to show the connections. I intended for these lines to appear on hover in the final interactive.

6.3

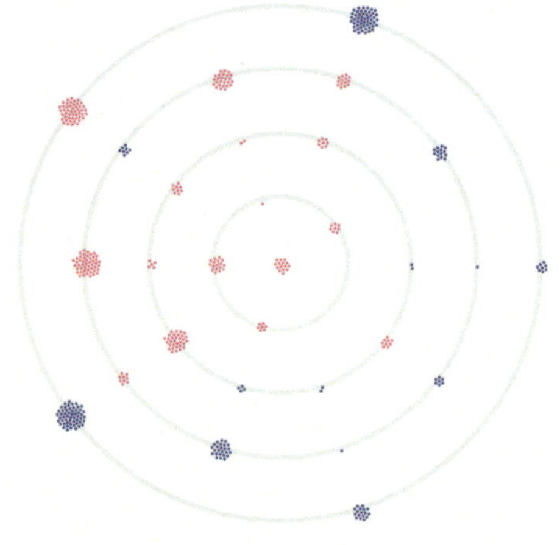

Figure 6.3

Spreading out all the different clusters of cultural elements belonging to the same set of domains. Blue is the default color, but selecting a specific domain would turn the associated clusters pink.

I was unsure if I could make the core idea of the five-way-Venn-diagram blobby shape work visually. It was time to test the design with the actual data.

Well, in short, I utterly failed to make the blobby shapes understandable. So don't worry if you can't pull meaning out of the following few figures. I first tried placing clusters of cultural elements along five concentric rings, as shown in figure 6.3. The cluster in the center contains the elements that belong to all five domains. The innermost ring holds elements that belong to four domains. The next ring contains elements belonging to three domains, and so on, until the outermost ring includes elements belonging to a single domain. In each ring, the elements are clustered by the combination of domains they belong to.

I exported this image to my iPad and started drawing blobby shapes to show which clusters of dots belonged to which set of domains (figure 6.4).

I tried many different versions, but I couldn't develop something that seemed to make sense, something I felt a viewer might easily understand or even want to look at. These all just looked… difficult. This is where I took a step back and truly evaluated the design. I realized that this idea of the blobby Venn diagrams was not the answer.

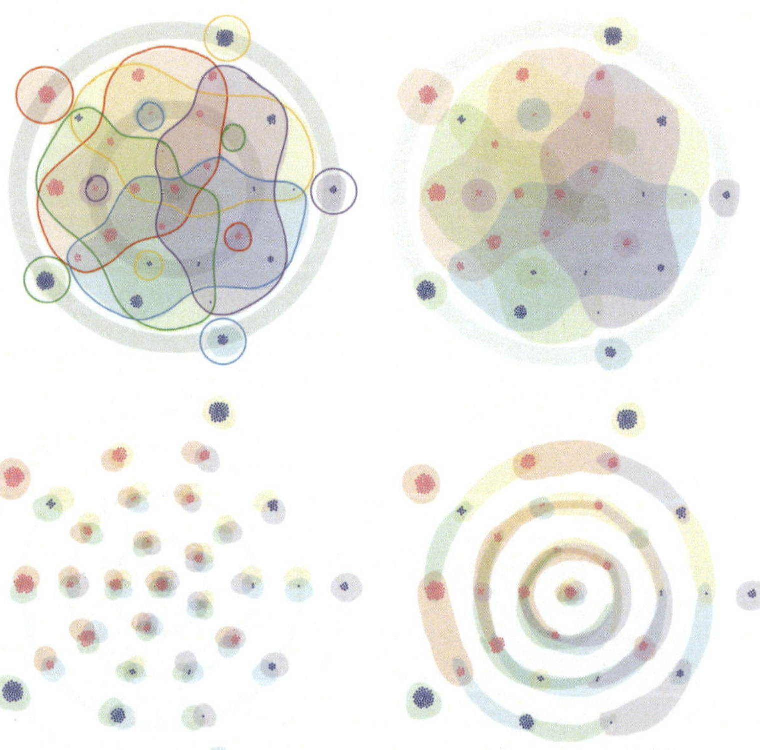

6.4

MOVING TO A DIFFERENT RING STRUCTURE

I returned to my notebook. On the left page of figure 6.5 are two rough attempts at adjusting the original idea. I placed five circles representing the five domains on an outermost ring. Lines would connect them to the smaller clusters of dots on the inner rings. Those lines would show which clusters belonged to which domains (instead of the blobby shapes).

Figure 6.4

Taking figure 6.3 and adding different types of "blobby shapes"; my attempts to show which cluters of cultural elements belonged to which set of domains.

And let's just pretend not to see what's going on at the top of the right page. I have no idea what I was thinking. But when you're exploring designs, nonsense sketches are completely fine.

I felt that the lines were an interesting new approach, but I didn't think that sticking with the sort-of Venn diagram layout of figure 6.3 in the center was the right approach. You can see where I headed next at the bottom of the right page in figure 6.5. If I couldn't make the clusters of dots insightful, what if I placed all the cultural elements along a big circle (note the outer ring of smaller dots) and connected each cultural element to its domains (the five bigger dots inside the ring) with a line? (I sadly don't remember what the innermost ring of small dots was supposed to represent.)

6.5

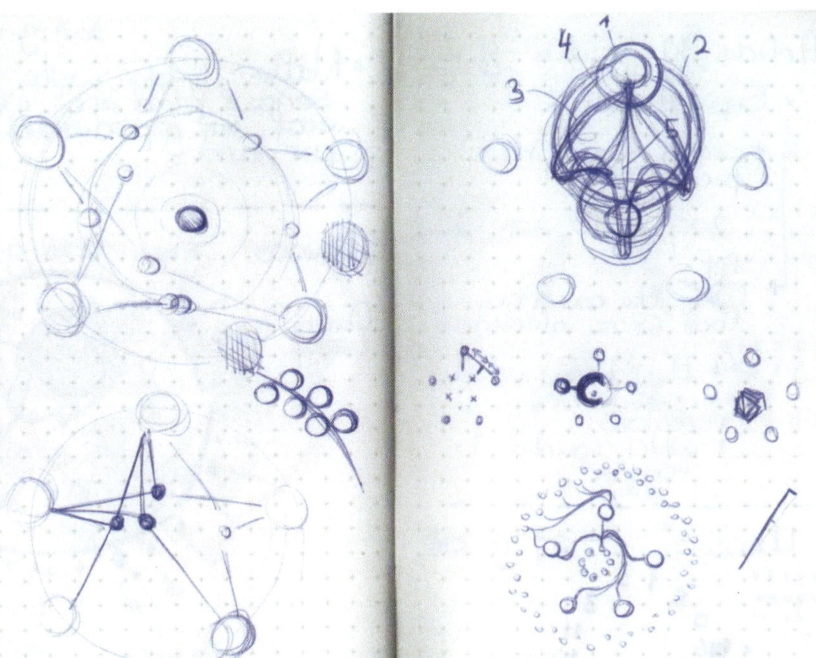

With this rough idea on the page, I turned to my computer again to test the concept using the actual data. I placed the cultural element dots in a giant ring. From experience, I knew that by offsetting each dot's location a little inward or outward, one after another (effectively creating a double ring), I could make each individual dot a little bigger than if I placed all of them at precisely the same radius. (See figure 6.6a for the version with all the dots at the same radius and 6.6b for the "offset" version.)

With this double ring concept on screen and the rough sketch in my notebook, I felt some creative momentum. Instead of five dots along the inside (from the sketch) I created arcs for the five domains. Furthermore, I realized I could take the ring of countries concept from my initial sketch (figure 6.2) and I added a third ring around the outside for the regions and countries, ending up with figure 6.7.

Figure 6.5

More sketches to find other ways to reveal the domains.

I wanted to make all the elements belonging to the same set of domains stand out better. Therefore, I applied the Gestalt principles of enclosure and proximity by placing cultural element dots with the same domains into boxes (enclosure) and adding a little padding between each box (proximity).

If you've not heard of the Gestalt principles before, I highly recommend looking into it, as this book isn't the place for a deep dive. They are straightforward to understand and extremely useful in data visualization to make your design more intuitive.

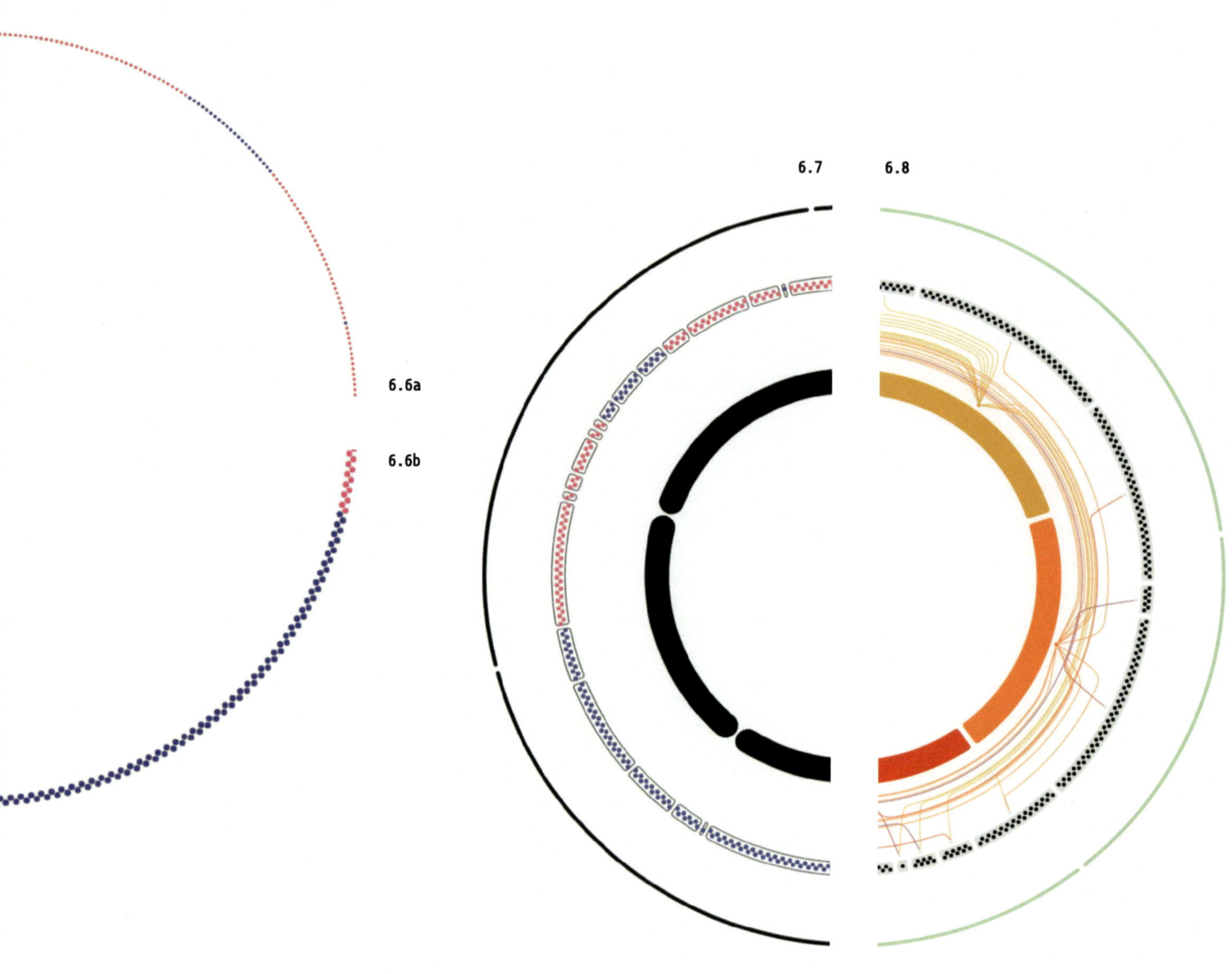

Figure 6.6a & b

Placing all of the cultural element dots in a ring (a) and offsetting them into a double ring (b).

Figure 6.7

Adding an outside ring to hold the countries and regions and an inside ring to hold the five domains. In the middle ring, boxes enclose all the cultural element dots that belong to the same set of domains.

I was happy with how this visual was starting to look! It was far from being done. However, with a sense for what I still needed to add, I could see its potential. The current shape was inviting and natural, like expanding ripples on water or rings in a tree trunk.

To show the connections, I pulled from an idea I had developed about a year earlier that used radial lines between rings. Here, those lines could link the middle ring of cultural elements to the inner ring of domains (see figure 6.8). They could also link the elements to the outside ring of countries (not yet visible in figure 6.8).

THE FINE-TUNING STAGE

With that, the abstract form of my visualization was complete: three rings of information, with lines running from the middle to both the inner and outer rings to reveal connections. Now, the fine-tuning began. This is something I can't really do by hand sketching. To refine the color palette, fonts, text positions, and other minor stylistic choices, I have to apply them to the visualization (generally using code) to see if they have a desired effect.

Figure 6.9 shows the final color palette for the five domains, which I based on the colors in the original visualization (figure 6.1). The separate countries are diamonds around the outside, grouped per region. Hovering over an arc showcases certain links, as demonstrated by the red lines tied to the "oral traditions and expressions" domain.

Another new detail is that I replaced each cultural element dot with a mini donut chart representing its domains. These later became pie charts, as the empty center had no added value. I did this partly to make it easier to see which domains each group of cultural elements belongs to, but also because I didn't know how to color them otherwise.

Figure 6.8

Connecting the groups of cultural elements (middle ring) to the domains (inner ring).

Figure 6.9a & b

A version with the final colors, countries, and text elements in place (a) and a zoom-in on the donut charts where the element dots have become three rows thick (b).

6.9b

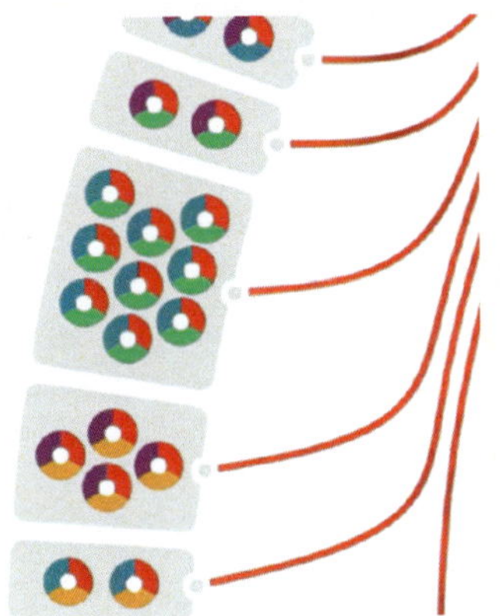

6.9a

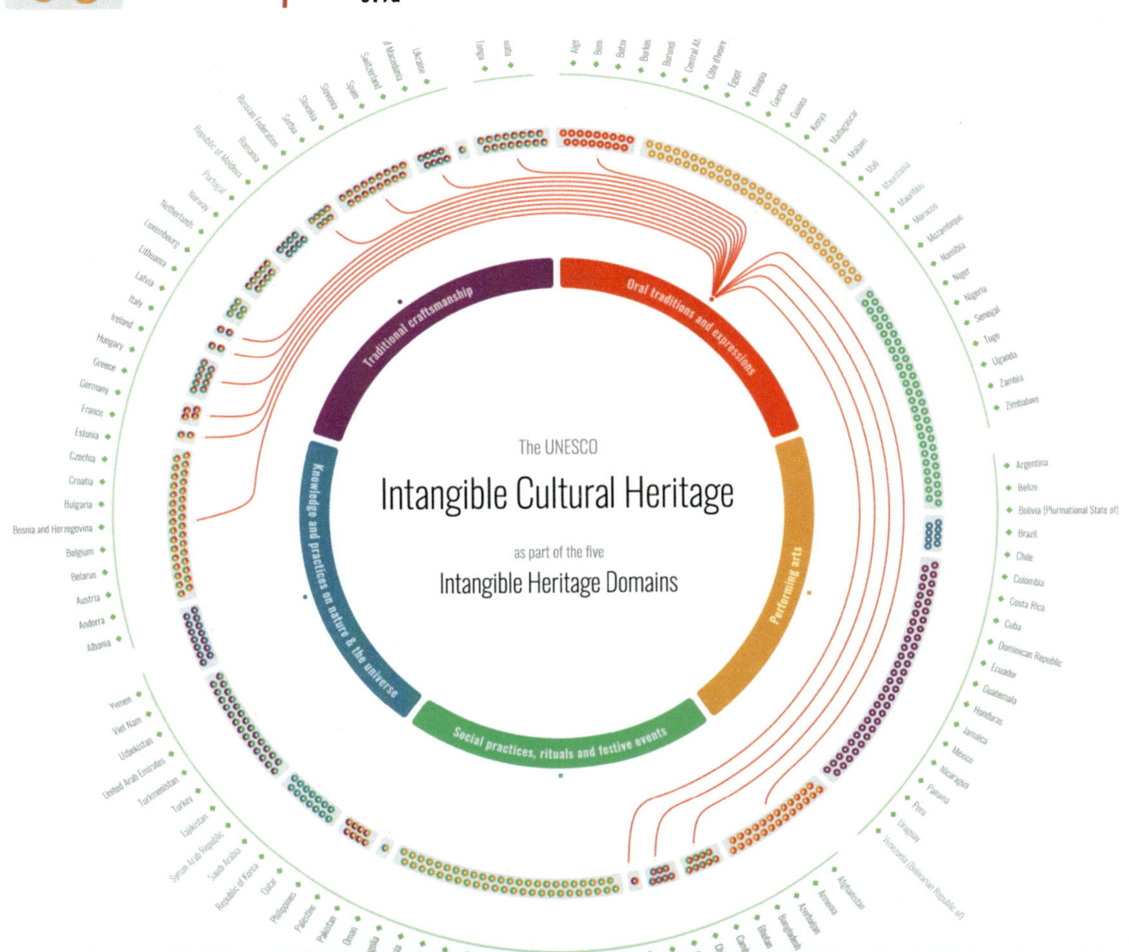

6.10

However, I felt the colors were hard to distinguish, so I made the elements ring thicker by bumping it from two rows of elements to three, thereby increasing the size of each dot (figure 6.10).

After more rounds of minor tweaking and refining the interactivity, the visualization was finished; see figure 6.11.

Figure 6.12 demonstrates what happens when you hover over the domain for social practices, rituals, and festive events: Lines appear, showing the cultural element clusters associated with that domain. All countries with at least one element assigned to that domain are also highlighted (in the sense that countries without that domain are faded out).

Embedding the pie charts into this custom visual is another example of placing one chart into another; a technique from Lesson 3.

Figure 6.13 shows an example of hovering over a country, Mongolia, revealing direct lines to that country's Intangible Cultural Heritage elements.

Finally, Figure 6.14 shows what happens when you hover over one of the cultural elements. The domains associated with that element become highlighted, along with the country or countries connected to it. (The version online also shows a photo of the element in the center.)

Figure 6.10

Going from two to three rows of elements created more area to enlarge the pie charts and better display their colors. The outside edge of each pie chart is the color of the primary domain of each element (if this is defined).

The final results in figures 6.11-14 are a custom data visualization creation, generated from my thought process that prioritized the data set and my goals. In this case, the goal was to reveal the domains and countries associated with each cultural element in an inviting way that made the user want to explore and learn.

Figure 6.11

The final result of the Intangible Cultural Heritage domain visualization using data from 2018.

I found my way to the final visualization by sketching in my notebook, evaluating the designs to assess which ones showed promise, and playing and iterating with the actual data on my screen. This wouldn't have been possible if I'd focused on making the data work in a specific chart form.

6.11

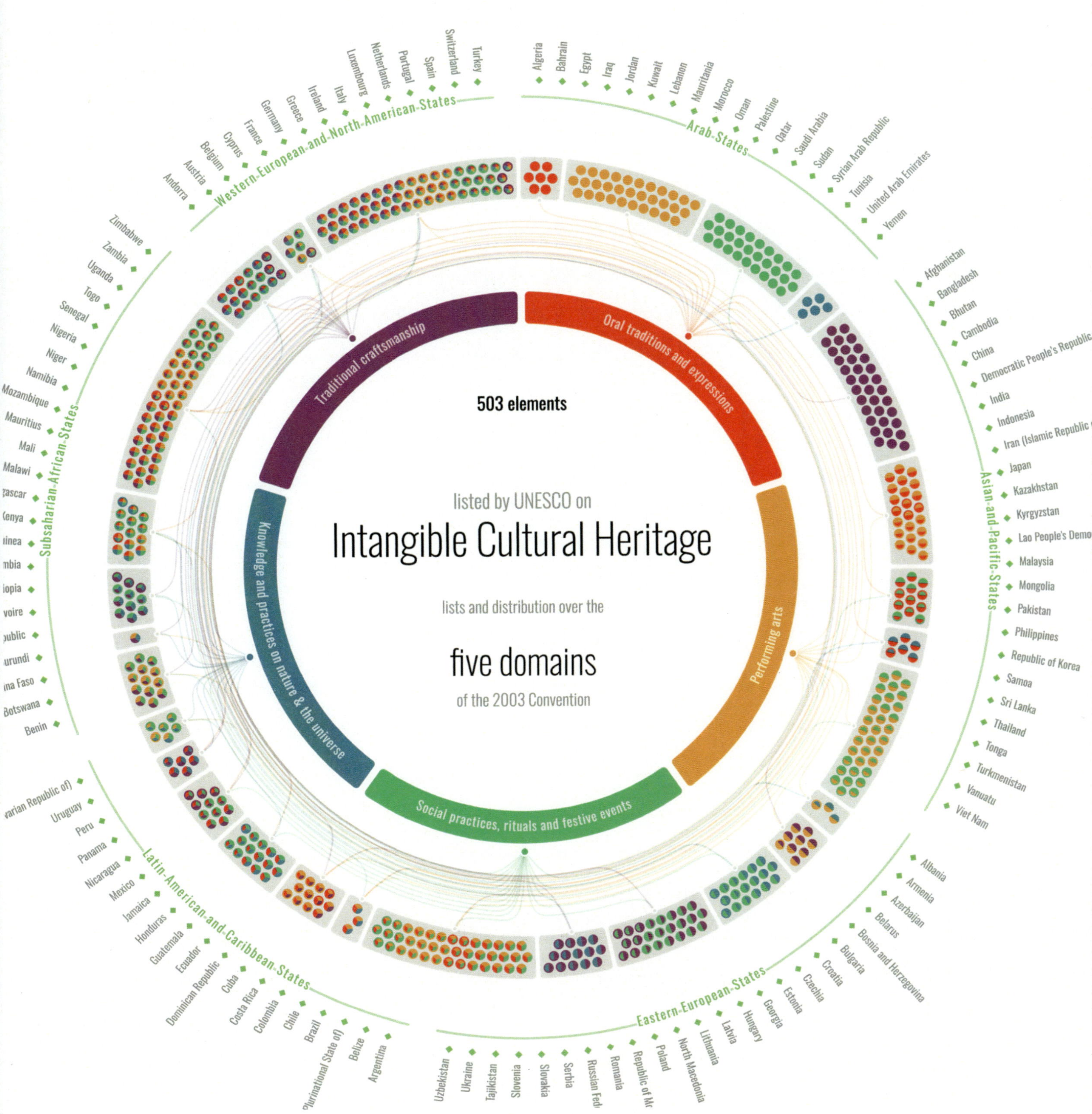
503 elements
listed by UNESCO on
Intangible Cultural Heritage
lists and distribution over the
five domains
of the 2003 Convention
Traditional craftsmanship
Oral traditions and expressions
Performing arts
Social practices, rituals and festive events
Knowledge and practices on nature & the universe
Western-European-and-North-American-States
Arab-States
Asian-and-Pacific-States
Eastern-European-States
Latin-American-and-Caribbean-States
Subsaharian-African-States

6.12

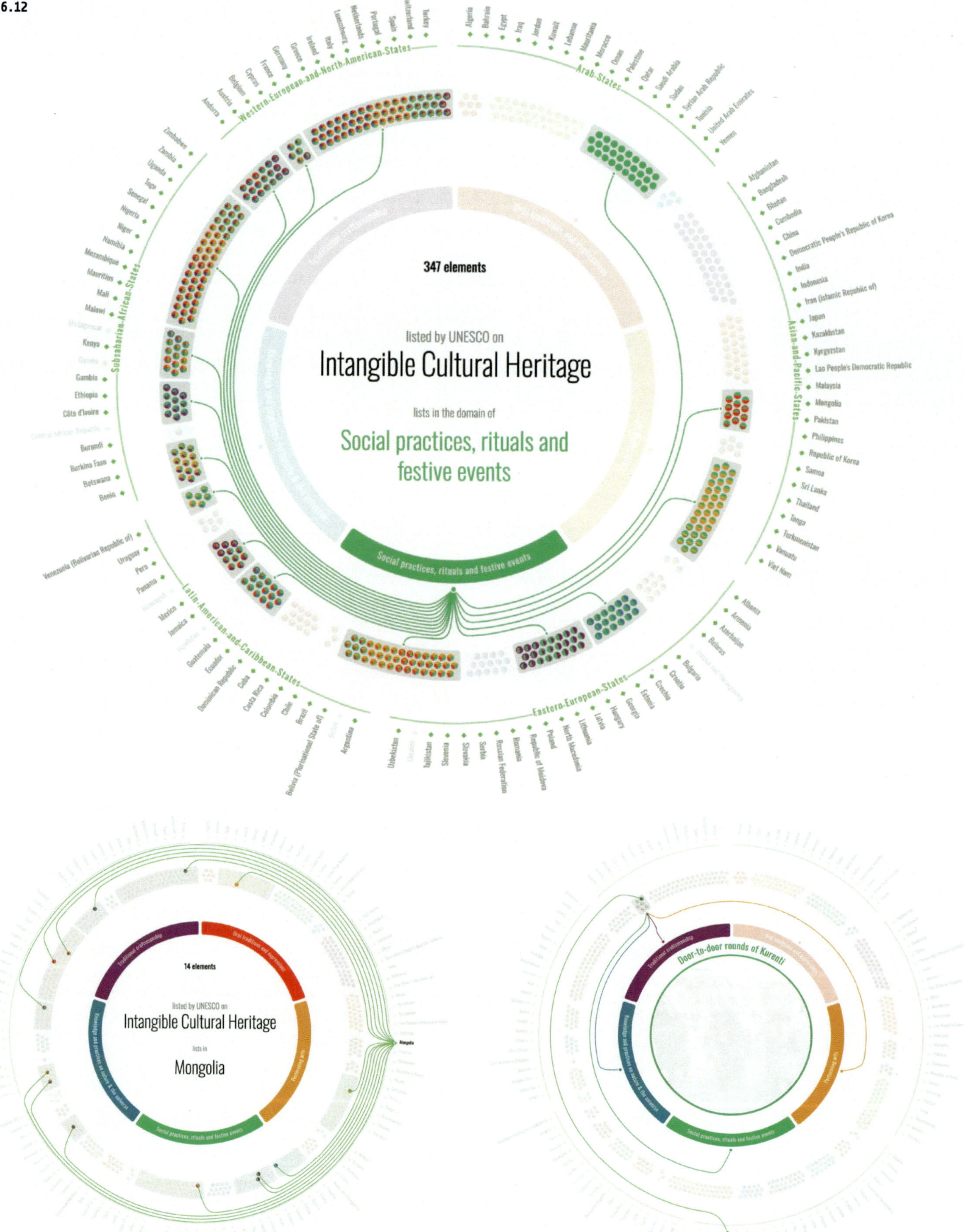

347 elements
listed by UNESCO on
Intangible Cultural Heritage
lists in the domain of
Social practices, rituals and festive events
Western-European-and-North-American-States
Arab-States
Asian-and-Pacific-States
Eastern-European-States
Latin-American-and-Caribbean-States
Subsaharian-African-States
Social practices, rituals and festive events
14 elements
listed by UNESCO on
Intangible Cultural Heritage
lists in
Mongolia
Traditional craftsmanship
Oral traditions and expressions
Performing arts
Social practices, rituals and festive events
Knowledge and practices on nature & the universe
Door-to-door rounds of Kurenti

6.13

6.14

Figure 6.12

Hovering over one of the big domains in the inner circle highlights all of the cultural element clusters and countries that are connected to that domain.

Figure 6.13

Hovering over a country shows lines to all of the cultural elements associated with that country.

Figure 6.14

Hovering over a cultural element shows lines to all of its domains, as well as its associated country or countries. A photo of the cultural element would also appear in the central circle.

In the end, choosing to think beyond conventional chart forms isn't about dismissing what works; if you end up with a traditional chart form, that is completely fine! The beauty of letting go of chart types is the freedom it gives you to explore and refine. By focusing on the data, the story and the goals for the project (rather than trying to fit within traditional chart structures), you give yourself room to create a visualization that speaks uniquely to the patterns and insights within your dataset. It's a process that might feel a bit unstructured at first, with sketches that might not all work out, but that's part of the discovery. Each iteration brings you closer to a design that captures both the complexity and essence of what you want to convey.

PART III

AIMING FOR

You've learned how to jazz up charts in small ways to make them more impactful. You've also learned how to step away from traditional chart types to explore more unconventional designs and come up with your own. These are the foundational skills you will need as you tackle the remaining lessons in this book.

At this point, you are halfway across the chart-to-art spectrum, and you've entered a vast space where you can really stretch your creativity. When I work in this space—aiming to be as creative as possible while still clearly conveying the story and trends in the data—I follow my personal motto: "Increase the visual diversity."

Increasing visual diversity means adding more variation to the design. In Lesson 4, you already saw how to make a grid of circles come to life by encoding them through visual channels such as size, color, and opacity. But encoding isn't the only way to enhance visual diversity.

In this third part of the book, I'll share my favorite techniques for increasing visual diversity. You will learn how to present data at the most granular level of detail available and you'll acquire strategies for revealing aggregated values, such as totals or averages, visually. You'll see how to add extra variables to the visual, to layer them on to the primary variables to provide deeper insights. Finally, you'll combine these skills and begin to embrace more variables and more data points—the ultimate source of visual diversity.

The payoff of this visual diversity approach is that it adds more context and depth to the end result. It reveals more nuances and side stories beyond the chart's key insights. You'll find plenty of examples of these benefits in the projects we'll explore in the following lessons.

At the end of this section, you'll have a firm grasp of what visual diversity means, how to increase it, and why it makes your visuals unique and more enjoyable to explore.

VISUAL

LESSON SEVEN

SHOW ALL

Show the most granular level of detail in the data set to supply a reader with intriguing context

One way to create visual diversity in a data visualization is to draw many visual elements, many points on the page. Therefore, whenever possible, I prefer to visualize the most granular level of detail I have in my data, rather than the aggregated values such as the sum or average. For example, in a visualization about daily air travel, I'd prefer to visualize each separate flight that occurred during a day instead of the total number of flights per airline per day. I love how using granular data gives me the largest number of visual elements that I can style in size, color, transparency, and more.

Using a granular level of detail increases visual diversity, and can reveal more context, nuances, stories, and patterns than if the data is aggregated into summary statistics. You can highlight a few of those "mini" stories with a textual annotation and let the interested reader continue to find their own insights.

Though you may not have noticed at the time, you've already seen several cases where I applied this technique. Recall, from Lesson 1, the "Top 2000" music visual (figure 1.4a), where each of the 2,000 songs is a circle, and the "Olympic Feathers" project (figure 1.5), where each of the gold medal winners is a tiny rectangle. There's a lot of data baked into those visuals!

In fact, the "Landscape of Power Flows" project from Lesson 5 (figure 5.10) has been the only instance where I didn't visualize the data set's most granular level of detail. The original data set had over 60 million data points—one value for every minute! I had to group the data in weekly averages to fit the result on my canvas.

THE DATA

7.1a

7.1b

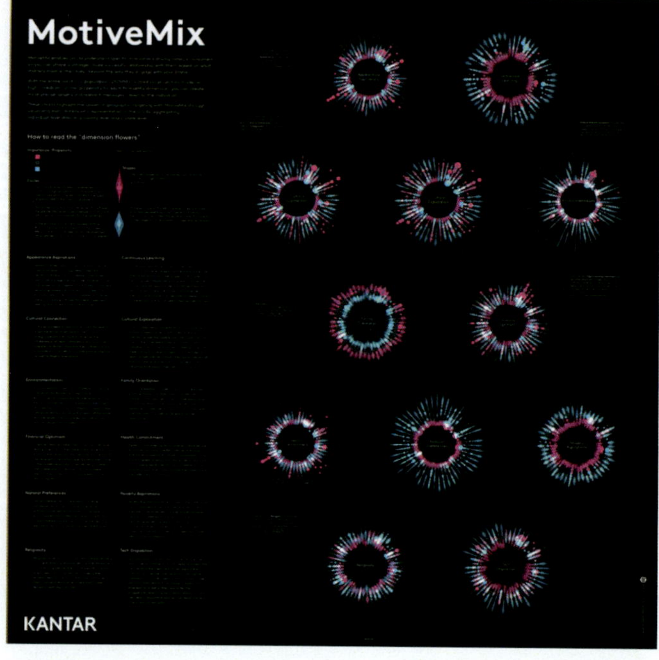

Turning US counties into bright flowers

BUSINESS | 2018 | KANTAR CONSULTING

visualcinnamon.com/portfolio/kantar-motivemix

Kantar Consulting, a market research advisory firm, asked me to visualize their MotiveMix data set. This data set looks at American consumers along 12 "attitudinal dimensions," such as tech disposition, environmentalism, and cultural connection, to better understand what is important to them.

The data set contained the percentage of each county's population with a low, medium, or high propensity for each attitudinal dimension. These three values together add up to 100%. Therefore, one county could hypothetically have 50% high propensity, 25% medium propensity, and 25% low propensity for appearance aspirations, 40% high, 30% medium, and 30% low for religiosity, and so on across all 12 dimensions.

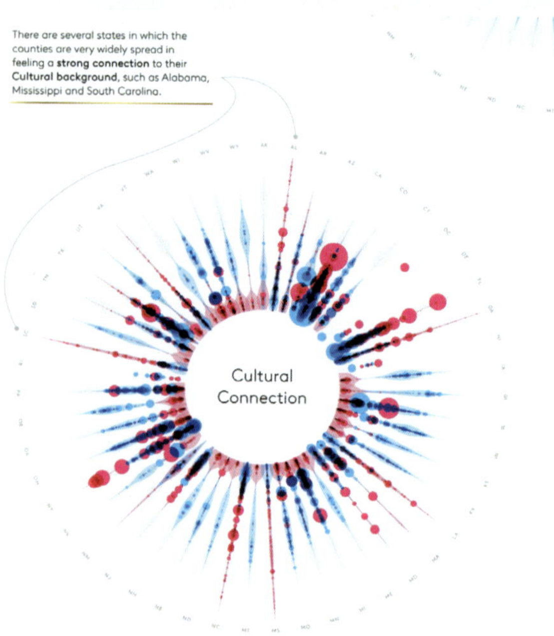

7.2

Figure 7.1a & b

The black version of the Kantar MotiveMix poster with 12 "dimensional flowers." Along the poster's left is an introduction, a legend, and explanations of each dimension (a) and a close-up (b).

Figure 7.2

Zooming in on the cultural connection flower in the white version of the poster.

The visual wasn't meant to have one central insight but instead reveal the breadth of the MotiveMix data—and the stories within. The final result would be hung in their office, to grab attention and spark conversations. It was a perfect opportunity to make a design that visualized the most granular level of detail available: the propensity percentages, per attitudinal dimension, per county.

In figure 7.1, you can see the final result of the black poster (there's also a white version, see figure 7.2). I represented each of the 12 attitudinal dimensions as a blue-magenta "flower." The US states are 51 spokes radiating outward from the center of each flower. Along each spoke, blue and magenta circles represent the counties in the state. Each county is shown twice on each spoke—one circle represents the county's low propensity percentage (in blue), and another circle represents the county's high propensity percentage (in magenta). The circle's size is scaled according to the population of the county. The farther away from the center, the higher the percentage.

I didn't draw the medium propensity values as circles, as I wanted to highlight the extremes. However, they are still in the visual as an almost transparent white violin plot along each spoke.

All those circles of different sizes, in two colors, partially overlapping, placed along spokes, create a lot of visual diversity. No flower is the same as another, as the underlying data is different. Without showing the data at this granularity, that meaningful texture would be lost.

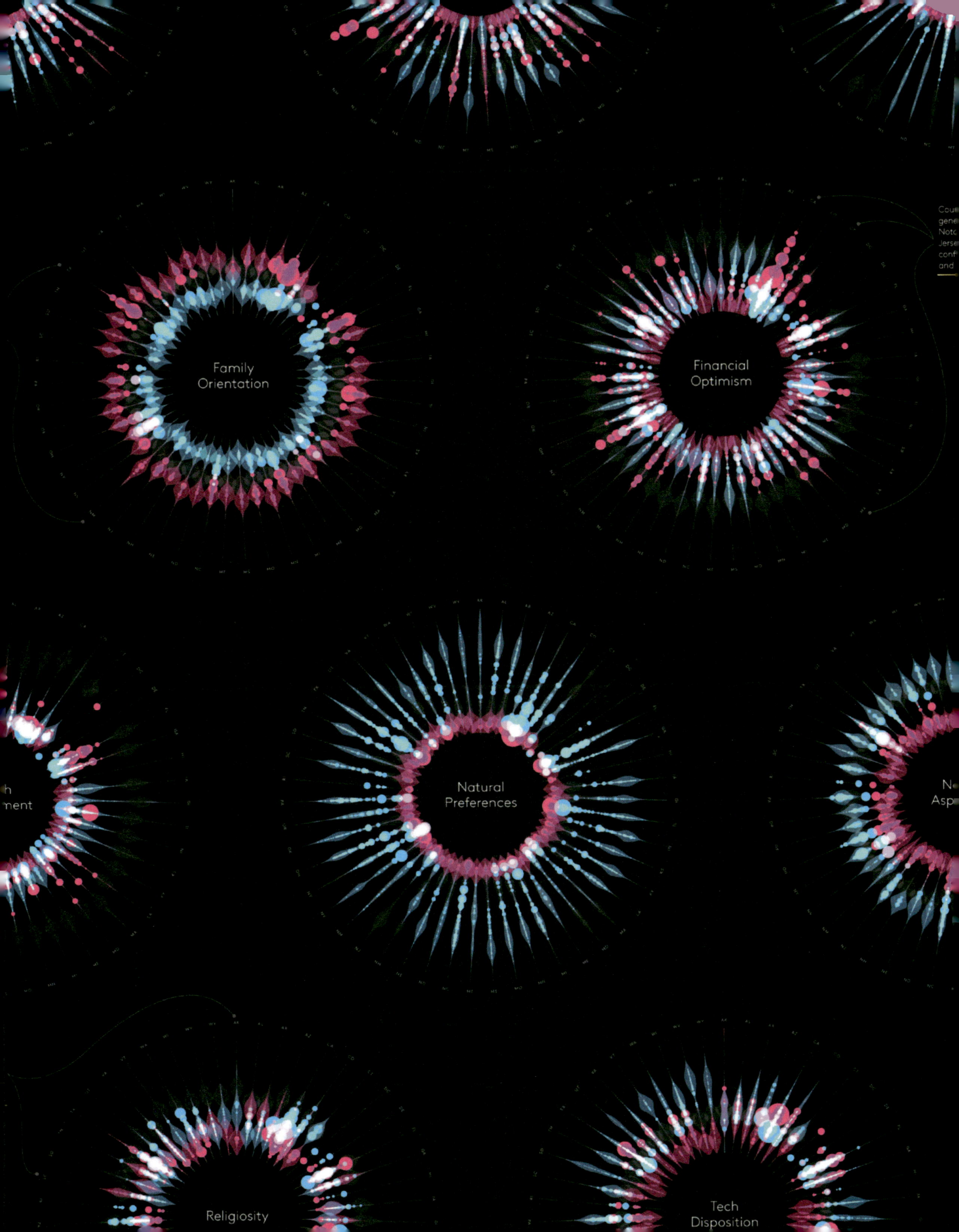

Family Orientation
Financial Optimism
Natural Preferences
Religiosity
Tech Disposition

7.3

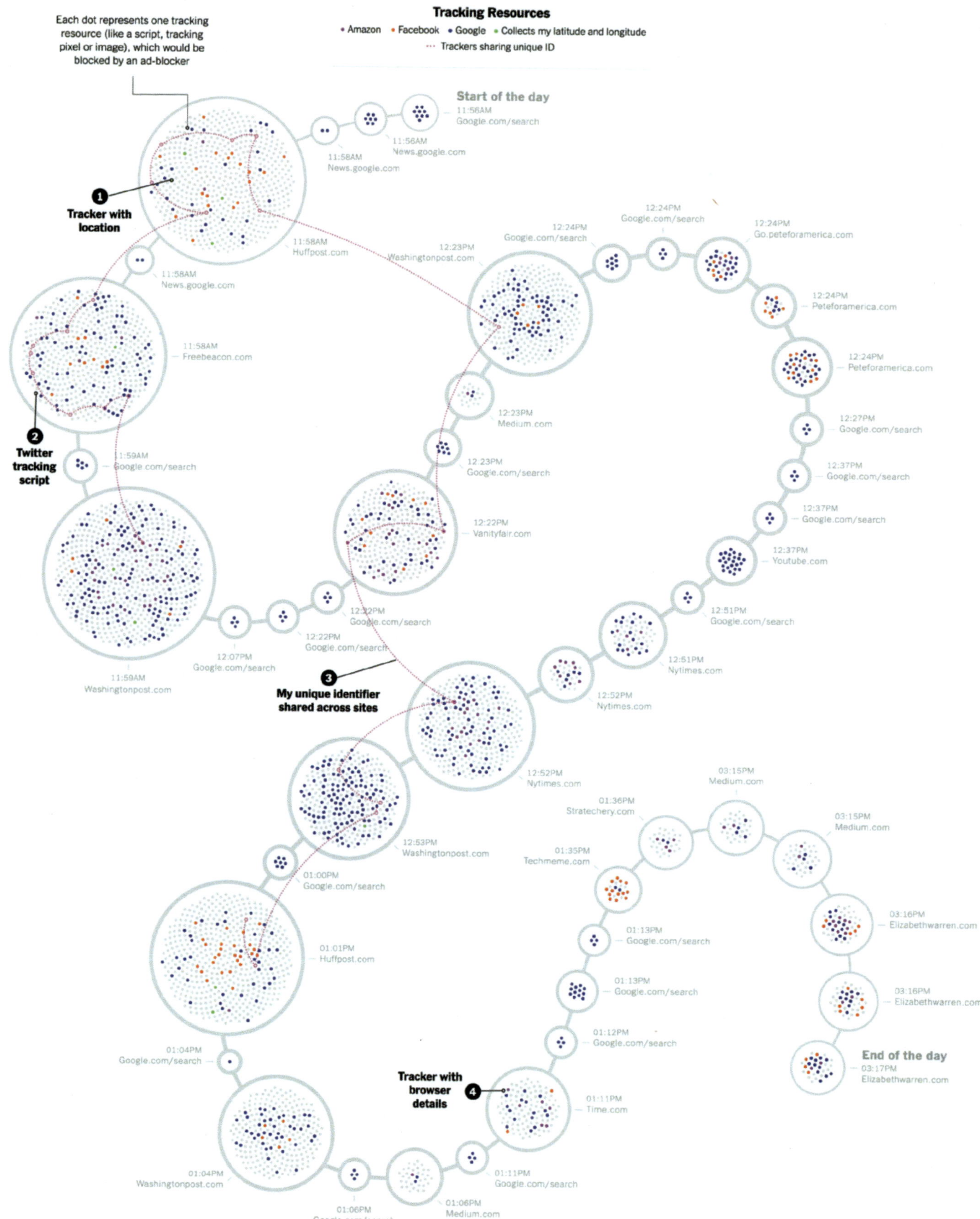

Tracking Resources
• Amazon • Facebook • Google • Collects my latitude and longitude
··· Trackers sharing unique ID
Each dot represents one tracking resource (like a script, tracking pixel or image), which would be blocked by an ad-blocker
Start of the day
11:56AM Google.com/search
11:56AM News.google.com
11:58AM News.google.com
11:58AM Huffpost.com
11:58AM News.google.com
11:58AM Freebeacon.com
11:59AM Google.com/search
11:59AM Washingtonpost.com
12:07PM Google.com/search
12:22PM Google.com/search
12:22PM Google.com/search
12:22PM Vanityfair.com
12:23PM Google.com/search
12:23PM Medium.com
12:23PM Washingtonpost.com
12:24PM Google.com/search
12:24PM Google.com/search
12:24PM Go.peteforamerica.com
12:24PM Peteforamerica.com
12:24PM Peteforamerica.com
12:27PM Google.com/search
12:37PM Google.com/search
12:37PM Google.com/search
12:37PM Youtube.com
12:51PM Google.com/search
12:51PM Nytimes.com
12:52PM Nytimes.com
12:52PM Nytimes.com
12:53PM Washingtonpost.com
01:00PM Google.com/search
01:01PM Huffpost.com
01:04PM Google.com/search
01:04PM Washingtonpost.com
01:06PM Google.com/search
01:06PM Medium.com
01:11PM Google.com/search
01:11PM Time.com
01:12PM Google.com/search
01:13PM Google.com/search
01:13PM Google.com/search
01:35PM Techmeme.com
01:36PM Stratechery.com
03:15PM Medium.com
03:15PM Medium.com
03:16PM Elizabethwarren.com
03:16PM Elizabethwarren.com
End of the day
03:17PM Elizabethwarren.com
1 Tracker with location
2 Twitter tracking script
3 My unique identifier shared across sites
4 Tracker with browser details

Some dimensions, like family orientation, have similar values across the states, while other dimensions, like financial optimism, are an explosion of different colors along each state's spoke (figure 7.1b), meaning that people across the US states are split on how important it is.

The annotations highlight interesting insights. They also serve as an entry point for the audience to dive in and better understand how the visual works so they can explore it on their own.

Figure 7.3

The desktop version of the visual for the "Digital Trackers" article in *The New York Times* showing all of the trackers grouped into circles according to the website on which they operated.

VISUAL GROUPING

Generally, when showing granular data, visually grouping the data points can help with the interpretation. In the previous case, the data was visually grouped by attitudinal dimension (the flower) and state (the spokes around each flower).

One of the most straightforward ways to execute visual grouping is to cluster all the visual marks and contain them within a bigger shape. I often do this by putting small circles or dots (the individual data points) inside a large circle (a common grouping). Let me show you two examples.

7.4

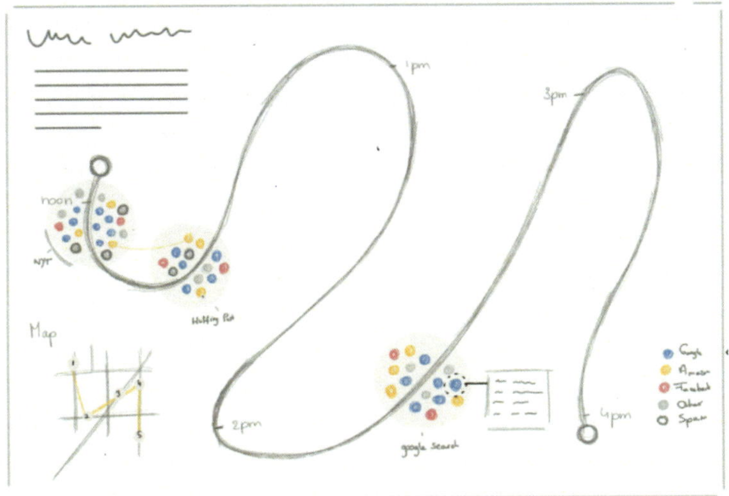

Figure 7.4

An early sketch for the design of the version that would appear across two pages in the printed edition of *The New York Times*.

Circles within circles

BUSINESS | 2019 | *THE NEW YORK TIMES*
nytimes.com/interactive/2019/08/23/opinion/data-internet-privacy-tracking.html

The New York Times ran a story about how websites track users' data. One of the newspaper's journalists installed a version of Firefox that monitors all the tracking resources (such as a script, tracking pixel, or image that an ad-blocker would block) on each visited website. This resulted in a data set of trackers, metadata about what they gathered, and from which domain or company they originated (e.g., Google, Facebook). The team working on the story was staggered by the obscene level of detail and scale of tracking, and they were looking for an eye-catching and illustrative visualization of this data that would be suitable for both print and online editions.

7.5a

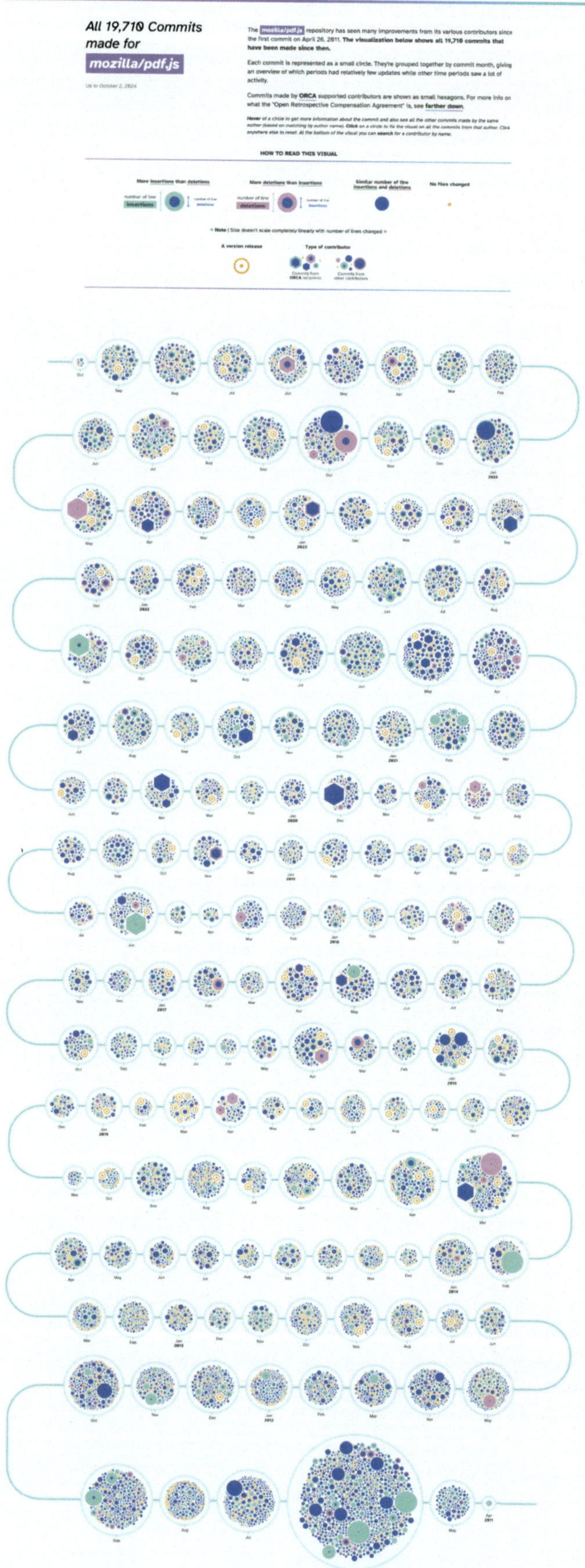

The final visual, figure 7.3, shows the full set of over a hundred trackers as dots, grouped into larger circles according to the website on which they operated.

Even more circles within circles

BUSINESS | 2024 | MOZILLA

nbremer.github.io/ORCA/commit-history

I created two visualizations to promote the launch of Mozilla's ORCA program. ORCA is an experimental funding model that provides compensation to open-source contributors. (The acronym stands for Open Retrospective Compensation Agreement.)

Mozilla had given ORCA funding to several non-employees who had made noteworthy contributions to the company's pdf.js repository on GitHub.

The visualization in figure 7.5 shows nearly 20,000 updates that changed pdf.js files (known in programming speak as "commits"). Each commit is a circle or a hexagon—depending on whether the contributor received ORCA funding—and is sized according to the number of lines of code that changed. Added lines are turquoise and removed lines are pink. But if a commit added and subtracted lines, both colors are nested in the shape.

I wanted to arrange the data on a timeline, so I clustered the commits into a larger circle by month and strung them together on a line that weaves from top to bottom (moving back in time). This visual grouping makes it easier to absorb the whole data set. However, it also reveals some interesting trends about lower and higher activity periods.

In both the website tracker and the ORCA examples, showing all of the underlying data points provides a lot more context to the whole story than only showing the *total* number of trackers per website or commits per month. In both cases, the technique increases visual diversity and makes each piece more creative and unique.

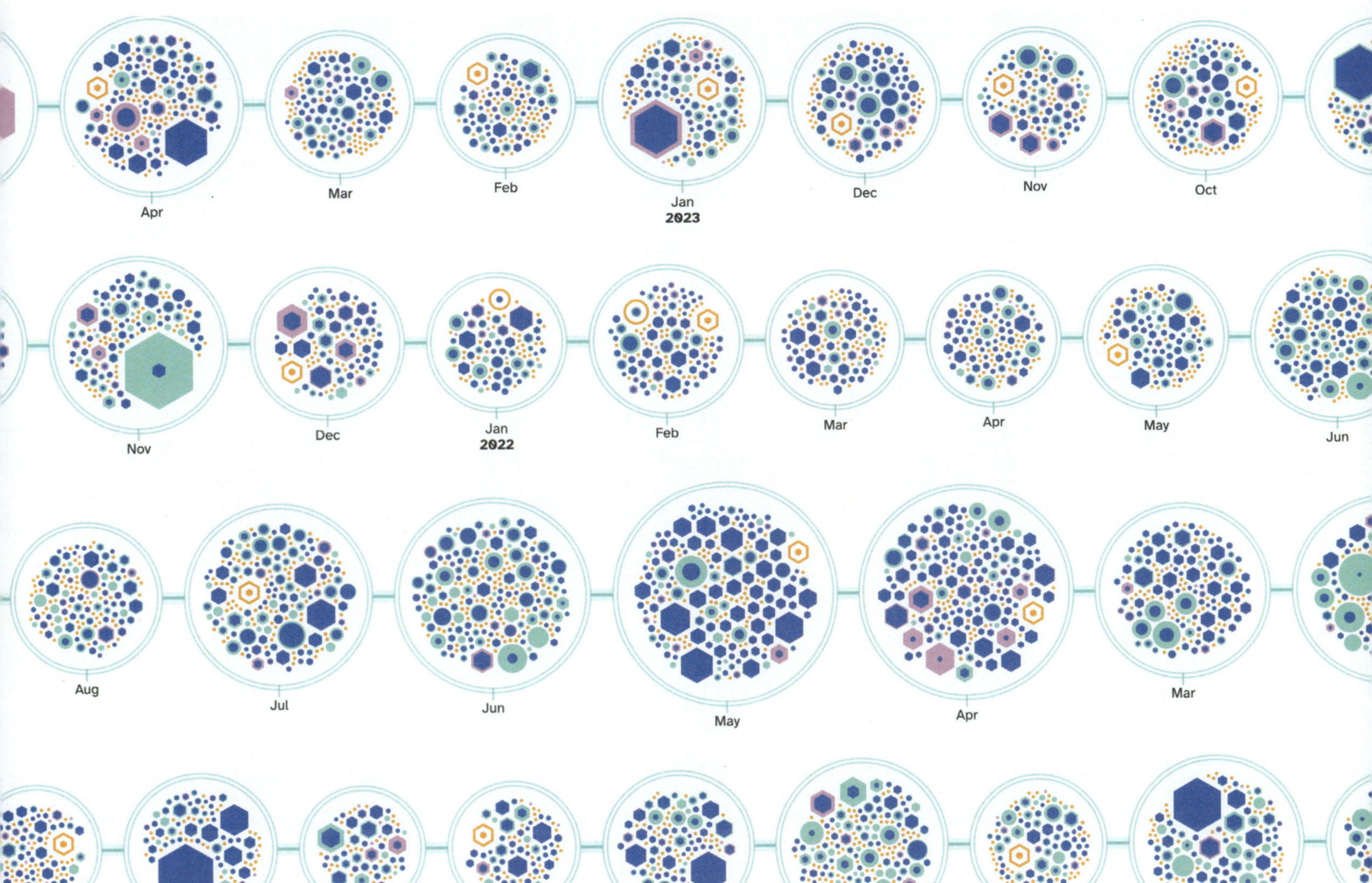

7.5b

ADDITIONAL (MINI) CHARTS OF GROUPED VALUES

Figure 7.5a & b

All of the nearly 20,000 commits made to Mozilla's pdf.js GitHub repository, clustered by month and organized in reverse chronological order (a), and a zoom in (b).

There are also times when it's beneficial to give the viewer more information about the grouped values, such as the averages or totals. In those cases, I like to add a mini chart—something straightforward, small and simple. It won't be the first thing people notice, but it will give them more context with time. And yes, you've seen this technique already in "The Top 2000 ❤ the 70s & 80s" from Lesson 1, which included small histograms (figure 1.4) about the changing interests in musical styles across the past 20 years of the list.

Animating hundreds of flights

BUSINESS | 2019 | LIGHTHOUSE REPORTS
vimeo.com/351673775

In 2019, Lighthouse Reports, a collaborative newsroom organization, worked with news organizations across Europe to reveal that the EU border control agency Frontex had significantly grown in scale over the 2010s. Using the Lighthouse Reports data, I created an animation of over 1,200 individual deportation flights between 2007 and early 2019.

Figure 7.6

A frame from the Frontex animation showing flights in early 2018, with the mini charts of funding and monthly flights along the bottom.

The animation displays the flights over time, with a dramatic uptick during the second half of the 2010s. I wanted to emphasize this increase, as it was an important part of the story. Therefore, as you can see in figure 7.6, I drew an inverted dotted bar chart of the number of flights per month. Above that is another mini line chart of Frontex's yearly budget, for extra context.

A GENTLE INTRODUCTION

In a few cases, I thought that showing all of the data was key because it gave a lot of interesting information, but it turned out that either the data or the visual itself was overwhelming and that a casual observer would need a bit of hand-holding. In these cases, I've eased the viewer into the full visual with a "gentle" introduction. For example, a (more simplified) chart might appear at the top, showing aggregated values or only a subset of the data. This chart would give the reader a taste of the data before they scroll down to the visualization with the entire data set.

From clustered circles to connected circles

BUSINESS | 2019 | GOOGLE NEWS LAB
WhyDoCatsAndDogs.visualcinnamon.com

I used a gentle introduction for the "Why Do Cats and Dogs…?" project from Lesson 5. As you may recall, my goal was to give insight into the most popular cat-related and dog-related questions asked on Google. The main visual, which revealed all the questions, looked quite daunting (figure 7.7).

Frontex: EU's Deportation Machine

The European Border and Coast Guard Agency has transformed from an unfashionable EU outpost in Warsaw into a super agency. Its growth has tracked Europe's migration anxiety with budgets expanding alongside its role in managing deportations. This growth will be supercharged in the coming years to match the political appetite for forced returns.

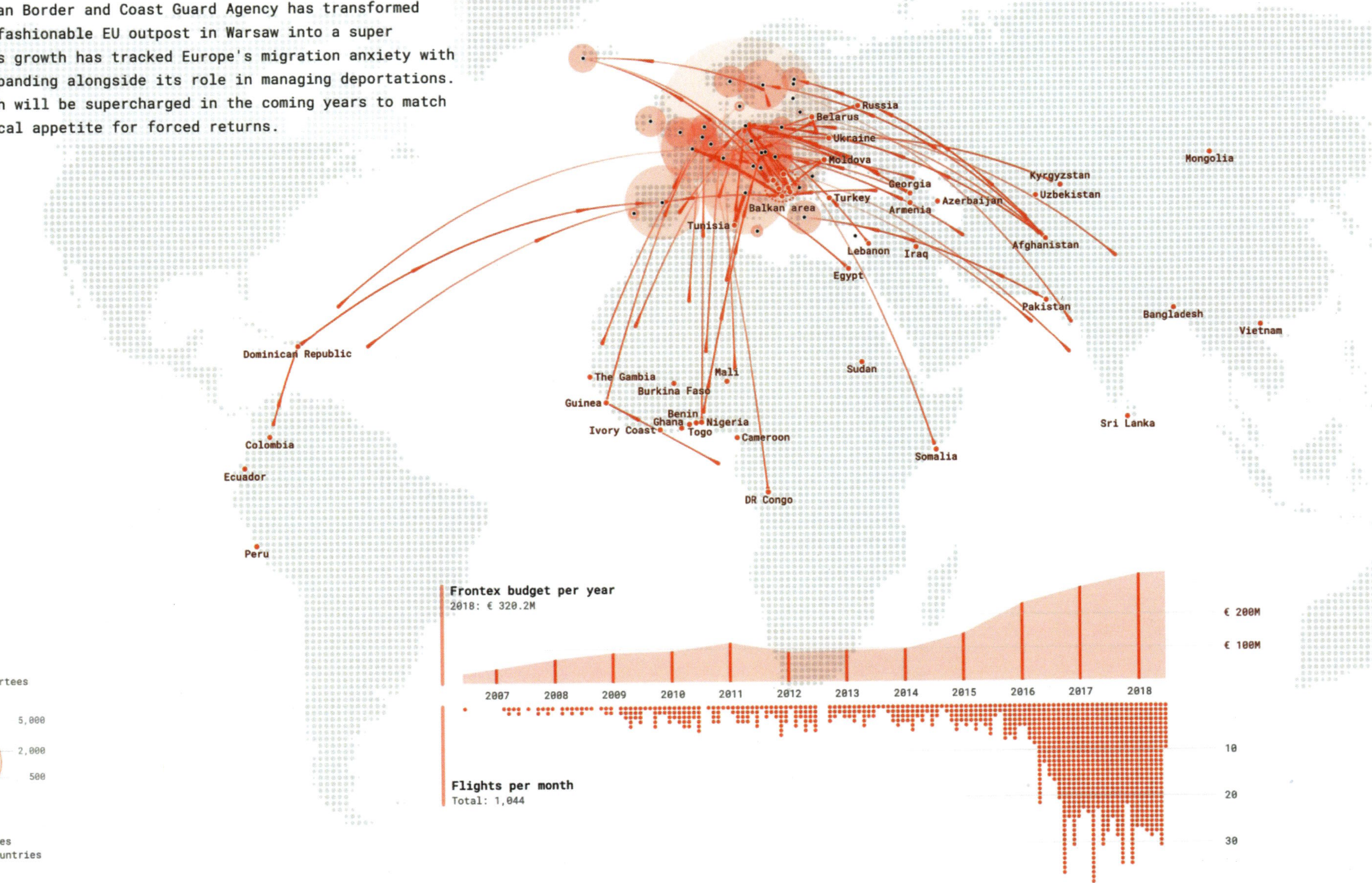

7.6

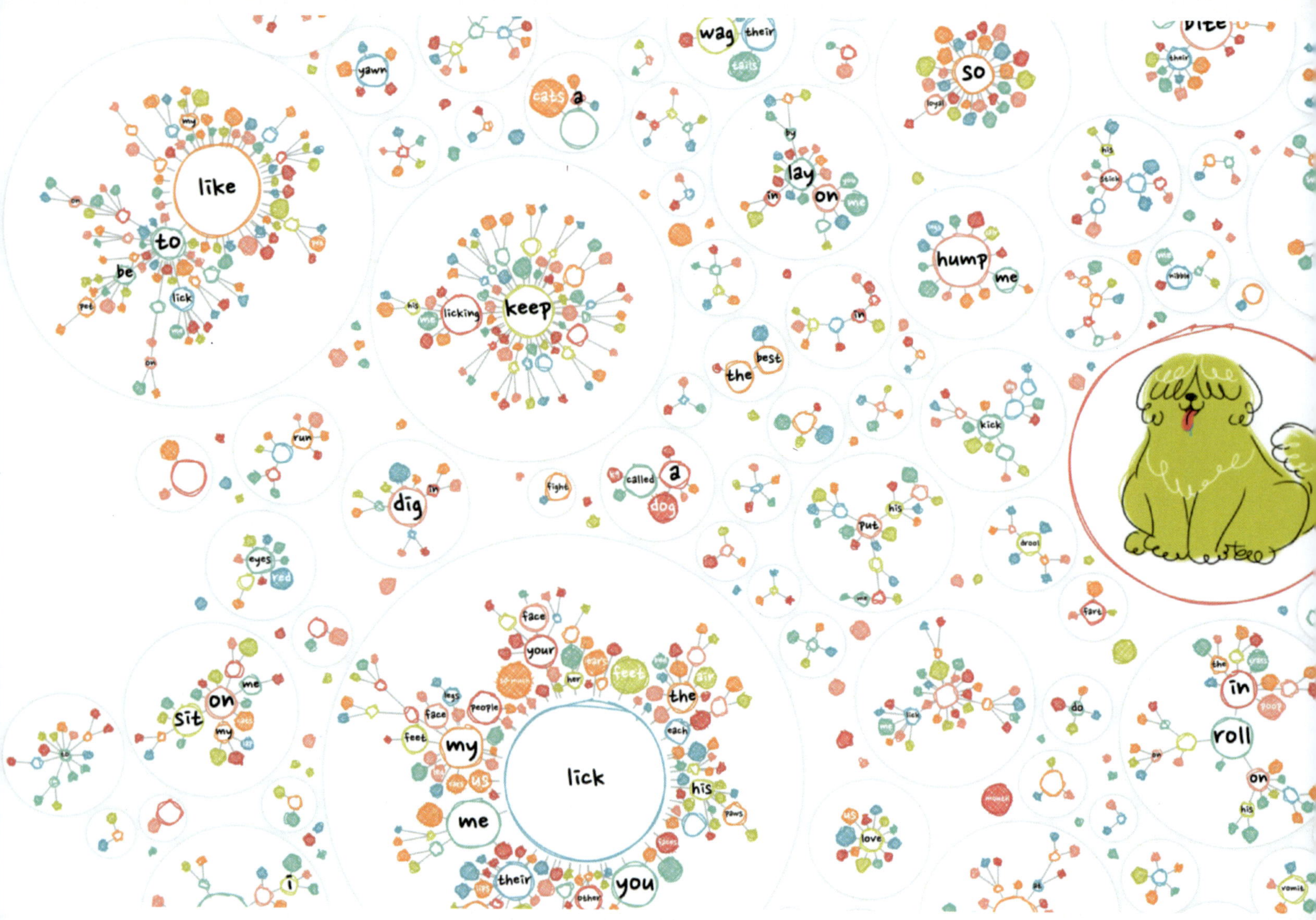

Figure 7.7

The word tree visual that revealed all of the most popular questions asked about dogs on Google. Central dog illustration by Juliana Chen.

Therefore, I created a more simplified visual using a subset of the data and placed it at the top of the article. I took the "circles within circles" approach I discussed earlier in this lesson. First, I analyzed the most common question themes for cats and dogs. Next, I selected the main words for each theme and grouped all of the questions that contained those words. In figure 7.8, you can see the result for the "likes and dislikes" theme for cats. (It hadn't been long since the "cat vs. cucumber" meme had gone viral.)

After scrolling through a few of these thematic visuals (accompanied by explanations), the reader is warmed up, ready to embrace the full word tree visual.

At this point, readers could explore the visualization on their own. But with so many data points, I realized that they may feel a bit lost at sea, even though they understood what the data represented.

7.7

That's where the interactivity came in. Besides adding a touch of playfulness to it all, the interactivity provided more detail and aided understanding. This treatment is widely useful, as it can help break down most types of complex visualizations. In this case, it was well worth the time investment required to program those features.

There are several factors that determine whether a visualization would benefit from having interactivity. I assess the following:

- **Complexity:** If the visualization is complex, I prefer to add at least a hover effect that highlights parts of the visual that relate to the hovered entity to help the audience understand it more easily (both images of figure 7.9).
- **Positioning:** I don't want to hide any of the key takeaways behind interactivity. Interactivity, such as a tooltip on hover or a highlight at the click of a button, should only reveal interesting extra details.

Figure 7.8

The first visual on the cats article that more gently introduces the reader to the data set with a more straightforward visual of clustered circles.

Figure 7.9a & b

Two examples of the interactive hovers; hovering over the word "poop" in the text highlights all the questions containing that word (a), and hovering over a circle in the full word tree highlights all of the downward word connections as the tooltip simultaneously spells out all the questions (b).

- **Resources:** What do the budget and deadline allow? This important question has the biggest impact on what's possible *in practice.* Ultimately, my work is limited by time and budget. Because of this, I will discuss the potential for interactivity with my clients during the negotiation phase. I'll give some examples of static visuals and dynamic ones and I'll give my advice for what I think works best for their needs. After that, the decision is up to them.

7.8

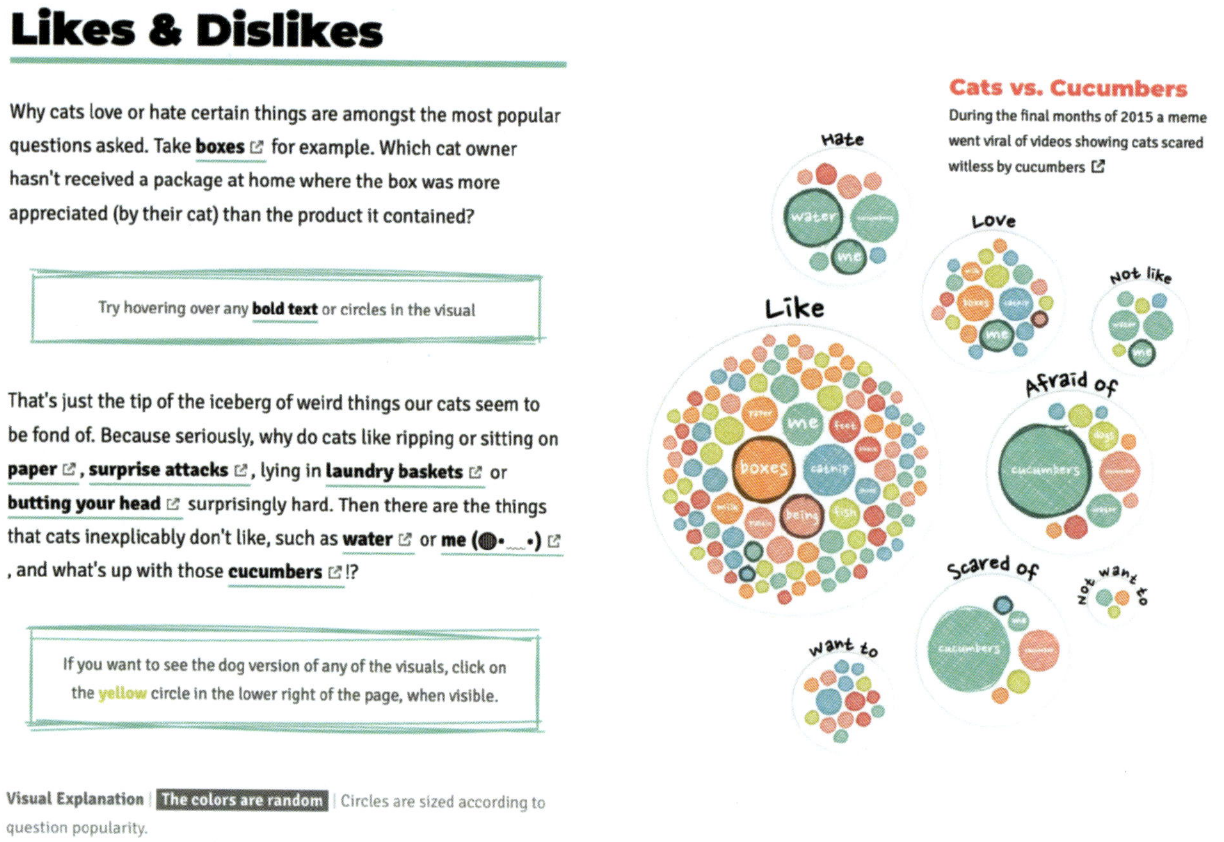

Likes & Dislikes

Why cats love or hate certain things are amongst the most popular questions asked. Take **boxes** for example. Which cat owner hasn't received a package at home where the box was more appreciated (by their cat) than the product it contained?

Try hovering over any **bold text** or circles in the visual

That's just the tip of the iceberg of weird things our cats seem to be fond of. Because seriously, why do cats like ripping or sitting on **paper**, **surprise attacks**, lying in **laundry baskets** or **butting your head** surprisingly hard. Then there are the things that cats inexplicably don't like, such as **water** or **me (●•___•)**, and what's up with those **cucumbers** !?

If you want to see the dog version of any of the visuals, click on the yellow circle in the lower right of the page, when visible.

Visual Explanation | The colors are random | Circles are sized according to question popularity.

Cats vs. Cucumbers

During the final months of 2015 a meme went viral of videos showing cats scared witless by cucumbers

Hate

water

me

Love

boxes

me

Not like

Like

me

boxes

catnip

Afraid of

cucumbers

Scared of

cucumbers

Not want to

want to

Why does a dog | Why do dogs | Why does my dog | Why is my dog

eat poop | eat their poop | eat cat poop | eat their own poop | eating poop | eat dog poop | eat poo | eat other dogs poop | eat shit...

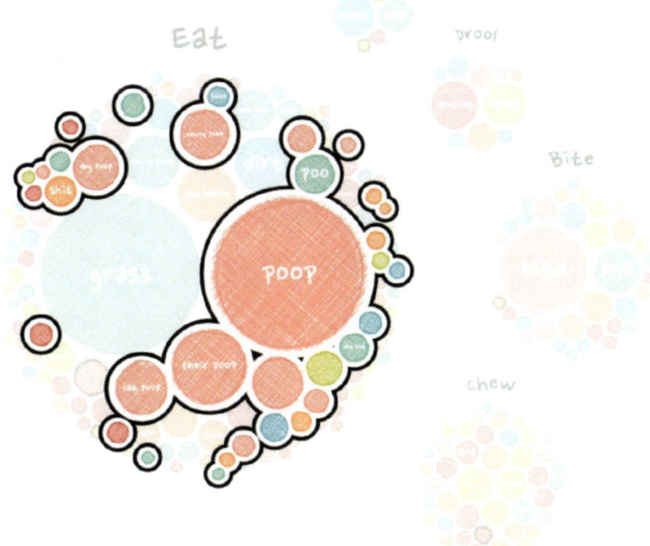

Eating & more

Questions about why dogs eat so many strange things aren't far behind licking in terms of popularity. Specifically, eating-related questions are dominated by why dogs like to **eat lots of unsavory things**. Especially **poop...**, and not only their own! Apparently **charcoal** is also a dish that some dogs can't stay away from.

Dogs do lots of other things with their mouth, such as chewing, nibbling or drooling. Although I would imagine dogs **nibbling on your kitten**, or **drooling in your car** isn't what you like to see happen.

Interestingly, for cats biting is a lot more popular than what they eat, while for dogs it's the other way around. I wonder if that says more about cats or dogs?

7.9a

Why do dogs | Why does my dog

like to...

bark at vacuums | be chased | be in the bathroom with you | be pet so much | be petted | be squashed in bed | be under blankets | be watched while eating | bite my hand | bite on the leash | bite tires | chew antlers | chew on bones | cuddle | dig in their water bowl | have something in his mouth | have their tummies rubbed | kick sheets | lay by your feet | lay on me | lay on my pregnant belly | lick babies | lick faces | lick me | lick on lips | lick

7.9b

The title of this lesson is "Show All of the Data" because it makes for a somewhat shorter title than the more nuanced "Show The Most Granular Level of Detail Available in the Data that Still Shows Interesting Patterns and Insights Without Getting Bogged Down Too Much in the Minute Details." But that should be your primary takeaway here.

Overall, the level of detail that you present depends on your goal and the intended audience. (There's always an "it depends.") Does your visual need to be quick and easy to grasp, or do you have the option to make it more creative, more customized? I always start from the most granular level available in the data and zoom out from there. Only when there's far too much data or it turns out I can't reveal the primary insight, do I consider going up a level and using grouped values.

But in short, when you have the option to be more creative, try to show all your data.

LESSON EIGHT

SHOW

If you need to show aggregated numbers, like averages or totals, reveal them using more granular data and clever design tricks

After the last lesson, you are hopefully feeling excited to play with all that rich, detailed data. But what do you do if you need to show higher-level aggregated numbers, like, for instance, the average salary within a company, the total sales of a supermarket, or the final score of a tournament? Fear not. In this lesson, I'm going to share ways to visualize granular data in a way that it actually showcases the top-level aggregated numbers.

You might be thinking, "Wait! Didn't we already do this in the last chapter by encircling or grouping clusters of data?" Well, you'd be correct. Apart from the "Frontex" case, all the other examples had some form of visual grouping. However, the main goal for those groupings wasn't to show the aggregated numbers but rather to offer some organizational focus and clarity. For the "dots within circles" examples of figures 7.3 and 7.5, the circles containing the dots do not scale precisely to the total value of the dots inside; they are only meant to create order.

VALUES WITH GRANULAR DATA

It's a subtle difference, but in this lesson, I want to highlight how you can apply the same concept of "showing all the data" when the true goal is to visualize the aggregated values or summary statistics of those data points. I admit though, that there may be cases where grouping for the sake of visual focus and grouping to show the aggregated values end up being one and the same. In the previous lesson, I used the word "grouping" because the data points were quite literally clustered into groups. In this lesson, I'll instead use "aggregation," because there's a deeper purpose to grouping the data—to show the totals, averages, medians, or other statistics.

Suppose, after running your analysis, you find that the aggregated values don't amount to many remaining data points. You may be reduced to only one number in the most limiting cases! One total value. One average. When this happens, try to visualize the data (at least) one level deeper than the topline aggregated numbers. Show totals per region, averages per industry, highs and lows per day, or whatever makes sense for your data. This will give you more material (and more data points) to make a creative and custom visual; it increases the visual diversity.

As with the previous lesson, the same major benefit of showing more detail holds here: I feel that "the average person," "the total sales," or "the longest time" only gives me a narrow glimpse at a bigger story. The scientist in me isn't as interested in the so-called "average person" (that doesn't exist). If I see a visual about "the average salary," I'd love to know if the underlying distribution has big outliers (like C-suite execs) that pull the average up and paint a more rosy picture for the company. I want to know how the underlying distribution looks. I want more context!

Therefore, when I visualize data, I also like to give the audience extra context when it's available. I visualize the main story but give people the ability to look deeper if they're interested and let them see the nuances of the aggregated values.

Brightly colored blobs

BUSINESS | 2020 | *UNEARTHED* & PUBLIC EYE

unearthed.greenpeace.org/2020/02/20/pesticides-croplife-hazardous-bayer-syngenta-health-bees

Figure 8.1a & b

The main visual (a) and a close-up (b) from the series of HHP articles showing CropLife companies' total sales, aggregated visually into those that are considered highly hazardous and those that are not.

In 2020, I worked for *Unearthed*, the journalistic arm of Greenpeace UK, and Public Eye, an NGO investigating human rights abuses by Swiss companies, to create visuals for several articles. The investigative journalists obtained data from a leading agribusiness intelligence firm about the chemical sales of the world's five largest agrochemical companies—all members of a lobby group called CropLife. They combined that data with an international list of "highly hazardous pesticides" (HHPs). Pesticides classed as "highly hazardous" are incredibly harmful to people, animals, and ecosystems.

8.1a

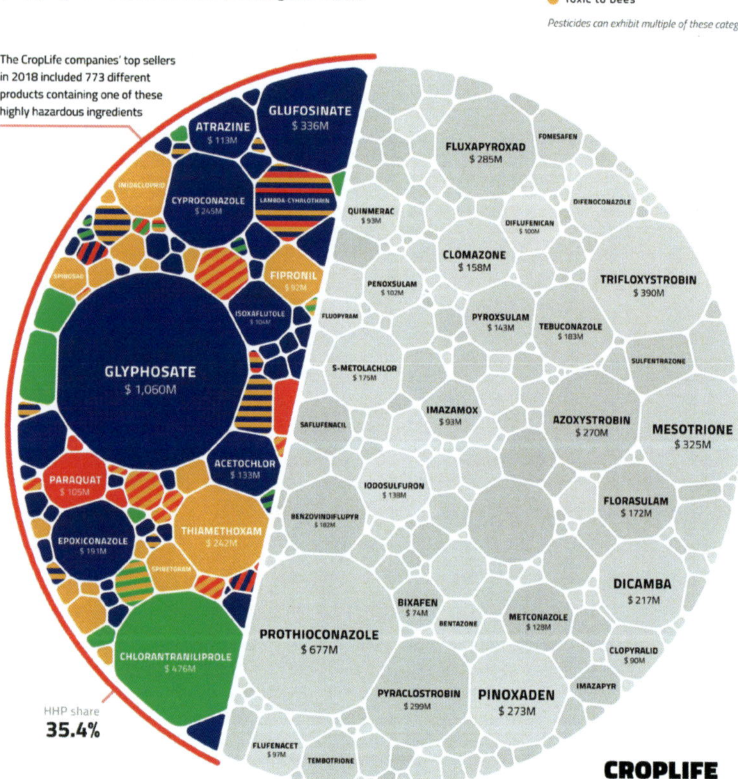

My goal was to illustrate the main takeaway from their analysis: Over one-third of the CropLife companies' total sales consisted of HHPs. A straightforward bar (or pie) chart with one section for the share of HHPs and another for the remaining sales would have sufficed. However, the article needed something bigger and more detailed to claim the page, give more context, stand out, and invite exploration. Thankfully, the underlying data went one level deeper, which allowed me to create a visual that was much more elaborate. Ultimately, I revealed the sales per pesticide, categorized into those that are hazardous or not, as shown in figure 8.1.

The chart type in this visualization is called a Voronoi treemap. The size of each "blob," each pesticide, is scaled according to its sales volume (the total sales from all the companies) and colored according to its associated hazards. Gray pesticides are considered non-hazardous.

I enjoy using Voronoi treemaps because of their unique polygons—each one has its own character. And, unlike standard treemaps,

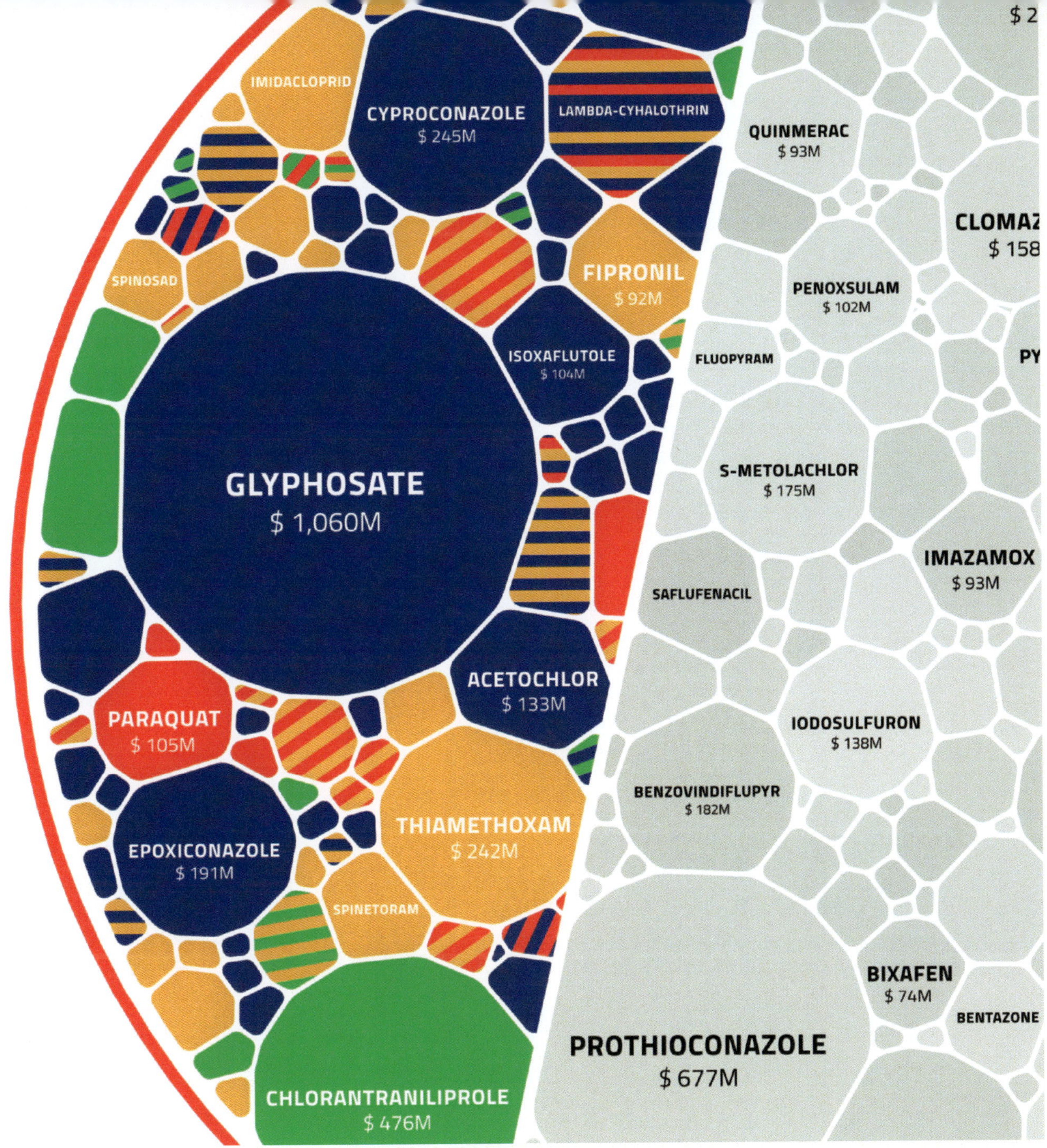

8.1b

Voronoi treemaps can be arranged into forms other than rectangles, such as circles.

The bright colors make it easy to see that the share of hazardous pesticides is significant. That was the primary takeaway from the investigation. However, readers have an opportunity to get more context and go deeper into the data. They'll see, for instance, that acutely toxic pesticides (in red) are still in use, that Glyphosate

Crops that drive world trade in hazardous pesticides

Unearthed and Public Eye analysed more than $23bn of agrochemical sales data for 2018 - about 40% of the global market - to identify sales of highly hazardous pesticides (HHPs). Across 12 crop groups analysed, those shown here accounted for more than four out of every five dollars spent on HHPs.

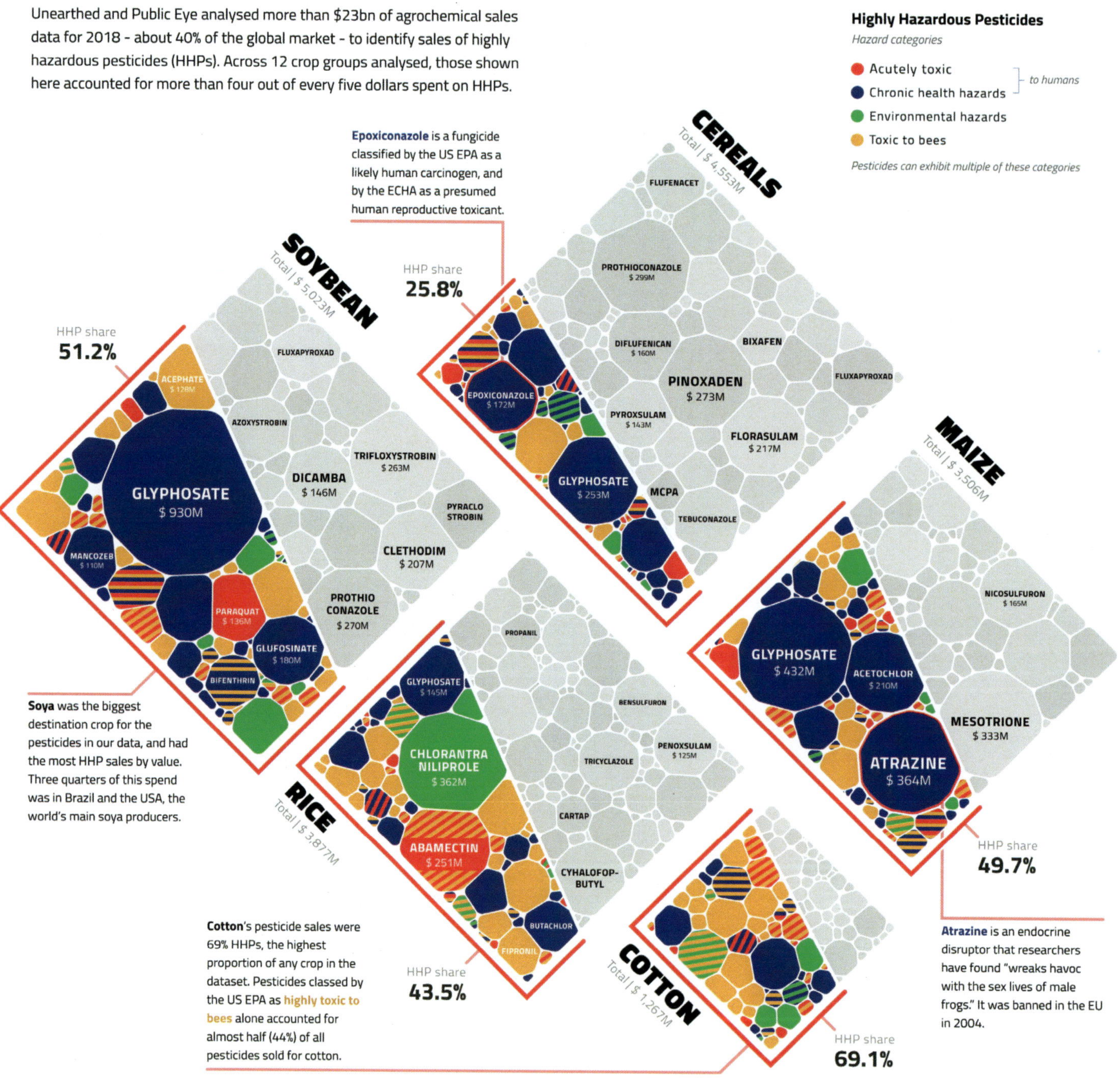

Epoxiconazole is a fungicide classified by the US EPA as a likely human carcinogen, and by the ECHA as a presumed human reproductive toxicant.

Soya was the biggest destination crop for the pesticides in our data, and had the most HHP sales by value. Three quarters of this spend was in Brazil and the USA, the world's main soya producers.

Cotton's pesticide sales were 69% HHPs, the highest proportion of any crop in the dataset. Pesticides classed by the US EPA as **highly toxic to bees** alone accounted for almost half (44%) of all pesticides sold for cotton.

Atrazine is an endocrine disruptor that researchers have found "wreaks havoc with the sex lives of male frogs." It was banned in the EU in 2004.

Figure 8.2

This visual appeared in a second article that covered pesticide sales per crop type.

is the biggest seller, and that some pesticides (with multi-colored stripes) can harm humans, the environment, and bees altogether.

Here again is an example of a design strategy that creates more visual diversity, more elements for the eyes to wander over and spend a little time investigating.

For a second article, I created a visual that splits the sales per crop type (figure 8.2). I manipulated the design so the data points fit into a diamond shape instead of a circle. These alterations signaled to the reader that the two graphics were for different articles, each with its own focus.

I had explored a different design earlier in the creation process (figure 8.3). I used small, scaled circles for the pesticides and grouped them in larger circles. Within each group, I placed the colored hazardous pesticides on the left and the benign gray ones on the right. However, I didn't like all the white space this created within the larger circles. I also felt that the split into the colored HHPs and gray not-HHP circles was more challenging to grasp. And, most importantly, the aggregated values got lost with the approach.

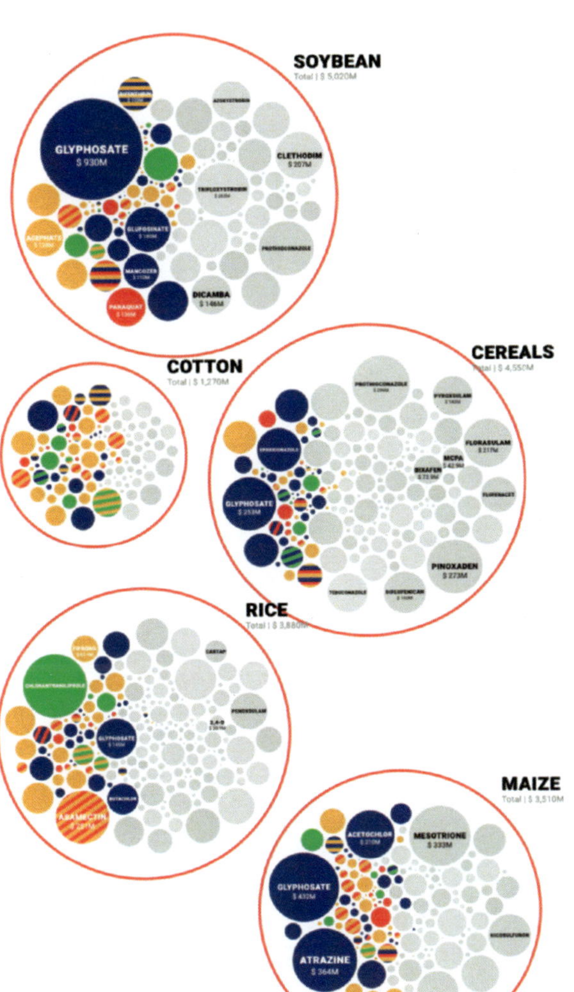

Figure 8.3

A draft design that shows each pesticide as a scaled circle, clustered by crop type. This treatment, with the colorful HHPs on the left of each grouping and gray non-hazardous pesticides on the right, does not immediately convey the overall share that is hazardous.

Clustering satellites into rectangles

BUSINESS | 2020 | *SCIENTIFIC AMERICAN*
scientificamerican.com/article/how-do-we-prevent-war-in-space

Scientific American asked me to visualize Earth's active satellites for a "Space Wars" article. The main goal was to convey which countries owned the satellites in each orbital region (e.g., low, medium, or geosynchronous orbit). I could have built a stacked bar chart of the countries with bars split by orbit, or vice versa.

8.3 However, I received the data for each satellite, which had a lot of extra interesting information, such as weight, age, category, and more. With nearly 3,000 active satellites in space at the time, I realized that I could plot each as a circle, scaled in size by weight, and styled based on that extra information.

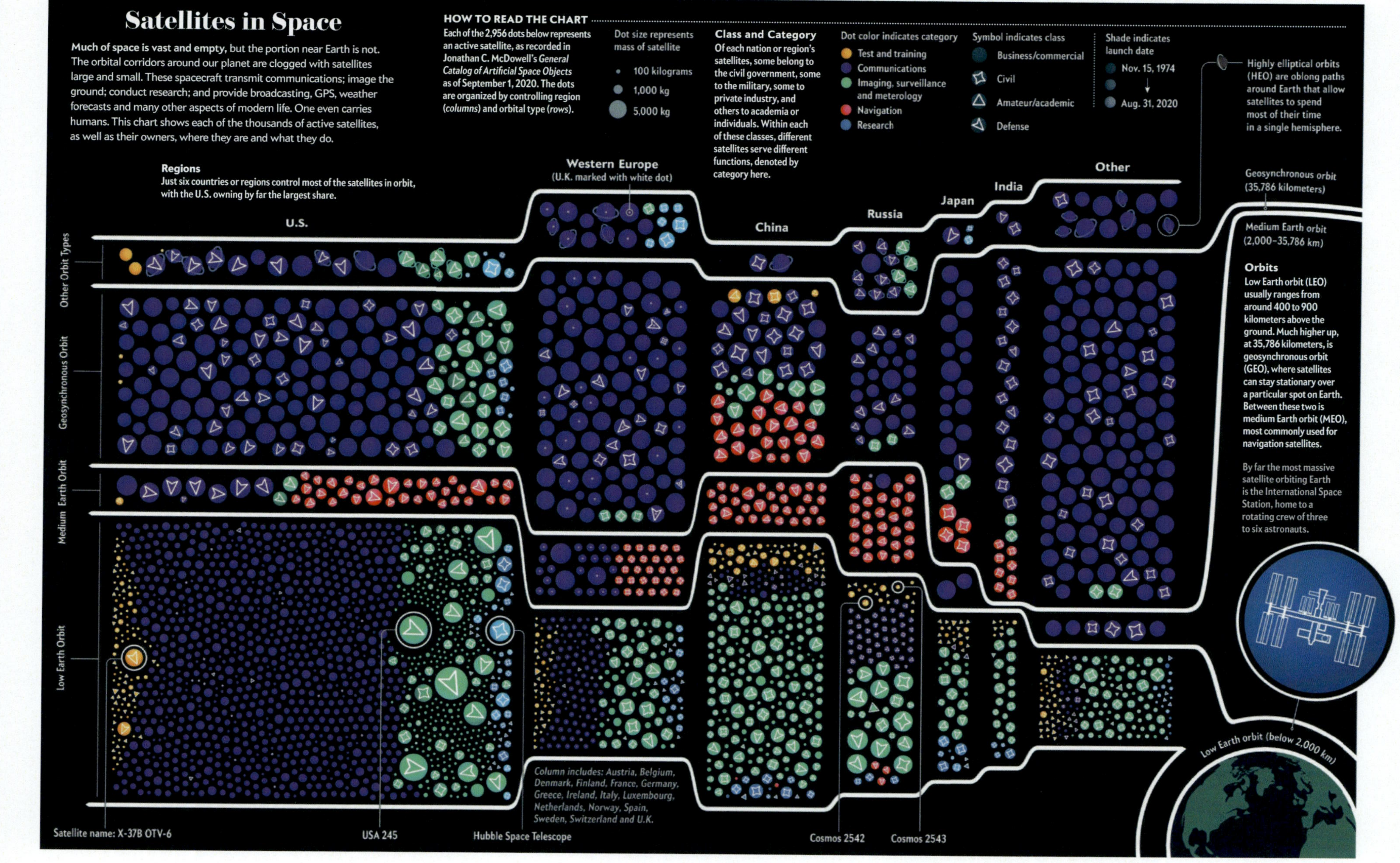

Satellites in Space
Much of space is vast and empty, but the portion near Earth is not. The orbital corridors around our planet are clogged with satellites large and small. These spacecraft transmit communications; image the ground; conduct research; and provide broadcasting, GPS, weather forecasts and many other aspects of modern life. One even carries humans. This chart shows each of the thousands of active satellites, as well as their owners, where they are and what they do.
HOW TO READ THE CHART
Each of the 2,956 dots below represents an active satellite, as recorded in Jonathan C. McDowell's *General Catalog of Artificial Space Objects* as of September 1, 2020. The dots are organized by controlling region (*columns*) and orbital type (*rows*).
Dot size represents mass of satellite
100 kilograms
1,000 kg
5,000 kg
Class and Category
Of each nation or region's satellites, some belong to the civil government, some to the military, some to private industry, and others to academia or individuals. Within each of these classes, different satellites serve different functions, denoted by category here.
Dot color indicates category
Test and training
Communications
Imaging, surveillance and meterology
Navigation
Research
Symbol indicates class
Business/commercial
Civil
Amateur/academic
Defense
Shade indicates launch date
Nov. 15, 1974
Aug. 31, 2020
Highly elliptical orbits (HEO) are oblong paths around Earth that allow satellites to spend most of their time in a single hemisphere.
Regions
Just six countries or regions control most of the satellites in orbit, with the U.S. owning by far the largest share.
U.S.
Western Europe
(U.K. marked with white dot)
China
Russia
Japan
India
Other
Other Orbit Types
Geosynchronous Orbit
Medium Earth Orbit
Low Earth Orbit
Geosynchronous orbit (35,786 kilometers)
Medium Earth orbit (2,000–35,786 km)
Orbits
Low Earth orbit (LEO) usually ranges from around 400 to 900 kilometers above the ground. Much higher up, at 35,786 kilometers, is geosynchronous orbit (GEO), where satellites can stay stationary over a particular spot on Earth. Between these two is medium Earth orbit (MEO), most commonly used for navigation satellites.
By far the most massive satellite orbiting Earth is the International Space Station, home to a rotating crew of three to six astronauts.
Low Earth orbit (below 2,000 km)
Column includes: Austria, Belgium, Denmark, Finland, France, Germany, Greece, Ireland, Italy, Luxembourg, Netherlands, Norway, Spain, Sweden, Switzerland and U.K.
Satellite name: X-37B OTV-6
USA 245
Hubble Space Telescope
Cosmos 2542
Cosmos 2543

8.4

Figure 8.4

The final result of the "Space Wars" visual revealing the nearly 3,000 active satellites in space, per country and orbital type.

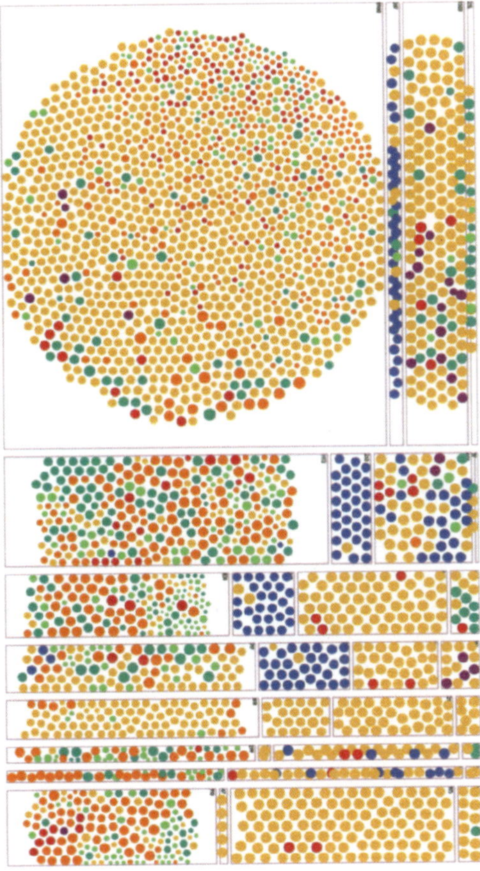

8.5

Figure 8.5

A work-in-progress screenshot displays all the rectangles still sized according to the "average satellite radius" process and how the actual satellite circles fit within them.

This visual uses techniques in Lesson 3's "Combine Charts" and Lesson 6's "Don't Think in Chart Types.

You may recall my sketches for this project (figure 5.6). In the final design (figure 8.4), I used something similar to a treemap, or Marimekko chart, which is akin to a two-dimensional stacked bar chart, where one variable scales to the width of the stacked bars, and a different variable scales to the height. The two main variables—the country and the orbit—become a grid of sorts: Countries run vertically, and orbits run horizontally. At each country-orbit intersection, I placed all the corresponding satellite circles. This layout shows that the United States has by far the most satellites, and so many tiny ones in low Earth orbit!

With so many circles, there's a lot of visual diversity. But there were other benefits to showing the individual satellites. For instance, I could specifically call out a few famous ones, like the Hubble Space Telescope (US column, low Earth orbit row), and the satellites mentioned in the story, such as the two Cosmos satellites (Russia column, low Earth orbit row). This makes it possible for a reader to compare these satellites to all the others, adding that extra layer of context.

To make this visual, I started with a general formula that approximated the amount of area on the page required to fit all the satellite circles, assuming that they were all the same "average" size. I then clustered the circles by country and orbit and I enclosed each cluster into a rectangle. Using that setup as a base, I had to manually increase or decrease the size of the rectangles (see figure 8.5 for a work in progress).

WHEN TO AGGREGATE WITHOUT SHOWING DETAILED DATA

As much as I've extolled the benefits of showing all the data (Lesson 7) or at least a moderately detailed view of the data (Lesson 8—up till this point), there are certainly cases where showing the aggregated values is the best approach. I find this happens when people need to understand the visual quickly, which means the aggregated values must be easier to identify (sometimes at the expense of creativity). It can also happen when there are enough aggregated values to be visually diverse, or there isn't enough room on the canvas to draw each underlying data point.

Figure 8.6

The final page of the "Satellite Surge" article, which visualized almost the same data as the "Space Wars" visual but aggregated the satellites to show just orbit and weight class groups.

Part of me is also sad for the stories that are "lost" in this version, such as the timeline of each separate satellite (which would reveal the oldest satellite that is still active, for example).

Aggregating the satellites into orbits and weights

BUSINESS | 2020 | *SCIENTIFIC AMERICAN*
scientificamerican.com/article/satellites-in-low-orbits-are-taking-over-the-skies

For example, a few months before working on the "Space Wars" visual, I used a slightly different version of the same data to create the image in figure 8.6 for a different *Scientific American* article. It shows how the number of satellites in space has grown, split by orbit type (color) and weight class (tint).

For one, there was not enough space on the page for each of the 2,000 satellites to have their own lines. Even if they could all fit, the lines would be too thin for the reader to decipher the color and shade. There was also already enough going on with the weight class bands overtaking each other at various places—as they are arranged by prevalence—especially in the yellow "lower low Earth orbit" lines. Therefore, I decided that aggregating the satellites to show the total by orbit and weight class was the optimal level of detail in this particular case.

Balancing the data details with higher-level aggregations in a visual manner allows the reader to explore the data's nuances, discovering patterns and stories beneath the surface. Therefore, my advice is to always consider whether showing the most granular level of detail can create a compelling visual, even when the main goal is to show the aggregated values.

GRAPHIC SCIENCE

Text by Mark Fischetti | Graphic by Nadieh Bremer

Satellite Surge

Low-orbit instruments are taking over the skies

For decades the number of satellites orbiting Earth rose at a gentle pace, but growth has soared recently. By July 2019 more than 2,200 satellites were aloft. In the 1980s and 1990s the action was in geosynchronous orbit (*blues*), says Jonathan McDowell, an astrophysicist at the Center for Astrophysics | Harvard & Smithsonian. But now the action is in the lowest Earth orbits (*yellows*), he notes, and increasingly dominated by young companies rather than government, military or academic owners. The uptick started around 2014, stemming largely from CubeSats—diminutive satellites, each lighter than two kilograms, that were lofted in small groups.

Today the push is from Starlink—constellations of satellites weighing 260 kilograms, being launched by SpaceX to deliver high-speed Internet. CubeSats are fulfilling a desire to observe changes on Earth every day. They could reveal, for example, how people were moving around Wuhan, China, during the coronavirus outbreak. And instead of Google Earth showing a driveway with a car from 10 years ago, it could capture a vehicle purchased last week.

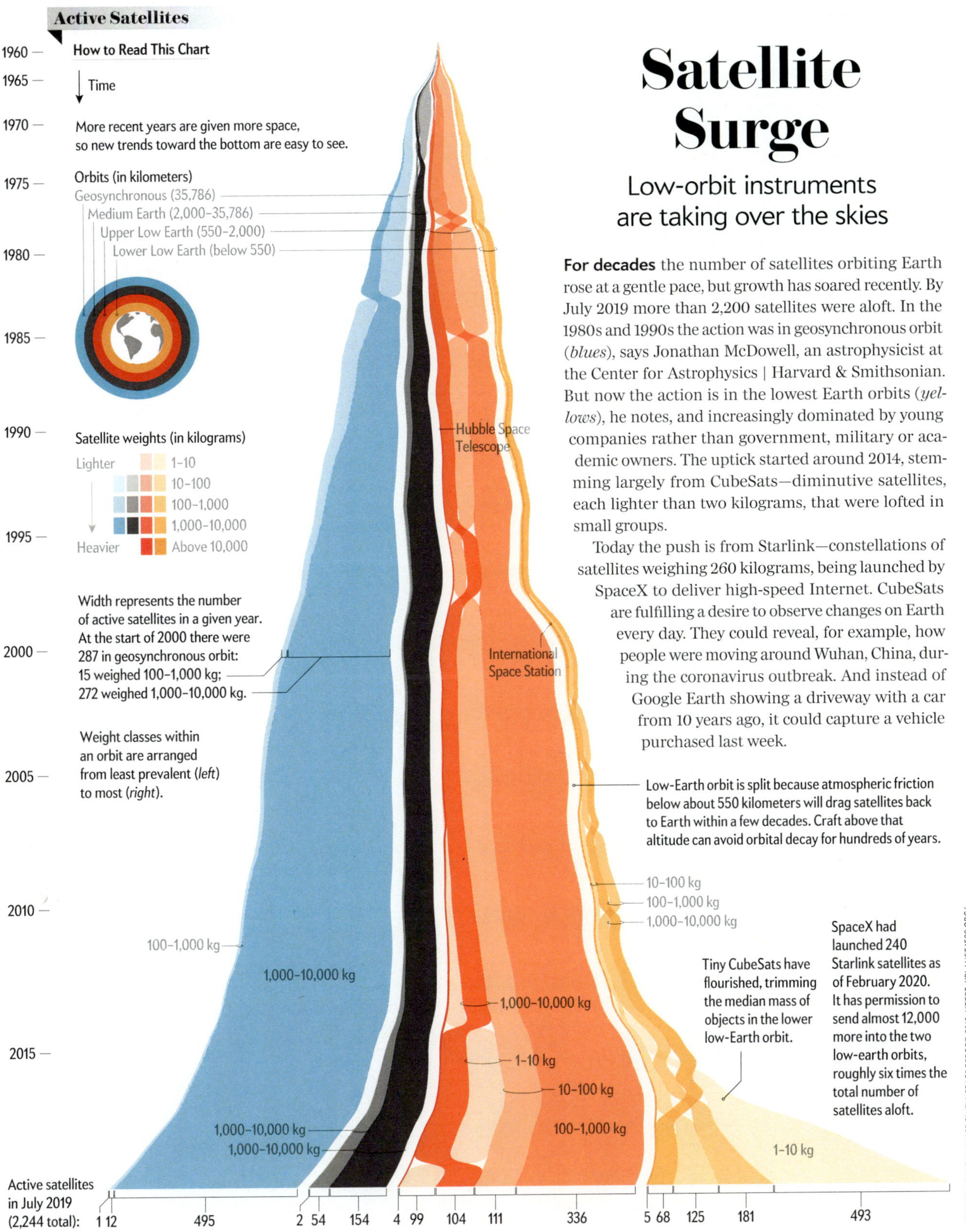

LESSON NINE

ADD MORE

Enhance your visuals by thoughtfully adding additional variables to provide greater depth and interest to the main story

I consider all the variables I have in the data, even if I can make the story's main point clear using only a few of them. The difference between this technique and what we've covered previously is that the visual diversity will stem from more data *categories,* not more data *items*. (If you think about this in spreadsheet terms, we're adding more columns of data instead of more rows of data.)

Working with variables requires some restraint. A key point for this lesson is to add only interesting variables that connect to the primary insight or that provide relevant context to each data point.

VARIABLES

Even with the same data set, what's interesting can vary based on the visual goal and audience. For example, when I visualized the 100 tallest skyscrapers, my focus was on height and location, along with relevant details like construction year and building function. Although the data set included other variables, such as materials and architect names, I left them out, as they didn't enhance the story I wanted to tell. However, if my goal had been to explore skyscrapers from an architectural perspective, details like the architect and materials would have been essential.

MY PROCESS FOR ADDING MORE VARIABLES

Let's look at variables in the context of two designs. I'll explain my thought process, reasons for making certain choices, and steps to add more variables.

Squeezing in as much information as possible

BUSINESS | 2020 | *SCIENTIFIC AMERICAN*
scientificamerican.com/article/how-do-we-prevent-war-in-space

Let's return to the "Space Wars" project (figure 9.1) with its 3,000 satellites. Satellites were clustered by country and orbital type. However, I had all of this fascinating information about each satellite, such as its weight, age, and much more. I needed to strike the right balance between visual intrigue and information overload.

My approach starts by deciding which variables would be interesting to add. I first order them from most to least vital to showing the main insight. I also consider which of the remaining variables would add interesting context. This will help me later when I consider how to add them to the visual and how prominent or subtle their encodings should be—I want the visual hierarchy (what the viewer notices first, what is easiest to read) to match the hierarchy of information.

I then look at the visual channels that are still available. As a reminder, a visual channel is a way to encode data. Color, shape, and size are visual channels, for example.

When I began building the "Space Wars" visualization, each satellite was a uniform circle. I positioned them on a loose grid of countries (columns) and orbits (rows). Next, I wanted to connect the remaining variables to visual channels to see which would pair nicely—or even metaphorically. I cannot overstate the power of good metaphors, especially when a visual gets more elaborate. With a good metaphor, it takes less effort for our minds to remember what the visual encoding means.

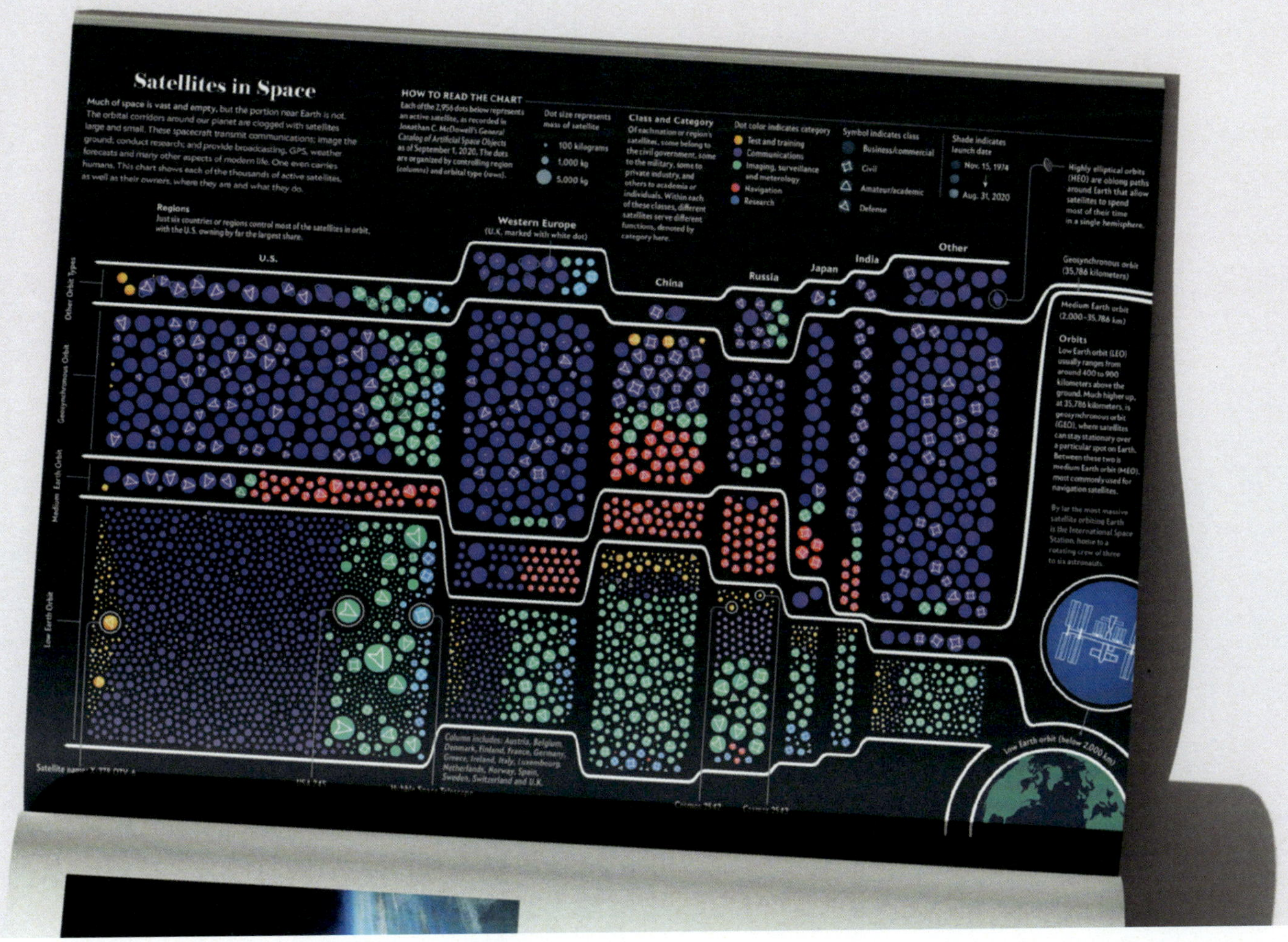

9.1

Figure 9.1

The "Space Wars" graphic.

For example, using circle size for the satellite's weight seemed like a good metaphor: the bigger, the heavier. (Variables that show weight, volume, height or some other physical characteristic generally work well for sizing your visual marks.)

Opacity made sense for age, where older satellites were more faded.

Next was the satellite's purpose (research, imaging, navigation, etc.). This variable didn't have an apparent visual metaphor. Nevertheless, I thought it was one of the most interesting extra variables since a satellite's purpose explains why it got shot into space in the first place! Therefore, I applied this variable to color—a very clear way to distinguish the satellites. Sometimes colors can be metaphorical so readers can deduce which category goes with which color, but that wasn't the case here; readers may need to keep referencing the legend to remember which color is which category.

Figure 9.2

Zooming in on the "Space Wars" graphic to better see the different encodings used to convey satellite variables like weight, purpose, and age.

Another variable was satellite class (such as defense or commercial). In 2020, the president initiated the United States Space Force, so it felt like a timely and relevant variable to encode. By this point, though, many of the more "standard" visual channels (position, color, and opacity) were already assigned. Changing the circles into other shapes seemed like a good option, and I couldn't resist using a shape inspired by the Space Force logo for the "defense" class as a tiny joke. However, after some tests I found that an icon inside a circle was more visually pleasing than altering the entire shape. For a final touch of finesse, I randomly oriented the circles.

I consciously did not assign an icon to the most common class (business/commercial). The absence of a visual marker can work just as well to distinguish a category, as long as all the other options do have an icon. My reason for this treatment in this case was to keep the visual from getting too busy.

The visual was already very robust, with multiple variables on display. But I still added a tiny ellipse around the few satellites with highly elliptical orbits. I very much enjoy ~~hiding~~ adding subtle yet clever details to a visualization, like small easter eggs, that reward people who do a more detailed inspection. I thought highlighting elliptical orbits was relatively low on the "interesting context" scale—someone else might have said it wasn't interesting enough to make the cut—but the astronomer in me still saw something there. What convinced me was the solid visual metaphor of the ellipse around the circle. Furthermore,

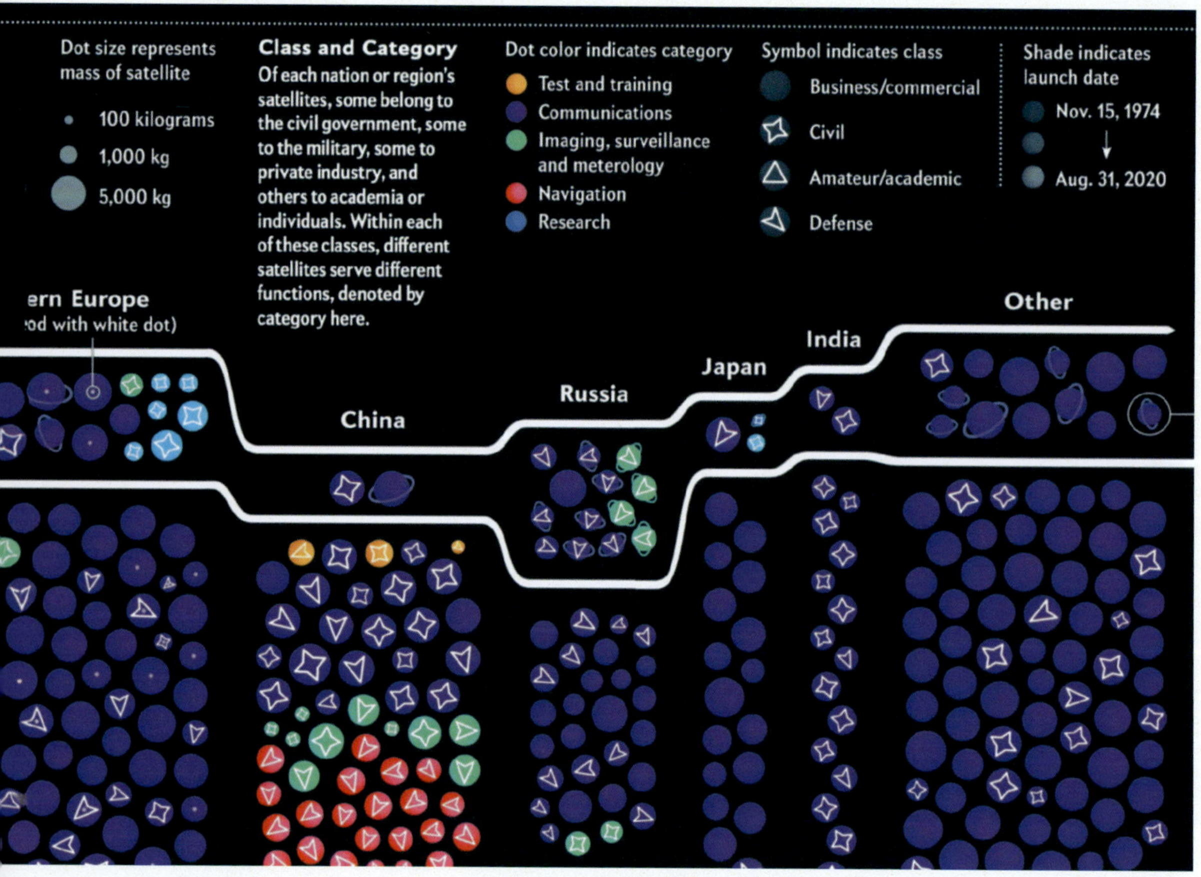

9.2

since only a few satellites had the ellipse, they didn't create a distraction (they might even pique someone's interest to figure out what the little ellipses even mean).

In the end, I left a bunch of variables on the cutting room floor, including satellite maneuverability, the scientific areas of the research satellites, and a lot of information about the launch (type of rocket thruster, number of stages, and so on).

Choosing variables is a balance between offering the most relevant information, complementing the existing visual encodings, and leveraging possible metaphors. But you also need to navigate constraints such as how and where it's displayed (a social media post or a large poster) and client requests (the colors or even the shapes you can use).

Beeswarms and epicenters

BUSINESS | 2024 | CÆMPUS

visualcinnamon.com/portfolio/amsterdam-startup-landscape

When the Amsterdam Center for Entrepreneurship (ACE), an Amsterdam startup incubator for students, researchers, and academics, relaunched and rebranded into Cæmpus, I created a visual entitled "Amsterdam Startup Landscape" about the startups that ACE and three of its affiliated Amsterdam Universities had coached.

Figure 9.3

The "Amsterdam Startup Landscape" slide that visualizes more than 300 startups that launched out of the three Amsterdam universities (left) and ACE (right).

Given that this visual focused on the history of the incubators, the most important variable was the founding year of the startups—more than 300 of them. Another important variable was the technology sector in which the startups operated. To effectively convey this information, I placed the founding year along the horizontal axis and the technology sectors along the vertical axis (assigning each technology to its own row). This layout leverages position as a visual channel. And it's one of the strongest visual channels, at that—statisticians at AT&T Bell Laboratories found in the 1980s that placement helps people very effectively interpret the information.

The result was a beeswarm chart, which shows how the data is distributed across categories without overlapping the points that belong on the same spot. In this case, each startup is positioned at its founding year but does not overlap with the others from the same year.

Figure 9.3 shows the final visual, optimized for a slide deck (hence the aspect ratio and large font size). Because ACE used a different

Amsterdam Startup Landscape

Placed according to founding year & technology, and sized by the number of employees and funding

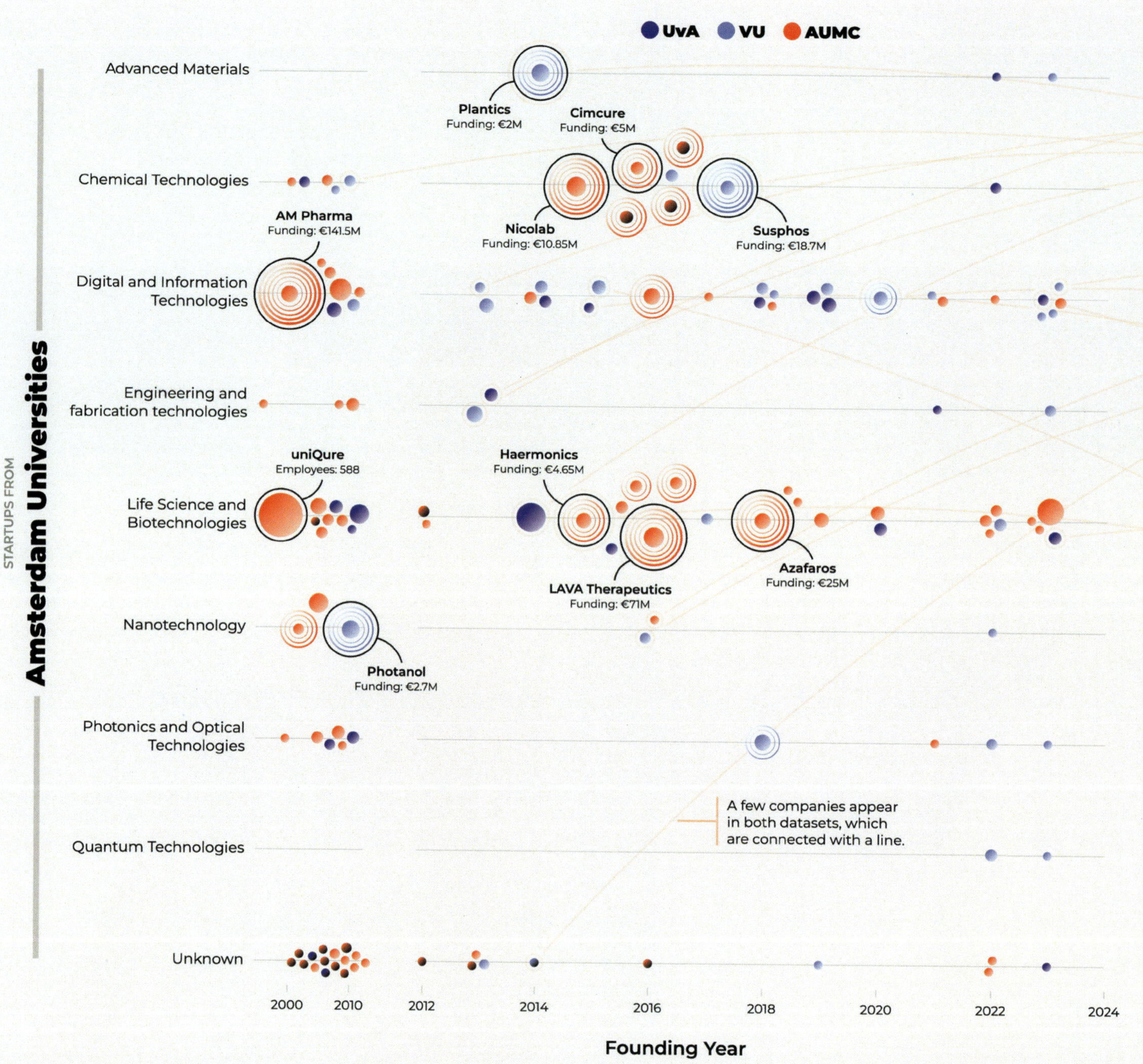

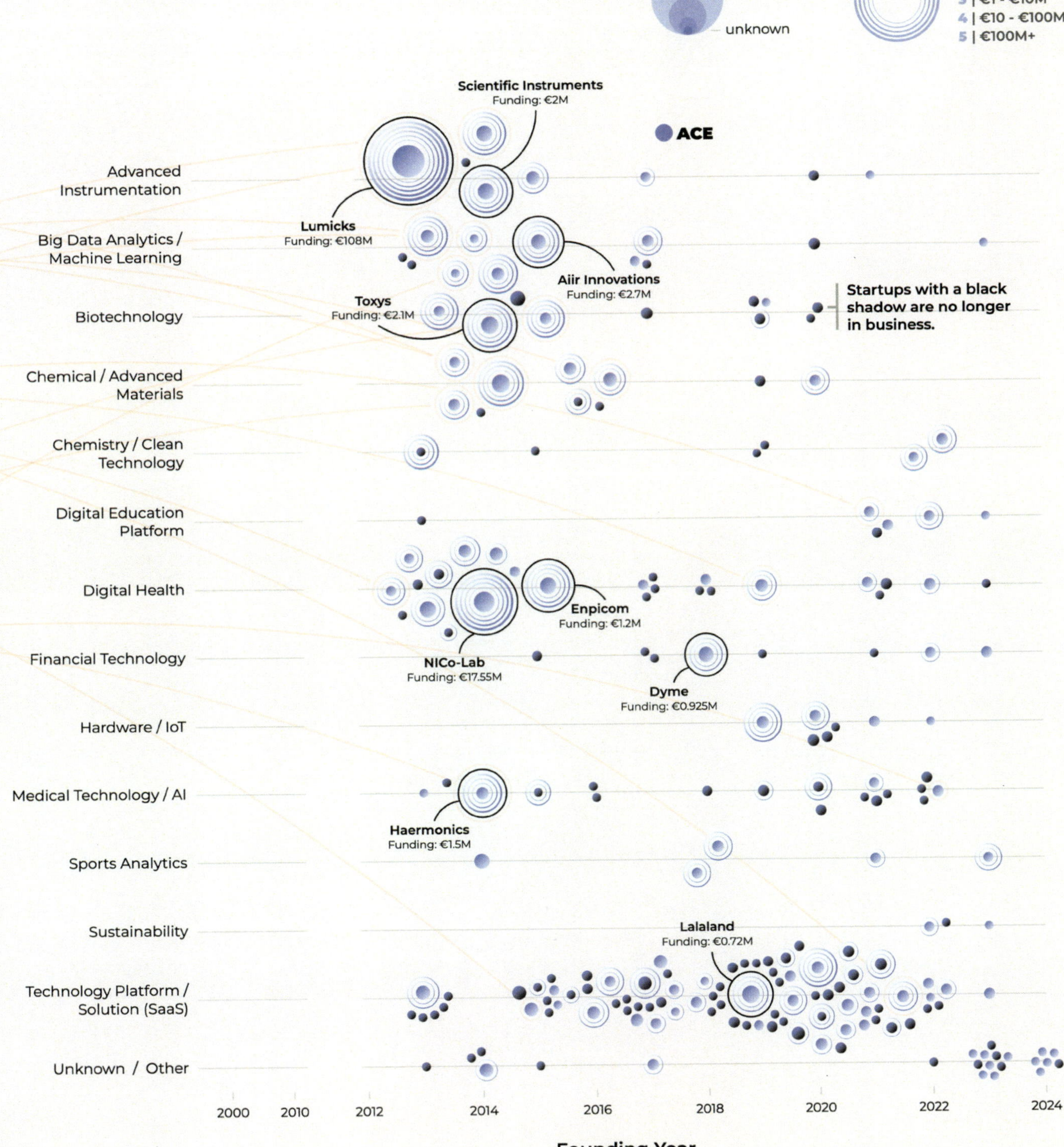

Employees
The larger the circle the more employees
unknown
Funding
number of rings
1 | €0 - €0.1M
2 | €0.1 - €1M
3 | €1 - €10M
4 | €10 - €100M
5 | €100M+
ACE
Scientific Instruments
Funding: €2M
Lumicks
Funding: €108M
Aiir Innovations
Funding: €2.7M
Toxys
Funding: €2.1M
Startups with a black shadow are no longer in business.
Enpicom
Funding: €1.2M
NICo-Lab
Funding: €17.55M
Dyme
Funding: €0.925M
Haermonics
Funding: €1.5M
Lalaland
Funding: €0.72M
Advanced Instrumentation
Big Data Analytics / Machine Learning
Biotechnology
Chemical / Advanced Materials
Chemistry / Clean Technology
Digital Education Platform
Digital Health
Financial Technology
Hardware / IoT
Medical Technology / AI
Sports Analytics
Sustainability
Technology Platform / Solution (SaaS)
Unknown / Other
STARTUPS FROM
ACE
2000
2010
2012
2014
2016
2018
2020
2022
2024
Founding Year

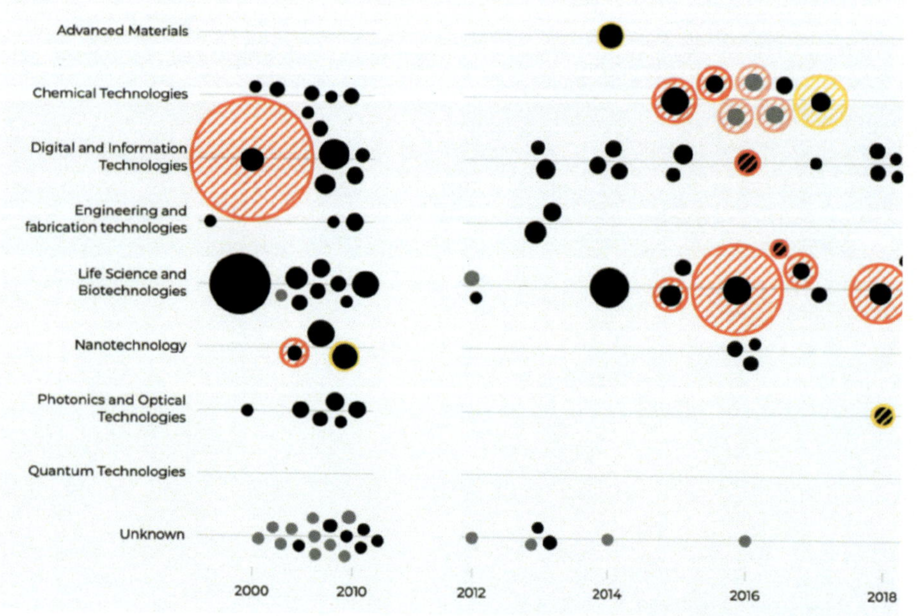

9.4

Figure 9.4

A work in progress where I was using hatched circles (on top of or behind the black employee-sized circle) to visualize the amount of funding a startup had received.

convention for technology sectors than the three universities, I split the slide to show both: universities on the left and ACE on the right.

Like the "Space Wars" visual before, I began with plain dots to represent the data points (startups). I tried to add many other variables about these startups to make the design more informational and visually intriguing. But I ran into a few problems. For instance, I wanted to show the funding received and encode it to the circle size. However, I realized that the data set contained too many zeros (funding is not something every company receives) or unknown amounts. Fortunately, the data set did have another suitable size variable: the number of employees.

Even though funding data wasn't available for most companies, it was important to show for the companies that did have this information, as this is seen as a measure of success. I initially tried adding a circle with hatched lines behind the dot. However, when the funding was small, it was hard to see the colorful funding circles on the black inner dots (figure 9.4). I tried several other ways to design the funding circle, but sadly, nothing solved the issue.

I then woke up on a Saturday with the idea to use outer rings instead of hatched circles; the more rings, the more funding. I immediately grabbed my laptop and implemented this idea. I liked how this treatment turned the funded startups into "epicenters," without interfering with the employee dot. I could then also give the inner employee dot and outer funding strokes the same color, to distinguish which university the startup was associated with.

I also knew which startups were still active—an interesting but not very uplifting variable. I first tried to give the inner employee dot of the out-of-business startups a black stroke, but they stood out too much. I eventually settled on a gradient that went from transparent in the top-left of the dot to full black toward the bottom-right (see figure 9.5). I called it "a black shadow." In contrast, the dots representing operational startups were opaque in the top left and transparent in the bottom right. It's noticeable, but not at all dominating.

Figure 9.5

A close-up of the "Amsterdam Startup Landscape" visual, where you can see several small circles with a "black shadow" indicating that they are no longer in business.

Finally, as a final and subtle touch, I connected the startups that appeared in both data sets with a thin, peach-colored line.

All these extra variables added more layers of information to the final result. At the Cæmpus relaunch event, we presented the visual to the audience and highlighted all the insights I'd pulled from the data. No one in attendance knew of my struggles to design those insights—that was my little secret.

9.5

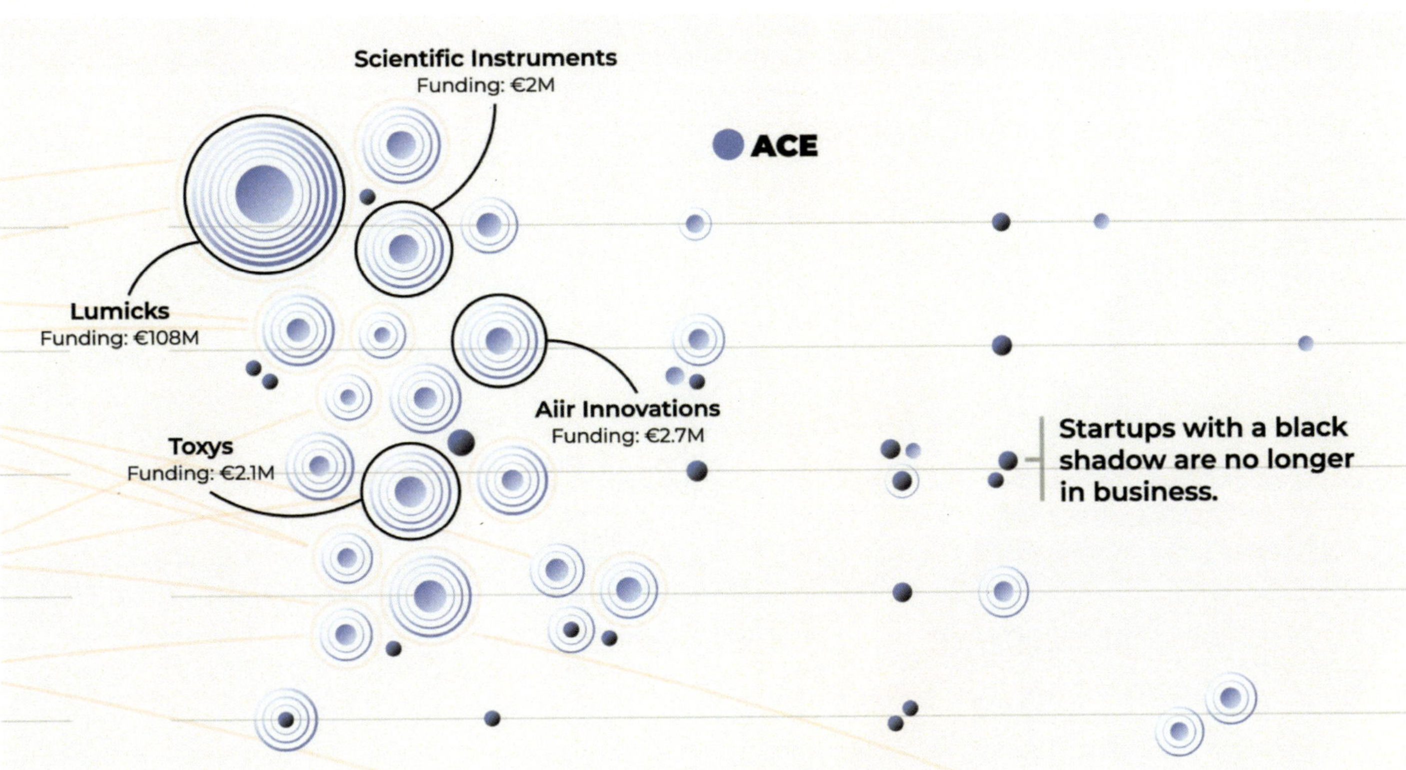

THE INFINITE WAYS TO ENCODE DATA

Some of the visual channels I see most often—and use most often myself—are:

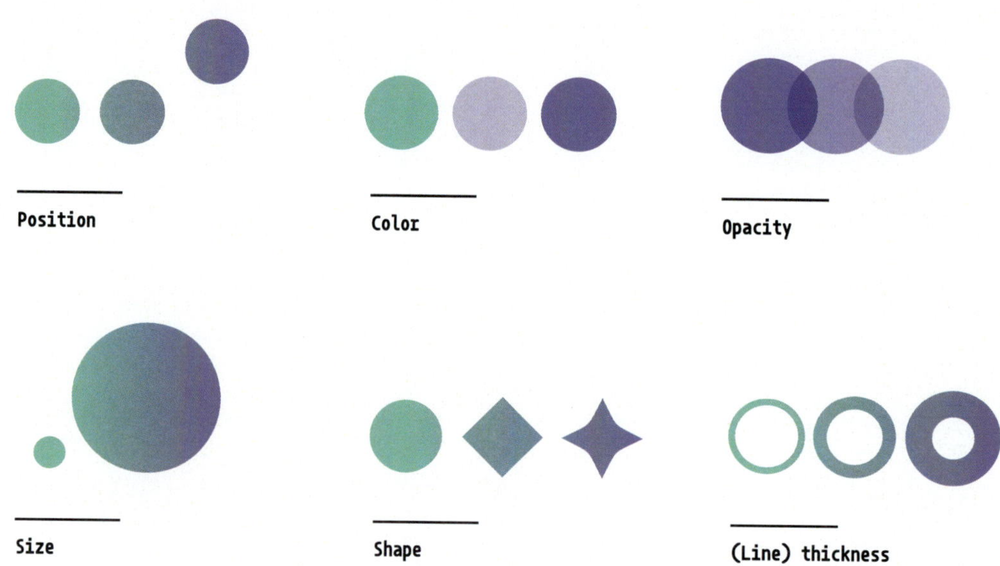

However, I'd say there are infinite ways to encode data. A short list of channels I've used in the past includes: the number of tiny dots around a central shape, edge blurriness, straight versus curved lines, sharp versus rounded angles, additional outer strokes (or even a whole mini donut chart around a central circle), glow, speed of movement, and so on.

Figure 9.6

The desktop version of the gravitational waves visual, with the outer circles scaled to the merger's mass, and positioned along a reverse chronological timeline. (The visual would get narrower and longer on mobile screens.)

And those feel like they're not even particularly inventive. I often see data visualization designers—who do more work by hand than by programming—finding the most unique ways to encode data into visual elements. As I mentioned in Lesson 5, drawing by hand lets you come up with more out-of-the-box ideas because you're not constrained by the options of your digital (drawing) program.

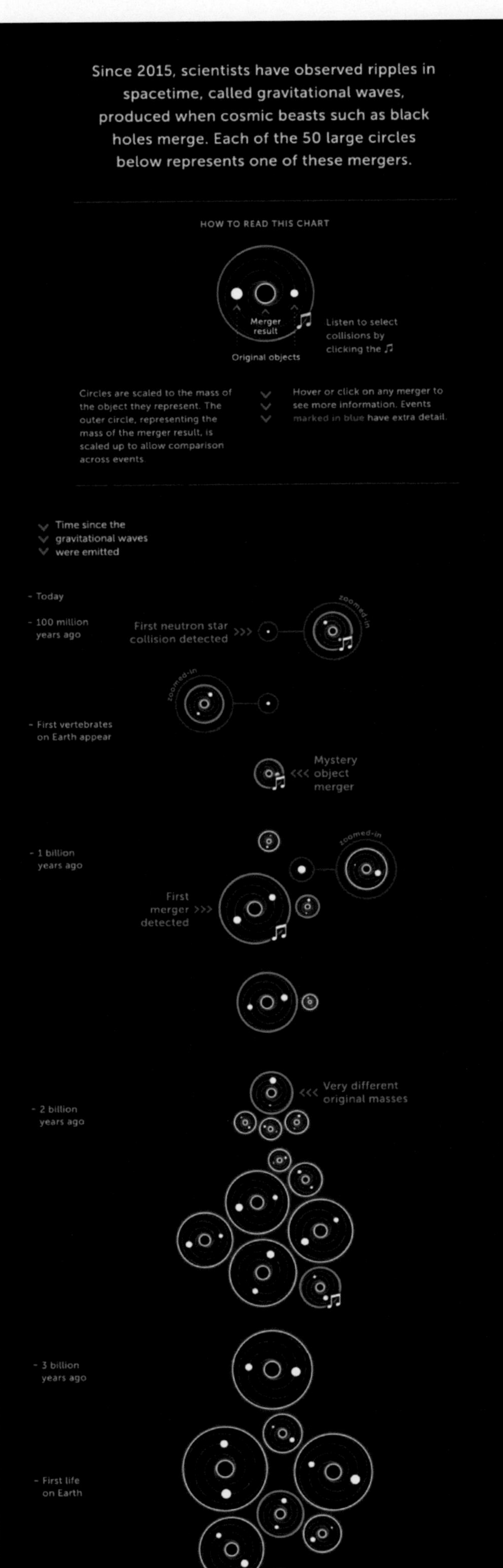

A mini scene inside each circle

BUSINESS | 2021 | *SCIENCE NEWS*
sciencenews.org/article/gravitational-waves-black-holes-spacetime-ligo-virgo

To close out this lesson, here's an example where I used extra variables in an unusual manner: presenting a whole "scene" within the data point.

For *Science News*, I created an interactive visual for online—and a static version for print—that highlighted gravitational wave events. These ripples through spacetime are caused by the violent collisions of black holes (and/or neutron stars) dating back billions of years.

Figure 9.6 shows the final result for the scrollable online visual—a series of 50 spirals representing gravitational wave events spotted between 2015 (when the first event was observed) and 2019. The outer circle, which contains the spirals, is scaled to the mass of the object that was born from the collision. The scroll was in reverse chronological order: The farther down the graphic, the further in the past the event happened. As with the "Amsterdam Startup Landscape," this visual is also a beeswarm, with circles clustering around a point in time but not overlapping.

The merger event occurs when two objects, usually black holes, spiral into each other, collide, and form a new (more massive) black hole. Therefore, I thought it would be interesting to show variables about the original two objects, as they can be different (neutron stars or black holes) and can have very different masses.

Figure 9.7 presents a rough sketch that illustrates my idea. Each gravitational wave is represented as a large white circle, scaled to reflect the mass of the merger object. At the center of each circle is the merger object itself, depicted on a smaller scale, while the two original objects orbit around it, also scaled according to their masses. The spiral patterns emphasize the concept of these objects spiraling into one another.

With this design, I couldn't resist creating an animation. When the viewer hovers over a circle, the original objects spiral into each other, forming one black hole. Although the animation was only a second or two, this made the visual more engaging to interact with and encouraged the reader to explore it a bit more.

Each gravitational wave had additional variables that I presented in popup text boxes. Incredibly, one variable was sonifications of some of the merger events, so I added a musical note icon in the lower right corner of the circles, prompting the viewer to click and listen.

In this project, I only added a few extra variables, the main one being the size/mass information about the two original objects. However, the unconventional way I added them, inspired by the actual physical event, created visual diversity and a strong metaphor to make the final result stand out.

Figure 9.7

The sketch for the gravitational waves visual. (I need to work on my spiral drawing skills.)

Figure 9.8

A pop-up text box that supplied more detailed information about the merger, as well as the rough location on the sky the merger happened.

9.7

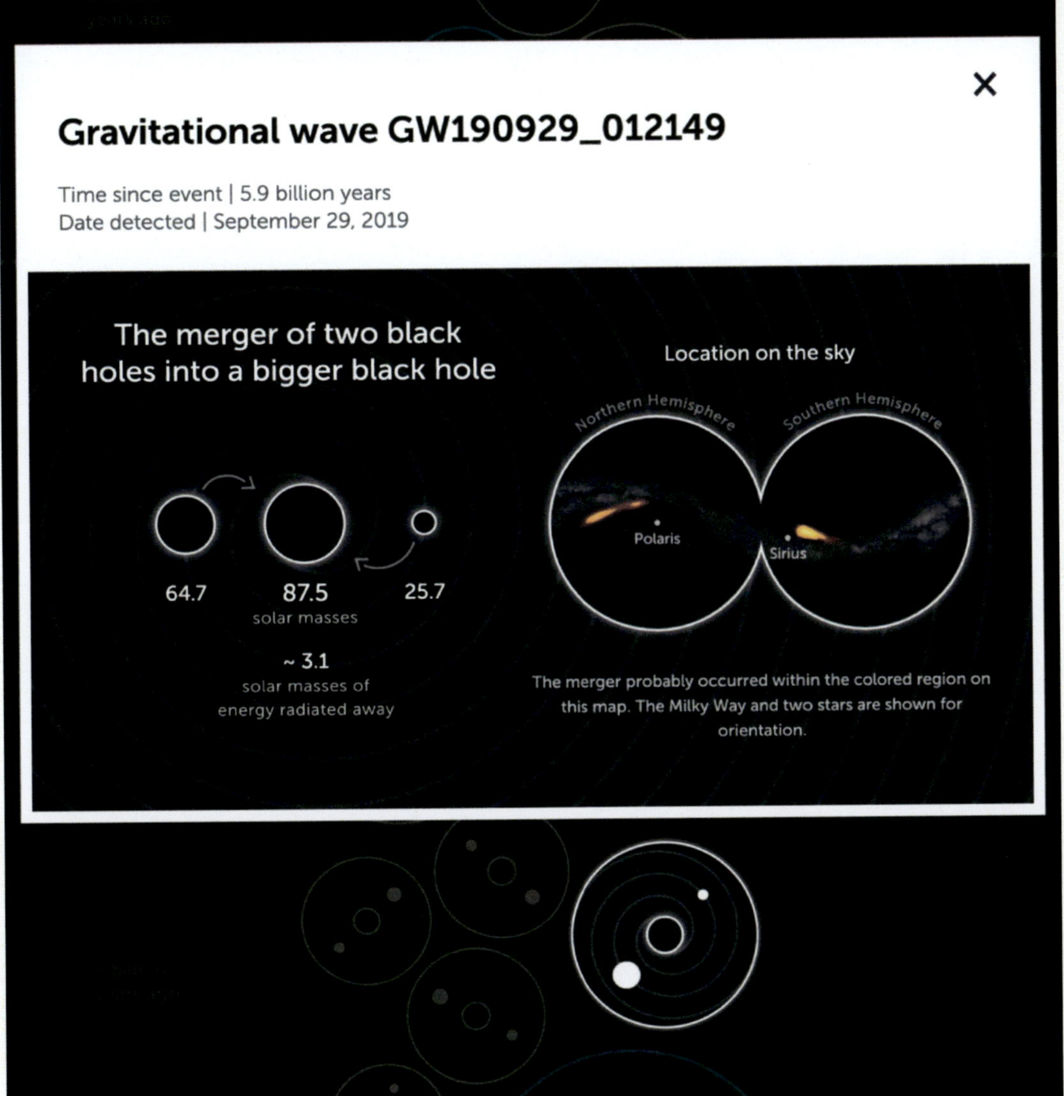

9.8

What your eyes have seen and the media you've been exposed to most recently will affect your thinking in the current moment. Your visuals today would probably look somewhat different if you had made them a few months or years ago (regardless of any new skills learned). That doesn't mean they would have been better or worse because there is no "best" option; part of it comes down to taste and what you know.

As you consider ways to visually encode data, especially the less conventional approaches, I recommend taking some time to think about your ideas and to sketch them out. Keep in mind that even though there are many ways to encode variables, not all are easy for the viewer to understand. This is why I put a heavy emphasis on metaphors; the stronger the encoding metaphor, the easier it is for the viewer to absorb all that information at once without feeling overwhelmed.

In the end, hitting the main point of your visual is most important. Adding the extra variables should not stand in the way of that. By keeping the original goal in mind, you can assess whether any additional variables truly work. And by finding visual channels that pair well with the variables, you can turn your visualization into something more engaging to look at.

REFINING YOUR USE OF COLOR

A nice-looking color palette can have a massive impact on a chart's visual appeal. That's why I always spend a good amount of time iterating colors (unless there are fixed color schemes demanded by the brand that I have to adhere to). However, there's so much more to color than just the color selection—once you start playing with options like gradients and color blending. These techniques can truly take your color game up a notch.

GRADIENTS

I'm a big fan of using gradients in my visuals to get a more refined result. Sometimes the color transitions are obvious, and sometimes they are so subtle that I might be the only one to notice.

Perhaps the best-known gradient method is to use two (or more) colors to fill a shape. Another method, often underused, is to apply a gradient along a line or a stroke. For example, a line connecting two circles of different colors can feature a gradient that seamlessly blends the colors of the circles (as in figure IV.1).

Gradients don't need to be multi-color; they can transition a single color to a lighter/darker or a more/less saturated version of that color. (See the solar panel line charts in figure 1.5.)

They can also have a tiny shift in hue, adding a pinch of red to an orange, for example. These gentle color changes provide a little extra visual dimension without being in your face (the satellite circles in figure 8.4 are all filled with a subtle gradient).

Figure IV.1

There is a lot to unpack in this interactive network visualization for Mozilla's ORCA project that shows how top contributors of pdf.js are connected to (other) repositories. But the one thing you should notice is that the lines are filled with gradients based on the colors of the connected circles. You can see and interact with the visual on *nbremer.github.io/ORCA/top-contributor-network*

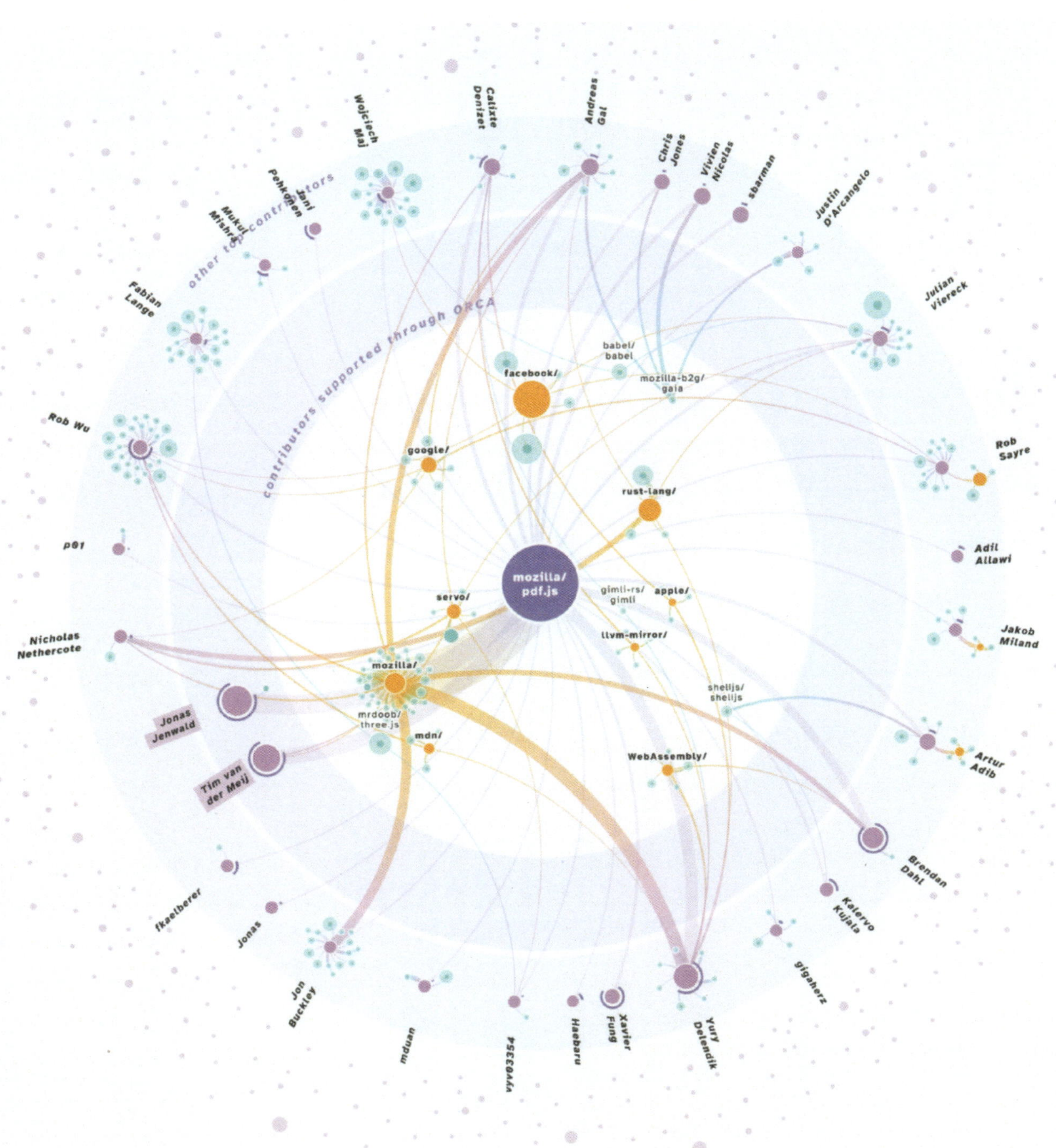

IV.1

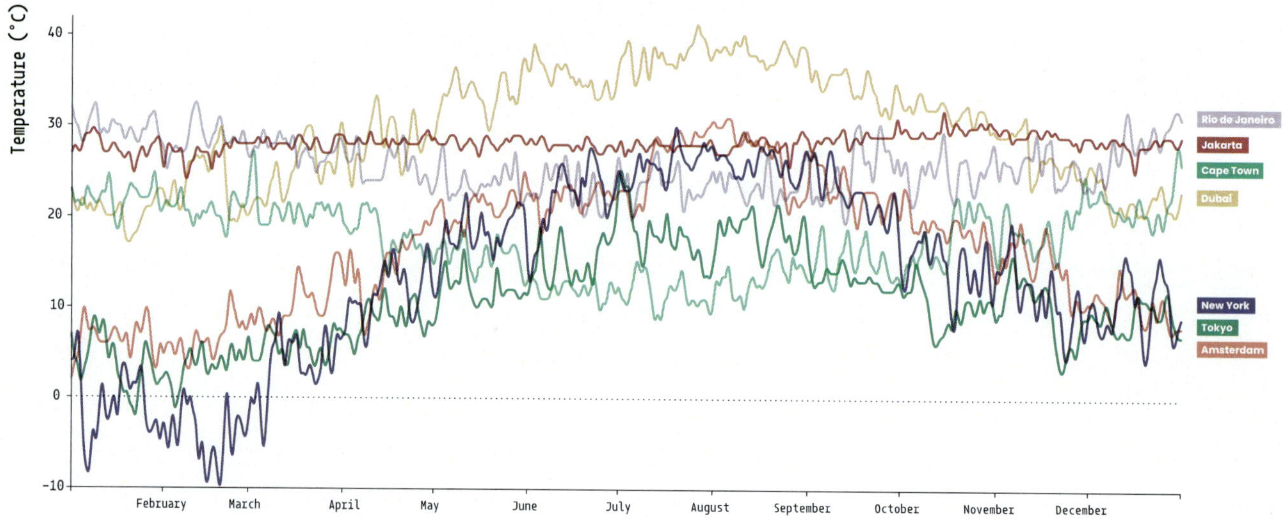

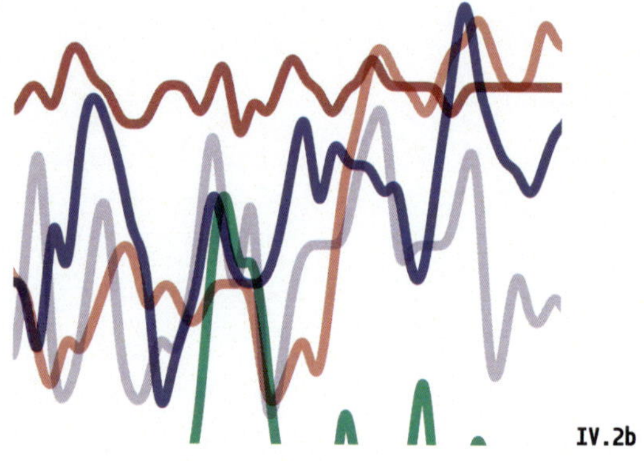

Figure IV.2a & b

A multi-color line chart of average daily temperatures for several places around the world. A *multiply* color blend mode allows colors to mix together when the lines intersect, making it impossible to see which line was drawn "on top" of another (a) with a zoom in to better see the color blending (b).

If the visual is a static and standalone piece (such as a poster) or doesn't need to color-coordinate with a website or dashboard, I like to apply a subtle gradient to my visuals' entire background. I usually go from the main color in the top-left to a slightly darker version in the lower-right corner of the canvas.

This is almost impossible to notice consciously, but it definitely adds a more refined touch to the whole design.

Finally, gradients don't need to transition from one tone to the other perfectly smoothly. Sometimes, I find that it looks better if I divide the gradient into discrete color steps. You can see my favorite example of this technique in the forthcoming baby births visual in figure 11.4. (Online tools such as the "Chroma.js Color Palette Helper" can help you determine the in-between colors based on the number of steps.)

COLOR BLENDING

With color blending, colors can mix in fascinating ways. The color of a shape will blend with the background and/or overlapping shapes according to a specific mathematical formula.

I find that color blending only works in a specific realm of options; too many layers of overlapping shapes often aren't appealing, but just the right number and balance can look amazing.

Even if you don't do it for the purely aesthetic effect it brings, I can still recommend applying a color blend when you have overlapping shapes. In the multi-color line chart of figure IV.2, I applied a so-called *multiply* blend mode to make line intersections a (darker) mix of both colors.

For a *multiply* blend mode, in more technical terms, the RGB value of one color is multiplied by the RGB value of another color. The formula applies to each of the three channels (red, green, and blue) separately. This results in a darker color, up to fully black. This is why having too many overlapping shapes doesn't work well with *multiply*: Add enough shapes on top of each other and the result will be all black.

Blending colors makes it impossible to know which line or shape is drawn "on top" of the other. It eliminates any bias that the order of drawing could have potentially created. I've used this tactic countless times, such as in the radial line charts of the upcoming pharmaceuticals visual in figure 10.2. It's pretty subtle—so much so that a reader probably won't truly notice it—which is a good thing!

Besides *multiply* blend mode, my other favorite color blend mode is *screen*, which is the inverse of *multiply* and makes colors lighter (the consumer opinions visual in figure 7.1). However, I also occasionally use *lighter* (resulting in a lighter color, but in a different way than *screen*), *lighten,* and *darken* (which retains either the lightest or the darkest color).

Using gradients and color blending enhances the color palette's appeal and effectiveness across the entire data visualization spectrum, from traditional charts to data art.

Normal [no color blend mode]

Blend mode [*multiply*]

IV.3

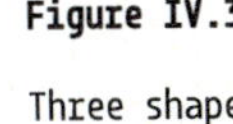

Figure IV.3

Three shapes overlapping without any color blending (top) and with a *multiply* blend mode applied (bottom); for the bottom version, it's impossible to tell which shape was placed on top of the others.

These blend modes may be named differently depending on the tool, and some tools might even have a larger set of blending options than what I've mentioned here.

LESSON TEN

BIG DATA SETS,

Bigger data sets lend themselves more easily to creative data visualization

The more data I have to work with, the more creative I can be. That's why I love working with big and diverse data sets. "Big" is somewhat subjective, but I consider it to be around 1,000 data values or more. In this lesson, I'm going to walk you through some of the biggest data sets I've ever had to work with to show you some extremes. But first, let's talk about getting into the right mindset to find and embrace all the data you can get your hands on.

Data sets tend to be big if they have many variables (columns), many data points (rows), or both. But they can also become big if you combine data sets together. The bigger the data set, the more options there will be to deploy the strategies from the previous three lessons: show all the data, use granular data to present aggregations, and include many variables. Combining these strategies can be extremely powerful and can yield a truly unique visual with both nuance and context.

BIG

POSSIBILITIES

Therefore, if you have an opportunity to increase the size of your data, don't pass it up. If your client asks, "I also have this extra information—do you want it?" or, "How far back in time do you want the data?," you should reply with, "I'd like everything that you can give me." Or better yet, proactively ask your client if more information is available: more variables, more history, or complementary data sets to enrich the main one. Perhaps you, yourself, can find a public data set to connect to the client's data!

You're not obligated to use all of it. After analyzing the data, you can always decide which supplemental variables to include, how much history to show, and where to possibly aggregate the data that's otherwise too detailed. Remember, you can always aggregate the data up (calculating means, totals, per day/week/category, etc.). But you can't drill down (e.g., from total sales to each separate sale) if the data set contains only aggregated values. So the more granular the data is, the more options you have.

Several projects I've discussed in previous chapters were more than big enough for me to pick and choose how to increase visual diversity, as the size and variety of the data set gave me multiple ways of approaching the design. But none were quite as large, or turned into something as complex, as the ones I'm about to show you.

The "Landscape of Power Flows" project from the end of Lesson 5 would've also fitted right at home in this Lesson.

Aggregating the data requires a bit of care. In some cases you should consider using a weighted average instead of a straight average. And some data are better presented as a median than an average (if there are extreme outliers, for example).

10.2

10.1a

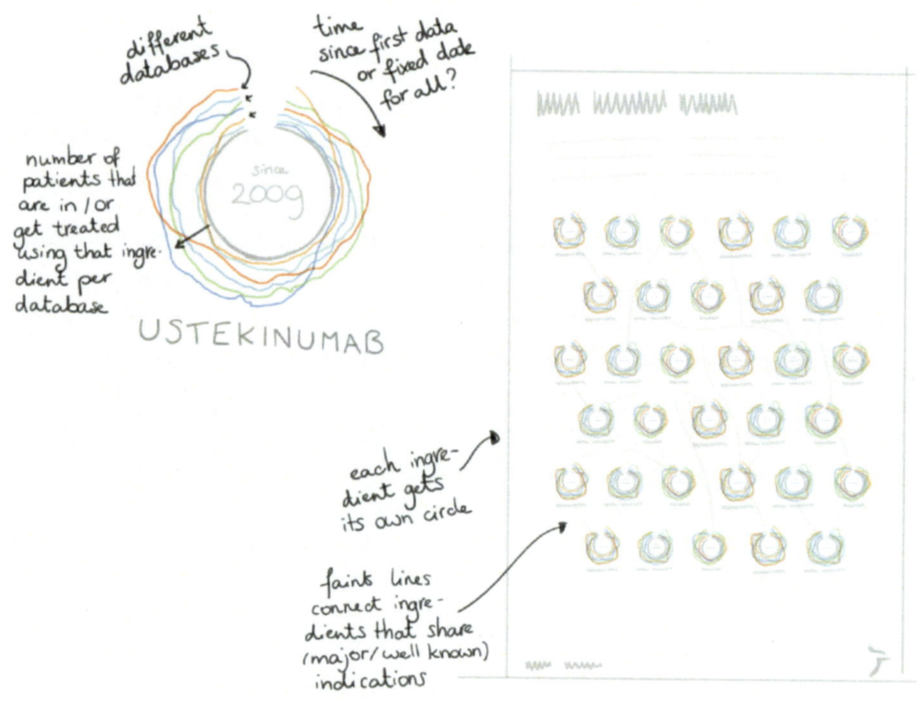

Layers of data aggregation in vibrant colors

BUSINESS | 2017 | JANSSEN

visualcinnamon.com/portfolio/janssen-product-portfolio

I created a large data-filled poster for Janssen, a pharmaceutical company. They wanted an A1-sized (about 84 cm or 33″ tall) poster to hang in their offices, showing the usage of their portfolio of drug products worldwide.

The data sets, some of which dated back to 1987, featured the products by active ingredients, such as Loperamide (anti-diarrheal) and Ketoconazole (anti-fungal), and the number of people exposed to each ingredient per month from 11 different healthcare record repositories across the US, Europe, Japan, and Australia. While I was grateful to have all the rich history, I ultimately decided to focus on the 2006 to 2016 decade: not too long to lose monthly trends and not too short to miss year-on-year trends. (It was also a period for which all of the 11 healthcare repositories had full data.)

10.1b

Figure 10.1a & b

Two design sketches that reveal the active ingredients in Janssen's drug products.

Following the steps I presented in Lesson 5 about sketching and presenting ideas to a client, I created multiple designs on how to reveal this information, combined in a slide deck. In figure 10.1, you can see sketches of two different concepts.

For the final poster, I ended up using a bit of both ideas (see the result in figure 10.2). I felt that the most granular data—the number of people exposed to each ingredient, per month, per repository—was the most fascinating to show. I made a hexagonal grid of radial line charts (from the sketch in figure 10.1a) for each ingredient, with one line per repository (though not all ingredients appeared in all repositories).

Little dots, dashed rings, and connected circles all convey variables that provide extra context and information (see figure 10.3a for a zoom-in on several circles).

A Real-World Exploration of the Janssen Product Portfolio

Epidemiology analysis of patient-level data shows Janssen's reach and impact on populations around the World

Driven by our commitment to patients, Janssen brings innovative products to people throughout the world. Janssen's product portfolio includes medicines across six therapeutic areas: cardiovascular & metabolism, immunology, infectious diseases & vaccines, neuroscience, oncology, and pulmonary arterial hypertension. Together, these medicines contain more than 90 active ingredients and used in more than 170 countries around the world.

The mission of Janssen Epidemiology Analytics is to collaborate with the Janssen Research and Development organization, within the Johnson & Johnson Family of Companies, and across the broader healthcare research community. The goal is to generate and disseminate real-world evidence about disease, health service utilization, and the effects of medical products through the analysis of healthcare data. Epidemiology uses a network of more than 10 healthcare databases, such as electronic health records and administrative claims, collectively representing over 450 million de-identified patient records.

We monitor the real-world utilization and study the effects of Janssen's medicines in North America, Europe and the Asia-Pacific region.

This visualization provides an overview of the ingredients within the Janssen product portfolio, and the extent to which those ingredients are observed across the network of healthcare data that is available throughout the Johnson & Johnson enterprise. The data offer insights into areas of future opportunities where Janssen Epidemiology can generate reliable real-world evidence to improve the lives of the patients we serve.

Active Ingredients in the Janssen Product Portfolio

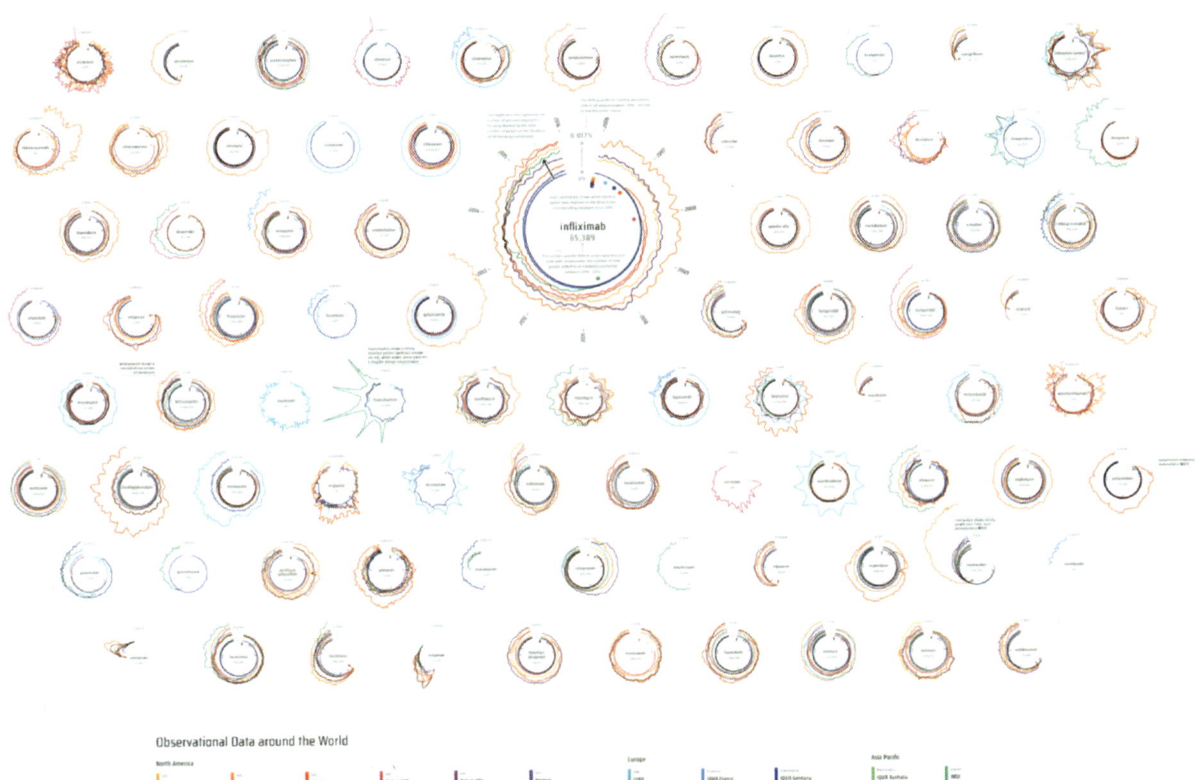

Observational Data around the World

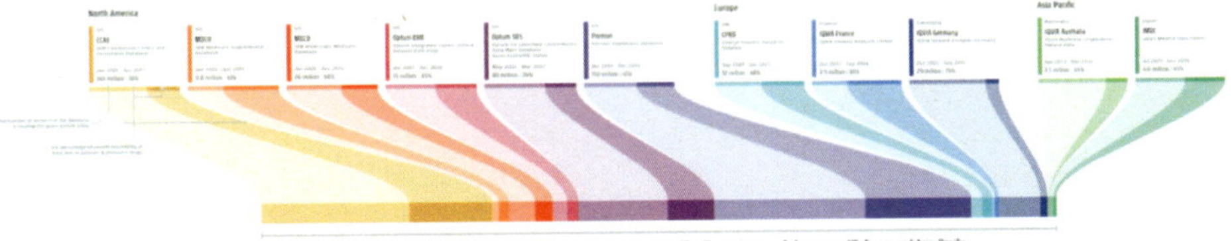

In total, Janssen Epidemiology Analytics conduct research on more than 460 million patient records from across US, Europe and Asia-Pacific

Therapeutic Area Landscape

Poster created by Nadieh Bremer | Visual Cinnamon

Analysis by Janssen Epidemiology Analytics: Patrick B. Ryan and Frank J. DeFalco

janssen

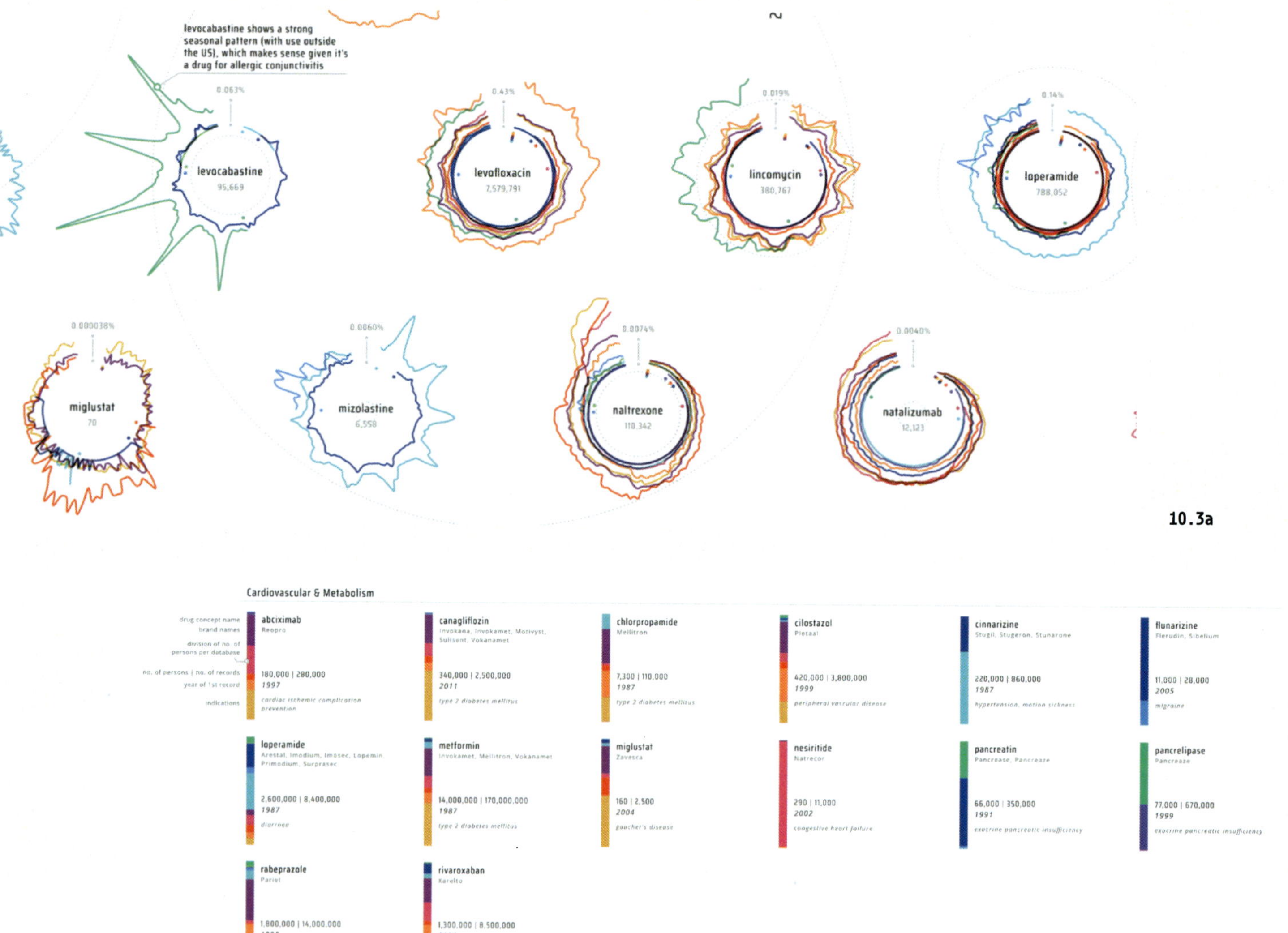

10.3a

10.3b

Figure 10.2

The final A1-sized poster titled "A Real-World Exploration of the Janssen Product Portfolio." There are endless details to explore.

Figure 10.3a & b

A close-up of the active ingredient circles from the top of the poster (a) and stacked bar charts of ingredients from the bottom of the poster (b).

However, I also felt that aggregations would reveal different kinds of insights. I therefore added two more sections to the poster. (This being at A1 size, I had quite a lot of space!) The middle section reveals the total number of people per repository, each in its own vibrant color as a horizontal stacked bar chart. This visual element performs double-duty, as both a bar chart and also a color legend for the entire poster. It's one of the first things the viewer will focus on, because the large splash of vibrant colors naturally draw the eye.

Finally, the poster displays a grid of all the ingredients again, this time grouped per medical field. Little stacked bar charts show the number of people per repository and per ingredient. Other information, such as drug names and health indications that are associated with the ingredient straddle the colorful bar (figure 10.3b).

This poster reveals the same data at three levels: the most granular level captures the data per month, per ingredient, per repository in the radial line charts at the top; a secondary level shows the totals per ingredient, per repository in the little stacked bar charts at the bottom; and finally, a tertiary level shows the totals per database as the central horizontal stacked bar chart.

On a (much smaller) computer screen, I would have had to split this into entirely separate visuals or only show the radial line charts. However, with such a large canvas, I could reveal the breadth of the data set and show Janssen employees layers upon layers of insights about the company's products.

10.4a

More than half a million observations

BUSINESS | 2020 | *PHYSICS TODAY*
doi.org/10.1063/PT.6.4.20200401a

In 2020, the Hubble Space Telescope celebrated its 30th anniversary. To commemorate this event, *Physics Today* wanted to visualize several stories based on an open source database that included all of Hubble's observations—about half a million of them!

I thoroughly investigated the data set using Python (to download the data via an API) and R (to analyze the data) to find possible angles for stories and visuals.

One thing was abundantly clear to me from the start: My goal was to showcase the enormous amount of work that Hubble has done by revealing the locations of all those hundreds of thousands of observations in the night sky. Plotting the data on a two-dimensional sky map would make the abstract idea of "an observation" more familiar.

Figure 10.4b shows the final poster with the sky map at the top. Each mark on the map is an observation. The observations are grouped by color into five kinds of "targets," such as blue for solar system objects and red for galaxies.

PHYSICS TODAY

Hubble's
30-year legacy

In the three decades since the space shuttle *Discovery* carried it into orbit on 24 April 1990, the *Hubble Space Telescope* has changed the way both astronomers and the general public understand the cosmos. Incorporating some 550 000 scientific observations from the Space Telescope Science Institute's comprehensive Barbara A. Mikulski Archive for Space Telescopes, this stereographic map charts the diverse astronomical objects that *Hubble* looked at from 1990 to 2019. The callouts link specific observing proposals with the celebrated images and discoveries they produced. With its instruments working well and demand for observing time as high as ever, *Hubble* is primed to continue exploring the universe through at least 2025.

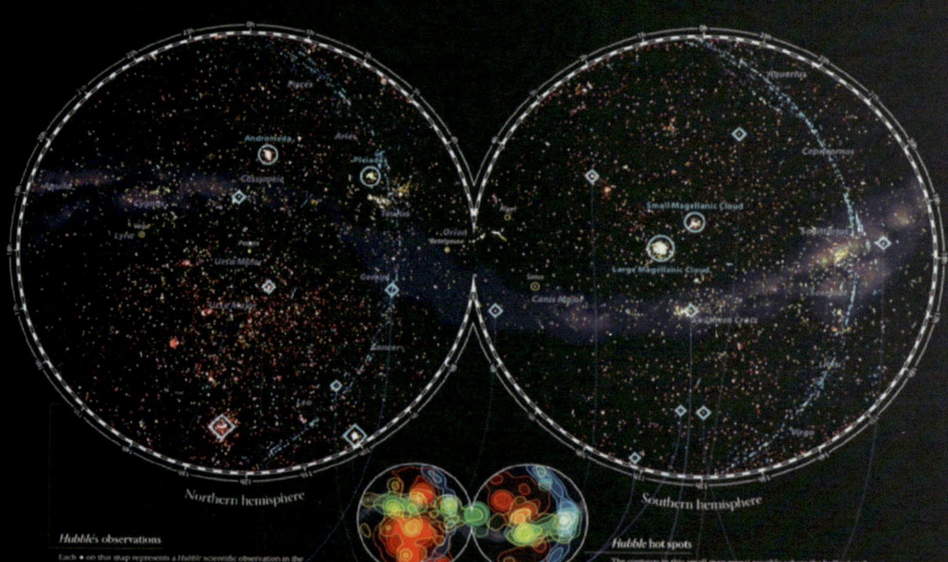

Hubble's observations

Each • on this map represents a *Hubble* scientific observation in the telescope data archive. The color signifies the main category of the observation target: • Star and • Stellar cluster, which include extrasolar planets; • Galaxy and • Cluster of galaxies, which include quasars and clusters that serve as gravitational lenses; interstellar medium, or • ISM, which includes planetary nebulae and supernova remnants; and • Solar system. Other observations are tagged as • Unidentified, such as the Hubble Deep Field surveys, or as • Calibration.

Some well-known stars and constellations are marked for context.

Hubble hot spots

The contours in this small map reveal roughly where the bulk of each category of target has been observed. Most stellar and ISM targets are in the disk of the Milky Way, so the observations cluster along the galactic plane. Many galaxy and galaxy cluster observations are made in the northern hemisphere because of the extensive catalog of targets already compiled by ground-based projects such as the Sloan Digital Sky Survey. Planets, moons, and other solar-system objects have been viewed at various positions along the ecliptic.

Proposal ID | Year of first observation | Title

Main classification(s) | Secondary classifications

Elliptical galaxy M87

Proposals 5267 and 5634 | 1994 | Velocity dispersions in the nucleus of M87

A quarter century after *Hubble* gazed at M87 to confirm whether supermassive black holes at the centers of galaxies exist, a network of radio telescopes directly imaged the galaxy's central black hole.

Galaxy | Elliptical galaxy; Nucleus
ISM extragalactic | Coronal gas

Spiral galaxy M81

Proposal 2227 | 1991 | Determination of the extragalactic distance scale

Measurements of Cepheid variable stars in M81 helped establish one rung of the cosmic distance ladder that has been used to estimate the age of the universe.

Galaxy | Spiral galaxy

Comet 2I/Borisov

Proposal 16009 | 2019 | Interstellar object C/2019 Q4

Over the past three years, *Hubble* has observed two objects in the solar system that are likely interstellar visitors, including this active comet.

Solar system | Comet; Interstellar comet

COSMOS

Proposal 9822 | 2003 | The COSMOS 2-Degree ACS Survey

Capturing more than 2 million galaxies over a 2-square-degree field, the Cosmic Evolution Survey is *Hubble's* largest-ever sky survey.

Cluster of galaxies | Blank sky
Unidentified | Parallel field

Fomalhaut b

Proposal 9862 | 2004 | ACS detection of substellar companions [...] via parallax and proper motion

The first exoplanet to be directly imaged follows a long, highly elliptical orbit around its host star.

Star | A0–A3 V–IV

Bubble Nebula

Hubble has returned multiple images of a young, massive star whose stellar wind has created a glowing bubble of heated gas that spans 7 light-years.

Jupiter

Proposal 13631 | 2014 | Dynamical change on Jupiter's Great Red Spot

Hubble has tracked the slow, steady diminution of the solar system's most famous anticyclone, the Great Red Spot (GRS).

Solar system | Planet Jupiter; GRS dynamics

V838 Monocerotis

Proposal 9587–88 and 9694 | 2002 | Imaging polarimetry of the light echo around V838 Monocerotis

Polarization measurements of light bouncing off a cocoon of dust helped scientists pin down the distance from Earth to the central red supergiant star, which briefly was one of the most luminous stars in the Local Group.

Star | Nova-like

Ultra Deep Field

Proposals 9978–9983 | 2003 | The Ultra Deep Field

By staring at a dark spot of sky for a cumulative 11.3 days, *Hubble* returned this view of about 10 000 galaxies, some of them dating back to when the universe was less than a billion years old.

Unidentified | Blank field; High-latitude field

NGC 3603

Proposal 10602 | 2005 | A complete multiplicity survey of galactic O[...] stars with ACS

Astronomers have analyzed some of the young, massive stars clustered in the nebula to help evaluate theoretical limits of stellar mass.

Stellar cluster | Star-forming region; OB association

Eagle Nebula

Proposal 10393 | 2004 | Hubble Heritage observations of Eagle Nebula

Among *Hubble's* most captivating cosmic subjects, first imaged in 1995, are the Pillars of Creation: billowing towers of cold gas and dust in a stellar nursery.

ISM | Planetary nebula

Antennae galaxies

Proposal 10188 | 2004 | In-depth study of the Antennae with NICMOS and ACS

The pair of merging galaxies offers a possible preview of the Milky Way's future merger with the Andromeda galaxy.

Galaxy | Interacting galaxy

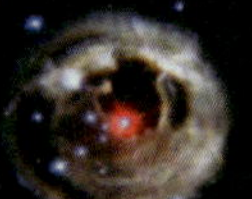

Data source Astroquery for *Hubble* science observations through 31 December 2019 in the Barbara A. Mikulski Archive for Space Telescopes

Image credits NASA, ESA, and the Hubble Heritage Team (STScI/AURA).
Additional credits: A. Simon/Goddard Space Flight Center and C. Go; H. E. Bond/STScI; S. Beckwith/STScI and the HUDF team; ESA/Hubble collaboration; B. Whitmore/STScI

Visualization Nadieh Bremer (Visual Cinnamon) created for *Physics Today*. Text by Andrew Grant.

10.4b

Figure 10.4a & b

The final poster for "Hubble's 30-year legacy" with more than 500,000 observations plotted on a map of the night sky (b), with a zoom in on the right half of the left hemisphere (a). A version also appeared in the April 2020 print issue *https://doi.org/10.1063/PT.3.4462.1*

Figure 10.5

A work in progress, where I was testing density contours instead of visualizing each separate observation. This eventually became a mini map below the main map.

The reader can see how Hubble has made observations all across the northern and southern skies. To help orient the viewer, some of the most well-known and groundbreaking observations were explicitly marked on the map and explained at the bottom of the poster. The audience could see, for example, where in the sky an iconic Hubble photo was taken.

There are so many trends and patterns in these locations that they already provide abundant visual diversity for readers to let their eyes wander. Coloring each observation to its target type added an interesting extra dimension. But beyond that, I needed to show restraint. Even though there were plenty of other great variables, the marks were simply too small to add more variables, more visual channels.

In this project, my goal was to convey the immense scale of Hubble's work and to make that scale feel tangible. Representing each observation with an individual mark creates this sense of vastness and significance—showing that Hubble has accomplished a monumental amount of work. Each tiny pinprick on the map represents a remarkable addition to our understanding of the universe.

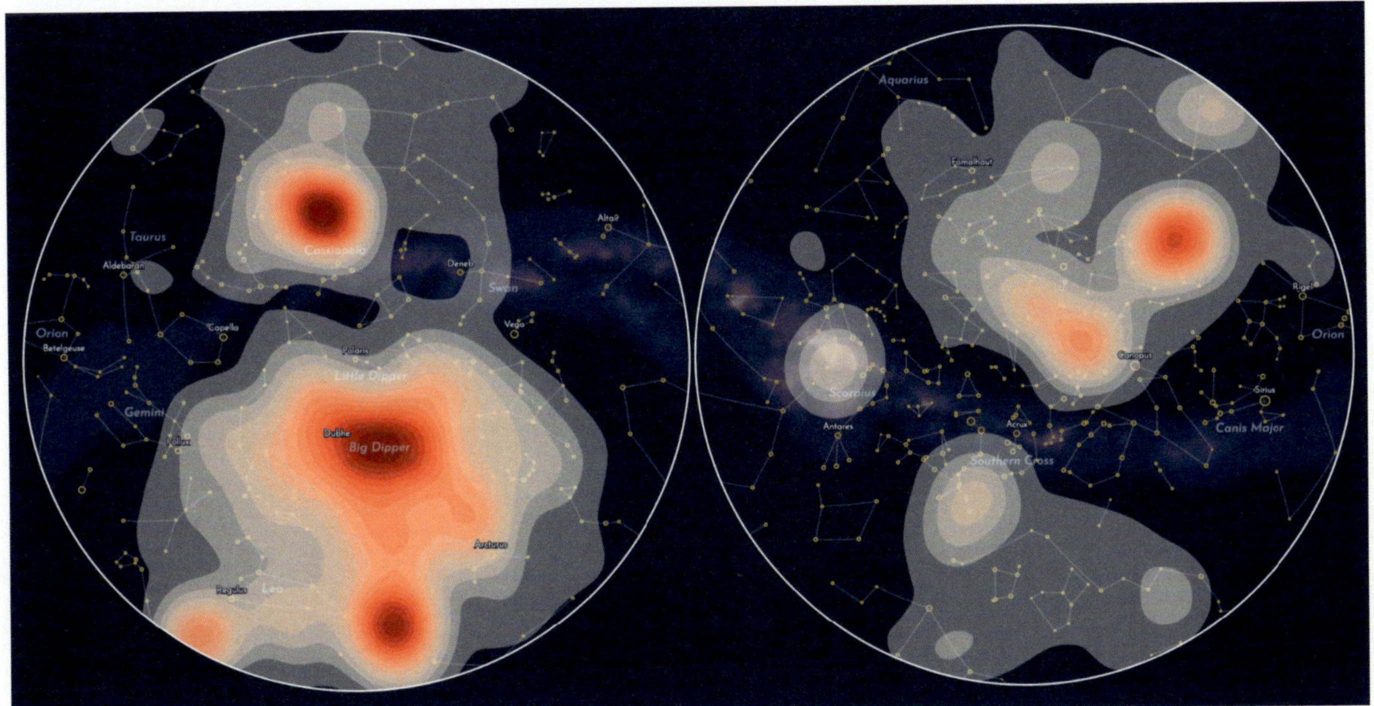

FULL DESIGN STORY

Wrapping music data into a giant circle

BUSINESS | 2020 | SONY MUSIC ENTERTAINMENT NETHERLANDS
medium.com/sony-music-data-insights/how-we-used-data-to-design-modern-record-certification-plaques-bc2c575a9fa3

When a single or an album reaches gold or platinum status, the artist is typically awarded a framed vinyl record—a tradition that originated around the middle of the last century—symbolizing the monumental achievement of captivating an audience on a massive scale. However, in these days of music streaming, Sony Music Entertainment Netherlands asked if I could develop a more data-driven, more data-art-inspired version of these celebratory plaques.

From the start, I knew I wanted to use the characteristics of the songs themselves, alongside the data about streams and chart entries, to create a unique data-based "fingerprint" for each song. I wanted to create something that reflected the shape of the original gold records: a portrait-style poster with a large vinyl—a large circle, in essence. (As I mentioned in Lesson 1, the topic of the data is often the best inspiration for ideas.)

Figure 10.6a & b

A snippet of sound that I converted into some simple visuals, shown as a "waveform" line chart visualization, with a line/wave drawn several times a second and then slowly fading away (a), and as a bar chart of binned frequencies, with low frequencies on the left and high ones on the right (b).

10.6a

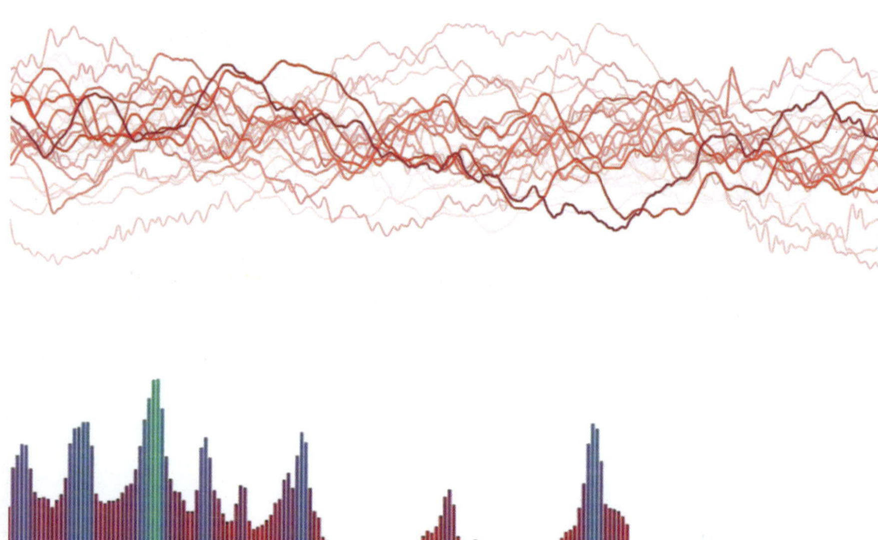

10.6b

Before sketching, I first investigated how to visualize music. I'd visualized data about music but never data directly based on a song's musicality. It took me a long while to extract audio and acoustic data and figure out how to visualize it. I had to learn about waveforms (similar to the wobbly line you see when interacting with Siri) and audio frequencies (figure 10.6). When dealing with this kind of data you generally split the song up into tiny sections of less than a second and transform the data from each little snippet of sound into either a waveform or frequency bars.

10.7a

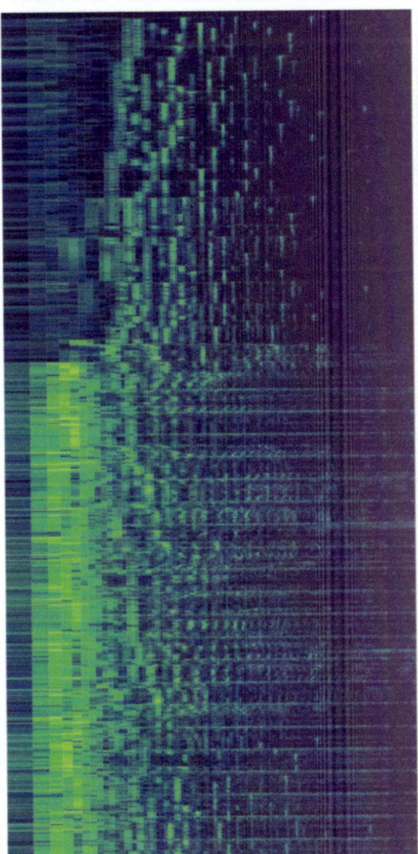

10.7b

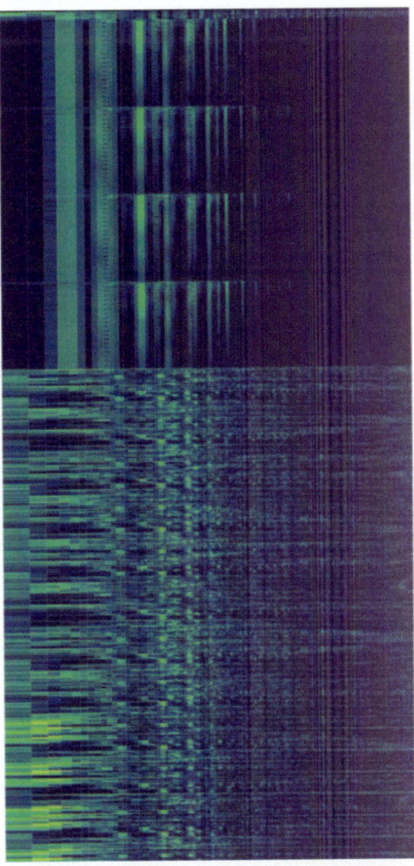

Figure 10.7a & b

The spectrogram of the first 30 or so seconds of "Dancing in the Moonlight" by Toploader (a) and "Harder Better Faster Stronger" by Daft Punk (b).

In case you're wondering why the rectangles along the left are longer than those along the right, I learned that humans don't perceive sound/notes/ frequencies in a linear fashion. Instead, our ears respond logarithmically to both the volume and frequency. Therefore, I applied a logarithmic scale to the bins, which stretched the low frequencies and squished the higher ones.

From the moment I saw my first bar chart dance on the screen, with the bars moving up and down to the music, I had a vague idea of what to do for an entire song. Later, while searching the web, I saw that my idea already had a name: spectrograms. In essence, spectrograms show the frequency bins along one axis and time along the other axis. Usually, color represents the value (or amplitude) of each frequency at each point in time.

Therefore, I took my single bar chart and turned it into my own version of a spectrogram (figure 10.7).

When I saw these results, especially when the rows of rectangles appeared in tandem with the music, I could see what I heard: the beats (along the left), the mid-tones, and the voices (in the middle and along the right). I was thrilled to start getting a unique "fingerprint" of each song.

Next was the "circle-ification" idea that I'd had in mind since the start, an ode to the gold records. There were several other benefits to a circular layout. For one thing, the rectangular form took up a lot of space—the images in figure 10.7a & b are only 30 seconds of a song. A circle offers about three times more space at the same height. Another reason was that most of the "action" occurs in the lower frequencies. By fanning the rectangle into a circle, the lower frequencies would get more space along the outside, whereas the rarely featured high frequencies would take up much less space in the center. In short, going from a rectangle to a circle gave me three important benefits: more data in less space, more emphasis on the data that matters, and a shape of a vinyl record. I wish circular forms always were such a clear win-win-win!

10.8

10.9

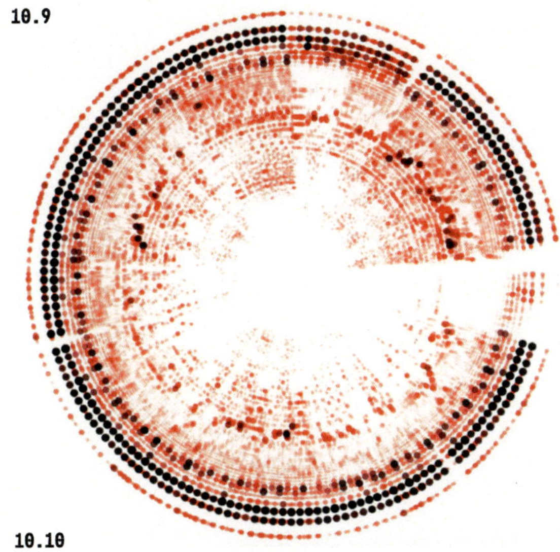

10.10

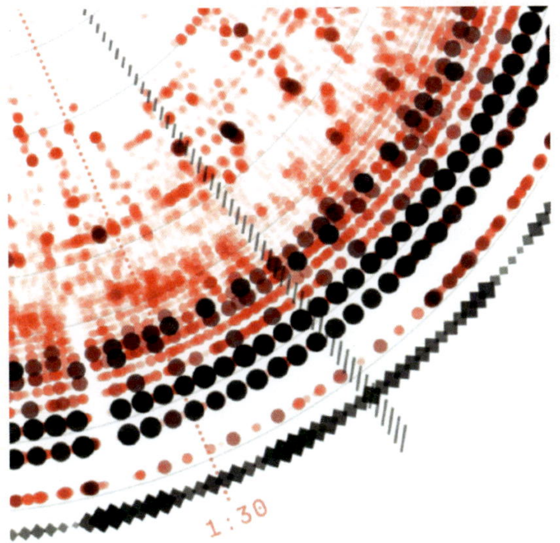

Figure 10.8

Fanning the timeline into a circle shape and turning the individual rectangles into circles.

Figure 10.9

The jump to a smaller circle scale that highlighted the structure of the song and a red color scale based on Sony Music's logo.

Figure 10.10

Adding black diamonds around the outside for Spotify's beats data and hatched dividers on top to signify the start of new musical sections.

Rectangles made sense in the previous rectangular layout. However, when going to a circular layout, this wouldn't be a good fit anymore. So I turned each little rectangle into a circle and set both the color and size to the amplitude of the bin (amplified encoding!). See figure 10.8 for the spectrogram of the entire song of "Adore You" by Harry Styles (the test song that I received from Sony to develop a prototype).

The circles in figure 10.8 were still too big, they created a lot of overlap which hid the song's "shape." And although the "viridis" color palette from yellow to dark purple is a great option to use for readability, it did not fit Sony's branding. I therefore adjusted both the size (shrunk the circles) and color (red, like the Sony Music logo), as shown in figure 10.9.

I thought about adding new colors to the palette, maybe red for the base frequencies and other colors for the midrange, for example. However, this visual would potentially be re-created for other artists, each with their own musical style and vibe, which meant the palette needed to remain rather minimal.

Next, I had access to a second data set about the music: the "audio analysis" from Spotify, which describes the song's structure and musical content. After looking into the many different variables available, I felt that the beats and sections—a song is divided into sections defined by large variations in rhythm or timbre—would add context to the circular spectrogram.

I visualized the beats as a black outer ring of diamonds (a different shape to make them stand out from the circles), sized to the beat confidence value given in the data. To mark the start of a section, I drew small hatched dividers on top of the circle, as shown in figure 10.10.

That was it in terms of visualizing the musical features, but there was still plenty left to say about the song, including the number of streams on Spotify, chart position per day across the countries, playlists it belonged to, and the music video's daily YouTube streams.

10.11

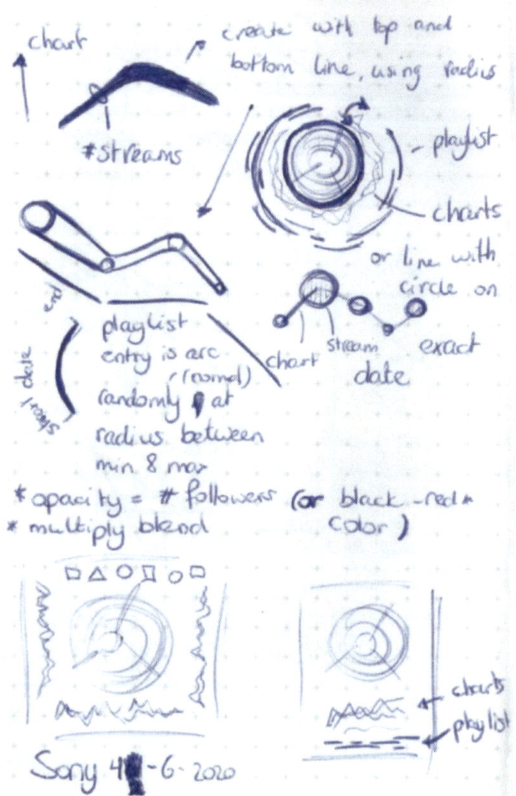

Weirdly, it was only at this point that I started sketching. I think it worked out this way because I knew from the start that I wanted something big and circular inspired by the vinyl of the gold record. There was already a solid concept to follow, even if the details only slowly became apparent along the way.

I started drawing some sketches to help me figure out how to incorporate the charting and streaming data sets (figure 10.11). The new data sets were all time series across several weeks. Since the existing visual had time running clockwise, I wanted to wrap the other data sets around the circle as well, making it even bigger, even though they would run along a different time scale than the central music circle (days instead of seconds).

I did some initial data exploration in R to get a sense of these data sets. The charting data yielded a lot of lines (one per country) going up and down across time. That would provide a lot of visual diversity!

I started by wrapping the charting data around the music circle (figure 10.12a). Next, I added the streams per day, encoded as line thickness, creating a more pleasing line shape, shown in figure 10.12b (while adding more context). Finally, using the same color palette as the central circle, I colored each line by the average number of streams (the higher the value, the darker the line).

To more clearly separate the central music circle from the outer charting lines, I added two large white circles with a (red) drop shadow in between, making it look like the inner circle was lying on top of the charting lines (figure 10.13). On each white circle,

10.12a

10.12b

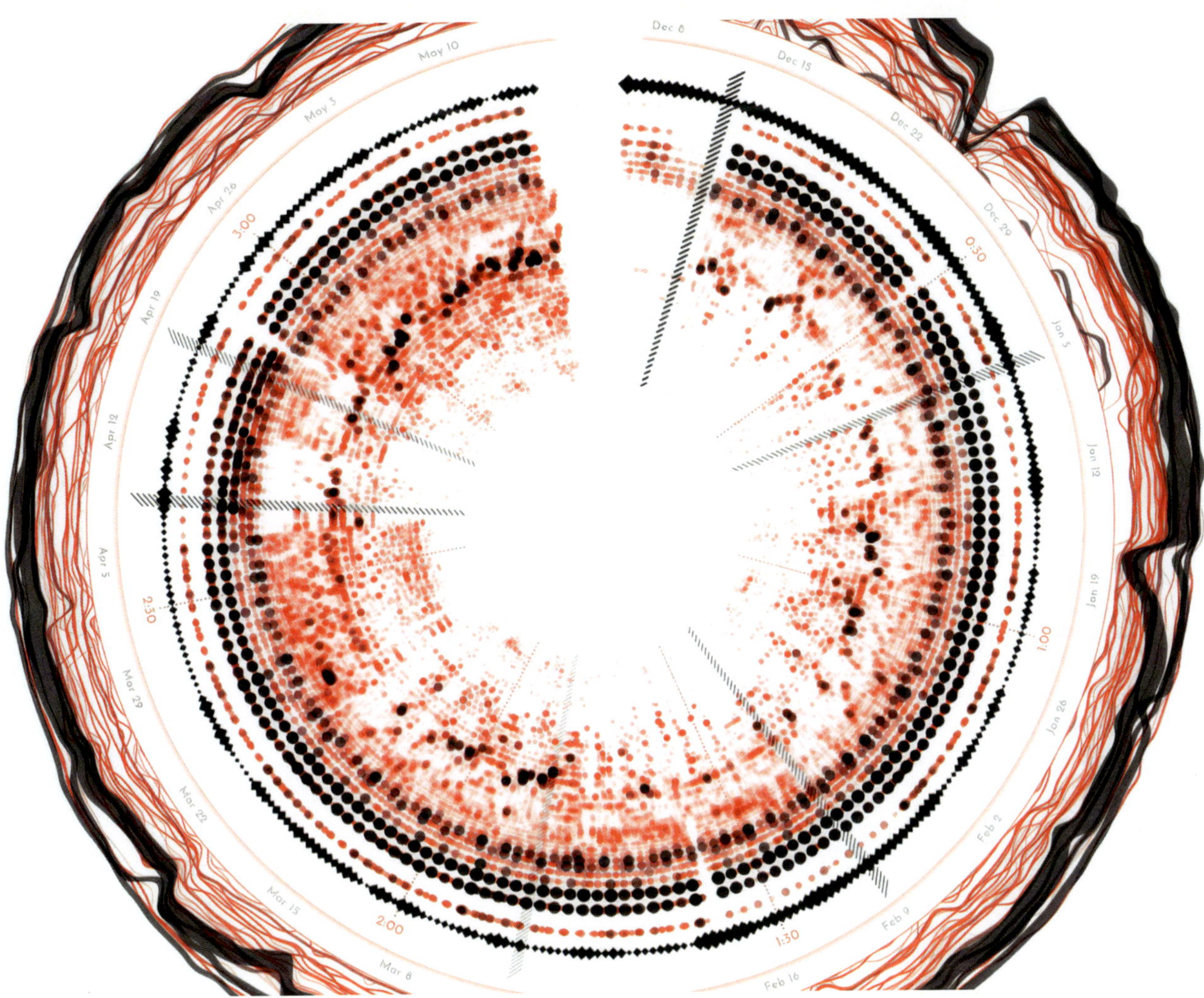

10.13

Figure 10.11

Sketching several ideas on how to visualize the streams, chart positions, and playlist data around the central circle.

Figure 10.12a & b

Wrapping the Spotify data around the music circle. Chart positions by country are the lines (a), and number of streams per day are represented by line thickness (b).

Figure 10.13

Two circles with red shadows separate the inner music circle from the outer charting lines and hold the two time axes: one in seconds for the inner song data and the other in weeks for the outer charting data.

I drew a time axis: one in 30-second intervals for the inner circle and the other in weekly intervals for the outer circle.

Next up was the Spotify playlist data. The first thing that came to mind was to draw one arc for each playlist, starting from the date the song was added to the playlist and running to the day it was removed. I layered the playlists in order of start date around the outside (figure 10.14).

Well, that didn't look visually appealing. All those unwavering lines didn't fit with the rest of the design style. However, it did reveal some insights: The song was added to many playlists at its release date and was removed after exactly one week.

10.14

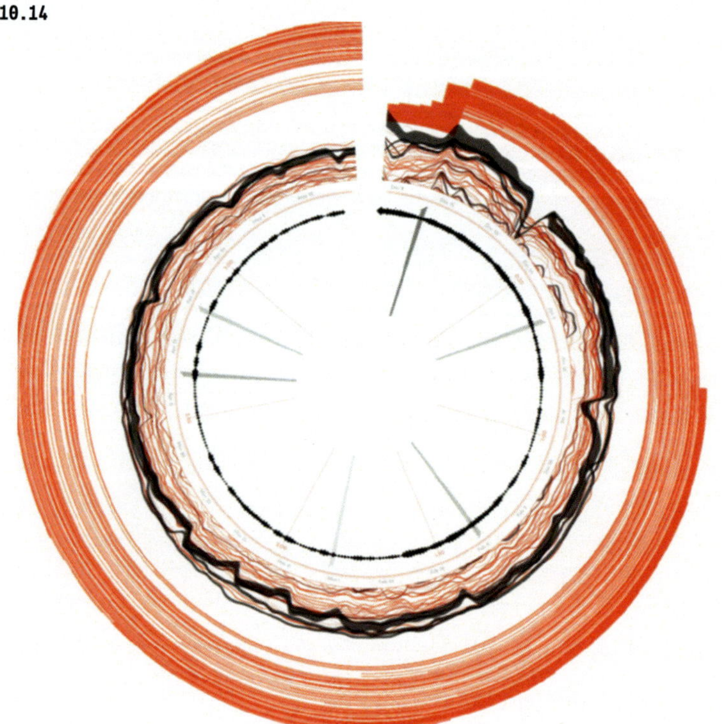

I tried some alternatives, such as showing the number of playlists with the song per day (figure 10.15a). However, there wasn't much happening. Simply put, the result looked boring. What about positioning each playlist randomly inside a band along the outside (figure 10.15b)? That wasn't it either—it was too dominant. I tried and tweaked so many things, even getting to the point where I thought that converting the straight arcs into sine waves could be the ticket (figure 10.15c). What was I thinking?

For my next idea, I moved the playlist section into the circle. The arcs looked more at home next to the inner white circles with the date axes (figure 10.16). That felt like an improvement, at least. However, I still didn't like how it looked—the playlists were still too visually dominant, yet in a boring way.

Figure 10.14

Adding the Spotify playlist data around the outside, with an arc per playlist running from the moment the song was added to the playlist until it was removed.

Figure 10.15a, b & c

Several other attempts to visualize the playlists around the outside, from grouping the playlists per date (a), to drawing separate arcs randomly distributed along an outer section (b), to using sine waves (c).

Figure 10.16

Situating the playlist arcs in between the inner music circle and the charting lines was a bit of a design improvement.

Because I couldn't think of anything else, I decided to let it go for the moment and focus on a different part of the visual. Mental separation has helped me tremendously on many projects because it gives my brain a break. Sometimes, when the rest of the visual gets more and more defined, I get a better grip on the overall design style, which gives me fresh ideas on how to tackle the more difficult sections.

I wanted to work with a completely different type of data set next; no more timelines. Therefore, I tackled Spotify's "audio features" (not to be confused with the "audio analysis" data set from before). This small data set contains several interesting values about the song as a whole. These are single numbers that quantify danceability, energy, and more.

I knew that adding a handful of these single values to the visual could be tricky, given the design style I'd applied to the rest of the data. But I was convinced that placing them in the middle, in some glyph-like form, would work. And with that, I embarked on my second doomed quest.

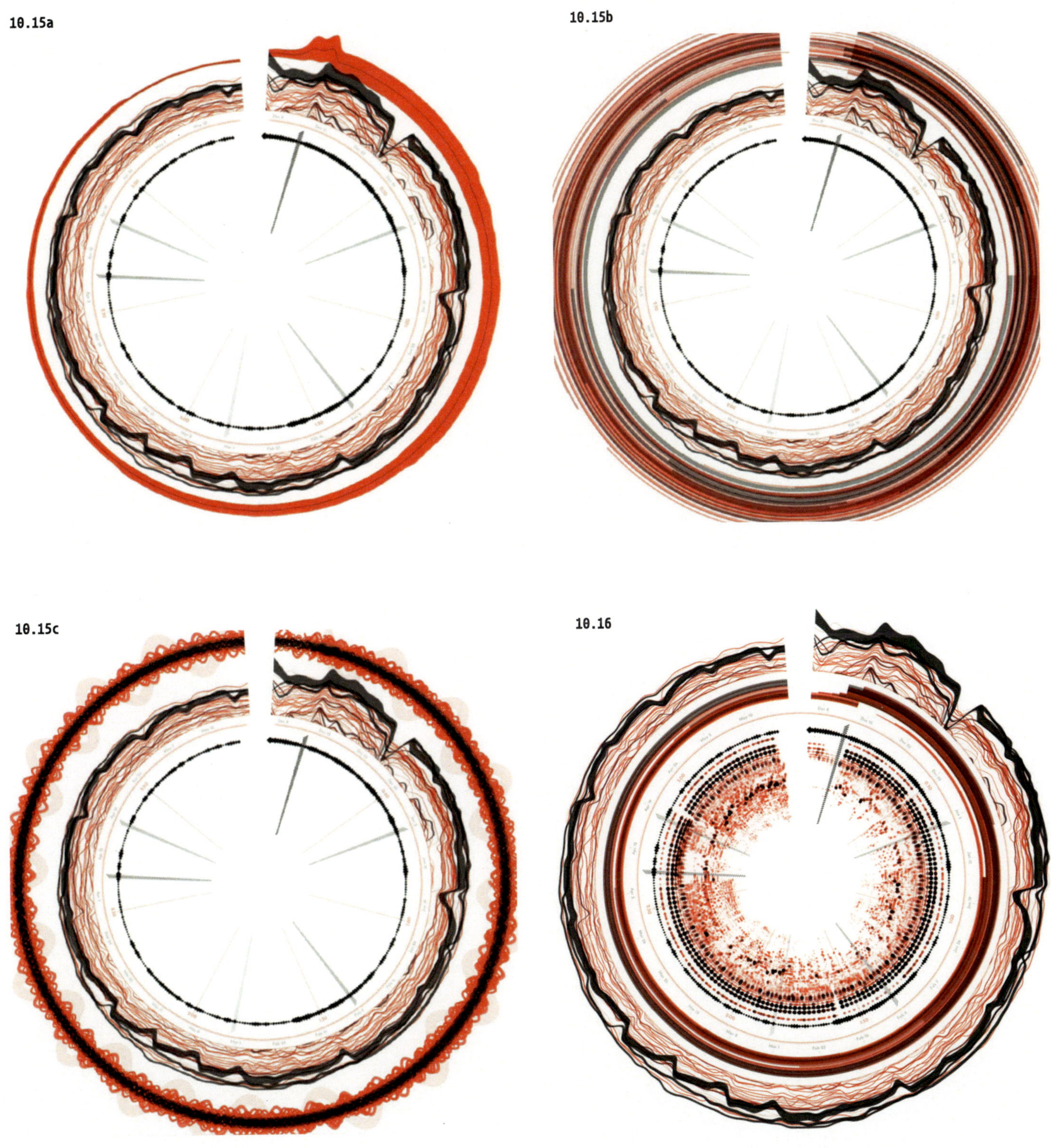
10.15a
10.15b
10.15c
10.16

10.17

Figure 10.17

Sketching various ways to visualize a collection of six numbers (on a scale from 0 to 1).

Figure 10.18

Adding five labels at the center for the different "audio feature" variables. The radiating circles increase in number and size for higher values.

Figure 10.19a, b & c

Trying other forms to visualize the "audio feature" data.

Figure 10.20

Visualizing the playlists as dots placed on the date the song was added.

After inspecting the available variables, I chose five to visualize: accousticness, danceability, energy, speechiness, and valence (sad to happy). All of the values were abstractly the same: a number between 0 and 1. I sketched several ideas to visualize these audio features in the center of the circle (figure 10.17).

I started with one of the most straightforward designs: stacks of circles increasing in size as they radiate outward from a central point (figure 10.18).

However, I didn't like it, for the same reason that I disliked the playlist arcs: it felt at odds with the style of the music circle around it.

I tried several of the other ideas from my sketch to make the innermost visual more complex. You can see several attempts in figure 10.19: petals (a), "fireworks" circles (b), and spirals (c).

However, I didn't like any of these results either.

Feeling frustrated with how things were going, I turned back to the Spotify playlist data with some renewed energy. All my previous attempts had shown that something with an arc, something that was drawn from the date the song was added to the date it was removed, didn't work. Therefore, I changed my tactic and put a dot on the date that the song was added to the playlist. After a bit of iteration, I colored the dots according to how long the song stayed on the playlist (darker was longer) and sized them to the number of playlist followers (figure 10.20).

That looked much better! Finally, something that seemed to work with the rest without being too visually dominant. It wasn't a 100% fit with the rest of the circle, but I liked it enough and was honestly out of ideas.

Going back to the "audio features" data again, it hit me that the variables had nothing to do with time, and therefore, it made sense to take them out of the big circle, which only featured time-related variables. And somehow, when I made that decision, things started to fall into place. I first created bar charts below the central circle, but I quickly saw that simple rectangles looked uninteresting. Therefore, I integrated the hatched design element from the musical sections so that the bars weren't solid blocks but hatched lines (figure 10.21).

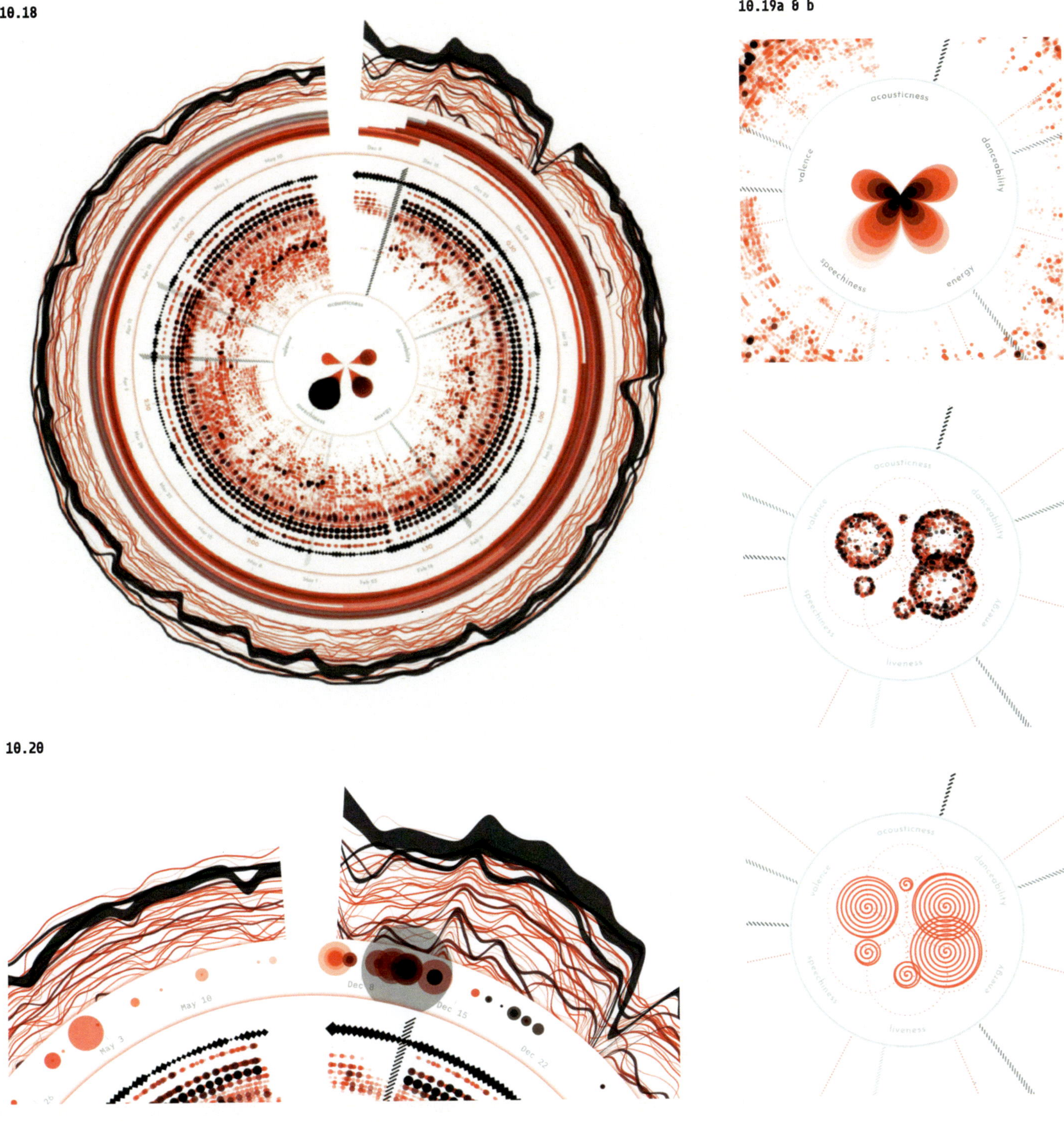

10.18

10.19a & b

10.20

10.19c

acousticness /
danceability ///////////////////
energy /////////////////////
speechiness /
valence ///////////////

10.21

Figure 10.21

Moving the "audio features" numbers out from the center and plotting them as hatched bar charts below the main circle, with the single gray hatch along the right subtly marking the maximum value.

Figure 10.22

Three mini charts on the right, showing daily Spotify streams, daily YouTube views, and total playlist additions.

It was technically the simplest iteration of the "audio features" that I had tried, but it felt completely right the moment I saw it appear on my screen.

I wanted to add more data to the empty section on the right side of the "audio features" bar chart. Some earlier data exploration revealed that there could be some interesting trends in daily streams, such as dips during weekends. Therefore, I visualized the total number of daily streams (for all countries) as a straightforward line chart. I kept the design very minimal, a simple red line, so as not to compete with the central circle.

I still had one untapped data set from Sony: the daily YouTube streams. I realized that this data complemented the Spotify streams line chart I had just created because it, too, was one metric: the total views, per day. It seemed fitting to add a second line for the YouTube views below the Spotify streams.

That left space for one more mini chart. I remembered that when I changed the playlist data from arcs to dots, it became hard to see how many playlists the song was added to on busy days because the dots overlap. (This mostly occurs around the song's release date.) Therefore, I created a tiny bar chart highlighting the number of playlists the track is added to over time (figure 10.22).

10.22

SPOTIFY AUDIO FEATURES

acousticness /
danceability ///////////////////
energy //////////////////////
speechiness ///
valence ////////////////
[sad = 0 / happy = 1]

chart eligible
spotify streams

youtube streams

spotify playlists
[no. of playlists added to]

Figure 10.23a & b

The final poster of Harry Styles's "Adore You."

These being tiny charts, I didn't want to convey the exact numbers—only the trend. I did label the highest value for context. We're often talking about millions of streams a day!

As this project veered into data art, the main goal was never to clearly visualize the exact numbers but to create something eye-catching that captured the "shape" of the data. Nevertheless, because the visual shows trends in the data, I added several small and unobtrusive legends outside the main circle (figure 10.23a).

With a working algorithm on "Adore You," I got several more songs to test, which highlighted a few problems (like data quirks that are unique to older songs). This took me a few more days to handle.

10.23a

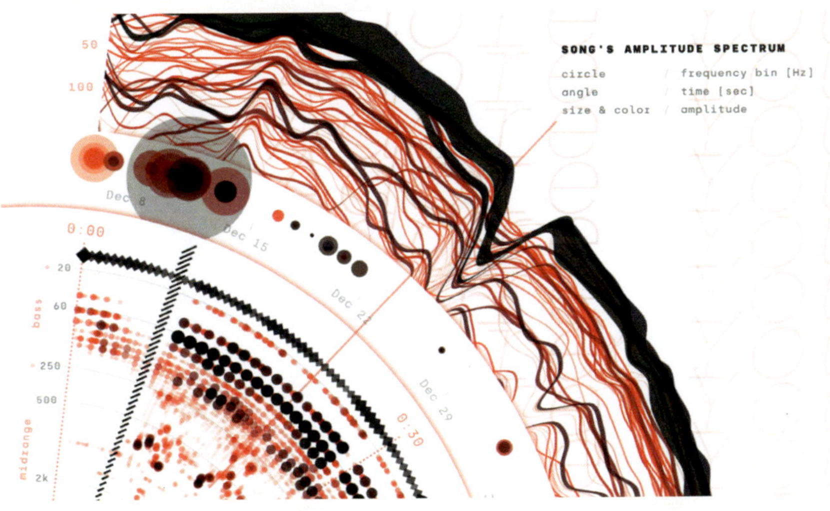

Looking at the resulting posters of all the test songs side by side, it was clear that the "data-based gold record poster system" gave unique results for each song and really brought out that distinctive "fingerprint" (figures 10.24 through 10.28).

After some more (endless) tweaks, ordering a test print of the intended 40 cm x 50 cm size—the size of an actual gold record—and making a few more minor changes based on the test print, the poster system was fully done!

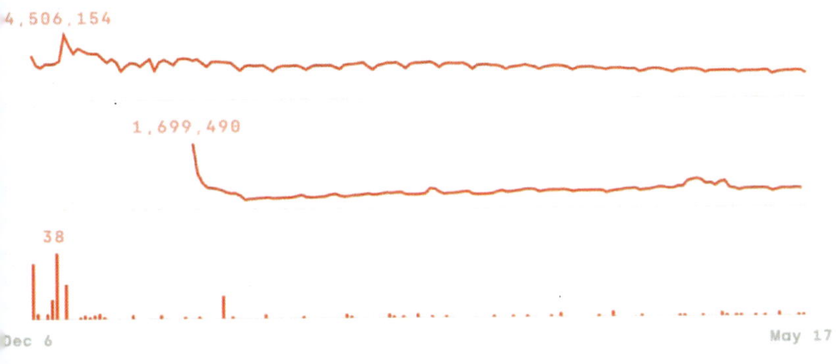

10.23b

Adore You

HARRY STYLES

SONG'S AMPLITUDE SPECTRUM

circle / frequency bin [Hz]
angle / time [sec]
size & color / amplitude

1
15
50
100

0:00
0:30
1:00
2:30
3:00

20
60
bass
250
500
midrange
2k
4k
6k Hz

Dec 8
Dec 15
Dec 22
Dec 29
Jan 5
Jan 12
Jan 19
Apr 5
Apr 12
Apr 19
Apr 26
May 3
May 10
May 17

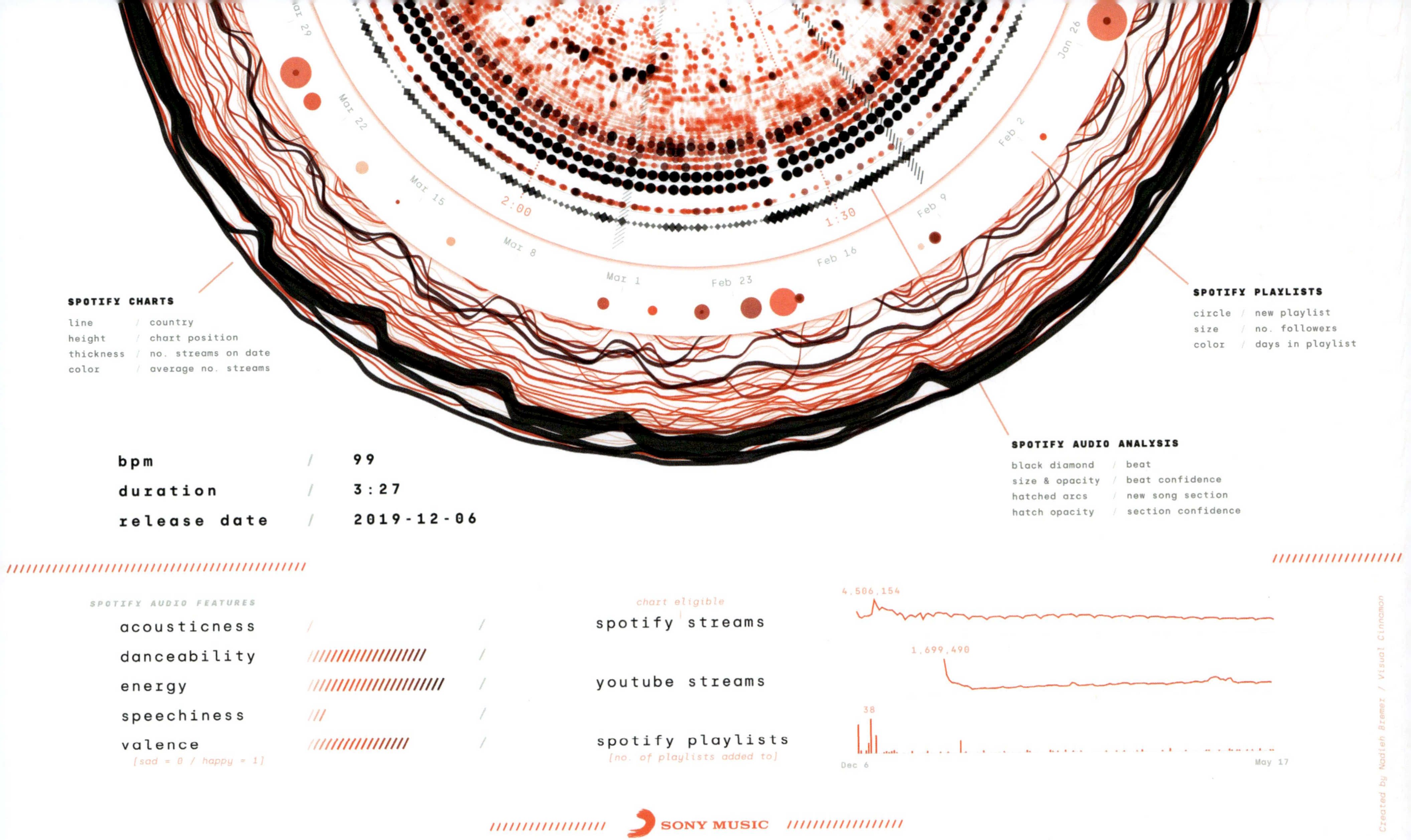

Mar 29

Mar 22

Mar 15

2:00

Mar 8

Mar 1

Feb 23

Feb 16

1:30

Feb 9

Feb 2

Jan 26

SPOTIFY CHARTS

line / country
height / chart position
thickness / no. streams on date
color / average no. streams

SPOTIFY PLAYLISTS

circle / new playlist
size / no. followers
color / days in playlist

SPOTIFY AUDIO ANALYSIS

black diamond / beat
size & opacity / beat confidence
hatched arcs / new song section
hatch opacity / section confidence

bpm	/	**99**
duration	/	**3:27**
release date	/	**2019-12-06**

SPOTIFY AUDIO FEATURES

acousticness / /
danceability ////////////////// /
energy ////////////////////// /
speechiness /// /
valence //////////////// /
[sad = 0 / happy = 1]

chart eligible
spotify streams — 4,506,154

youtube streams — 1,699,490

spotify playlists — 38
[no. of playlists added to]

Dec 6 — May 17

SONY MUSIC

Created by Nadieh Bremer / Visual Cinnamon

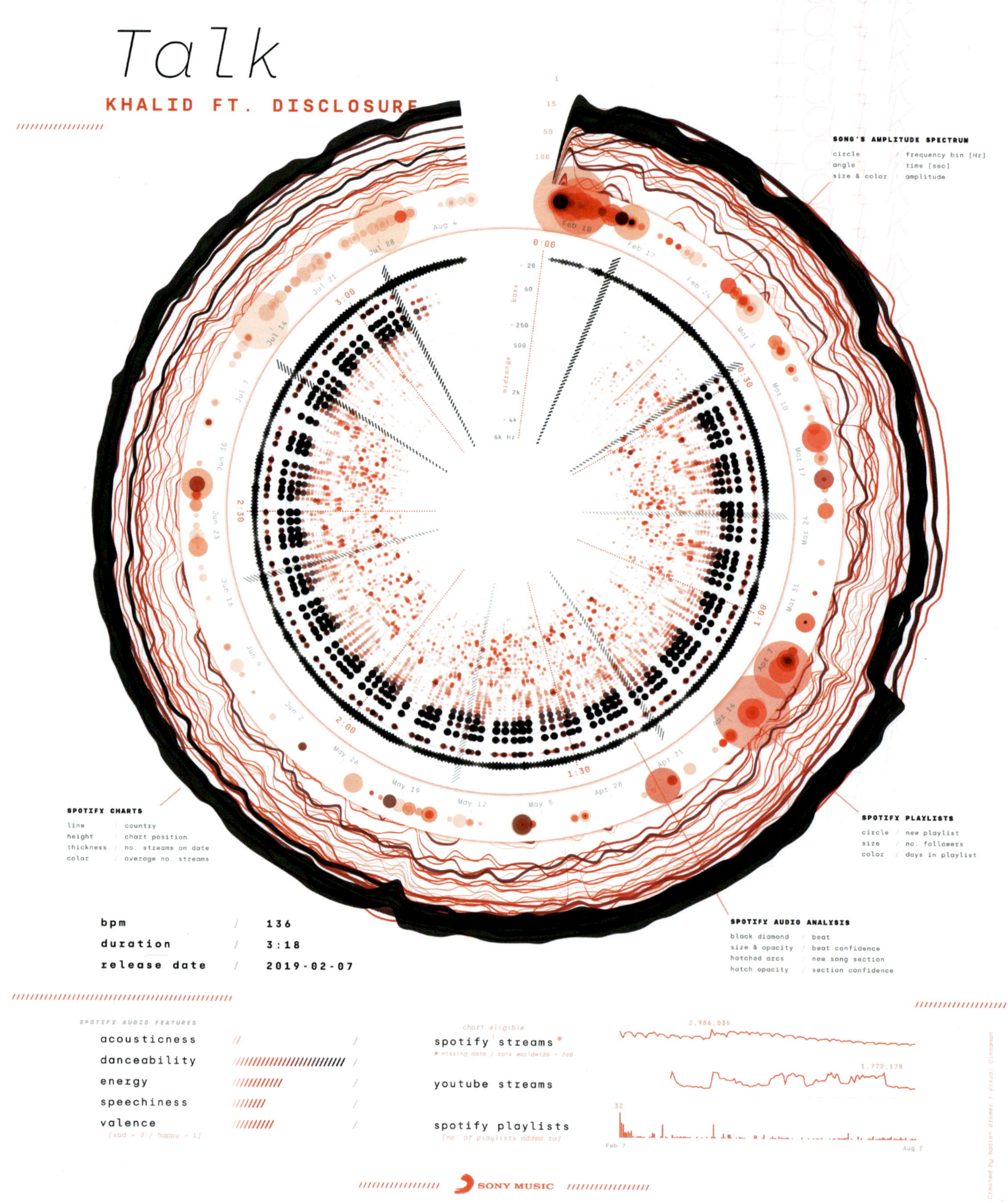
Talk
KHALID FT. DISCLOSURE
SONG'S AMPLITUDE SPECTRUM
circle / frequency bin [Hz]
angle / time [sec]
size & color / amplitude
SPOTIFY CHARTS
line / country
height / chart position
thickness / no. streams on date
color / average no. streams
SPOTIFY PLAYLISTS
circle / new playlist
size / no. followers
color / days in playlist
SPOTIFY AUDIO ANALYSIS
black diamond / beat
size & opacity / beat confidence
hatched arcs / new song section
hatch opacity / section confidence
bpm / 136
duration / 3:18
release date / 2019-02-07
SPOTIFY AUDIO FEATURES
acousticness
danceability
energy
speechiness
valence
[sad = 0 / happy = 1]
chart eligible
spotify streams *
* missing data / rank worldwide > 200
2,986,035
youtube streams
1,772,178
spotify playlists
[no. of playlists added to]
32
Feb 7
Aug 7
SONY MUSIC
Created by Nadieh Bremer / Visual Cinnamon

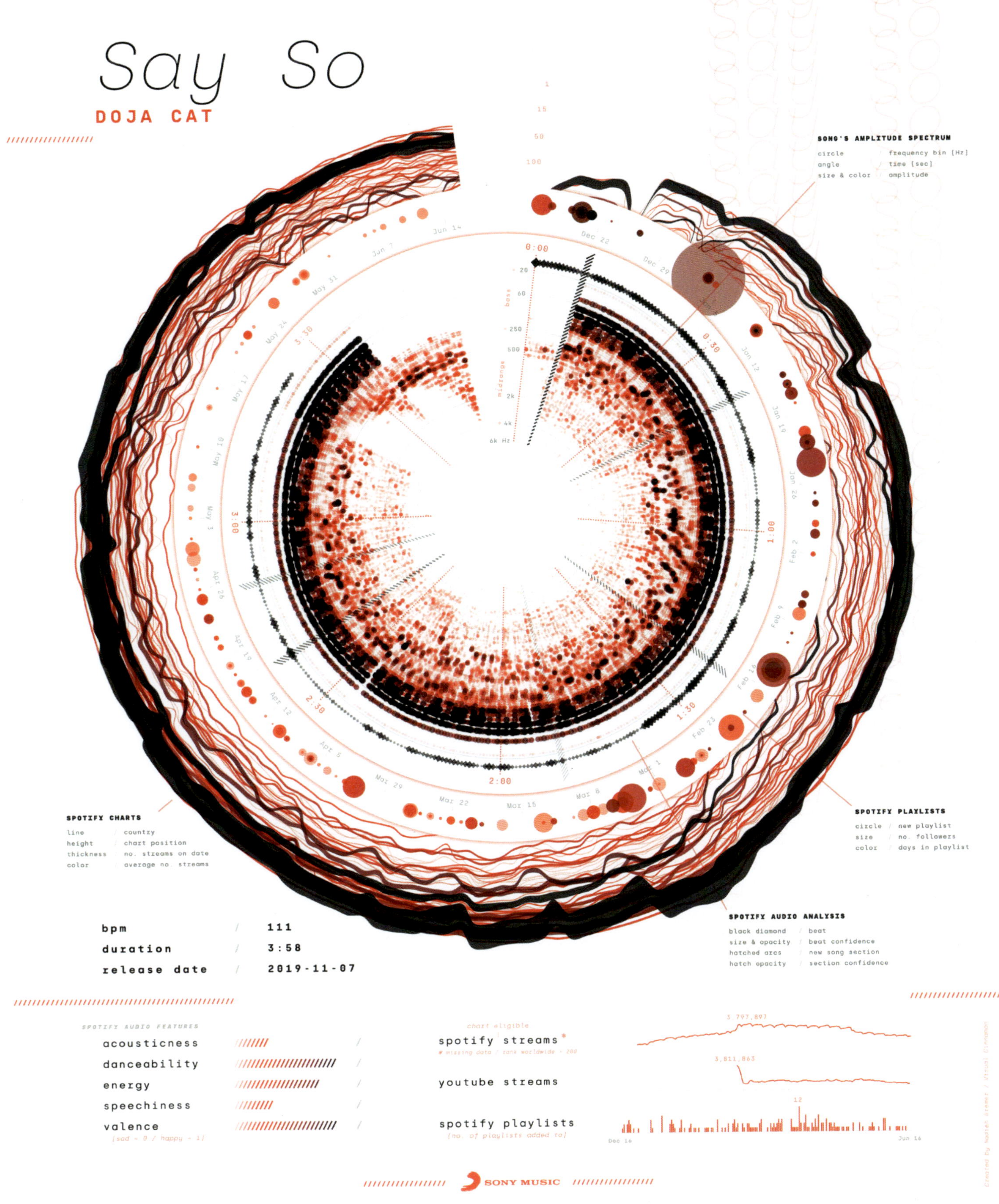

Say So
DOJA CAT
SONG'S AMPLITUDE SPECTRUM
circle / frequency bin [Hz]
angle / time [sec]
size & color / amplitude
SPOTIFY CHARTS
line / country
height / chart position
thickness / no. streams on date
color / average no. streams
SPOTIFY PLAYLISTS
circle / new playlist
size / no. followers
color / days in playlist
SPOTIFY AUDIO ANALYSIS
black diamond / beat
size & opacity / beat confidence
hatched arcs / new song section
hatch opacity / section confidence
bpm / 111
duration / 3:58
release date / 2019-11-07
SPOTIFY AUDIO FEATURES
acousticness
danceability
energy
speechiness
valence
[sad = 0 / happy = 1]
chart eligible
spotify streams *
* missing data / rank worldwide > 200
3,797,897
youtube streams
3,811,863
spotify playlists
[no. of playlists added to]
12
Dec 16
Jun 16
SONY MUSIC

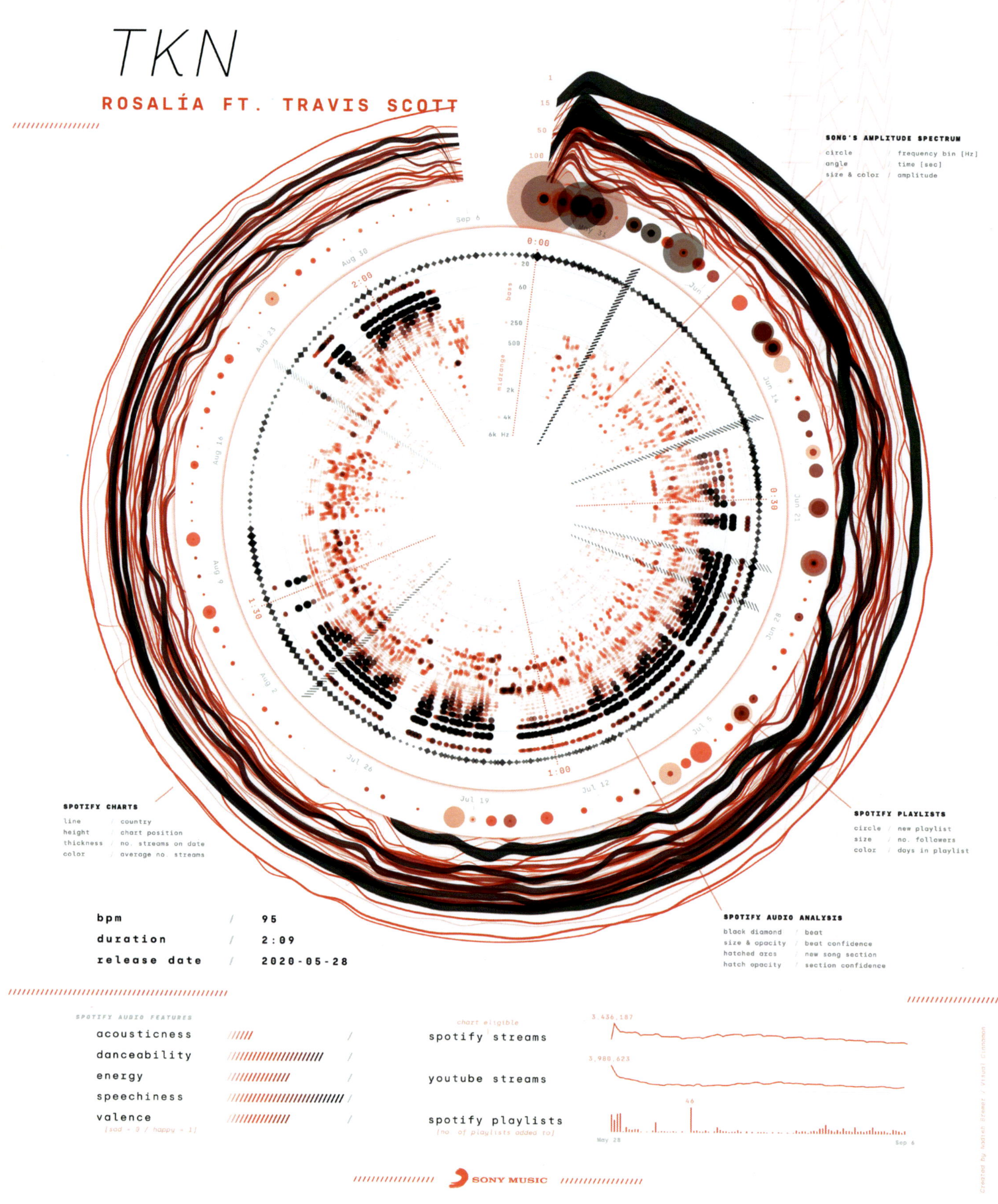

TKN
ROSALÍA FT. TRAVIS SCOTT
SONG'S AMPLITUDE SPECTRUM
circle / frequency bin [Hz]
angle / time [sec]
size & color / amplitude
SPOTIFY CHARTS
line / country
height / chart position
thickness / no. streams on date
color / average no. streams
SPOTIFY PLAYLISTS
circle / new playlist
size / no. followers
color / days in playlist
SPOTIFY AUDIO ANALYSIS
black diamond / beat
size & opacity / beat confidence
hatched arcs / new song section
hatch opacity / section confidence
bpm / 95
duration / 2:09
release date / 2020-05-28
SPOTIFY AUDIO FEATURES
acousticness
danceability
energy
speechiness
valence
[sad = 0 / happy = 1]
chart eligible
spotify streams
3,436,187
youtube streams
3,980,623
spotify playlists
[no. of playlists added to]
46
May 28
Sep 6
SONY MUSIC

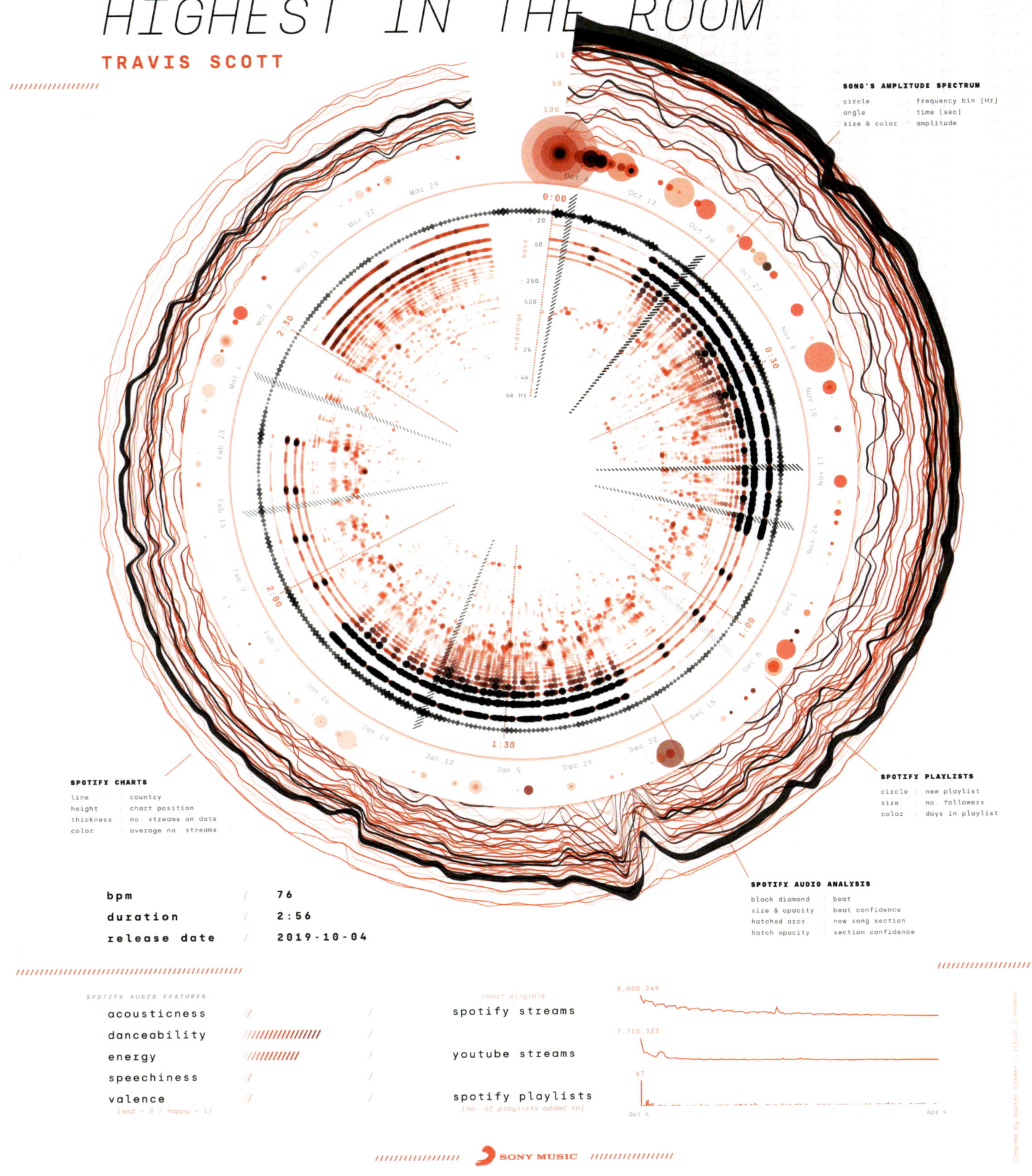
HIGHEST IN THE ROOM
TRAVIS SCOTT
SONG'S AMPLITUDE SPECTRUM
circle / frequency bin [Hz]
angle / time [sec]
size & color / amplitude
SPOTIFY CHARTS
line / country
height / chart position
thickness / no. streams on date
color / average no. streams
SPOTIFY PLAYLISTS
circle / new playlist
size / no. followers
color / days in playlist
SPOTIFY AUDIO ANALYSIS
black diamond / beat
size & opacity / beat confidence
hatched arcs / new song section
hatch opacity / section confidence
0:00
0:30
1:00
1:30
2:00
2:30
bpm / 76
duration / 2:56
release date / 2019-10-04
SPOTIFY AUDIO FEATURES
acousticness
danceability
energy
speechiness
valence
(sad = 0 / happy = 1)
chart eligible
spotify streams
youtube streams
spotify playlists
(no. of playlists added to)
8,000,249
7,715,323
67
Oct 4
Apr 4
SONY MUSIC

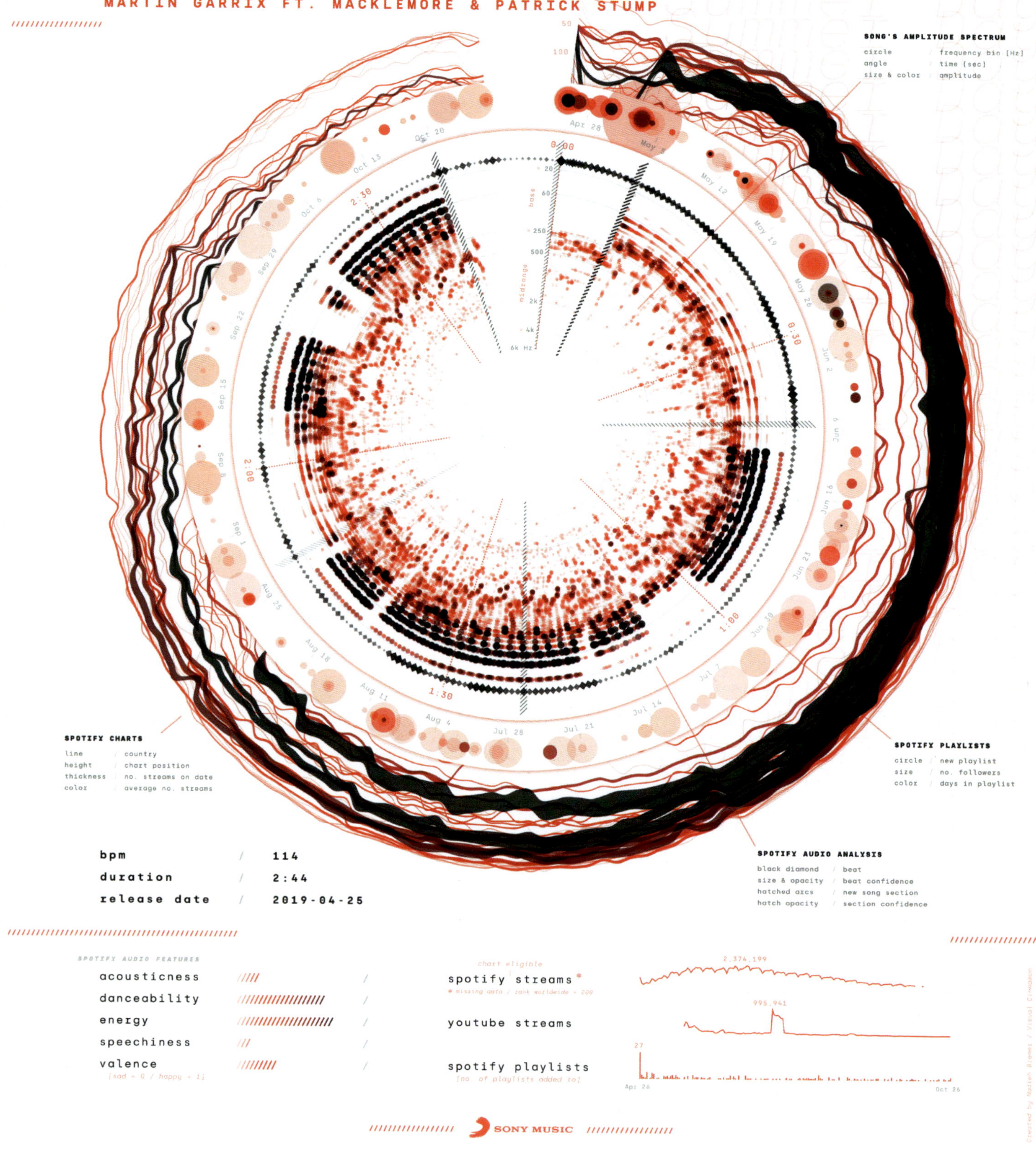

Summer Days
MARTIN GARRIX FT. MACKLEMORE & PATRICK STUMP
SONG'S AMPLITUDE SPECTRUM
circle / frequency bin [Hz]
angle / time [sec]
size & color / amplitude
SPOTIFY CHARTS
line / country
height / chart position
thickness / no. streams on date
color / average no. streams
SPOTIFY PLAYLISTS
circle / new playlist
size / no. followers
color / days in playlist
SPOTIFY AUDIO ANALYSIS
black diamond / beat
size & opacity / beat confidence
hatched arcs / new song section
hatch opacity / section confidence
bpm / 114
duration / 2:44
release date / 2019-04-25
SPOTIFY AUDIO FEATURES
acousticness
danceability
energy
speechiness
valence
[sad = 0 / happy = 1]
chart eligible
spotify streams *
* missing data / rank worldwide > 200
2,374,199
youtube streams
995,941
spotify playlists
[no. of playlists added to]
27
Apr 26
Oct 26
SONY MUSIC
Created by Nadieh Bremer / Visual Cinnamon

Figure 10.24

The poster for "Talk" by Khalid, featuring Disclosure, stands out thanks to the clear and separated beats.

Figure 10.25

The poster for "Say So" by Doja Cat.

Figure 10.26

The poster for "TKN" by Rosalía, featuring Travis Scott.

Figure 10.27

The poster for "HIGHEST IN THE ROOM" by Travis Scott.

Figure 10.28

The poster for "Summer Days" by Martin Garrix, featuring Macklemore and Patrick Stump.

If you've never worked with really large data sets and are feeling apprehensive, I'm here to calm your nerves a bit. With the benefit of software and programming tools, you can automate the placement of thousands or even millions of visual marks—although most data visualizations will contain far less than that. If you can get your software or coding program to do your bidding for one data point, you can generally automate that process for the other thousands of them. There's no need to fear large data sets; instead, get excited! See them for the treasure troves of information they are, the potential for creative visualizations they hold, and the extra context and nuance they can add to tell the best visual stories.

One small asterisk on the advantages of bigger and more diverse data sets is that, funnily enough, once you move all the way to data art, the size of the data doesn't really matter anymore in terms of how creative you can make it. Bigger data sets tend to be optimal when you're working in that sweet spot where you can be creatively free yet still need to convey some form of trends and patterns; when you still have a "constraint" to make the data readable. Once you cross into the art space-which we will in the next chapter-and there's no longer any need to show data values, you can do the wildest things with only a few data points.

CREATIVE LEGENDS

As your data visualizations become more creative, your legends may need to follow suit. A basic list of colored circles with labels might no longer be sufficient to explain more complex visuals.

V.1a

Hubble's observations

Each ◆ on this map represents a *Hubble* scientific observation in the telescope data archive. The color signifies the main category of the observation target: ◆ *Star* and ◆ *Stellar cluster*, which include extrasolar planets; ◆ *Galaxy* and ◆ *Cluster of galaxies*, which include quasars and clusters that serve as gravitational lenses; interstellar medium, or ◆ *ISM*, which includes planetary nebulae and supernova remnants; and ◆ *Solar system*. Other observations are tagged as ◆ *Unidentified*, such as the Hubble Deep Field surveys, or as ◆ *Calibration*.

Some well-known stars and constellations are marked for context.

THE WELL-KNOWN LEGEND STYLES

Let's start with some standard legend types, which are typically placed outside the main chart. These legends can be as simple as coloring words within a short text, as shown in figure V.1a from the Hubble project in Lesson 10. Alternatively, a minimalist approach might list visual channels and their meanings in plain text, like in figure V.1b from the music poster project in Lesson 10.

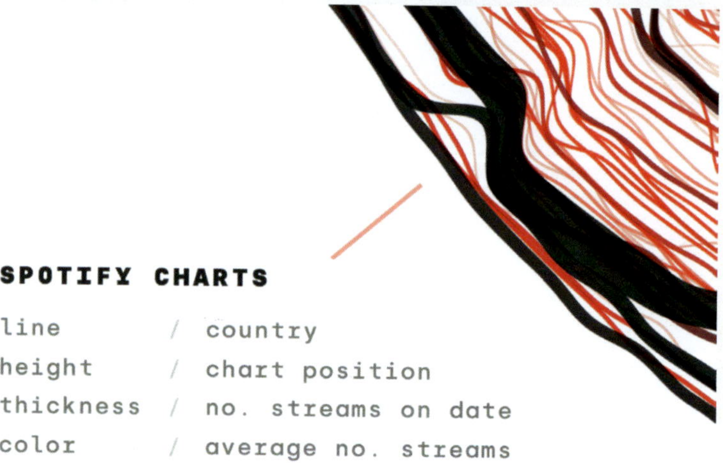

V.1b

V.2a

Position in Top 2000

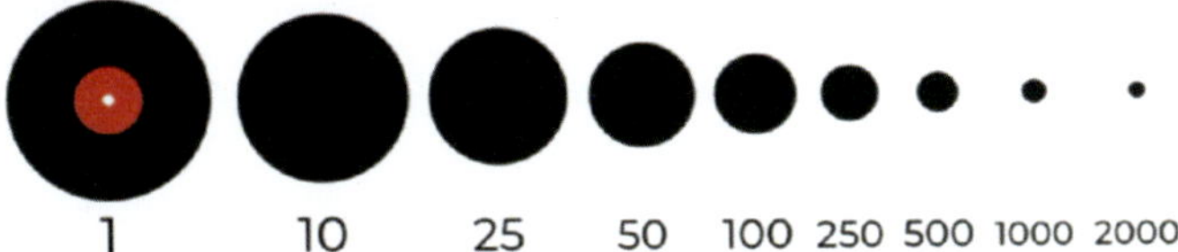

Highest position reached in weekly Top 40

never reached
the top 40*

Number of deportees
per EU country

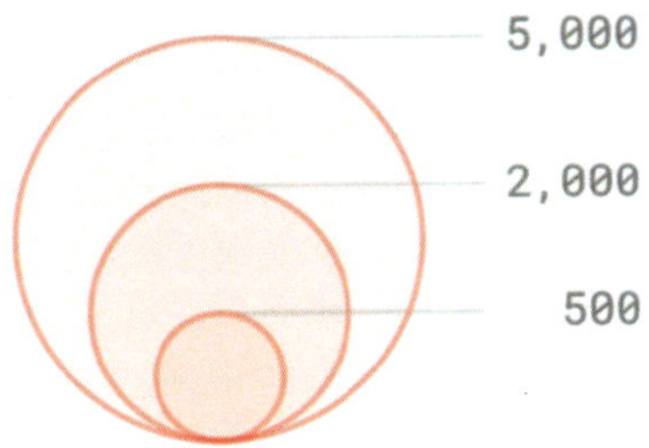

● EU member states
● Destination countries

V.2b

Figure V.1a & b

Two text-based legends: one that colors the categories within a paragraph (a), and one that lists the visual channels and their meanings in plain text (b).

Figure V.2a & b

Two more common legend types positioned beside the main visual, indicating circle size and color for the "The Top 2000 ❤ the 70s & 80s" project (a) and the Lighthouse Reports deportation visual (b).

A more traditional approach is to place icons alongside the visualization (often in some list form), as seen in figure V.2a for the "Top 2000" music songs project in Lesson 1 and figure V.2b for the deportation flights project in Lesson 7.

CUSTOM "OUTSIDE THE CHART" LEGENDS

When the visual has a unique design, you might need to convey more than color or size alone. In these cases, software's default legend options often fall short, requiring you to create your own legend to place next to the visual. Using a vector tool like Affinity Designer or Adobe Illustrator can make it easier to create these highly custom designs. Figures V.3a and V.3b show two examples of these more elaborate legends from

V.3a

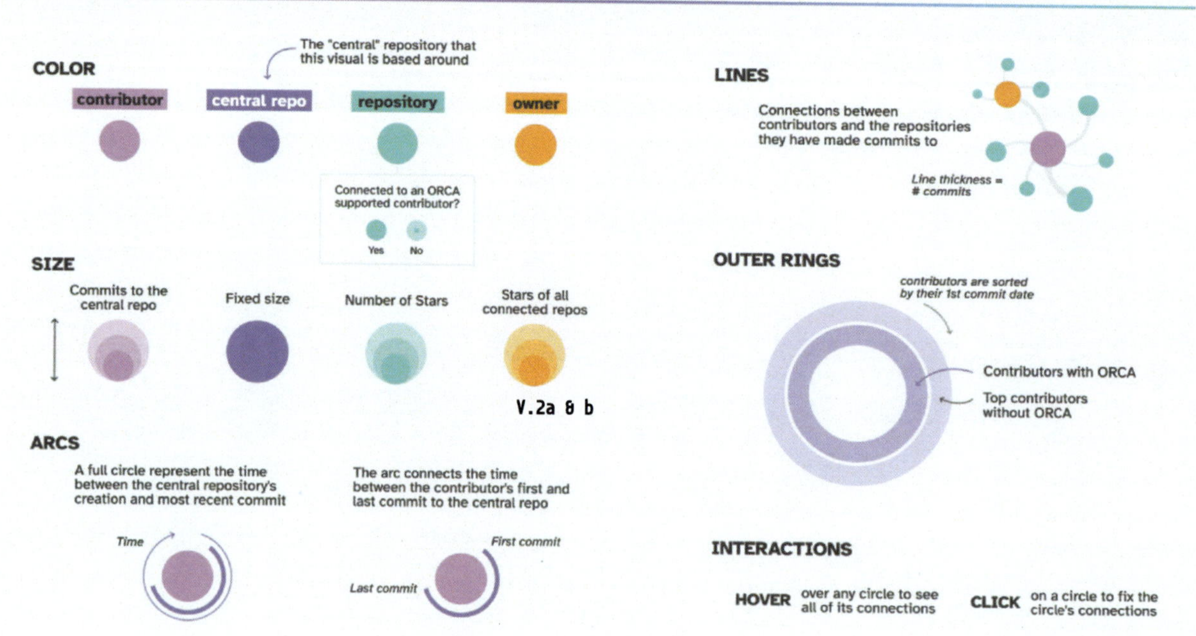

V.2a & b

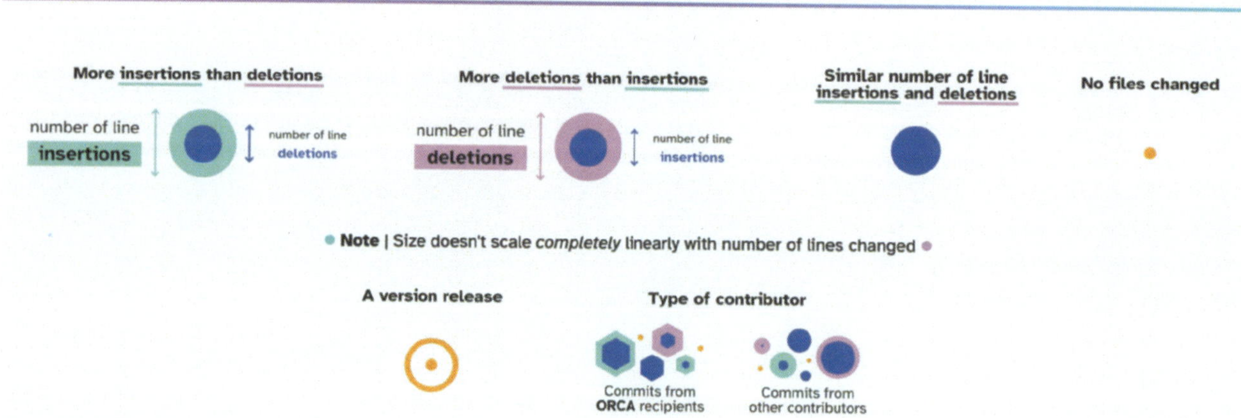

V.3b

Figure V.3a & b

Highly custom legends for the two ORCA projects, manually crafted using vector drawing software and positioned outside the main visuals.

the ORCA projects mentioned in Mini Chapter IV and Lesson 7. For these more elaborate legend designs, simple hand-drawn sketches helped me conceptualize the layout.

TAKING A SLICE FROM THE MAIN VISUAL

While I prefer to incorporate legends within the visualization itself, often there isn't enough space available. If your design is too complex to be captured in a simple custom legend, consider taking a direct slice of the main visual, placing it alongside the chart, and annotating its various elements.

You can see an example in figure V.4 for the consumer propensities project in Lesson 7, where I used one of the state "spokes" from the main visual to explain what it all meant. Although this legend is text-heavy, sometimes detailed explanations are necessary. The Olympic gold medals project in Lesson 3 also uses this technique (bottom-left of figure 3.4).

For the power grid project at the end of Lesson 5, I created a separate legend (figure V.5) to avoid distracting viewers from the main piece. (You can see the legend as the little rectangle off to the right in figure 5.10a.) This comprehensive legend combines elements from the main visual with small but detailed annotations.

PLACING THE LEGEND INSIDE THE VISUAL

Although generally my most challenging to create, legends that are integrated directly within the chart can improve readability and are therefore my favorite approach. By embedding the legend, the viewer doesn't need to shift focus between the chart and an external key. In line charts, for example, it's now common to place labels next to the lines rather than in a separate legend (as in the cinnamon-yogurt chart from figure III.1).

One favorite example is the Janssen pharmaceuticals project poster in Lesson 10,

V.4

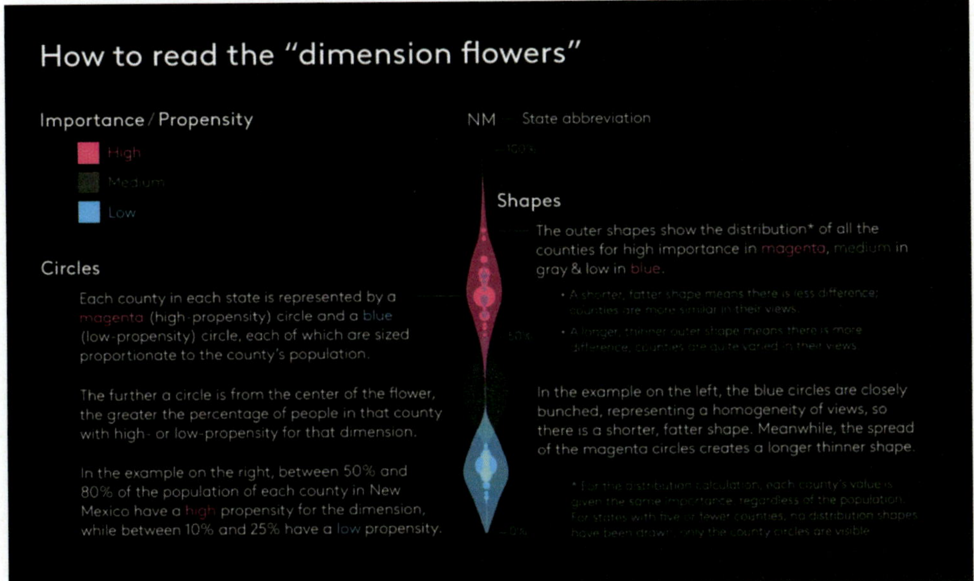

Figure V.4

A single "spoke" from the Kantar visual about consumer propensities serves as a legend, with annotations explaining each detail.

Figure V.5

An elaborate legend for Swissgrid's "Landscape of Power Flows" project, merging various elements from the main visualization.

V.5

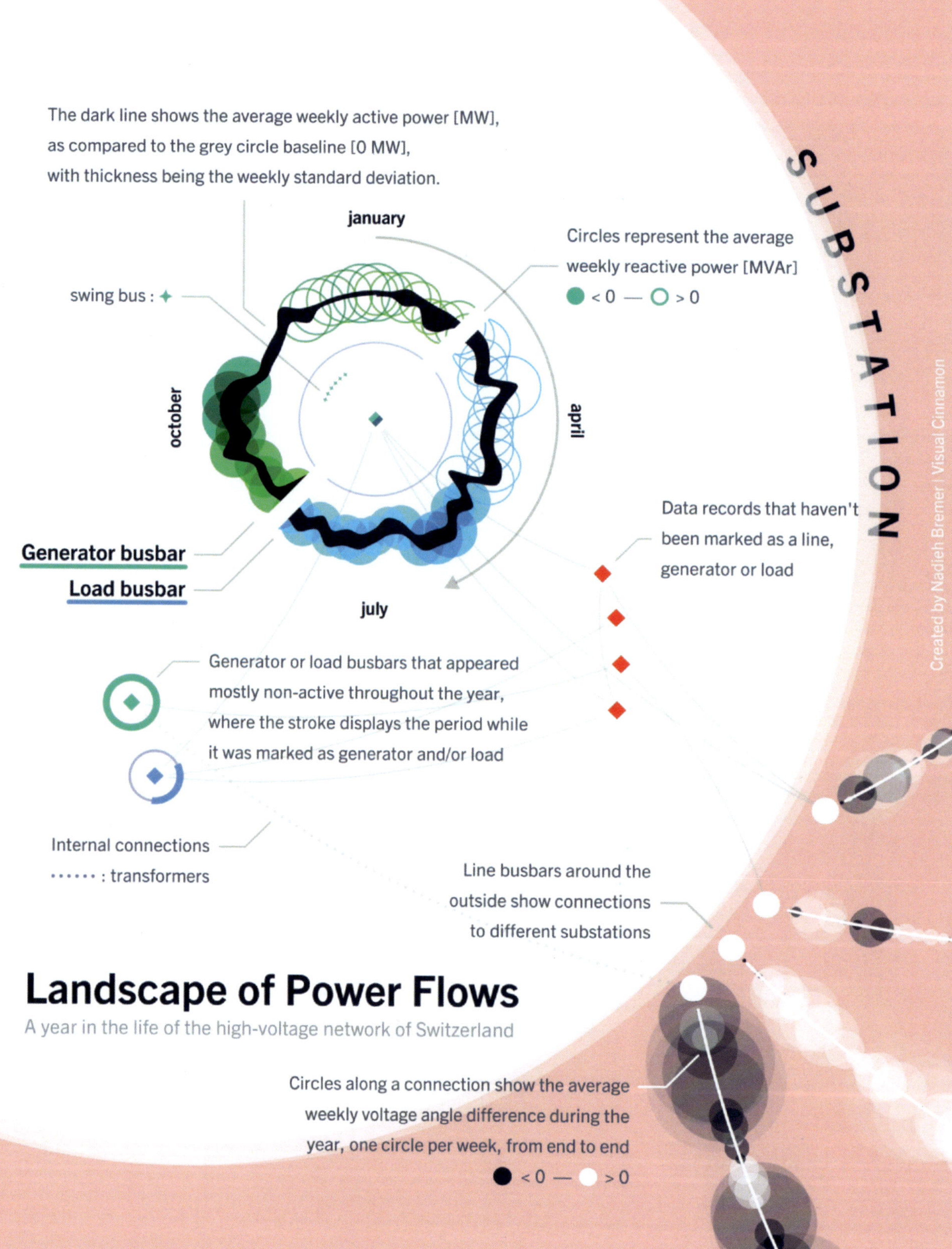

Landscape of Power Flows

A year in the life of the high-voltage network of Switzerland

where I placed a larger version of a radial line chart in the center, expanding it to fit annotations that explain each element in the charts (figure V.6).

In an extreme case, I turned a legend into a chart itself (figure V.7). That same Janssen poster includes a color legend for healthcare repositories; each colored vertical bar has texts next to it, describing the name of the repository and other metadata. I added a horizontal stacked bar chart showing the volume of records in each repository and connected it to the color legend with flowing lines. This added a dynamic centerpiece to the poster, drawing viewers' attention to the color meanings before they explored other elements.

As we transition from Part III to the data art explorations in Part IV, legends will play a smaller role. But for the creative data visualizations seen thus far, unique charts often require custom legends. Hopefully, the techniques here provide inspiration for designing legends that enhance your visualizations.

V.6

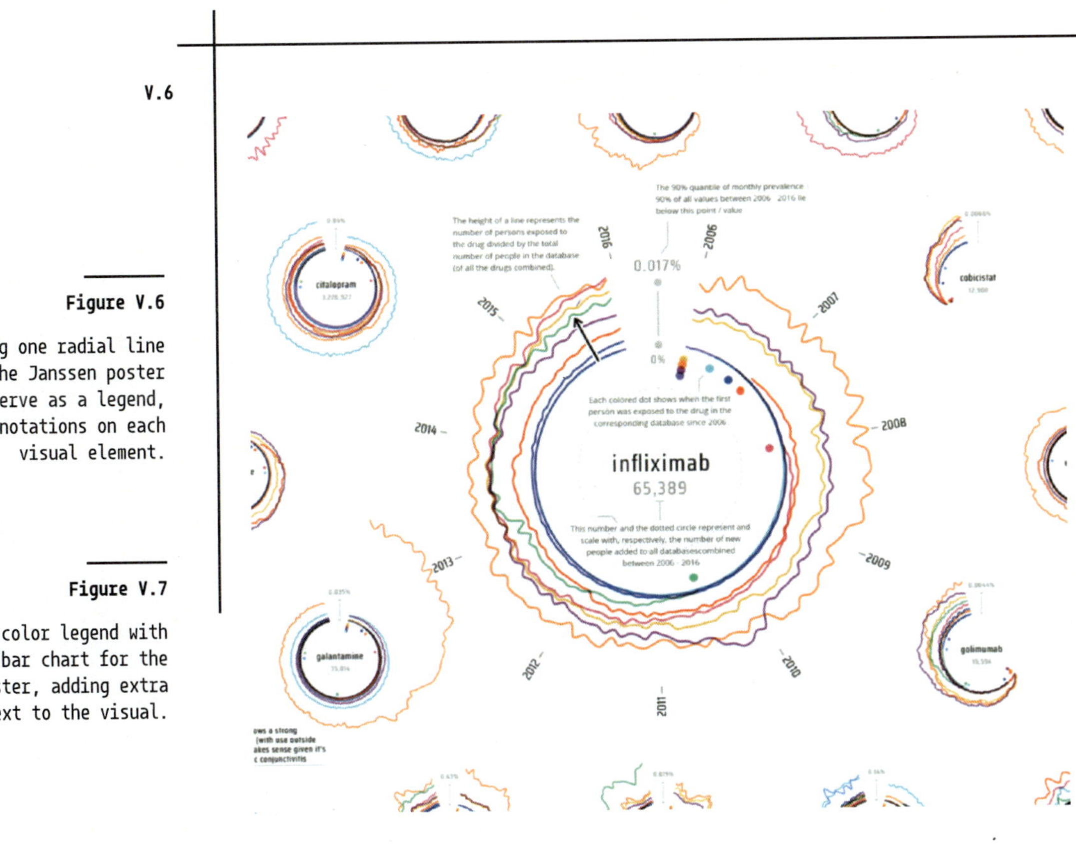

Figure V.6

Enlarging one radial line chart within the Janssen poster to serve as a legend, with annotations on each visual element.

Figure V.7

Merging the color legend with a stacked bar chart for the Janssen poster, adding extra context to the visual.

V.7

Observational Data around the World

In total, Janssen Epidemiology Analytics conduct research on more than 469 million patient records from across US, Europe and Asia-Pacific

DIVING INTO

Although I'm passionate about uncovering hidden stories in data and sharing them visually, I also love transforming data into art. When we step into the realm of art, the goal is no longer about conveying the exact values; it's more about evoking an emotion. You can let go of the "constraints" of traditional visual encoding—such as scaling by size or color—to make data readable. Instead, you have the freedom to choose whatever approach you feel works best for the story you want to tell. No more need for legends or explanations on how to read each part of the visual if you don't want them.

I'd say that in data art, there are no rules, apart from using *some* data, in *some* way. Although you can use any medium you like—I've seen data artists employ Play-Doh, knitting, balloons, and more—the focus of this section will be on the digital data art created with a computer.

We'll start by exploring how to leverage design, aesthetics, and other creative aspects from your hobbies, interests, and other disciplines. I'll then show you how randomness can be your best friend when you want to add more nuance and

DATA

some surprises to your design. And because it's evident at this point that I love circles, I'll come back around to the very first lesson about using inspiration from the dat set and the topic—but in the context of data art.

After these lessons, you'll have some footholds to get started with data art yourself, and even if you have no desire to create art, you'll be able to apply the lessons—subtly—to bring more finesse to your data visualizations.

LESSON ELEVEN

FIND INSPIRATION

Pull artistic inspiration—as well as techniques and tools—from other creative areas of your life to give your data visuals some flair

What grabs your attention?

You, and just about every other human, react to things that are exciting, new, or unexpected. However, I think many would agree that data visualization doesn't carry a reputation of excitement or surprise—especially on the visual design side—among the general public. This is understandable; a minimalistic approach will generally convey data insights quicker and more efficiently than a bespoke one, because the viewer will feel comfortable and familiar with its design. The downside is that if you only look at existing data visualizations for inspiration, you are severely limiting the options available to you.

FROM YOUR INTERESTS

This lesson doesn't contain data art. In a way, it is straddling the line right before making data art, where you are using outside inspiration to make very creative design choices and elevate your data visualizations. I don't explicitly talk about data art in the coming examples, but I am using inspiration from paper art and generative art as a gentle introduction to the data art we'll explore in the next two lessons.

This is why I actively seek inspiration outside the data visualization fields. The intriguing and beautiful creative influences that I find won't specifically dictate how to place my data, but will steer the style, the overall design, or the layout of the entire piece.

The fields from which you draw inspiration should be personal to you. I can't give you a list or tell you to "look into these specific fields or tools." You can only create such a list for yourself. In this lesson, I'll demonstrate how this technique can work. I will share three fields and a software tool that I'm personally drawn to for style inspiration. You'll notice that incorporating elements from these fields gave my data visualization designs a special touch.

11.1

PAPER ART

I like paper. In various forms. I see paper as the analog version of the 2D computer screen I face so often. There's this inherent flatness to it, but it's tangible, and real, with a texture and a pliability that make it 3D. Therefore, I'm not surprised that paper became a major inspiration for one of my most well-known visuals when I started freelancing in 2017.

Gradients like stacked paper cuttings

BUSINESS | 2017 | *SCIENTIFIC AMERICAN*
scientificamerican.com/blog/sa-visual/why-are-so-many-babies-born-around-8-00-a-m

Zan Armstrong, a wonderful data visualization specialist, scientist, and friend, found some fascinating trends in the average number of babies born in the United States per week, per day, and yes, even per minute. (For instance, there's a significant spike in births around 8:00 a.m. due to the prevalence of prescheduled C-sections.) *Scientific American* asked her to turn this data set into a page for their "Graphic Science" section, and she asked for my collaboration on the visual side.

The design evolved from a straight line chart to a radial area chart, as the data held a cyclical pattern (see figure 11.2). Time ran clockwise, with midnight at the top. The average number of babies born per minute was a baseline circle (in yellow). At first, we filled in the area between this baseline circle and the actual number of babies born each minute with green-blue and orange-red gradients to better reveal lows and highs throughout the day.

Although I'm a huge fan of gradients, I didn't quite like the look in this particular case. I could only describe it as feeling too "sleek" because the smooth gradients dominated the visual. I tried several things, such as turning the area chart into a bar chart (figure 11.3) to break up the wall of color, but nothing felt like a great solution.

Figure 11.1

Two images of pen plots I made using my AxiDraw V3/A3 machine. I make a design on the computer and use the machine to draw it out on actual paper with any pen I might fancy.

Figure 11.2

A radial area chart where the (yellow) baseline circle represents the average number of births per minute. The colored area, showing the actual number of babies born, is filled with a color gradient-green-blue for below average and orange-red for above average.

Figure 11.3

Testing a radial bar chart option to break up the wall of color.

Figure 11.4

The gradient is separated into discrete color steps. There is a subtle drop shadow on each step to mimic 3D layers of stacked colored paper.

I then thought to cut the gradients into discrete color steps as if each color were a sheet of paper layered on the one below it. To enhance that effect, I added a slight drop shadow to each colored ring to mimic the shadow cast by real stacked papers. I immediately liked this result from a design perspective (figure 11.4).

In typical bar and line charts, it's relatively easy to compare two points, even if they are far apart, because the axes are straight; it's much harder to make that comparison on circular charts. However, the discrete color circles addressed this—they made it much easier to compare various points along the circle, as the number of color rings signal the distance from the yellow baseline.

After several more iterations to perfect the details, we also crafted versions of the visual to illustrate birth trends over a week and across a year. The final page, as it appeared in *Scientific American*, is shown in figure 11.5.

11.2

11.3

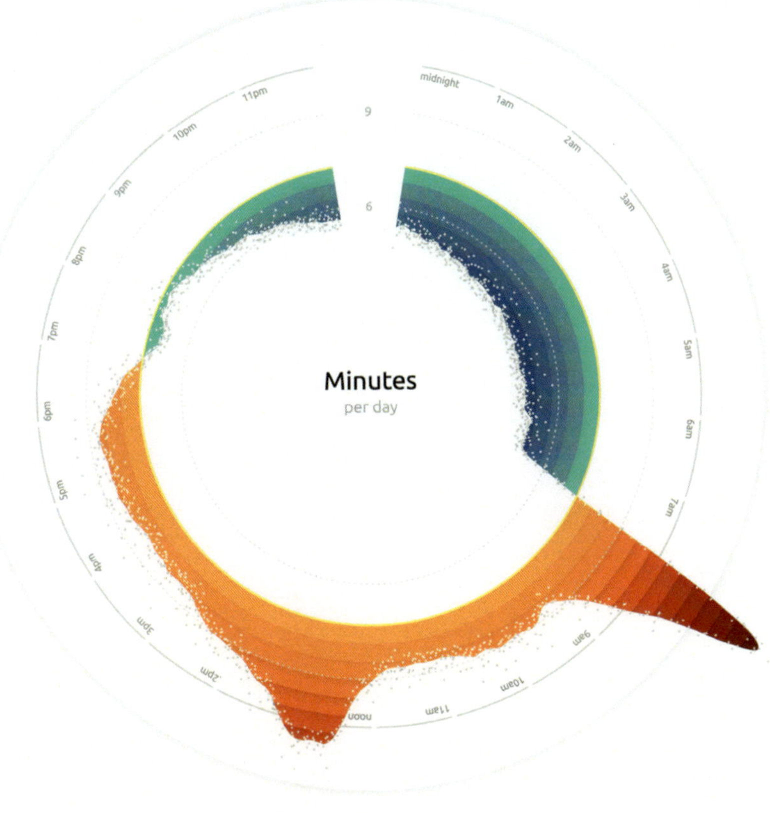

11.4

GRAPHIC SCIENCE

The Baby Spike

Births peak on weekdays during daytime work hours

Two generations ago babies were born pretty much spontaneously, around the clock. But today in the U.S., about half of all births are cesarean sections prescheduled by Mom or deliveries induced by doctors concerned about the mother's or baby's health. These medical procedures have skewed the days of the week, and hours of the day, during which those little bundles of joy arrive.

The procedures dominate because more than 98 percent of infants are born in a hospital, despite what seems to be the rising popularity of home births. Far more babies now arrive on weekdays than on weekends, most between 8 A.M. and 6 P.M. "We can't schedule spontaneous labor, obviously," says Neel Shah, a physician and professor at Harvard Medical School. "But we can schedule delivery."

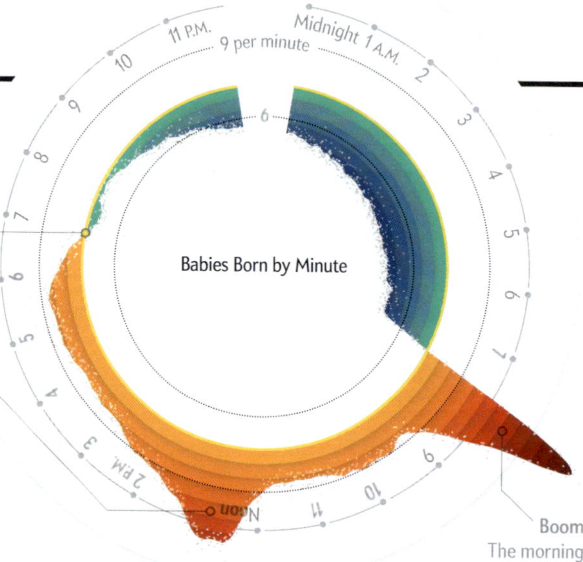

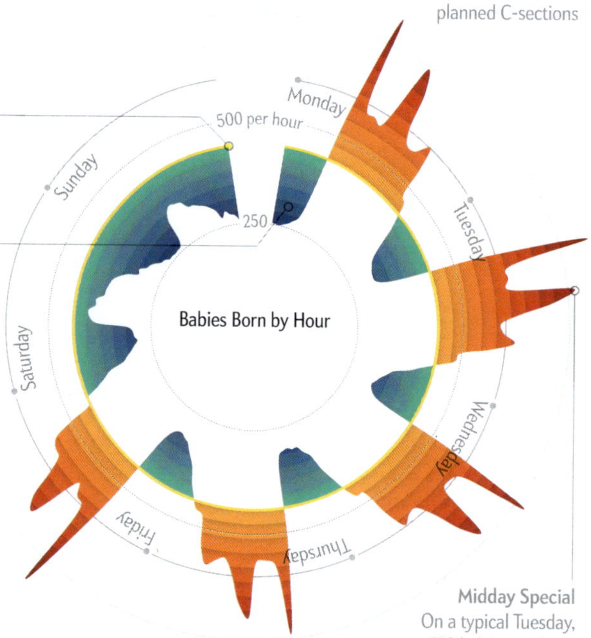

—Mark Fischetti and Zan Armstrong

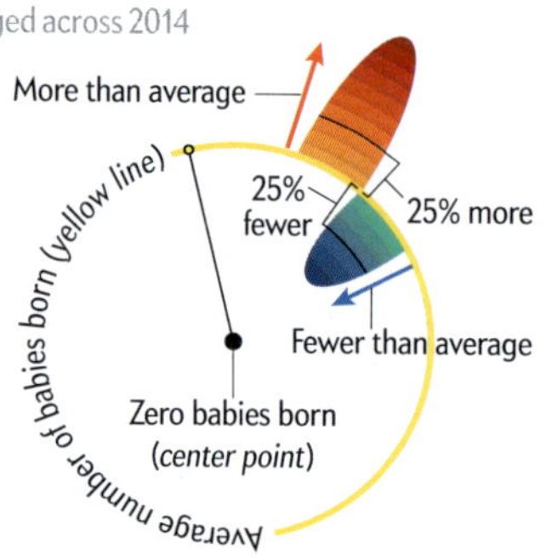

SOURCES: FIVETHIRTYEIGHT, FROM DATA SUPPLIED BY U.S. SOCIAL SECURITY ADMINISTRATION (week data); CENTERS FOR DISEASE CONTROL AND PREVENTION (minute and hour data)

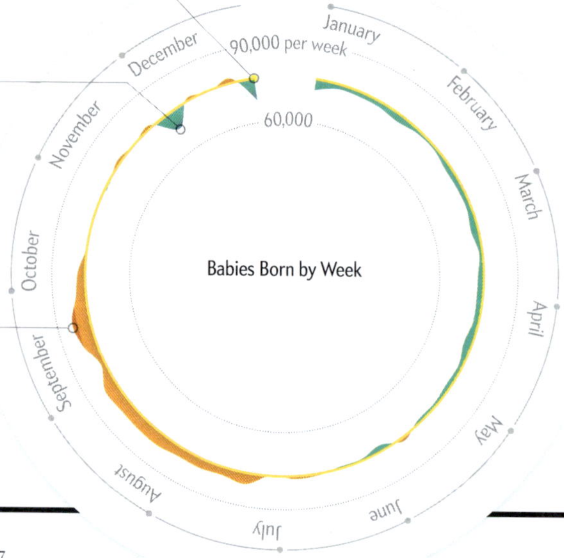

Graphic by Nadieh Bremer and Zan Armstrong

GENERATIVE ART

Figure 11.5

The final page of "The Baby Spike" in *Scientific American*, featuring circular charts for the number of babies born each minute over the course of a day (top), each hour over a week (middle), and each day over a year (bottom).

Generative art is any creative work—musical, visual, literary, etc.—produced using an autonomous system. This system is generally non-human and can independently determine (visual) characteristics that would otherwise require input from the artist. Rolling a dice to decide if, for example, a line should be yellow, green, or blue, is one type of autonomous system. Here, I want to focus on generative art created with a computer.

I see generative art as a collaboration between an artist and the computer. The artist programs algorithms and rules that establish certain style parameters and also determine when the computer can autonomously make style choices. As a very straightforward example, the artist can write a function to place several circles on the canvas. However, they will let the computer determine precisely where those circles are drawn. They could even program it so that the number of circles and the size and color of the circles are determined by the computer. The computer makes its "decisions" by generating random numbers that set its path through the algorithm (e.g., "Set the x-position of this circle to a random value between 0 and the width of the canvas,"

11.6a

11.6b

11.6c

or "randomly pick a color from this predefined color palette and apply it to the circle.") The artist generally knows the kind of style that will come out. Still, it's (usually) impossible to know precisely how it will look—will the circles be evenly distributed or all bunched in a corner? The craziest part is that there can easily be millions of different outcomes, all originating from the same lines of code.

Figure 11.6a, b & c

A few examples of my generative art collections: vibrant spirals in "Twistings / Explore" (a); capturing the chaos of our inner minds with "Fleeting Thoughts" (b); and a mid-century modern design for the "wavʌves" collection (c).

Especially for designers who program, there is considerable overlap between generative art and data art. My process for creating generative art is the same as data art but without the data. Instead of data, I use functions that supply random numbers to determine all the visual choices. (I'll explain more about what this entails in the next lesson.)

My main reason for working on generative art is that it allows me to simply create freely and flexibly—and not have to think about what data-based story to tell. I can clear my mind from tasks like gathering and cleaning data and can focus more on the design without worrying about legends or annotations. It helps me to flex my artistic muscles and experiment with visual styles that don't always work for formal data presentations.

11.7

Embracing the taboo with 3D bars

PERSONAL | 2023 | *NIGHTINGALE* MAGAZINE
visualcinnamon.com/portfolio/skyscrapers

I've noticed that my data visualization designs use elements from my generative artwork. I can lift the techniques or design elements from a generative art piece and infuse them (often subtly) into a data visualization.

As an example, figure 11.7 shows some outputs from my "Obscured" generative art collection. The visual uses only tiny dots, many millions of them, to create fields of overlapping triangles. The triangles may appear opaque, patterned, or shaded, but all these textures are actually dots at different densities.

Figure 11.7

Several pieces from the "Obscured" collection that use millions of dots to draw colorful fields of overlapping triangles. See more at *visualcinnamon.com/art/obscured*

Figure 11.8

Filling the 3D bars, representing skyscrapers, with a gradient made from tiny dots; the deeper the red, the older the building.

As a reader of the Data Visualization Society's *Nightingale* publication, I wanted to submit an article for their printed magazine. When I heard that an upcoming issue would be about "guidelines"—which, as you can probably tell by now, I think are very helpful but can be bent and broken—I definitely had some thoughts to share.

I wanted to tackle extreme guidelines—the so-called "best practices" that had effectively become hard rules. I thought, what taboos exist in the data visualization profession? Adding 3D effects is definitely considered a taboo because the added dimension makes it much harder to accurately compare values, such as the height in a bar chart.

My mind instantly went to a data set about the 100 tallest skyscrapers I'd encountered recently. Displaying a skyscraper as a 3D bar? Outrageous! But it's such a strong metaphor! Perhaps, I wondered, a 3D effect could work if building height was not the primary focus. I checked the data, and my instinct proved correct. Apart from the tallest building, the Burj Khalifa, and the other top four, all the skyscrapers in the data set were not very different in height. Other insights from the data analysis, such as their location, use, and age, were more interesting. Since comparing heights wasn't the primary goal, I felt this was a perfect opportunity to embrace the 3D bars to evoke the shape of a skyscraper.

During the design phase, I filled the bars with a red-to-transparent gradient. The more red, the older the building. But for a bit more finesse—and because I thought it would be a good fit for the style of a printed magazine—I didn't use the standard (smooth) gradient option. Instead, I reused the "gradient by dots" technique I learned while making "Obscured," as shown in figure 11.8.

11.8

11.9b

Figure 11.9a & b

My visualization about the tallest skyscrapers, printed in the third issue of *Nightingale* magazine. Courtesy *Nightingale*, the Journal of the Data Visualization Society, Issue 3.

It's subtle, but I found the granulated effect much more visually pleasing. I liked that the dotted gradient created a stronger depth effect by making the separate "skyscrapers" stand out more from one another.

Figure 11.9 shows the final result, and I was delighted that the visual and accompanying article got accepted for publication. Indeed, it is possible to bend the rules and embrace taboos under the right circumstances.

Because I anticipated that some readers would want to have some information about the exact heights nonetheless, I added a little "proper" 2D bar chart along the right edge listing all 100 skyscrapers in order of height, and another along the left edge that showed the skyscrapers by year of completion. (Remember the "additional (mini) charts of grouped values" from Lesson 7.)

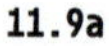

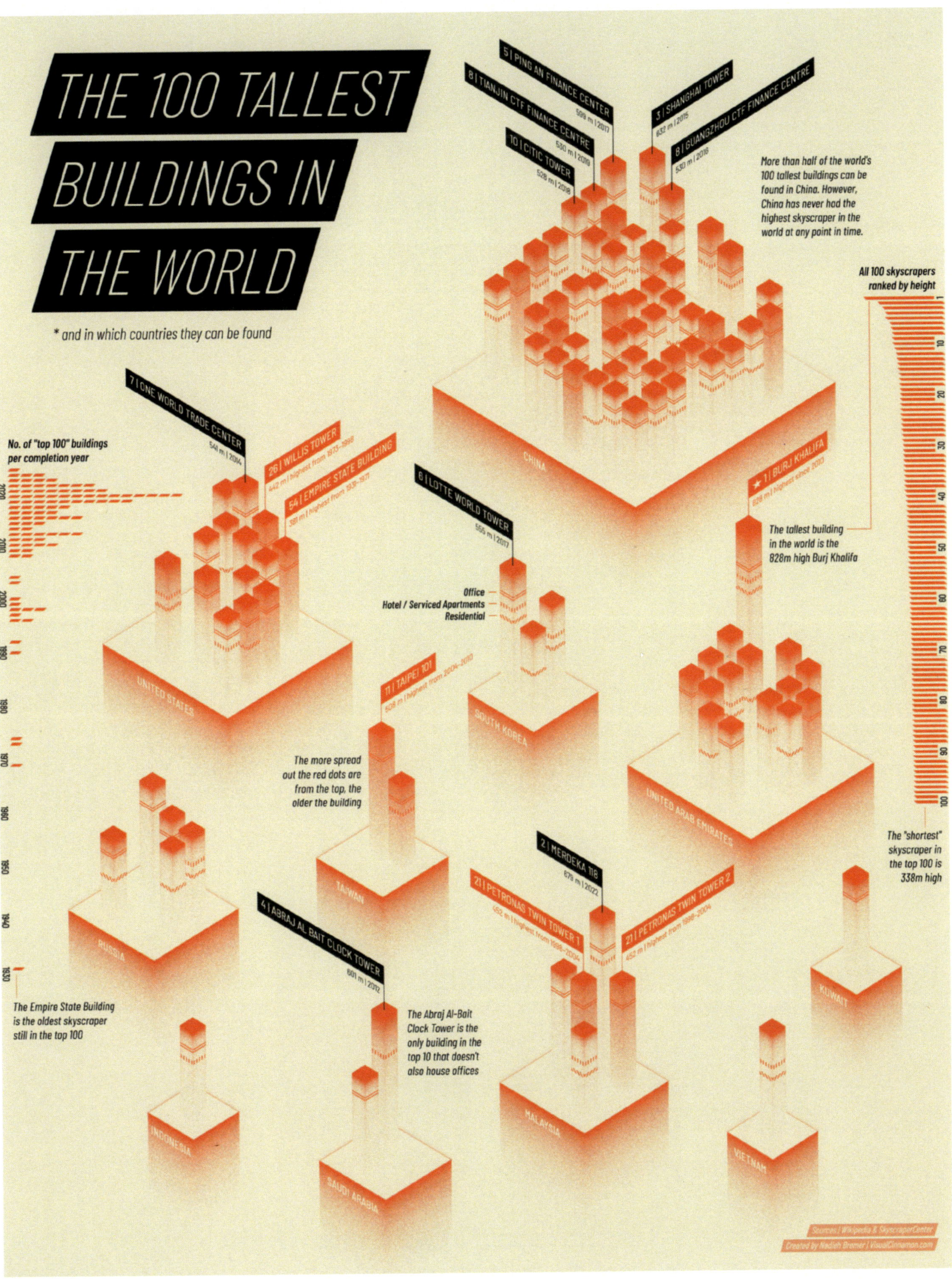

THE 100 TALLEST BUILDINGS IN THE WORLD
* and in which countries they can be found
5 | PING AN FINANCE CENTER
599 m | 2017
8 | TIANJIN CTF FINANCE CENTRE
530 m | 2019
10 | CITIC TOWER
528 m | 2018
3 | SHANGHAI TOWER
632 m | 2015
8 | GUANGZHOU CTF FINANCE CENTRE
530 m | 2016
More than half of the world's 100 tallest buildings can be found in China. However, China has never had the highest skyscraper in the world at any point in time.
All 100 skyscrapers ranked by height
CHINA
7 | ONE WORLD TRADE CENTER
541 m | 2014
26 | WILLIS TOWER
442 m | highest from 1973–1998
54 | EMPIRE STATE BUILDING
381 m | highest from 1931–1971
No. of "top 100" buildings per completion year
6 | LOTTE WORLD TOWER
555 m | 2017
★ 1 | BURJ KHALIFA
828 m | highest since 2010
The tallest building in the world is the 828m high Burj Khalifa
Office
Hotel / Serviced Apartments
Residential
UNITED STATES
SOUTH KOREA
11 | TAIPEI 101
508 m | highest from 2004–2010
The more spread out the red dots are from the top, the older the building
UNITED ARAB EMIRATES
The "shortest" skyscraper in the top 100 is 338m high
TAIWAN
RUSSIA
2 | MERDEKA 118
679 m | 2022
21 | PETRONAS TWIN TOWER 1
452 m | highest from 1998–2004
21 | PETRONAS TWIN TOWER 2
452 m | highest from 1998–2004
4 | ABRAJ AL BAIT CLOCK TOWER
601 m | 2012
KUWAIT
The Empire State Building is the oldest skyscraper still in the top 100
The Abraj Al-Bait Clock Tower is the only building in the top 10 that doesn't also house offices
INDONESIA
MALAYSIA
VIETNAM
SAUDI ARABIA
Sources | Wikipedia & SkyscraperCenter
Created by Nadieh Bremer | VisualCinnamon.com

GRAPHIC DESIGN

Graphic design, as a field, is a goldmine of inspiration for me. I'm often jealous of graphic designers' mastery of shapes, colors, and composition. I'm particularly drawn to posters and websites, but I also keep my eyes on marketing materials, magazines, and other content that requires well-designed layout and typography.

For a long time, I'd wanted to create a project inspired by 3D graphic design—particularly something bubbly, cute, and vividly colorful with soft, velvety textures. Unfortunately, my usual tools, D3.js and the (2D) HTML5 canvas API, couldn't achieve this 3D effect (despite D3's name perhaps suggesting otherwise). While I still enjoy the "flat" 2D designs these tools allow me to create, I was eager to expand my skill set. Writing this book became the perfect catalyst to finally dive into a proper 3D project using Blender—a tool I'd wanted to learn for years.

3D spheres along a glowing line

PERSONAL | 2024 | THE BEST SELLING NINTENDO SWITCH GAMES
visualcinnamon.com/portfolio/best-selling-nintendo-switch-games

I usually establish specific goals for my visual, the data stories I want to tell, when I start a new (personal) project. This case was different. I merely wanted a straightforward data set that could allow me to learn

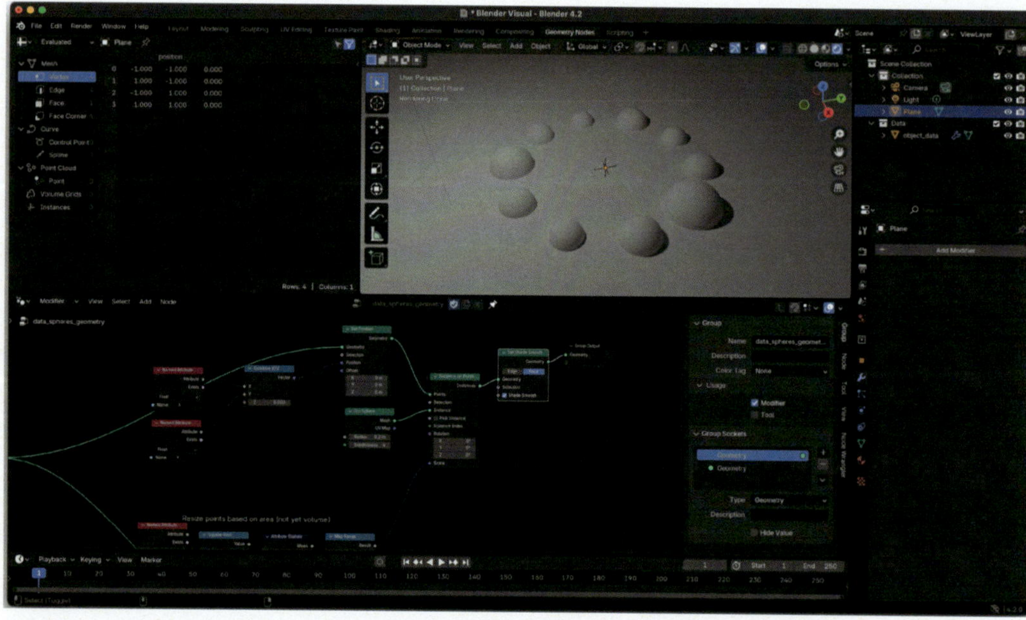

11.10

the tool. I thought about my hobbies, which led me to a list of the top 10 best selling Nintendo Switch games.

I wasn't going into Blender completely blind. I followed a tutorial in 2019 that yielded "the donut" (the "hello world" of Blender, although involving many steps). This gave me a little confidence but, importantly, a modicum of familiarity when I opened the program in 2024 and was confronted with all the tabs, views, and options.

I would say that Blender is best used with a mouse to make things "by hand." However, I wanted to use programming as much as possible, as I knew I'd likely want to visualize hundreds of data points in the future. Thankfully, there is also a Python API to control Blender, though its programming interface leaves something to be desired.

I still remember how it took me a whole week to make my first interactive scatter plot with D3 many years ago. I often thought back on that experience during this project, as my progress was slow, especially at the start. After two days of watching (and rewatching) many tutorials and asking an AI chatbot for help with the Blender Python code, I finally executed—and understood—the first step: loading my data set into Blender!

Figure 11.10

A screenshot of Blender, where I placed 10 spheres representing the top Nintendo Switch games in a circle. The spheres are scaled by the number of copies sold.

Things sped up after that, thankfully. I quickly learned how to create 3D spheres, scale their radius according to the number of units sold, and place them at a specific location. At first, I positioned the spheres in a circular formation (figure 11.10), ordered in no particular fashion, but once I got the hang of things, I instead placed them along a timescale in order of each game's release date. I figured out how to add text and played around with textures to give the spheres different looks—glossy white ceramic, copper, lava, and so on—encoded by game genre. I loved how I could make the timeline glow! And how I could make the title a white text on a white background, with a shadow to make it readable.

It took me a week overall (just like my first D3 visual) to achieve the final result, shown in figure 11.11. The top-down view is a throwback to

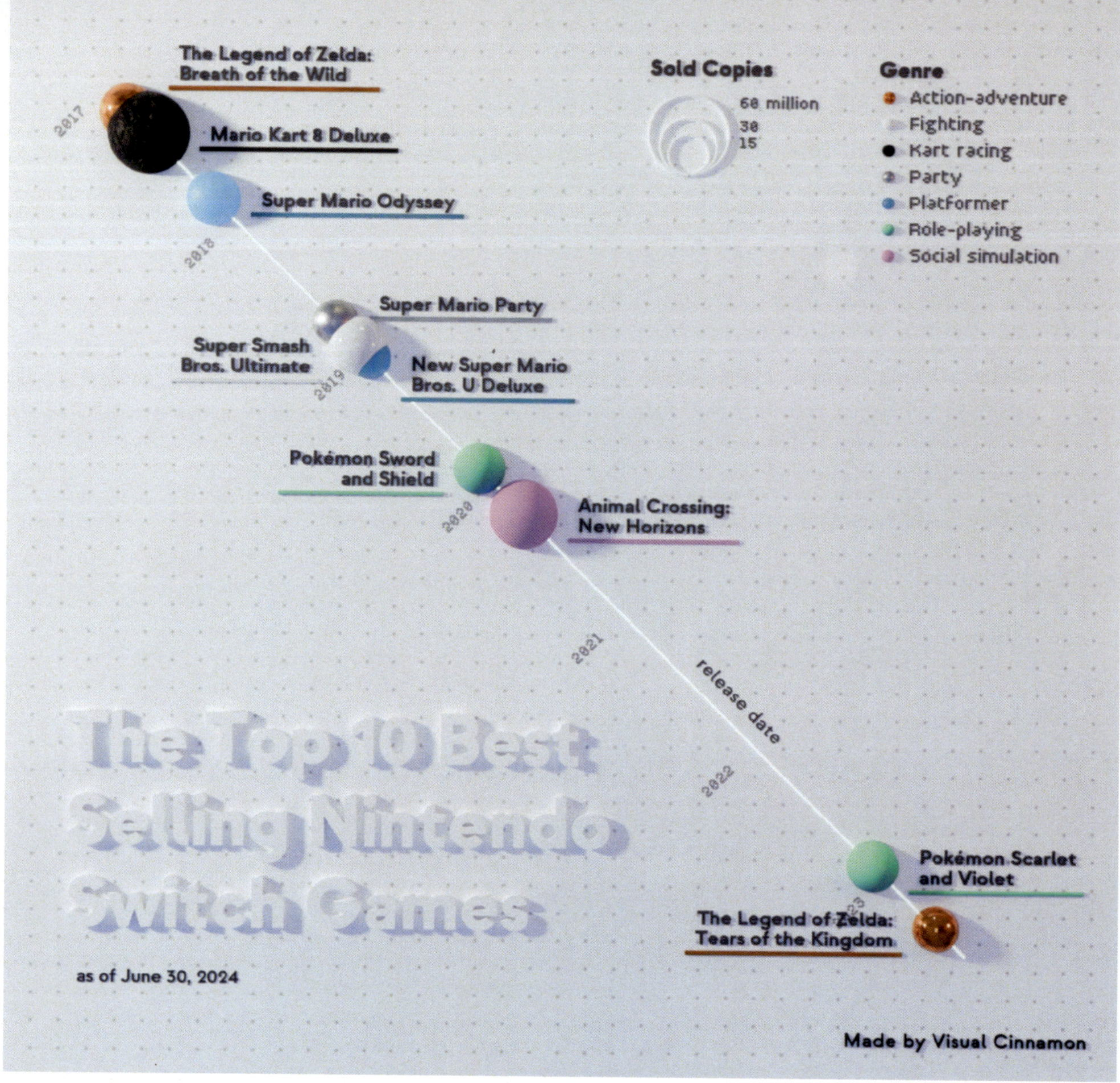

11.11

Figure 11.11

The final result of my first data visualization created with Blender showing the top 10 best selling Nintendo Switch games.

Figure 11.12a & b

Two more shots of the visual that highlight my reasons for wanting to learn Blender: to better show the 3D and shadow effect of the various elements (a) and to test the unique materials that can be used, such as "distressed copper" (b).

the standard 2D style, but the 3D aspect, the realistic lighting, and the material textures turn it into something a little more lively and fun.

I did stray a little from the "cute, bubbly" 3D graphic design style that I initially aimed for when I applied the lava and copper textures. But I think, overall, the final result definitely feels inspired by it, especially with the vibrant colors, the soft shadows, and the velvet texture of those pink and green spheres.

It was a frustrating experience at the start when everything was so new. However, things improved considerably once I got the hang of the program and the first spheres appeared in the scene. By the end, I looked forward to creating another data visualization with Blender.

11.12a

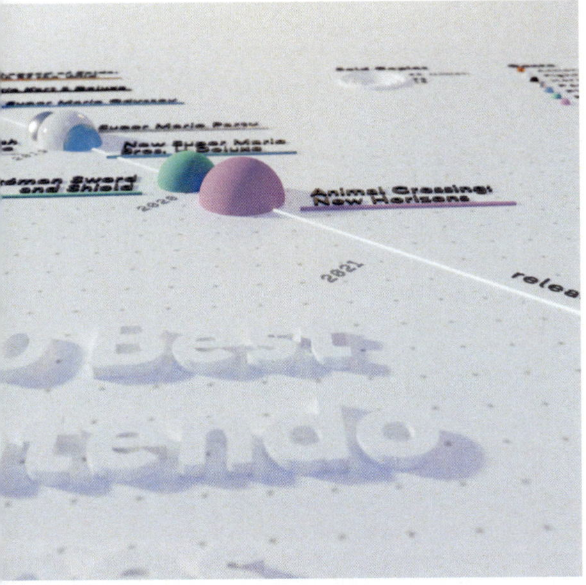

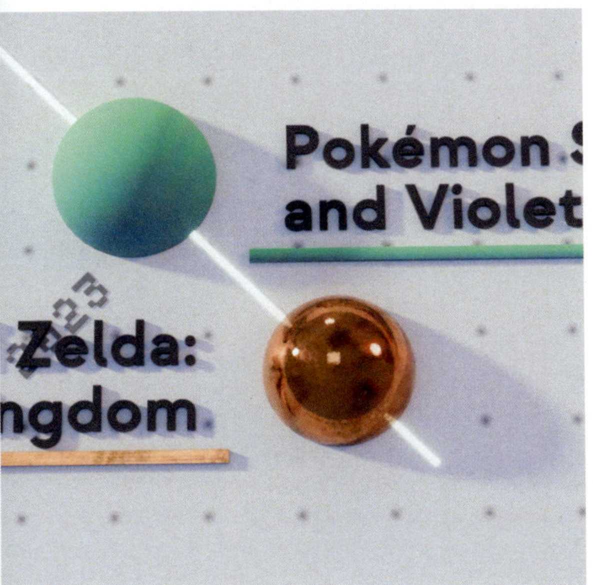

11.12b

Many other fields have inspired my data visualization designs. Space is perhaps an obvious one, from the gorgeous images of the Hubble and James Webb Telescopes to the retro space posters (from the space race era of the 1950s). I also love natural history illustrations and spirographs.

I would therefore advise you to be consciously aware of what your fields of interest are and what tools you want to learn. (You'll know because you'll feel envious of the amazing work other people are creating with them.)

My advice: Save photos, images, and even magazine pages that you find inspirational. As you're working on a new data visualization design, something from those other fields may just spark an idea. Or, if you want to be more proactive, look at those collections of saved images and see if anything from them, a particular design aspect, for example, would work with your current project.

LESSON TWELVE

ADD

Randomness broadens your visual possibilities and will reveal unexpected, refreshing outcomes

In general, as I move more toward data art, I become increasingly adventurous in leaving visual elements to chance. Being open to that kind of randomness will greatly broaden your space of visual possibilities. And having more possibilities will make it easier for you to create that visual diversity that I spoke so much about in Part III—especially when the available data is limited, and you need variation beyond what the data alone can provide.

Folding randomness into the design process adds an element of surprise—for you and also for your audience. Both parties benefit: You, the creator, can experiment and play more freely, producing unexpected elements that will improve the final result and thereby engage the viewer more.

The more randomness you allow, the less you can foresee all the possible outcomes. Sometimes, this leads to a completely unexpected outcome. Although it depends on your taste, I generally find that truly outlandish results wind up on the cutting room floor. But, occasionally, I find some out-there results so fascinating that I pivot the design toward them.

There is no one way to integrate randomness, but I prefer the following two options:

- **I apply random values directly.** For example, looking back at the "Highly Hazardous Pesticides" visual from figures 8.1 and 8.2, I set the opacity for every gray blob to a random number between 0.6 and 1, creating a field of gray blobs that were all slightly different.
- **I establish design rules that react to random values.** For example, a rule might say, "If the random value is lower than 0.5, the circle will be pink. Otherwise, it will be yellow."
    - These rules can have multiple layers of randomness: "... Otherwise, choose a color randomly from a set of five options."

RANDOMNESS INTO THE MIX

There are many ways to get a random number. Analog methods include flipping a coin, rolling a dice, or drawing numbers from a hat. But digital tools, like data analysis programs and programming languages (e.g., Excel, Python, JavaScript) with random-number generator functions, are generally faster and more convenient. (Technically speaking, they generate pseudo-random numbers based on a defined algorithm—not entirely on chance. But this is sufficient enough for my needs).

Although I applied randomness in subtle ways in some previous data visualization projects, the technique really shines in data art. So, without further ado, from here on out, it's time to kiss those legends goodbye!

If your design tool doesn't have a random-number generator, you can get creative by adding columns to your data set that contain only random values. These "dummy variables" can then be used in your visualization tool of choice. For instance, you might add a dummy variable with random values between 0.6 and 1 to set the opacity of each circle in your design. Another variable with random values between 0 and 1 could be used to color each circle: Assign pink to values less than 0.5 and yellow to values above 0.5.

Grids like growing minerals

PERSONAL | 2022 | ANHEDRA
visualcinnamon.com/art/anhedra

Figure 12.1

Some initial results from grids of random geometric shapes.

Ok, this project isn't technically data art; it's generative art; no data was used. It's made entirely with algorithms and random values. However, what happened at the start of this project is my clearest example of being surprised—that is, seeing an unexpected outcome that changed the entire direction of the project.

I originally aimed to create a collection of grids with simple geometric shapes, randomly assigned in position, color, and orientation (see some tests in figure 12.1).

The code I had written to create the grid already used a lot of random elements within the grid design (cell size, grid size, and color, for instance) and the shapes' design (orientation, color, and placement). At some point, I thought it would be nice to have some color coordination, where adjacent shapes would have a higher chance of being the same

12.1

12.2

Figure 12.2

A seemingly simple color coordination function created an unexpected but fascinating effect of large color areas.

Figure 12.3

Several outputs from the "Anhedra" collection.

color, so they would appear to be merged. I wrote a quick, but far from perfect, piece of code to get an initial sense. However, what appeared on my screen was quite shocking (figure 12.2).

I had anticipated that neighboring shapes would occasionally share the same color. Instead, I was taken aback by the large areas of pinks, blues, whites, oranges, and greens. The colors had seemingly grown, stretching and bleeding across the densest areas of the grid. It reminded me of how minerals can grow. I completely pivoted from my original idea and dove straight into finding more ways to let color "grow."

This eventually led to the "Anhedra" collection, featuring several hundred unique outputs. (See figure 12.3 for a few examples.)

12.3

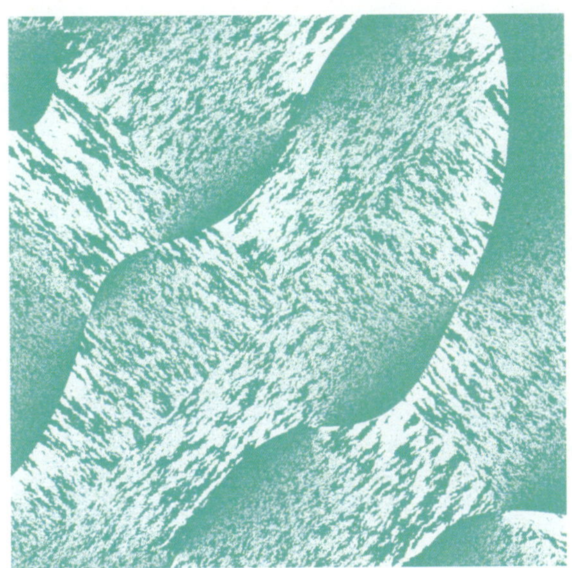

FULL DESIGN STORY

I want to take you along on the full creation journey of a 1,000-piece data art collection I made for UNICEF where data and randomness worked together in various ways.

Kingdoms of vibrant blocks

BUSINESS | 2021 | UNICEF

patchwork-kingdoms.com

UNICEF's Giga project aims to connect all of the world's schools to the internet. This access can significantly benefit the students, fostering digital skills and providing online learning resources. To raise funds, they wanted to create a digital art collection to sell. Since a large part of the Giga project consisted of gathering information about all the schools in the world, including where they are located and whether they have internet, the UNICEF team wished to feature this data in the art.

Figure 12.4

My father's childhood building block set that I fondly played with as a kid.

I wanted to go for a design style that would evoke nostalgia for childhood and feel natural in a child's bedroom (remember lesson 1, about finding inspiration from the data's topic). However, with the schools spread worldwide, I also wanted the design elements to be universally recognized. At first, I thought of drawing the schools on a stylized map, visualizing the digitally connected schools in some kind of giant web. However, I quickly realized that the essence of the data wasn't geographical. In a way, it didn't truly matter where the schools were. It was about whether or not they had internet access. And thus, I explored other options.

12.4

I started thinking about basic shapes—triangles, circles, squares—which reminded me of my father's wooden building blocks that I'd played with as a kid, creating entire cities from these versatile shapes (figure 12.4, tying back to the previous lesson about leveraging designs and structures from things outside the field of data visualization). Not only were these toys a direct tie to childhood in a universal sense, but these blocks could connect together to form something greater.

I also learned that Mary Blair created "It's a Small World" for UNICEF at the 1964 World's Fair; so finding this source of inspiration was a good sign!

With this idea of "cities built from simple building blocks," I started looking for inspiration online. It didn't take me long to come across the beautiful concept art that Mary Blair made for Disney's "It's a Small World," which immediately resonated with me. It was the same general concept as the wooden building blocks, with squares, rectangles, and other shapes placed together to form a (2D) city. She had decorated each shape with dots, lines, stars, and more.

An idea started to form in my head: Each school would be represented as a single building block, a tiny square. The schools already connected to the internet would have vibrant colors and complex decorations. The schools not yet connected would have more muted colors and only simple decorations.

I would then stack all those squares together to make them look like cities. However, there would be a divide, a "digital divide." The schools already connected to the internet would stack up together, forming a city in the normal sense. The schools not yet connected would instead stack down, forming a hidden upside-down city. This concept came from fairy tales that I remember, with upside-down or hidden cities below the ground.

12.5

Figure 12.5

The sketch for my concept, where each school is a building block (a square). The blocks stack together to form two cities; schools connected to the internet are upright on top. Those that are not are upside down on the bottom.

I drew a rough sketch to convey my idea (see figure 12.5) and presented it (along with my explanation) to the UNICEF team. Thankfully, they loved the idea, and thus, I continued to work on the design.

While this was very much a data-driven project, let me share the many ways I infused randomness into the process.

When I started working with the team at the end of 2021, they knew the internet connection status of about 283,000 schools across 21 countries (most of which are in the developing world), the connection speed, and type of connection available.

12.6a **12.6b**

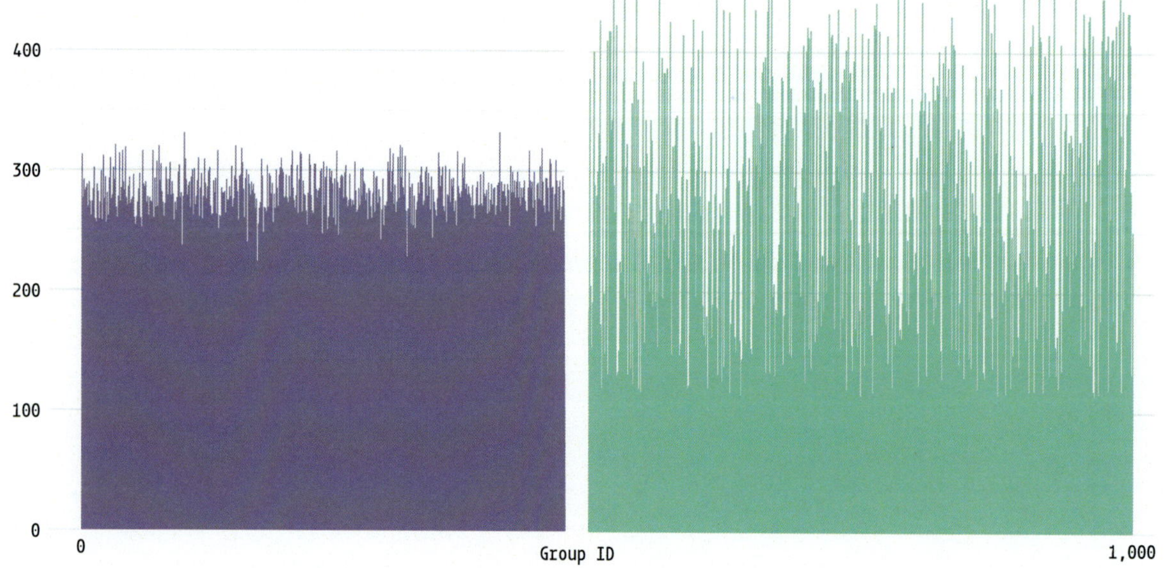

Figure 12.6a & b

The number of schools per group (the y-axis) was too close to the average of 283 for the 1,000 groups (a). The adjusted allocation assigns anywhere between 100 and 450 schools to each group (b).

Figure 12.7a & b

Creating a grid and stacking all the squares from the black baseline, either upward (for the schools connected to the internet) or downward (for those that aren't).

I wanted to spread those 283,000 schools across the collection. We settled on 1,000 unique artworks, and no school would appear more than once throughout the collection, meaning an average of 283 schools would be featured on each piece.

To start, I grouped the schools by randomly assigning them to a number between 1 and 1,000. However, of the 1,000 groups, most wound up having between 250 and 300 schools assigned to them (see figure 12.6a). I wanted more diversity—I wanted some art pieces to have about 100 building blocks and others to have more than 400! This would ensure that the collection would have both "villages" and "metropolises." Therefore, I adjusted the random allocation function to have a much wider spread (figure 12.6b).

12.7a

12.7b

12.8

After assigning each school to one of the 1,000 groups, it was time to start stacking. I began by setting up a grid for each group. The larger the number of schools, the more rows and columns I needed.

Then, I looked at how many schools in each group were connected to the internet versus not connected. I used the ratio between the size of these two groups to place the "digital divide," the black line in figure 12.7. This black line is the baseline from which I would stack the schools either upwards (connected to the internet) or downwards (not connected).

Each block got assigned to a certain column randomly, placing it on the next available cell in the column (either at the top for the connected schools, or at the bottom for the unconnected ones). This produced "towers" of varying heights. I created a more realistic "big city" skyline for the upright cities by adjusting the placement odds to be higher for the middle columns. This put higher towers more in the center, as you can see in figure 12.7.

With the city structure ready, it was time to decorate the building blocks. I wanted to use simple geometric shapes such as circles, squares, rectangles, and triangles in different combinations. I drew over 100 little boxes in a notebook and slowly filled them with designs (figure 12.8).

Figure 12.8

A page full of little squares with ideas for decorations using combinations of simple geometric shapes.

I intended to use my large assortment of decorations to encode information about the schools, but I knew that the data set's variables didn't have lots of unique values. So, I began by assigning a random decoration to each block and then seeing how I could incorporate some data-based rules to determine which school would get which decoration. For example, I realized that some of my decorations stemmed from the same underlying design, but ranged from simple to more detailed: one circle in the center versus two circles or even three. That could be encoded to the school's internet speed: the higher the speed, the more detailed the decoration (figure 12.9).

Figure 12.9

Adding circles to each school, where design complexity–the number of circles in this case–is determined by the internet speed; the faster the internet connection, the more circles inside a square.

Figure 12.10a & b

Adding increasingly more types of decorations to the cities.

Figure 12.11

Sketching decorations that could be combined in rows, columns, squares, or crosses to sync up into a bigger design.

Figure 12.12

A test showing "combined" symbols in the upper city.

After spending a few days digitally recreating all the hand-drawn decorations, I ended up with 51 unique decorative symbols, each with between one and five "levels of complexity," many of which you can see in figure 12.10.

Schools without internet, in the upside-down cities, always had the simplest designs. I had considered leaving them all completely blank, as they didn't have any internet speed, but I didn't think that was visually appealing.

The data set sometimes had information about the cellular services in the area of the school—2G, 3G, or even 4G availability. The schools that didn't have internet but were in an area with a cellular network got building blocks with color-filled shapes (rather than stroked outlines). This signaled that the schools had the potential to become connected to the internet, and that they could cross the divide with some help.

Although the schools were placed randomly in the grid, there were times when adjacent schools had something in common, like a shared country or internet connection type. When that happened,

12.9

12.10a

12.10b

12.11

I wanted to give those schools a shared decoration. Back to my notebook I went, this time to sketch out shapes and patterns that could be oriented or rotated so that they would sync up with their neighbors to create something more special (figure 12.11).

Figure 12.12 shows the idea in action. It's a test to see how schools that are adjacent and with common characteristics could be "fused" to each through their decorations, making it look like a larger, single decoration.

I decided that the 10% of schools with the highest internet speed would be assigned a flower shape. However, if two of those high-speed internet schools were side by side, their blocks would together become a rainbow, the ultimate children's symbol of positivity! (There's one in figure 12.12.)

With the decorations finished, it was time to work on the roofs. I had, at this point, added some elementary triangles on top of the buildings, but I wanted something that would complement the detailed decorations within the squares.

12.12

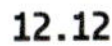

I returned to my notebook for the third time and started sketching roof designs ("turrets," I called them) that were one square wide. These would be assigned randomly. However, I also wanted to create multi-square options in case two or three adjacent towers were the same height (figure 12.13).

As the turrets materialized on my screen, I truly started seeing each of the cities as fairytale-like "kingdoms" (figure 12.14).

One thing I love about randomness is that you can get clever yet unintentional results. For instance, the decorations and the turrets in figure 12.15 sync up in shape and color. The pink tulip symbol on the left is an illusion, made from a block with a pink semicircle and a turret with pink quarter circles.

As I talked with the team at UNICEF, we thought it would be nice if all the 1,000 artworks were "linked" somehow. I imagined a map showing all of these kingdoms. I decided to lay out all of them on a grid of 40 by 25, giving each kingdom four direct neighbors (apart from those on the edges). I made a background motif, inspired by topographic lines. Figure 12.16a shows a test background for one artwork, while 12.16b shows how this subtle motif creates a shared background for the individual kingdoms.

Figure 12.13

Sketching different "turret" designs to top each tower.

Figure 12.14

Adding various turret designs turned the upright cities into kingdoms.

Figure 12.15a & b

Two examples of the building-block decorations and the turret designs syncing up in shape and color to create a seamless look.

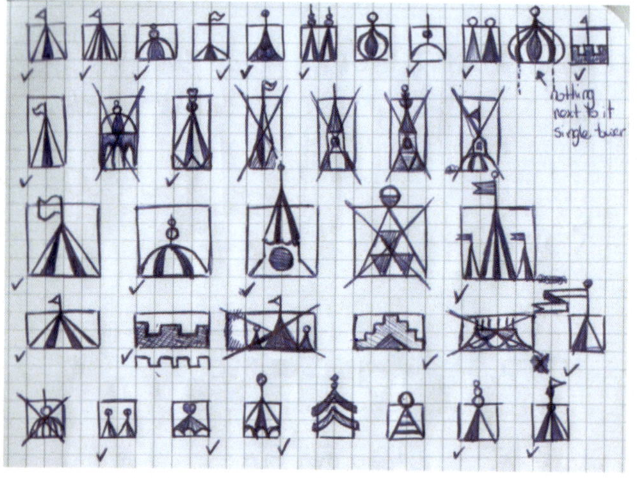

12.13

12.14

7.4b

12.15a

12.15b

12.16a

12.16b

Figure 12.16a & b

The topography-inspired background motif (a) and how it connects the backgrounds of the four kingdoms in a seamless way (b).

Figure 12.17a, b, c & d

Some examples from the final color palettes and their names: Fruit Loops (a), Crystal Palace (b), Unicorn (c), and Slime (d).

And then came the color palettes. I may have spent a whole week trying out colors. I have screenshots from hundreds of tests. It's a rather tedious process, whether creating a palette from scratch, or starting from some form of inspiration such as an image, turning it into a palette, and then tweaking it to fit your design. In both cases, I often find myself throwing out color palettes and trying something new—over, and over.

For this project, I wanted a variety of palettes. I wound up using a lot of colors from (retro) pixel art video games as inspiration, as these generally have quite vibrant hues (and perhaps because they stirred up some childhood nostalgia).

12.17a

12.17b

12.17c

12.17d

Figure 12.18a, b, c & d

Examples of special results among the 1,000 kingdoms: a "lighten" color blend mode on a "Unicorn" color palette (a); a single-decoration kingdom (apart from some windows and doors) (b); and kingdoms with only schools connected to the internet (c), and only schools not connected (d).

I ultimately settled on 24 color palettes, which would be assigned randomly across the kingdoms (see four options in figure 12.17). However, some palettes had a higher chance of being selected than others. I also added one small easter egg—kingdoms with the red palette, the green palette, and the blue palette would always be neighbors to allude to the RGB color model.

And finally, with 1,000 pieces, there is a lot of potential to purposely create a few very special results. For example, I added a small chance in the algorithm that a "color blending" technique would be applied (figure 12.18a). I added another small chance that all of a kingdom's turrets would be topped with little hearts. And another small chance that

12.18a

12.18b

12.18c

12.18d

12.20

Figure 12.19

A selection of 77 Patchwork Kingdoms.

Figure 12.20

Patchwork Kingdom #403 | Bultacindal.

one decoration would be applied throughout, in all its levels of complexity (figure 12.18b).

Furthermore, during the data preparation phase, I deliberately created 10 groups that contained schools that were either all connected to the internet (figure 12.18c) or not connected (figure 12.18d), while also adding a sun or moon to their backgrounds. And remember those schools with missing data? Well, I turned them into birds and clouds, but depending on the color palette, they could also become bats, snowflakes, stars, and a few other shapes.

And that's how the "Patchwork Kingdoms" collection came into existence. It was a very engaging project that took nearly three very dedicated months to create, partly because I couldn't stop myself from adding more and more to it.

Those who want to go the extra mile with color palettes, especially when the colors aren't (fully) defined by the data, should think about the distribution of colors. Some palettes look "okay" if you apply all the colors with equal chance. However, they look great if certain colors appear more than others. For instance, I find that palettes can look much better when a very light or very dark color is applied less frequently.

I used the data in as many ways as I could to encode visual aspects. However, using the school's data alone wouldn't have given me enough options to create 1,000 unique artworks; I needed more visual diversity in each piece. Therefore, I enhanced the visual channels with randomness and created something more interesting.

Ultimately, you don't need to know any of this to appreciate the final artwork. The explanation behind the art might lead to a higher appreciation of the piece, but it's not required. This was one of my main reasons for choosing such an abstract data art approach for this collection.

The UNICEF supporters who would buy the art weren't necessarily interested in any data aspect (all of the 1,000 pieces were sold!). Still, it was important to UNICEF's Giga team to use the data that they painstakingly collected. Therefore, data art was a wonderful means to create something visually unique and inviting, evoking a sense of childhood wonder. The pieces were perfect to hang in a child's bedroom while (secretly) being based on data.

Using randomness in data art allows me to explore a vast universe of visual possibilities, while still keeping within the design direction I'm aiming for. I can fine-tune the range of randomness I allow—requesting values between 0.2 and 0.4, for example, instead of a full range from 0 to 1—to create various outcomes and choose the one that fits my vision.

I will say that randomness is not required to make (digital) data art. When I don't apply randomness, I'm directing the computer to create my vision; everything on the screen is there according to something I consciously added. When I apply it, however, I feel like I'm working *together* with the computer to find visually exciting outcomes, while staying close to the underlying concept I have in mind. At this stage of my career, I'm using the latter approach much more often when aiming for more creativity and visual appeal.

Randomness increases visual diversity without needing more data. And that's true for data art and for data visualization, as we saw with the random circle orientations in the "Space Wars" graphics in figure 8.4. Therefore, randomness is an incredibly valuable tool to have in your belt, as it works wonders when you want a more detailed design.

SKETCHING YOUR DATA ART IDEAS

Data visualization and data art accomplish different goals. And so, it's natural that the sketching process (introduced in Lesson 5) is different as well.

Data visualization is about encoding the data; it's about making the data insightful; it's about how well the numbers transform into visual elements. And it's because of these objectives that I advise people to create sketches for their data visualizations in the first place.

Data art, on the other hand, is about the thoughts and emotions that the artwork evokes. So, instead of sketching to find shapes and forms that convey data insights, you should sketch to convey the general concepts—even if they are abstract. For me, a data art concept is usually so simplified, so nebulous, that I can draw it in an area of my sketchbook that's no bigger than a credit card.

For example, figure VI.1a shows the sketch for a project I'll explore in more detail in the upcoming lesson. The concept was to "hide" data about several natural elements (Earth, wind, water, etc.) in the negative space while lines representing the elements filled the positive space. I wanted to program the lines to appear flowy and free—except they could not overlap with the sections of negative space that held the data. The design would be quite abstract, and the simple depiction in this sketch was all I needed to convey the idea.

My data art sketches are usually nebulous for two reasons:

- I don't yet know how the visual design will look, which was the case for my "Elemental Flows" project, figure VI.1a.
- I'm unable to draw the intricacies I have in mind, which was the case with my "Marble

Figure VI.1a & b

The sketch (a) and a collage of the results of "Elemental Flows" (b). I only drew the underlying idea I had in mind: data, as circles, hidden in the negative space as "something" flows around it.

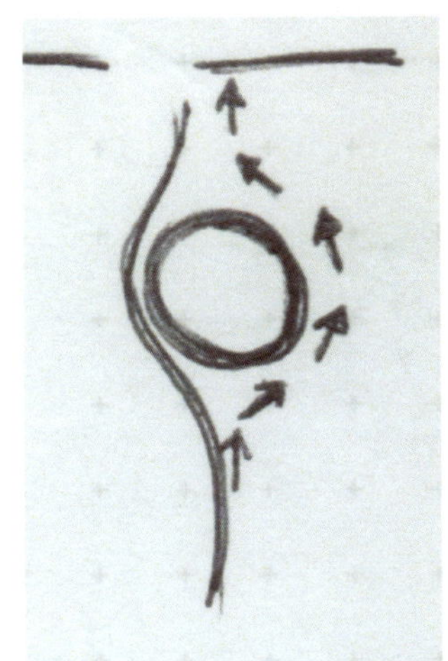

VI.1a

VI.1b

VI.2a

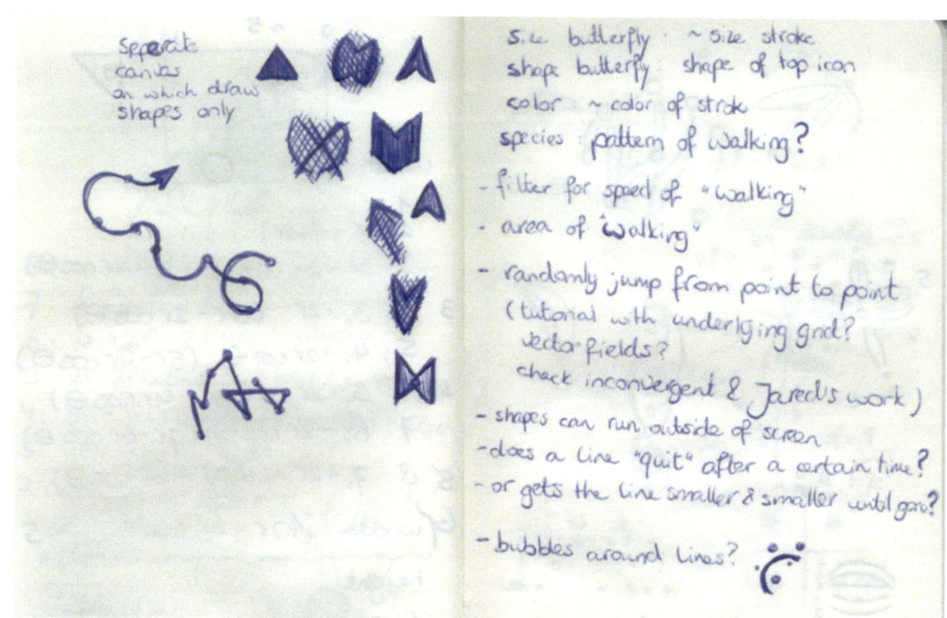
Seperate canvas on which draw shapes only
Size butterfly : ~ size stroke
shape butterfly : shape of top icon
color : ~ color of stroke
species : pattern of walking?
- filter for speed of "walking"
- area of "walking"
- randomly jump from point to point
(tutorial with underlying grid?
vector fields?
check inconvergent & Jared's work)
- shapes can run outside of screen
- does a line "quit" after a certain time?
- or gets the line smaller & smaller until gone?
- bubbles around lines?

VI.2b

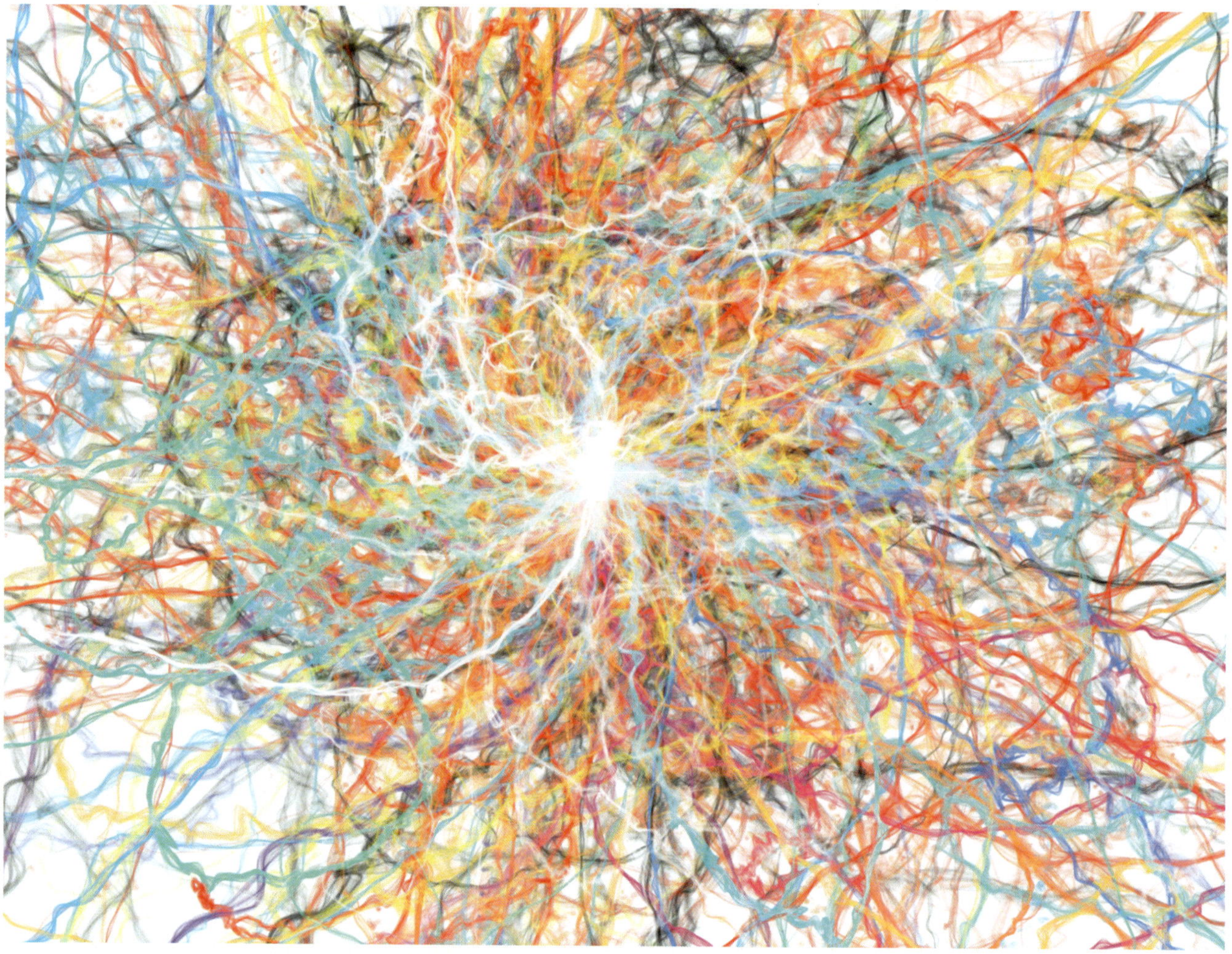

Butterflies" project. For example, I tried to sketch a "subtly flowing line" in figure VI.2a but couldn't make it look like what I was roughly imagining. I therefore stopped sketching and instead focused on writing down my thoughts.

As with "Elemental Flows," "Marble Butterflies," and most data art, the design and the visual details—the color palette, shapes, and other principles of artistic composition—are always more important than with data visualization. The design idea and its execution are all that you have; there are no data values, no interesting data trends that can mask how bland the chart looks (yes, I'm looking at you, bar chart races). And the visual design execution only happens when you're creating and iterating the work—not during the sketching phase.

Given the challenge of sketching data art, I suggest you write out your ideas and anything about the design that you want to keep in mind or test later, as I did in figure VI.2a, instead of trying to capture it all in sketches that can't properly convey the subtleties.

I'd also recommend spending extra time curating a mood board of inspirational images for a data art project—that is, more time than for a typical data visualization project. Since data art relies heavily on design, having a rich collection of detailed reference material can help you focus on the style you're aiming to achieve. Mood boards are a touchstone during the creation process, particularly when you get pulled into suboptimal tangents (as often happens to me) or when your current design isn't yet looking like anything special and you feel like you'll never get to anything that looks beautiful (also typically me). I find that, as an additional benefit, you can use these inspirational images to more properly convey the idea to your clients. (As you might imagine, my typical mini sketch alone isn't enough for anyone but myself to see the idea's true potential.)

In short, don't be surprised if your data art sketches are extraordinarily simple or look nothing like what you have in mind, as the example figures in this chapter show from my own experience. Focus on getting the bare-bones idea on the page and also rely on written notes and a well-curated set of inspirational images to be your beacons throughout the design phase.

Notice from both figures how the concept of the initial tiny sketch and the final result is the same. Yet clearly, the sketches lack details of the visual design.

Figure VI.2a & b

The sketch (a) and a final result (b) of "Marble Butterflies." The entire design and creation process is in my book *Data Sketches*, but you can find the animated version online at *marblebutterflies.visualcinnamon.com*

LESSON THIRTEEN

LET THE SUBJECT

In data art, the overarching theme or topic of the data holds more design significance than the precise figures

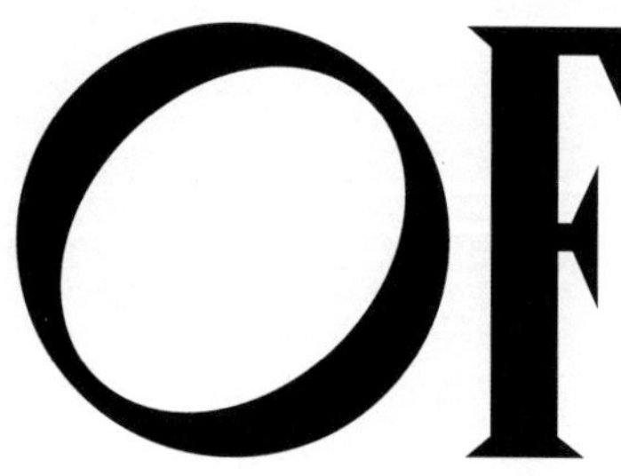

I mentioned in the very first lesson that the topic of the data is a key source of inspiration in my data visualization designs. However, with data art, when there is less, or even no need to convey the exact values and insights, when chart forms no longer (have to) make sense, I'm drawn even more to the subject matter to guide my design choices.

For one thing, a topic often gives both a constraint and a starting point, which is particularly helpful when I feel lost in the "ocean of all possibilities." Furthermore, I find it easier to connect with a data art piece, especially a digital one, if the design and the data have some relationship, some metaphor that links the data and design.

Now, if you want to keep things abstract, go right ahead. As I mentioned in the introduction to Part IV, there are no rules in data art—and I'm not presenting this lesson as such. My goal here is to introduce the "topical" approach that I follow. It's simply another data art strategy that could be helpful—particularly to anyone just venturing into data art for the first time.

In a way, this final lesson brings us back to the very first lesson. It looks at the same concept but from the other end of the chart-to-art spectrum. Lesson 1 showed how to apply thematic design to make a straightforward chart more unique and noticeable. Coming full circle, I want to show several examples of how to take that approach into the world of data art.

THE DATA GUIDE YOUR DESIGN

Thematic design should be subtle when applied to the ordinary charts so that it doesn't overwhelm the data and insights you're trying to convey. With data art, it's the opposite: Thematic design should be quite bold and can even be very literal.

Revealing star paths

PERSONAL | 2021 | THE WANDERINGS OF STARS
visualcinnamon.com/art/wanderings-of-stars

The stars above us, which appear eternally fixed in our sky, are always on the move. I wanted to make people realize that fact—stars move, not on a human timescale, but on a cosmic one.

Because the stars are extremely far apart, I wanted to project all the 3D positions of the stars "down" onto the surface of a sphere, to visually bring them closer together. It also fits with how we see the stars from our location on Earth—without depth—as if they were indeed all projected onto a 2D sphere.

Figure 13.1

"The Wanderings of Stars | Future" gives a sense of how the movements of the stars will pull apart and warp our current constellations as time moves 400,000 years into the future.

Since I was aiming to create a static piece, I couldn't rely on animation to show star movements. Instead, as a proxy for this motion, I drew each of the Western constellation's lines—the so-called stick figures—at various time intervals. As the stars gradually drift apart, the original constellations become almost unrecognizable.

The visual focused on the shapes of the stick figures and how those shapes transformed over time. Therefore, every line connected two stars, as opposed to connecting the positions of the same star as it moved. The latter would result in straight lines on the sphere, which would be more like an actual "data visualization." The connecting lines sweep across the space, as the two ends of the line follow two different stars. This creates more color and forms unique shapes as each pair of stars move.

Figure 13.2a & b

"The Wanderings of Stars | Present" (a), which visualizes the star movements from 200,000 years in the past to 200,000 years in the future; and "Past" (b), which looks 400,000 years into the past.

This approach is focused on creating something visually beautiful. Most importantly, all of these colorful and oddly stretched-out shapes across the sphere are not trying to highlight the actual path of star movement, but instead, make it apparent that stars move in the first place.

The final collection has three pieces. In figure 13.1, you can see "Future" which shows how stars will move 400,000 years forward in time. I used a color palette inspired by the control dashboards from various sci-fi movies.

There is also "Present" that looks into both the past and future, 200,000 years in both ways. It is colored vibrantly like flowers, since the present is always fleeting (figure 13.2a). Finally, there is the third piece to complete the collection, called "Past," which goes back 400,000 years (figure 13.2b), using more muted colors. Its reds and blues nod to colors that

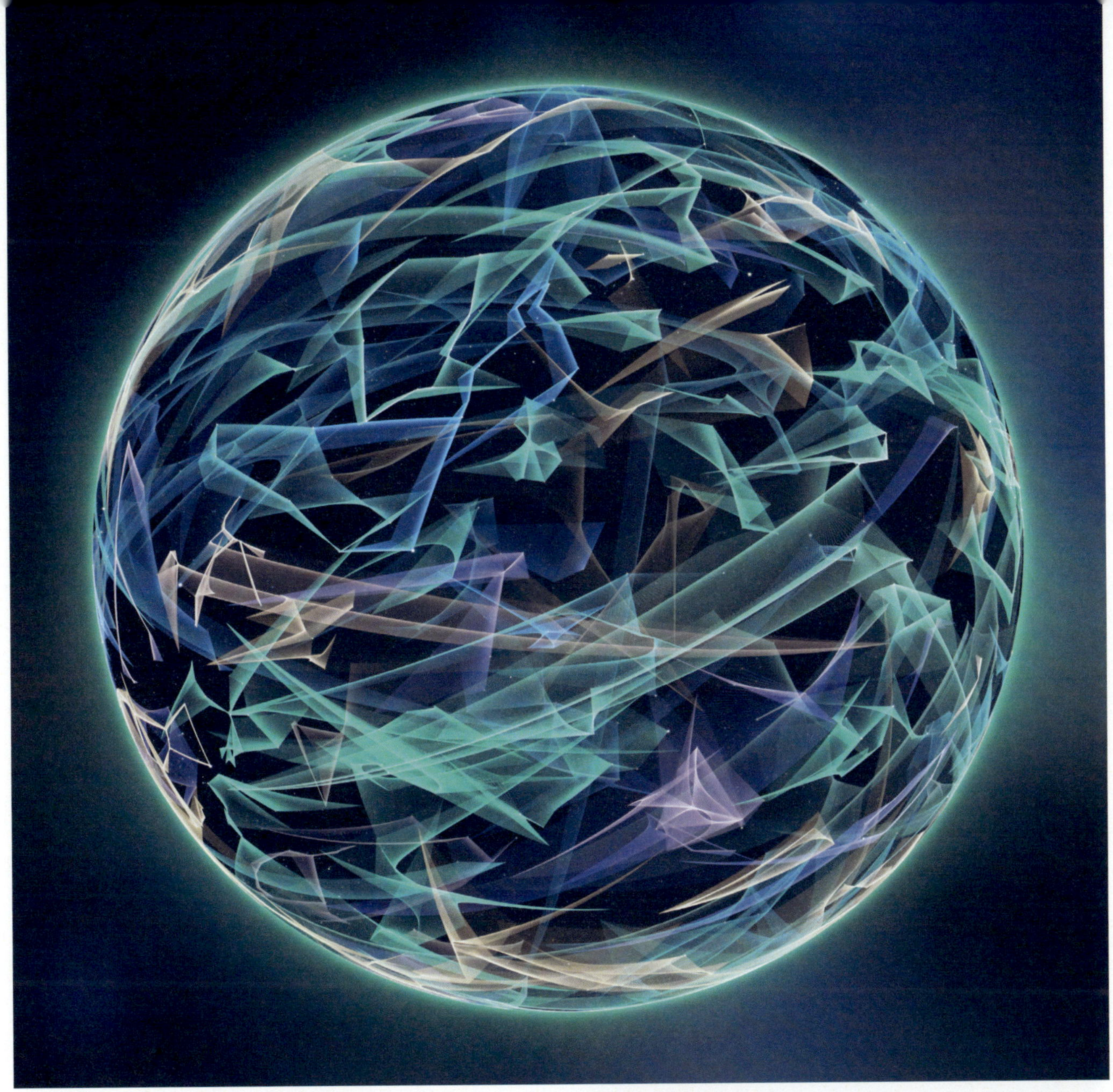

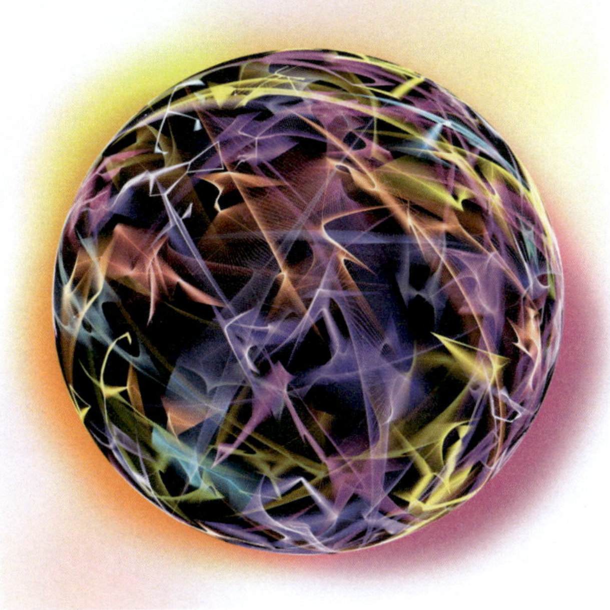

13.2a

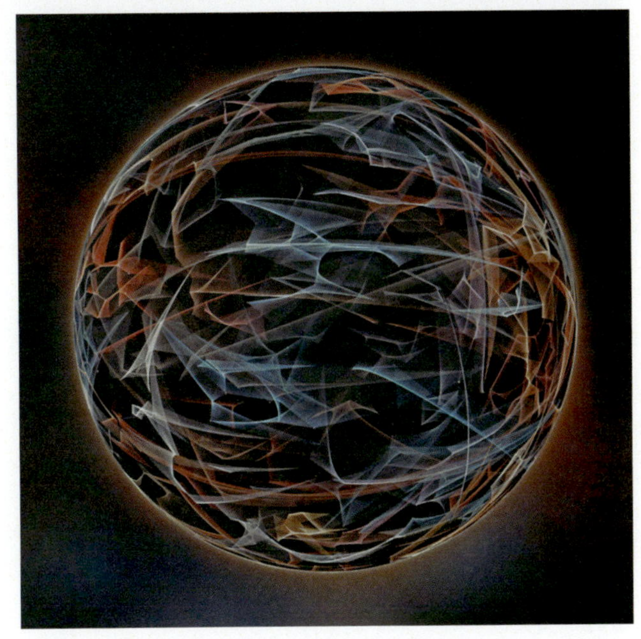

13.2b

are often found in retro space posters from the middle of the previous century. I also applied a subtle grainy texture on top.

It's debatable whether the design is "inspired by" the constellations or if it's simply a literal application of plotting star positions and their connecting lines. Regardless, this project serves as an example that you can be quite literal in applying the topic while still creating data art.

Hiding the data

PERSONAL | 2021 | ELEMENTAL FLOWS
visualcinnamon.com/art/elemental-flows

Figure 13.3a, b & c

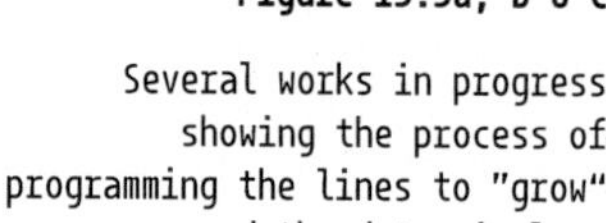

Several works in progress showing the process of programming the lines to "grow" around the data circles.

In 2021, I was working with a data set about the number of trees per country when I got an idea for a new personal project. The tree data made me think about nature and the planet. I thought about the elements of earth, water, fire, and air. I wanted to try and capture these in a data art collection by using data sets about the density of trees, the amount of rainfall, the hours of sunshine, and the air quality.

I developed a concept to abstractly represent these elements and "hide" the data in the visual. The key was to draw "something" that captured the essence of the element—but it could not overlap with any negative spaces that contained the data. After some initial brainstorming, I realized that flow fields, like the one I made for the Fab Academy light intensity project (figure 4.8), were well suited for this project due to their natural, wavy appearance.

13.3a

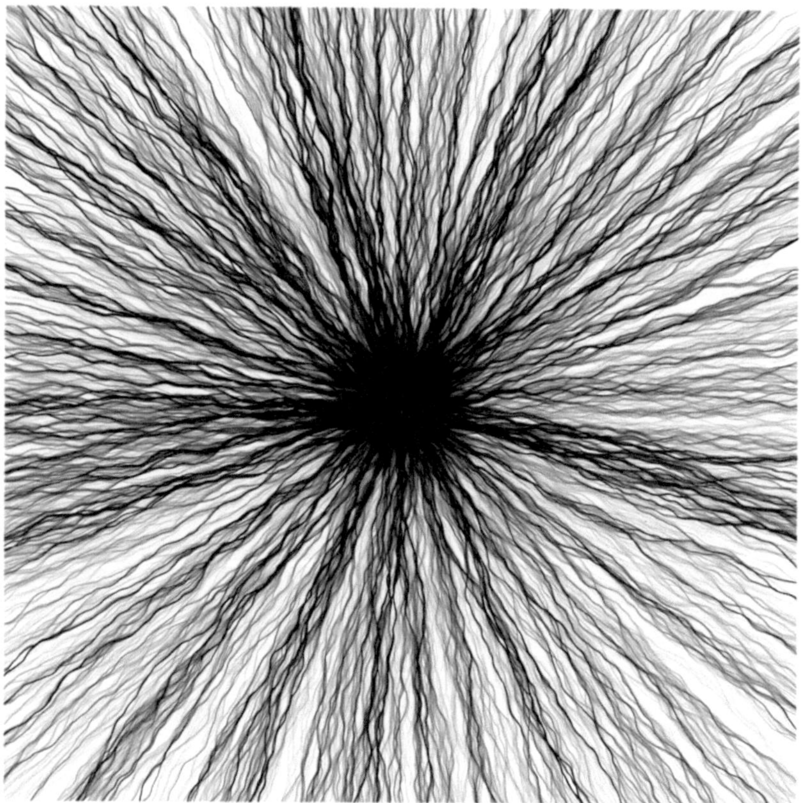

13.3b

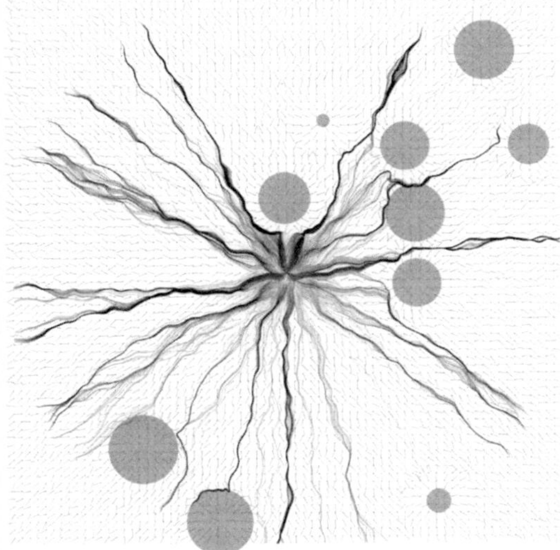

13.3c

Starting with Earth, I wanted the flows to resemble tree branches growing around the data. I turned tree density data (number of trees per square kilometer in nearly 30 high-population countries) into scaled circles. How I laid these circles out on the canvas is a detail I promised I would only ever share with the owner of the piece, so I'll keep that a secret!

These circles are "hidden" on the canvas—like transparent ghosts. As the tree branches expand outward from the center of the visual, they do not intersect with the circles. Instead, the branches weave around them, creating a unique interaction between the data and the visual design.

The easy part was growing the lines outward from the center in a wiggly, branch-like manner (figure 13.3a). Next, I introduced the data circles and had to make the lines flow around them (figure 13.3b, where the circles are visible in gray, so I could see how well my algorithm was working). This took me hours upon hours to get right. I did learn a lot of fascinating math along the way about attractors and other concepts that I've since forgotten.

Ultimately, I managed to get the effect that I wanted. Once satisfied with the general feel of the branches, there was endless fine-tuning, from colors to small details (such as randomly adding tiny leaves along the branches) to create the design in figure 13.4, where the data circles are part of the negative space.

The heavy lifting was behind me. The flow field algorithm worked, giving me a structure—and some confidence—to tackle the other elements. Nevertheless, I took a fair amount of time to think about how I wanted to capture the essence of each remaining element. For water (figure 13.5), I made the lines wavier and let them swirl in a spiral pattern, mimicking a whirlpool. The whirlpool flows around data circles representing average yearly rainfall in the capital cities of the same 30 countries. It's a bit harder to see the circles in the negative space in this design, but they are there, diverting the flow of the water.

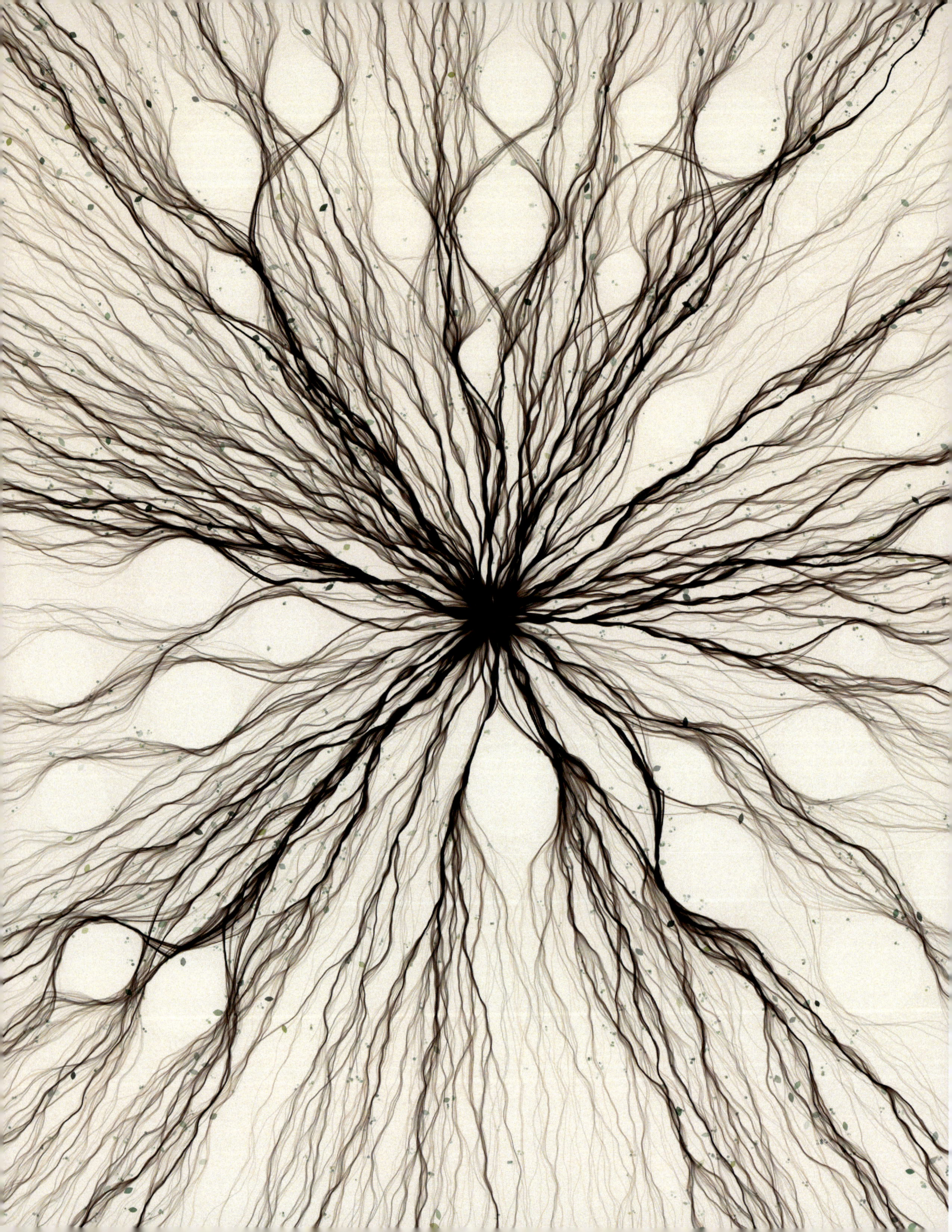

13.4

Figure 13.4

The final result of the "Earth" piece in the "Elemental Flows" collection.

Figure 13.5

The "Water" piece, which holds information about yearly rainfall in 30 cities. The data is hidden in transparent circles that divert the flow of water.

Figure 13.6

The "Sun" piece, representing the element of fire. The underlying data set is about the average yearly amount of sunshine in capital cities.

Figure 13.7

The "Air" piece, where the clouds need to twist and flow around hidden circles that are scaled to the air quality in 30 capital cities.

Figure 13.8

The final element, "Digital," where the lines turn only along straight angles.

For the fire element (figure 13.6), I wanted to draw the sun's rays radiating outward, conveying a sense of blistering heat. For the data circles, I used average yearly hours of sunshine in the capital cities. This time, when the rays hit any circle, they are reflected as straight lines (like light). This reflection effect makes the "hidden" circles much more visible here. It seems as if they are drawn, but they are still only negative spaces, showing the background.

For air (figure 13.7), I tweaked the flow field to create a series of vortices—perfect for cloud-like wisps of air. Like the roots and the water, the airflow is diverted around the hidden circles. The underlying data is about air quality in the cities.

I could have stopped there. However, in today's Western society, I feel that there's something else we can't live without: Technology. Therefore, I made a fifth piece for the "digital element" (figure 13.8) in which the lines are only allowed to turn at straight angles—a rigid design inspired by a computer's binary workings. There is no data hidden in this piece. Instead, I created the circles by placing them in a spiral formation and enlarging them as they get farther from the center.

The designs of these five pieces fundamentally represent the topic of each data set: Water looks like water, and air looks like clouds. The inspiration is clear, as there's no doubt which piece represents which element.

13.5

13.7

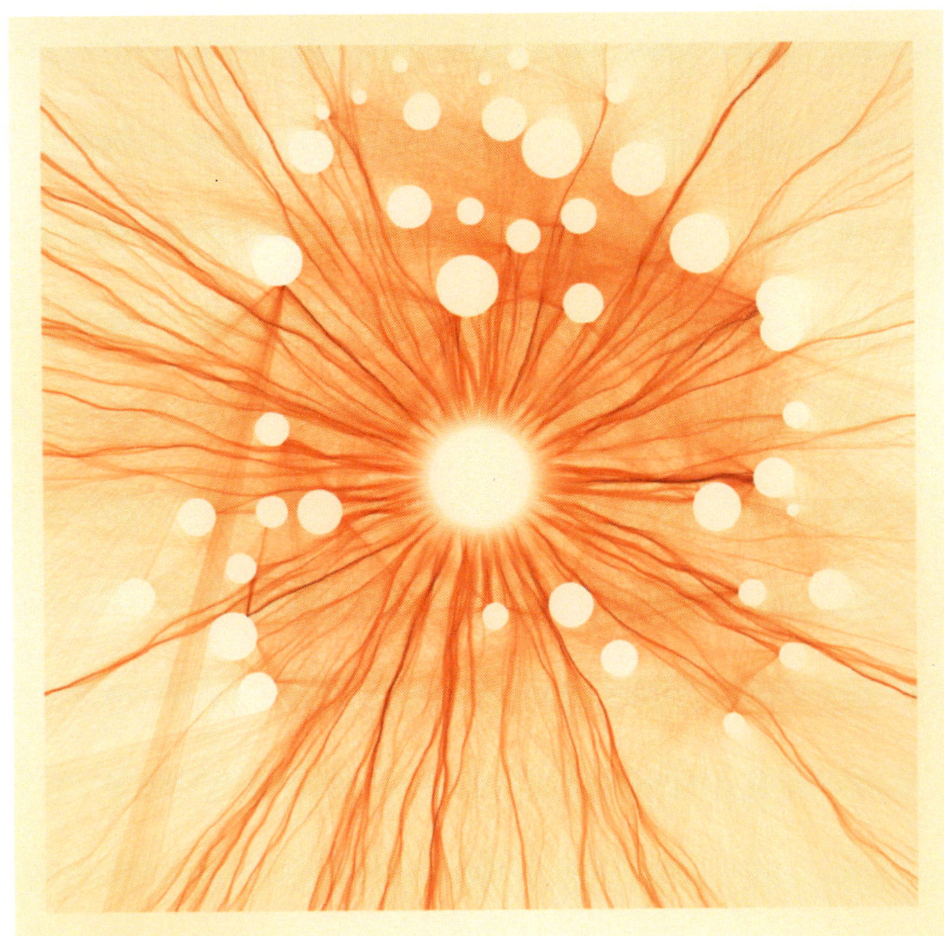

13.6

13.8

Spirals of exoplanets

PERSONAL | 2021 | THE ESSENCE OF US
visualcinnamon.com/art/the-essence-of-us

Figure 13.9

The first frame from "The Essence of Us," showing more than 5,000 exoplanets as spirals around a central white circle representing Earth.

Figure 13.10a & b

Two works in progress, where I was setting up the spiral arms (a) and playing with different ways to visualize the exoplanets, such as with circular shapes along the spiral arms (b).

I was asked to create an art piece for an exhibition on culture. The astronomer in me began mulling ideas about human culture: If an outside alien civilization put all of us together into one box, what would we look like? What defines human culture as a whole? This idea of an "alien perspective" eventually led me to think of exoplanets (planets outside of our solar system) and how, with the discovery of exoplanets in the early 1990s, we got one step closer to discovering where else life might exist. This prompted me to visualize all the exoplanets discovered to date as a stand-in for all the possible civilizations—and cultures—in our Milky Way.

Instead of taking a literal approach, like visualizing each exoplanet as a circle, I chose a more abstract route. Drawing inspiration from the spiral

13.9

13.10a

13.10b

shape of our Milky Way, I imagined how we and all those exoplanets are moving around a common center.

I symbolically positioned us, Earth, in the center, as it's a human tendency to see ourselves as the center of everything. Every exoplanet became one spiral line wrapping around it (figure 13.9). Data about the exoplanets (size, orbital period, etc.) map to the various visual aspects of the spiral. For example, the first planets discovered are the lines starting closest to the center.

Each piece in the exhibition would be displayed on its own large screen, allowing me to incorporate animation. I made each spiral rotate very slowly around the center at slightly different speeds.

For the visual design—the colors, the shapes, the strokes—I took inspiration from the Memphis design style of the early 1990s (think: bold, contrasting colors with lots of purples, blues, and yellows, geometric shapes and black block shadows) as that was when the first exoplanet was discovered.

I didn't—and still don't—expect anyone to gain insight into the exoplanets data. Instead, I intended to create this slow-moving piece that you can stare into, getting drawn into the center like a black hole, and simply ponder that initial question: What defines human culture as a whole?

Visualizing food in abstract ways

BUSINESS | 2024 | FHI360
intake.org/news/country-stories-inspire-motivating-gdqs-data-action

FHI360, a nonprofit human development organization, has developed a set of globally appropriate nutrition metrics to assess diet quality among women of reproductive age. It's called the Global Diet Quality Score (GDQS). As part of its work, FHI360 released a report showing how countries have meaningfully used GDQS data to advance diet quality. I got to create a collection of six data artworks to accompany this report—the main cover and five chapter covers.

The data set held information about which foods—and from which GDQS categories—thousands of people worldwide had eaten on a given day. The GDQS contains 25 different food categories, such as "red meat," "dark green leafy vegetables," "sweets and ice cream," and "low-fat dairy."

13.11

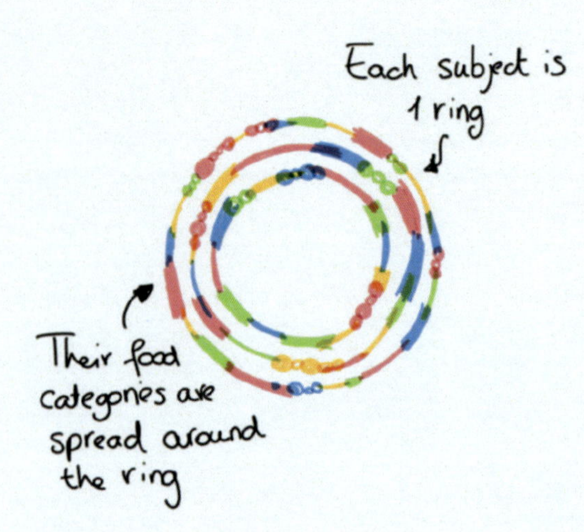

Figure 13.11

My simple sketch of the concept.

Figure 13.12

The final cornerstone piece of the GDQS collection that uses all 25 GDQS categories © 2024 FHI 360, used with permission.

After analyzing the data, I started brainstorming. With the data being about food, I imagined different ingredients being combined into a dish, creating something more than the sum of its parts. The concept of a dish made me think of plates and bowls: simple circles when seen from above. This concept felt entirely right and elegant—as I find is often the case for metaphors that connect to simple geometric shapes.

The team and I settled on a circular motif featuring a different visual mark for each of the 25 GDQS categories. (Figure 13.11 shows the basic sketch for the idea.) The circle had many rings within it—one ring per person at a randomly assigned radius—and the marks within the ring showed which of the GDQS categories that person had eaten during the observed 24-hour time window. Thousands of rings together on the canvas formed a beautifully intricate "plate." You can see the result in figure 13.12.

How I'd create a cohesive set for the five chapter-cover artworks wasn't immediately clear. I looked at the GDQS food items again and noticed

13.13a

13.13b

13.13c

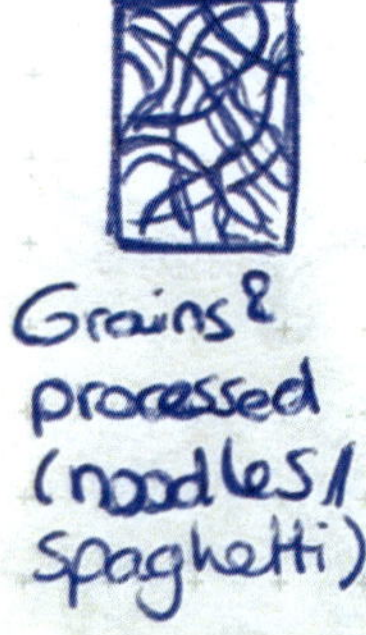

13.13d

13.13e

13.13f

Figure 13.13a, b, c, d, e & f

Sketches of the main cover and the five abstract images for the chapter covers, representing each food group.

that I could group them into five overarching categories:

- Animal source foods
- Whole foods (ingredients that are not very processed and generally more healthy, such as whole grain noodles)
- Vegetables, roots, and tubers
- Fruits
- Sweets, snacks, and processed foods

I decided to use these food categories to make each of the five artworks.

To make each piece more visually distinct, I wanted to adjust each of them in ways that reflected their respective food groups. I drew tiny (portrait-style) page outlines in my already tiny notebook and filled them with possible ideas (see the figures in 13.13). Perhaps I could turn the "sweet, snacks, and processed foods" category into a spiral inspired by those giant lollipops (figure 13.13f). "Vegetables, roots, and tubers" could have a wobbly circle inspired by lettuce (figure 13.13d). After some attempts, I realized I didn't want to use specific shapes, such as a schematic banana; I wanted it to be more abstract.

Eventually, I found patterns for the three remaining categories: slightly wavy lines for the "animal source foods," inspired by muscle cells (figure 13.13b), wavy criss-crossing lines for the "whole foods," inspired by noodles and spaghetti (figure 13.13c), and quarter circles for the "fruit" category, inspired by fruit slices (figure 13.13e). Figure 13.14 shows the final results for the five chapter-cover artworks.

13.14a, b, c & d

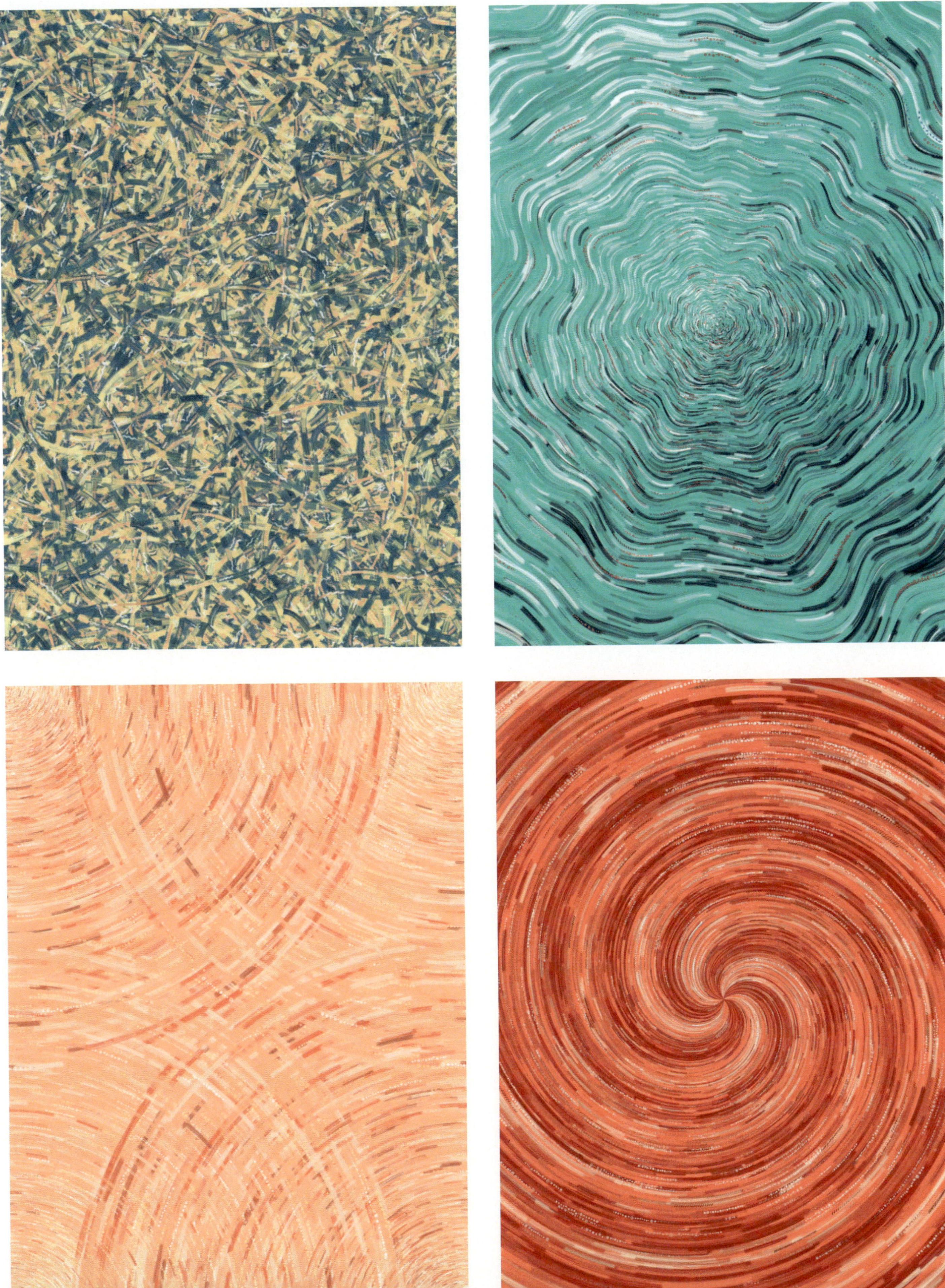

13.14e

The four projects discussed in this lesson demonstrate that there are many different ways in which the subject or topic of the data can significantly affect the design of the artwork. These examples also show how initial ideas and concepts can flow and evolve in strange ways.

Although I don't have a defined, linear process when creating data art, I would say there are two keys to success:

Figure 13.14a, b, c, d & e

The five chapter-cover artworks, each based on a group of GDQS categories: animal source foods (a); whole foods (b); vegetables, roots, and tubers (c); fruits (d); and sweets, snacks, and processed foods (e) © 2024 FHI 360, used with permission.

- Jot down all your thoughts related to the data's subject or theme. They can be very specific images or broad concepts. Consider, for instance, New York City's Central Park Squirrel Census data. What pops into your mind? For me: squirrels, squirrel tails (or just an "S"-shape), nuts (schematic shapes inspired by nuts?), trees (inspiration for a possible layout of the data), orange/green/brown color palette, leaves, cuteness (in terms of colors and fonts), nature, and on and on. Yes, this is my stream of consciousness. It's messy. But it's a great place to start.

- Try picking out the ideas that spark "something"—a quick flash of an idea, a vision, an emotion—and see if you can flesh it out into descriptions or sketches. If you're feeling stuck, ask whether the idea gives you a general concept for the art piece. If so, can you draw the rough design? Or can you perhaps find some inspirational images to accompany the idea? Keep probing, keep refining—and, eventually, something will stand out.

But, of course, data art is a free and freeing discipline.
Choose the best path for you, because there's no wrong way.

THINK OUTSIDE THE CHART

Reflecting on the journey

We've now journeyed through the complete spectrum from ordinary charts to data art, exploring how creativity can transform data into something remarkable at each stage. With that, we've come to the end of *CHART*—the lessons, tips, and experiences that I wanted to share with you.

We began by enhancing ordinary charts, drawing inspiration from the data set's topic, variables and values to make even the simplest visuals more unique. We then expanded our options by considering less common chart types and combining different charts in the same visual. By that point, we were ready to think beyond chart types, to break the mold of default settings.

Moving forward, we saw how hand-drawn sketches could open up new directions in our designs. We explored practical techniques such as amplified encodings, showing more granular data, and then using that granular data to show aggregate values.

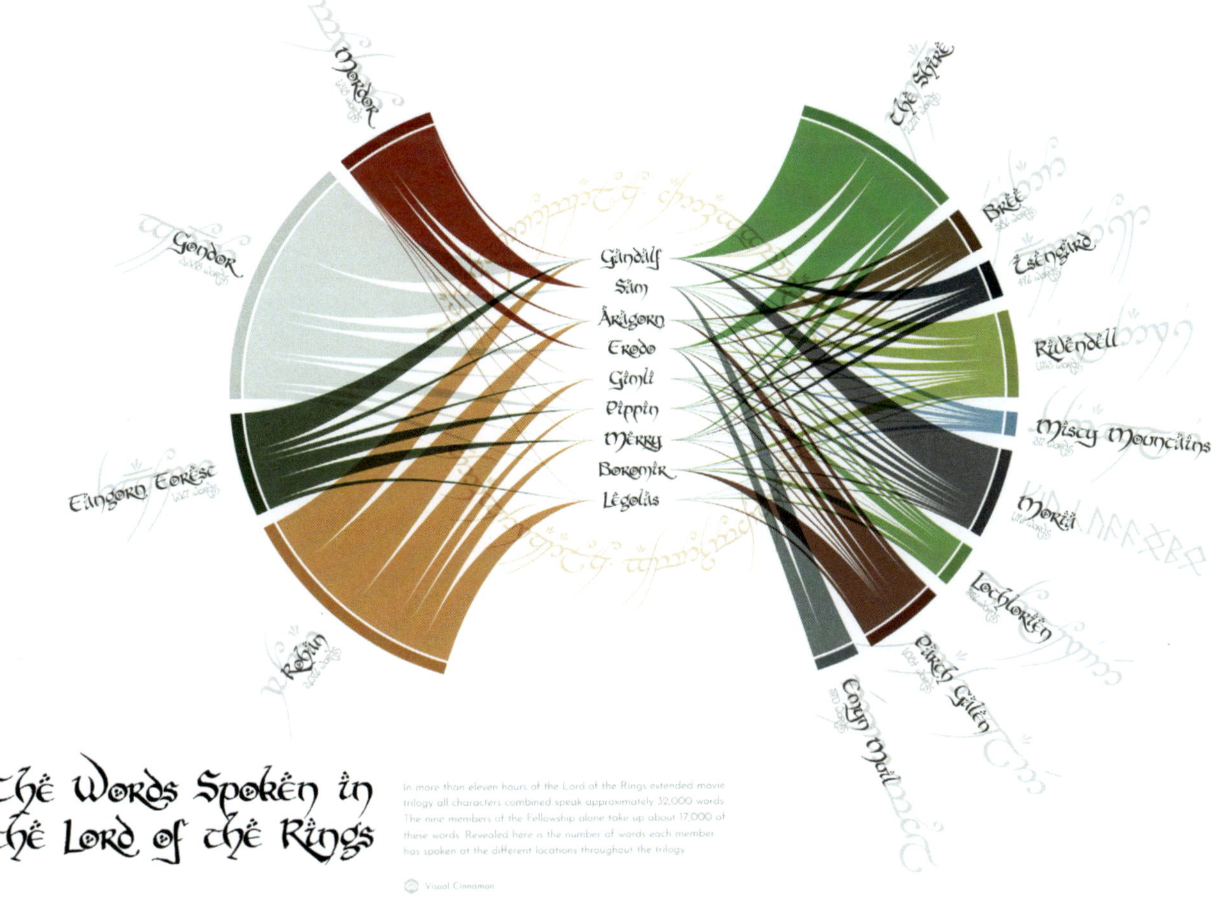

0.15

Figure 0.15

A visualization about the words spoken by the Fellowship characters in the Lord of the Rings movies at the different locations in the fantastical realm of Middle Earth. I created this for "Data Sketches" in 2016-around the time I started getting comfortable creating custom charts. See the interactive version at *lotr.visualcinnamon.com*

In addition, we added complementary variables to enrich the context and nuance of the data stories we want to tell—all while discovering the creative potential of larger data sets.

Finally, we entered the world of data art, where familiar rules fade, and the focus shifts to evoking emotions. Here, we saw the value of pulling inspiration from personal interests and embracing randomness for novel outcomes. The end of the journey brought us full circle as we, once again, found that the topic of the data can steer an artwork's design and composition—and perhaps even be more influential to the creative process than with data visualizations.

The ultimate goal of this journey is to help you be as expressive and boundless with data visuals as you would with any other art form. These lessons are therefore not rules, and most certainly not the only way to be creative with data visualization. Rather, they are tools to help you go beyond the mundane—in your own way—and present data in a way that will leave a lasting effect on your audience.

Thank you for joining me on this path, and may your own explorations lead to data visuals that captivate and inspire. Keep thinking outside the CHART!

ACKNOWLEDGMENTS

After the release of *Data Sketches* in 2021, I thought I would never write another book, and especially not within five years. And yet, here you hold my second book, released only four years after the first.

At the start of 2023, I was invited by Outlier, a conference organized by the Data Visualization Society, to give a keynote presentation. It was quite the honor, and I knew I wanted to make it special. I asked myself what would be most valuable to share with an audience of fellow data visualization enthusiasts. It hit me that I had been immersed in the world of data visualization for nearly a decade. That sparked an idea: I would share all my favorite techniques to make charts stand out, to make them beautiful. After all, that's what I consider my "selling point"—and what brings me the most joy.

I spent several weeks crafting lessons and transforming them into a slideshow presentation. But as I refined it, I wasn't feeling confident. I ran a test version of the presentation by my dear friend and *Data Sketches* co-creator, Shirley Wu. Her reaction was immediate: "My gosh, Nadieh, there's SO much! I can't absorb all of this in just 45 minutes!" And she was absolutely right! Reluctantly, I had to cut down on the number of examples and trim the lessons for the presentation.

After delivering the keynote at Outlier, Jason Forrest, a friend and the editor-in-chief of *Nightingale* magazine, came up to me and finally said out loud what I had been quietly thinking for a while: "You know, I think your presentation would work much better as a book."

Soon after, my editor from *Data Sketches* reached out to see if Shirley and I wanted to make an updated version. I replied, "Actually, I have an idea for a new book," and found myself, once again, strapped into the writing roller coaster.

As it takes much more than just the writer to get a book out there, I want to sincerely thank everyone who helped me along the way.

To my writing coach and fabulous line editor, Emily Barone, without whom this book would be full of long-winded introductions, sentences with more than eight commas, and unexplained thought processes.

To Julie Brunet, aka datacitron, the creative force who took my bland manuscript of words and images and turned it into the masterfully designed publication you're holding now.

To my publisher and editor Elliott Morsia (and the staff at CRC Press) for all the help he provided along the way, not in the least with gathering the various image permissions, but also with enduring dozens of my emails asking what might be possible in terms of colors, paper, printing, and more.

To Alberto Cairo for his unwavering support throughout my career and advice while writing this book.

To Tamara Munzner for being the champion in getting *Data Sketches* published in the first place and for cheerleading this second book.

To the four reviewers of my book proposal whose honest opinions provided me with excellent feedback and gave me the confidence that there was a place for it: Jen Christiansen, Moritz Stefaner, Valentina D'Efilippo, and the fourth anonymous person.

To all of those who signed up for the beta reading and the 100 who spent some of their precious time supplying feedback on my book. I wish I could name you all, but I want to expressly thank Dr. Bettina Hüttenrauch, Gabrielle Schroeder, Kenneth van Wanrooij, Neil Richards, Nuria Altimir, Nurşah Ayhan, Steven Nijman,

and Zan Armstrong for their extremely robust and on-point feedback that went beyond anything I was expecting.

To all the companies that let me use the work I'd created for them so I could show practical business examples to accompany each lesson: Adyen, alis_, Cæmpus, Deloitte, FHI360, Google News Lab, *Greenpeace Unearthed,* Janssen, Kantar Consulting, Lighthouse Reports, Mozilla, *Physics Today,* Public Eye, *Science News, Scientific American*, Sony Music Entertainment Netherlands, Swayable, Swissgrid, *The New York Times,* Transavia, UNESCO and UNICEF.

Figure 0.16

My two cats make sure I get enough time away from my laptop to play with them. (Twix is the one demanding attention here while I tried to photograph a map that I created as a personal project.)

To Sara Sprinkhuizen, my brilliant friend who mentioned naming this book "CHART" as if there was no title more obvious than that (I'd spent hours brainstorming ideas before this.)

To Shirley Wu, my data visualization soulmate, for being my dear, dear friend since 2016 and going through all the ups and downs with me since then. For her never-ending enthusiasm and eagerness to take bold steps. For her partnership in our "Data Sketches" project and her courage to turn it into a book, without which I would have never considered writing a book on my own.

Finally, a thank you to my love, Ralph, for keeping me sane while I tried to balance writing a book with client work and an extensive house renovation. (I wrote every word while we lived in the basement.)

And, of course, my two cats, Twix and Skittles, for all the cuddles and zen vibes they gave me; not that they made it easier to type with their heads and paws draped over my arm.

CASE STUDY METADATA LIST

HOW TO READ

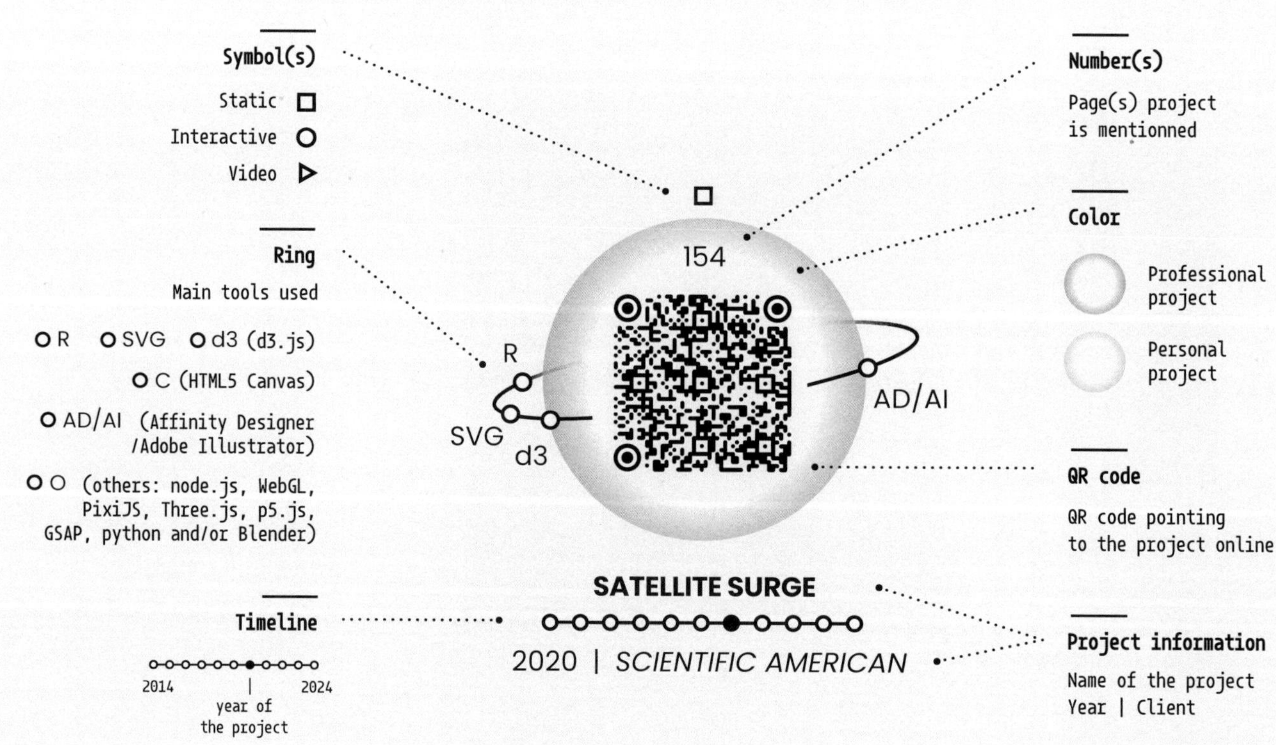

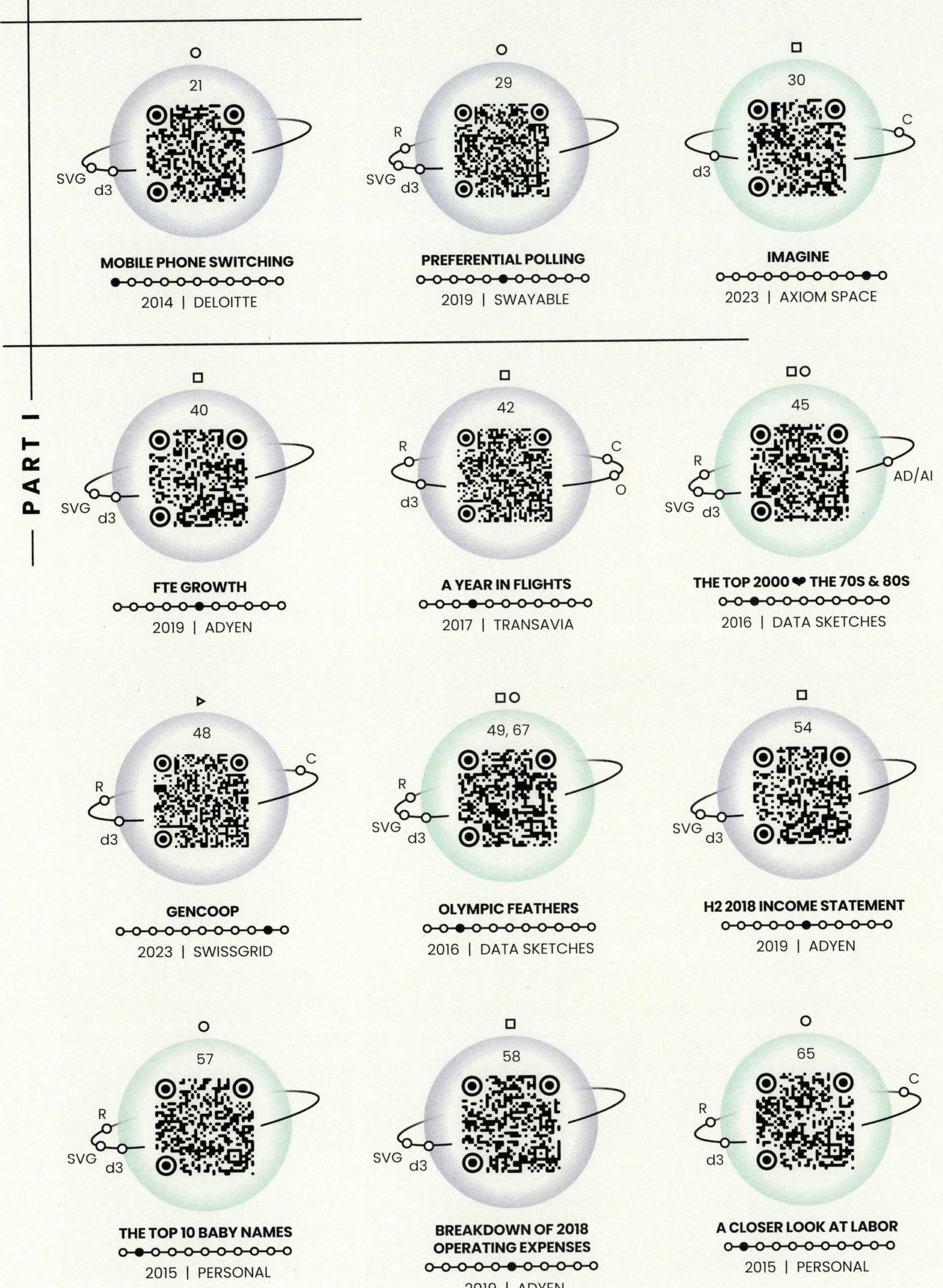
PART I
21
SVG
d3
MOBILE PHONE SWITCHING
2014 | DELOITTE
29
R
SVG
d3
PREFERENTIAL POLLING
2019 | SWAYABLE
30
C
d3
IMAGINE
2023 | AXIOM SPACE
40
SVG
d3
FTE GROWTH
2019 | ADYEN
42
R
C
d3
O
A YEAR IN FLIGHTS
2017 | TRANSAVIA
45
R
SVG
d3
AD/AI
THE TOP 2000 ❤ THE 70S & 80S
2016 | DATA SKETCHES
48
R
C
d3
GENCOOP
2023 | SWISSGRID
49, 67
R
SVG
d3
OLYMPIC FEATHERS
2016 | DATA SKETCHES
54
SVG
d3
H2 2018 INCOME STATEMENT
2019 | ADYEN
57
R
SVG
d3
THE TOP 10 BABY NAMES
2015 | PERSONAL
58
SVG
d3
BREAKDOWN OF 2018 OPERATING EXPENSES
2019 | ADYEN
65
R
C
d3
A CLOSER LOOK AT LABOR
2015 | PERSONAL

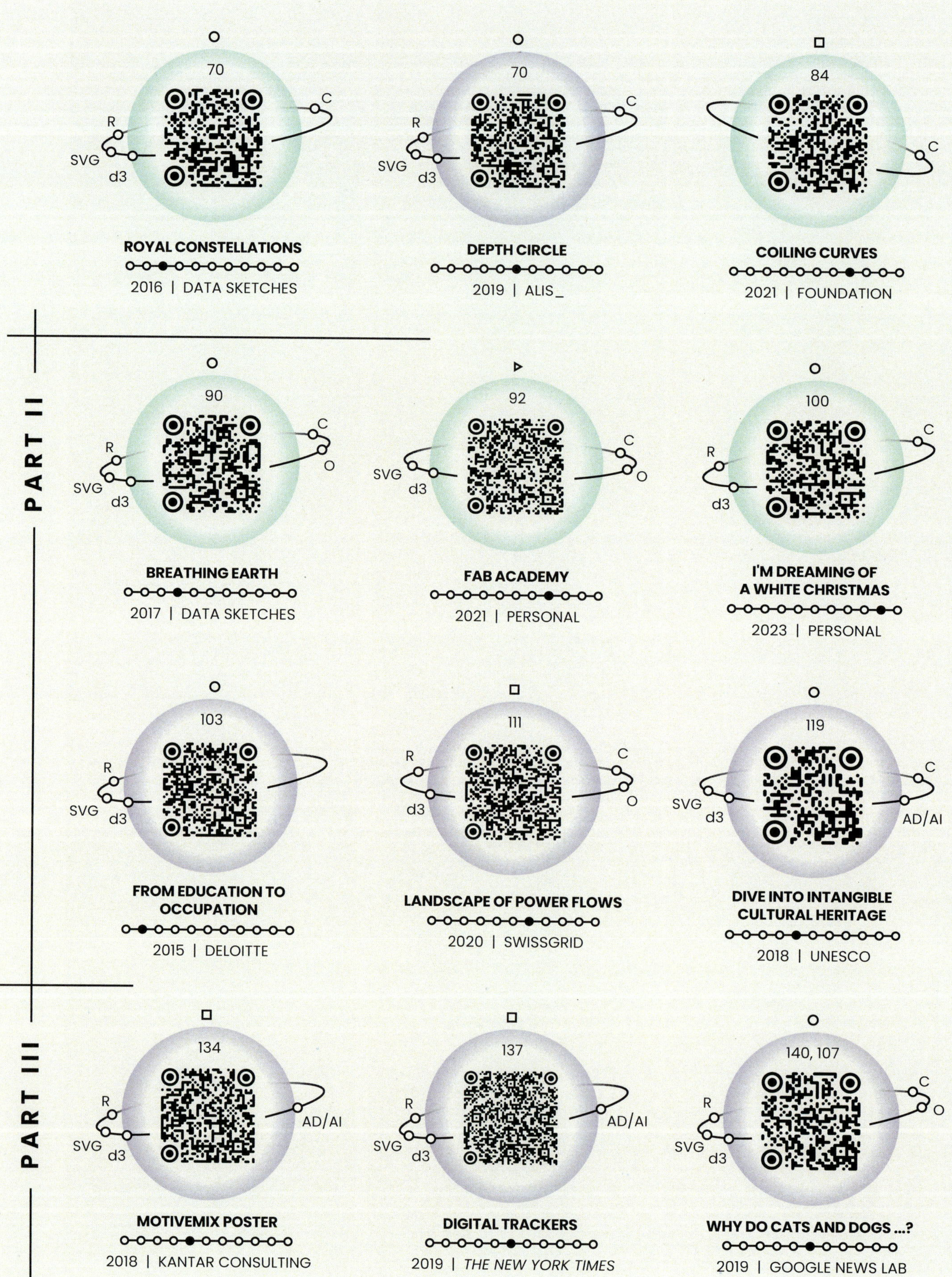

70
R
SVG
d3
C
ROYAL CONSTELLATIONS
2016 | DATA SKETCHES
70
R
SVG
d3
C
DEPTH CIRCLE
2019 | ALIS_
84
C
COILING CURVES
2021 | FOUNDATION
PART II
90
R
SVG
d3
C
O
BREATHING EARTH
2017 | DATA SKETCHES
92
SVG
d3
C
O
FAB ACADEMY
2021 | PERSONAL
100
R
d3
C
I'M DREAMING OF
A WHITE CHRISTMAS
2023 | PERSONAL
103
R
SVG
d3
FROM EDUCATION TO
OCCUPATION
2015 | DELOITTE
111
R
d3
C
O
LANDSCAPE OF POWER FLOWS
2020 | SWISSGRID
119
SVG
d3
C
AD/AI
DIVE INTO INTANGIBLE
CULTURAL HERITAGE
2018 | UNESCO
PART III
134
R
SVG
d3
AD/AI
MOTIVEMIX POSTER
2018 | KANTAR CONSULTING
137
R
SVG
d3
AD/AI
DIGITAL TRACKERS
2019 | THE NEW YORK TIMES
140, 107
R
SVG
d3
C
O
WHY DO CATS AND DOGS ...?
2019 | GOOGLE NEWS LAB

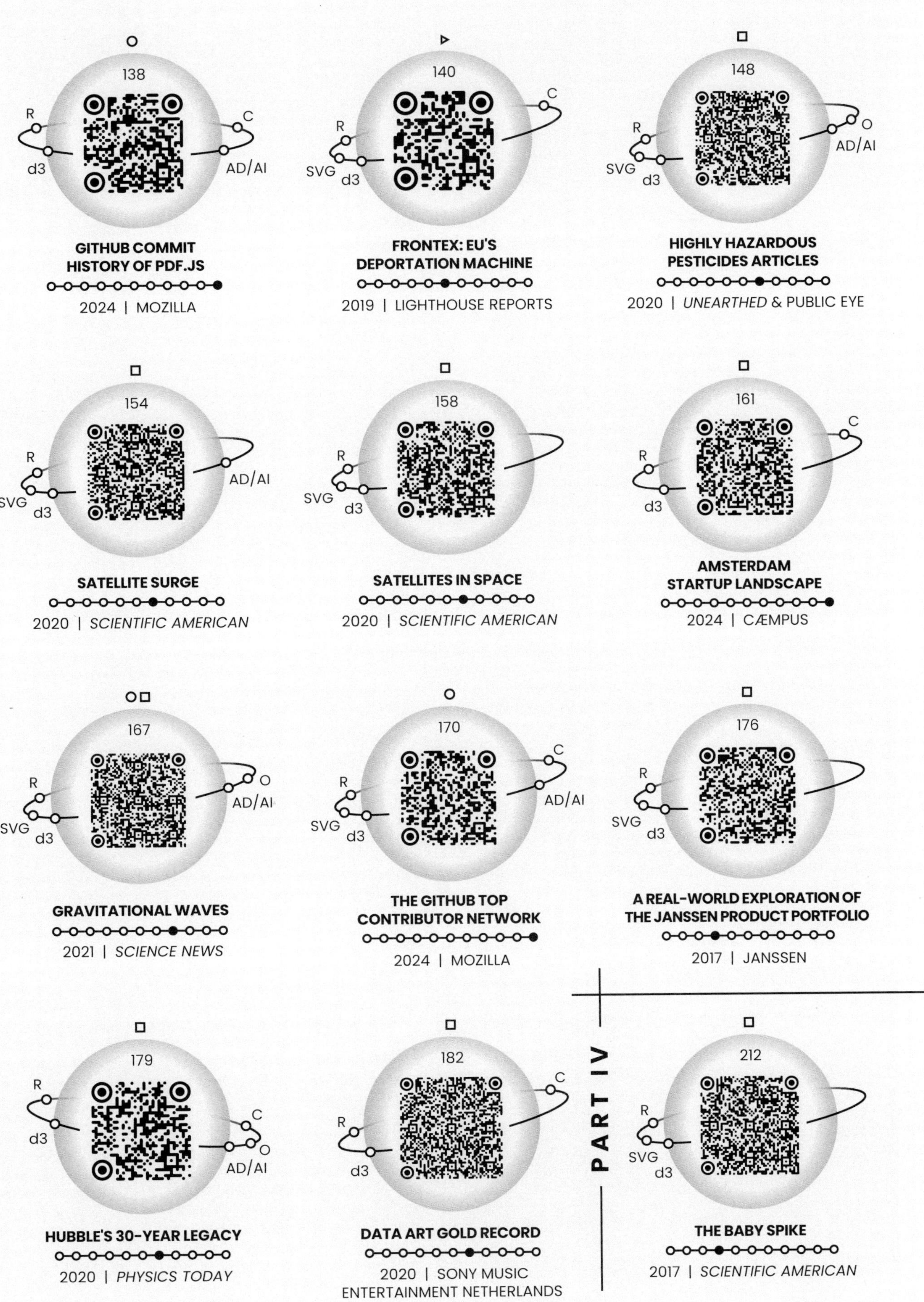

138
R
C
d3
AD/AI
GITHUB COMMIT HISTORY OF PDF.JS
2024 | MOZILLA
140
C
R
SVG
d3
FRONTEX: EU'S DEPORTATION MACHINE
2019 | LIGHTHOUSE REPORTS
148
R
O
AD/AI
SVG
d3
HIGHLY HAZARDOUS PESTICIDES ARTICLES
2020 | UNEARTHED & PUBLIC EYE
154
R
AD/AI
SVG
d3
SATELLITE SURGE
2020 | SCIENTIFIC AMERICAN
158
R
SVG
d3
SATELLITES IN SPACE
2020 | SCIENTIFIC AMERICAN
161
C
R
d3
AMSTERDAM STARTUP LANDSCAPE
2024 | CÆMPUS
167
R
O
AD/AI
SVG
d3
GRAVITATIONAL WAVES
2021 | SCIENCE NEWS
170
C
R
AD/AI
SVG
d3
THE GITHUB TOP CONTRIBUTOR NETWORK
2024 | MOZILLA
176
R
SVG
d3
A REAL-WORLD EXPLORATION OF THE JANSSEN PRODUCT PORTFOLIO
2017 | JANSSEN
PART IV
179
R
C
d3
O
AD/AI
HUBBLE'S 30-YEAR LEGACY
2020 | PHYSICS TODAY
182
C
R
d3
DATA ART GOLD RECORD
2020 | SONY MUSIC ENTERTAINMENT NETHERLANDS
212
R
SVG
d3
THE BABY SPIKE
2017 | SCIENTIFIC AMERICAN

215
d3
C
TWISTINGS / EXPLORE
2022 | FXHASH
215
C
O
FLEETING THOUGHTS
2023 | ALBA
215
C
WAV∧VES
2023 | FERAL FILE
218
C
OBSCURED
2022 | C-VERSO
218
R
d3
C
AD/AI
EMBRACING THE TABOO
2023 | NIGHTINGALE MAGAZINE
222
O
THE BEST SELLING
NINTENDO SWITCH GAMES
2024 | PERSONAL
228
C
O
ANHEDRA
2022 | GEN.ART
232
R
d3
C
PATCHWORK KINGDOMS
2021 | UNICEF
248
R
d3
C
MARBLE BUTTERFLIES
2017 | DATA SKETCHES
252
R
d3
C
THE WANDERINGS OF STARS
2021 | FOUNDATION
254, 247
R
d3
C
ELEMENTAL FLOWS
2021 | FOUNDATION
260
R
d3
C
THE ESSENCE OF US
2021 | PERSONAL

THE GLOBAL DIET QUALITY SCORE COLLECTION

2024 | FHI360

THE WORDS SPOKEN IN THE LORD OF THE RINGS

2016 | DATA SKETCHES

INDEX

A

D

F

H

I

J

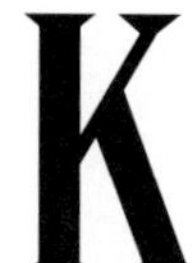

L

M

P

T

U